HUMAN NATURE AND THE FRENCH REVOLUTION

Polygons: Cultural Diversities and Intersections
General Editor: **Lieve Spaas**, *Professor of French Cultural Studies, Kingston University*

This series presents book length studies, single or multi-authored, which explore the divergencies and disparities that emerge during the transmission of cultural and social practices. Focussing on the significant topics, themes and motifs in different societies at different stages of their history, this series contributes to a better understanding of the interaction between cultures and societies.

Volume 1: *Reynard the Fox: Social Engagement and Cultural Metamorphoses in the Beast Epic from the Middle Ages to the Present*
Edited by Kenneth Varty

Volume 2: *Echoes of Narcissus*
Edited by Lieve Spaas in association with Trista Selous

Volume 3: *Human Nature and the French Revolution: From the Enlightenment to the Napoleonic Code*
Xavier Martin, translated from the French by Patrick Corcoran

Volume 4: *Secret Spaces, Forbidden Places: Rethinking Culture*
Edited by Fran Lloyd and Catherine O'Brien

Volume 5: *Relative Points of View: Linguistic Representations of Culture*
Edited by Magda Stroinska

Volume 6: *Expanding Suburbia: Reviewing Suburban Narratives*
Edited by Roger Webster

HUMAN NATURE AND THE FRENCH REVOLUTION

From the Enlightenment to the Napoleonic Code

Xavier Martin

translated from the French by Patrick Corcoran

Berghahn Books
New York • Oxford

First published in 2001 by **Berghahn Books**

www.BerghahnBooks.com

© French edition 1994 Editions Dominique Martin Morin

Originally published as
Nature humaine et révolution française

© English-language edition
2001 Berghahn Books Inc. New York/Oxford

Translated from the French by Patrick Corcoran
The translation of this book has been made possible thanks to a subsidy from the 'Ministère français de l'Education nationale, de l'Enseignement supérieur et da la Recherche'

All rights reserved.
No part of this publication may be reproduced in any form or by any means without the written permission of Berghahn Books.

Library of Congress Cataloging-in-Publication Data

Martin, Xavier.
    [Nature humaine et Révolution française. English
    Human nature and the French Revolution : from the Enlightenment to the Napoleonic Code / Xavier Martin ; translated from the French by Patrick Corcoran.
        p. cm. -- (Polygons ; v. 3)
    Includes bibliographical references
    ISBN 1-57181-709-3 (alk. paper)
    1. Philosophical anthropology--France--History--18th century. 2. Enlightenment--France. 3. France--History--Revolution, 1789–1799. I. Title. II. Series.

BD450.M277313 2000.R44 2001
128'.0944'09033--dc.21

00-049349

British Library Cataloguing in Publication Data

A catalogue record for this book is available from the British Library.

Printed in the United States on acid-free paper.

ISBN 1-57181-709-3 (hardback)

Contents

Foreword	vii
Notes on Translation	ix
Abbreviations	x
1. Human Nature	1
2. Helvétius and d'Holbach	5
3. Voltaire	15
4. Rousseau	35
5. Pedagogy and Politics	73
6. Mirabeau and Sieyès	83
7. The Audacity of the Philanthropists	103
8. Robespierre	121
9. Making an Impression	141
10. Cabanis and Destutt de Tracy	149
11. La Réveillière-Lépeaux and Leclerc	173
12. Supervised Sovereignty	189
13. Madame de Staël and Constant	197
14. Bonaparte: *Idéologue?*	209
15. The Napoleonic Code	251

Conclusion	271
Bibliography	277
Index	285

Foreword

The present study grew out of a conference paper given at the Société d'Histoire du Droit (Legal History Society, Paris) in April 1993.[1] Originally, it was meant to be the first chapter of a work which would probably have borne the same title, and for which a number of further chapters were already mapped out. However the internal dynamics of the argument, and the various issues which the conference itself brought to light, made it necessary to expand the whole undertaking into the form of a book. Its very origins then should make it quite clear that the resulting volume makes no claim to being in any way a definitive statement on the matter.

What view of man did the French revolutionaries, in essence, hold? Anyone who purports to be interested in 'the rights of man' which the Revolution is generally considered to have ushered in, could be expected to see this question as crucial, and yet surprisingly it is rarely raised. I myself came across it through the happenstance of my work as a legal historian, and not without feeling very early on that the realities which we are introduced to, when we peruse even the more well known of the original sources, tend to differ markedly from the official, shall we say 'academic' discourse, which enjoys favour among lawyers but equally – and very frequently too – among historians and students of literature, or philosophers and students of politics. For the question, by its very nature, cuts across many disciplines.

A number of ideas or hypotheses, formulated over a period of many years and as a result of various contacts, led, in the fullness of time, to a set of rather strange conclusions, the coherence and the explicatory value of which seem to me to have stood not only the test of time but also a form of scrutiny all the more rigorous in that it was often judiciously circumspect. Feedback received from students proved to be a stimulus to this research, as did the numerous *colloquia*, organised here and there to celebrate the bicentenary of the French Revolution. These provided opportunities to 'test' the results in a scientific context and, sometimes too, to make the organisers of such *colloquia* themselves rather testy.

Indeed, many aspects of the study which follows are likely to be considered surprising. And just as the historiographical view of the Revolution cultivated in France seems to play an organic role in helping to determine certain forms of the national consciousness, so any departure from the academic norm in these matters is perceived as an attack on intellectual comfort, which very often implies an attack on comforts of a less immaterial kind. But some readers may quite naturally be sincerely surprised at the conclusions which this book draws and which vie with one another to be included in its own *conclusion*. If that be so then let them remember that 'philosophy is the daughter of wonderment'.

Note

1. "*Unbeknownst to them*. The Civil Code as a social control mechanism?" Conference chaired by Professor Olivier Guillot.

Notes on Translation

Throughout the text certain words which have no direct equivalent in English, or which are commonly encountered in their French form by English readers, have not been translated but have been maintained in French either in quotation marks (e.g. 'vicaire savoyard') or in italics (e.g. *Tribunat, idéologie* et cetera).

All quotations from secondary sources, whether in the body of the text or in the notes, are my own translations.

All titles of books, articles, conference papers et cetera have not been translated but appear in the language of origin.

In the notes, any comments from the translator appear in square brackets.

Patrick Corcoran
Translator

ABBREVIATIONS

C.O.P.L.F. Corpus des Œuvres de Philosophie en Langue française (Collection published by Éditions Fayard)

N.B.O.H. Under the direction of J. Massin, *Napoléon Bonaparte, L'Œuvre et l'Histoire*, 12 Vols., Paris, 1969–71.

The title of older books is generally followed by an indication in brackets of the date of their first edition or the approximate date of composition.

Words in italics in quotations almost always indicate emphasis which the author has chosen to make. Exceptions are distinguished by the abbreviation (w.u.o.): word(s) underlined in the original.

Chapter 1

Human Nature

In May 1803, at the time when the French Civil Code was being drafted, one of the orators of the *Tribunat*, in seeking to justify the granting of a legal concession allowing inherited property to be disposed of between brothers, makes the following statement: 'It is sufficient that one brother, although incapable of loving his sibling, should at least realise that his hatred should not be openly declared, and these feelings which are rooted in convention, will eventually become *a matter of habit* for him and little by little, and so to speak unbeknownst to himself, he will be led towards more friendly feelings'[1] *Unbeknownst to himself.* In February 1804, one of his colleagues, while vaunting the fact that goods which form part of a woman's dowry remain inalienable and that this is an effective means of protecting an ageing lady from the rapaciousness of the family circle, explains himself thus: 'In the uselessness of her decrepitude and in the all too common weakened state of affections and most sacred memories, it is important that it should never be possible to separate her from this dowry which becomes more and more vital to her with each passing day, *even if it only serve as a bait*, a coveted object which works upon even the most virtuous individuals unbeknownst to themselves'. *Unbeknownst to themselves.* And he hammers the point home: 'Yes, even if it be the case that self-interest is here being dressed up in the guise of respect and affection, the ageing lady and mother of the family will nonetheless enjoy *this final sweet illusion*', meaning: the timely illusion on the part of this ancient, decrepit but far from impecunious woman of being loved by her family for her own sake.²

The pattern which thus emerges, and which in fact appears to be at the very heart of the elaboration of the Civil Code, is that of a legislator manipulating the fabric of humanity as though it were a *purely passive substance*, with the express aim of creating the sort of society which he has chosen to engineer. His efforts make full use of that mainspring of human nature: self-interest, and suggest that the totality of interpersonal relationships can be founded on inheritance laws which resemble forms of implicit blackmail, yet which mechanistically foster the development of good social habits. There is a grain of sand in the works, however: female irrationality and the fact that self-interest seems to work only in fits and starts where women are concerned. That is why, in 1804, when another member of the *Tribunat* is seeking to maintain that a wife is legally subordinate to her husband, he rails against 'her weakness, her goodness, her dangerous sensitivity', pointing out: 'These are the real enemies which constantly assail her and against which she must be protected *unbeknownst to herself* and even against her own free will'.³

That the compilers of the Civil Code should have taken it upon themselves to decide what is good for women, unbeknownst to them, is hardly surprising, but that such an endeavour should, as we have seen, have also encompassed the male sex is another matter. It is rather more likely, it would seem, to lead us to cast doubt upon that deeply ingrained belief held by many specialists, that what lies at the very heart of the Napoleonic Code is an overzealously optimistic view of mankind and an absolute confidence in the sovereignty of his free will.⁴ This leads us to suggest that it might be useful to hazard an explanatory hypothesis. It is based on two initial premises that should not provoke too many howls of protest. The first is that the principles which underpin the drafting of the French Civil Code (1800–04) possibly have a direct relationship to those which gave rise to the French Revolution (1789–99). The second is that the principles which come into play during the Revolution are perhaps directly related to those which were in evidence in Enlightenment philosophy. The unambitiousness of these initial premises indicates that our aim is to proceed carefully. Our project entails little more than a sort of meditative, but sometimes very surprising, trip around the site of an archaeological dig. Many of the sections visited will be only glimpsed even though they may deserve more thorough consideration.

The anthropology of the Enlightenment is of central concern here. Under the guise of scientific thought it propagates an idea of the inner man as nothing more than a pure and simple *passivity* that can be manipulated as the need arises, and if possible unbeknownst to himself, so that social harmony may prevail. This manipulation, it is believed, can be undertaken without moral side-effects and without too much technical difficulty. Having been trained to teach more or less the opposite point of view, and having done so more than most, I am not unaware of the fact that such a view may lack appeal for many people. And yet, I was eventually obliged to accept the fact that we are here dealing with what looks like a commonplace of Enlightenment thinking.

Without going back to absolute beginnings, it is worth remarking that the basis of such a conception of man is mechanistic and sensualist and for these reasons tends, at very least, towards the materialist. Indeed the tendency is to believe that in all aspects of human life there is not so much as the smallest detail that can escape the control of a cosmic determinism channelled into the laws of motion. In so far as this applies to man, the result is *sensualism*, that is to say, the belief that the reality of man's innermost being is nothing other than a series of purely chemical reactions to the sensations which he experiences. This idea is of capital importance and its implications will be far-reaching. By the very nature of things, and given the range of sources appealed to, these implications will be something of a leitmotif throughout this book. They include: firstly, the negation, or at least a serious questioning, of the existence of any active principle in human beings, of any deliberative faculty that can be distinguished from the mechanical interplay of sense experiences; secondly, the logical tendency to deny any nonmaterial dimension to man or any decisive boundary line separating him from the animal kingdom; and thirdly, the deliberate negation of human will, of free will and of notions of responsibility, and consequently of human dignity – so many negations which will be of interest to those with a mind of a legal bent or those who consider themselves as belonging to polite society. They will perhaps be of even greater interest to those who do not consider themselves to be gentlefolk at all, and who are usually classed as quite the opposite, since this whole frame of reference somewhat undermines the usefulness of any such classifications. This frame of reference is indeed one of the major factors allowing the 'progressives' of that time to discredit and render outdated the whole Catholic tradition. The anthropological perspective of that tradition was probably obscure precisely because it was medieval, but it taught exactly the opposite viewpoint, postulating that there was an active principle at work in all men and thereby providing a basis for a worldview which was contrary in every respect to that posited by the age of Enlightenment.[5]

It is probably true to say that this latter point of view seems to be expressed at times in little more than a whisper: in the first place because it is difficult to consistently present a thoroughly materialist point of view, and secondly because the threat of censorship that is always in the air is conducive to a prudent attitude and then, too, because the authors themselves recognise the pernicious effect of their theories on the fabric of society in that they question the very notion of individual responsibility, and finally because everyone has the right to hesitate and to waver between deism and atheism, or to profess an interest in the souls of animals with the sole intention of indirectly arguing that the soul of man is little different et cetera. But these recantations are of little real importance. What really matters is that the reductive tendencies we have outlined are in fact expressed everywhere (and often ring true) to the extent that they substantially influence a number of very important writers and not just the out-and-out materialists with whom we shall begin.

Notes

1. *Archives Parlementaires*, 2/5/85/2, Favard, to the *Corps Législatif*, on the Title relating to gifts bestowed among the living and testaments, 13th floréal year XI, 3 May 1803.
2. *Archives Parlementaires*, 2/5/435/2, Carrion-Nisas, to the *Tribunat*, against the bill concerning marriage contracts and the respective rights of spouses, 19th pluviôse year XII, 9 February 1804.
3. *Archives Parlementaires*, 2/6/165/2, Lahary, to the *Corps Législatif*, on the bill concerning forced expropriation, 28th ventôse year XII, 19 March 1804.
4. On this subject, see my own study 'The mythology of the Napoleonic Code', *Himeji International Forum of Law and Politics* (University Dokkyo, Himeji, Japan) no. 1, (1993): 27–38.
5. Saint Thomas Aquinas, *Summa Theologica*, I-IIae, Prol.: 'Homo factus ad imaginem Dei dicitur, secundum quod per imaginem significatur intellectuale et arbitrio liberum, et per se potestativum; (...) ipse est suorum operum principium, quasi liberum arbitrium habens, et suorum operum potestatem" Cf. E. Gilson, *Le Thomisme*, 6th edn, Paris, 1979, 264–5 et circa.

Chapter 2

Helvétius and d'Holbach

It is to the *Encyclopédistes*: especially Helvétius and d'Holbach, that we must turn if we wish to find materialist anthropologists of any real importance. Helvétius (1715–71) provoked an enormous scandal around his name by resolutely accepting the materialist doctrine in his two books *De l'Esprit*, (1758) and the intentionally posthumously published, *De l'Homme*, (1773).[1] 'In men, physical sensation is everything', he writes, 'feeling is all',[2] In other words, nothing in the mind of man goes beyond the biological interplay of sense experiences, 'in humankind the soul is nothing more than the capacity to feel'.[3] And he is not afraid to be absolutely explicit: 'In all cases, *judgement* is *feeling*', he insists.[4] 'Once that has been posited, all the operations of the mind can be reduced to pure sensations. Why then should we claim to have a capacity to judge which is somehow distinct from a capacity to feel?'.[5] 'Any judgement is never anything more than a way of *expressing feelings which have been experienced*'.[6] 'Any idea whatsoever can therefore, in the final analysis, *always* be reduced to physical sensations or physical realities'.[7] 'Physical sensitivity (that is to say: the capacity to receive sense experiences) is therefore the sole driving force of mankind',[8] and it is quite 'useless to suggest that we have other faculties'.[9]

By the same token, all human behaviour can be explained by the notion of self-interest, which, Helvétius insists, is itself reducible to physical need. 'In the moral universe, as in the physical universe, there exists one single principle which drives us and that principle can be no other than that of self-interest'.[10] This is the case, for example, with friendship which in theory can be totally explained by reference to the advantages which we hope to gain from it: 'Friendship, like avarice, pride, ambition and the other passions, is directly ascribable to our physical capacity to feel';[11] and it is at this point that he explains that a very clever man, in the presence of two good friends, can be in 'no doubt that in predicting the exact moment when these two friends will cease to be mutually useful to each other, can simultaneously calculate the exact moment when their friendship will end, just as an astronomer can predict the exact moment of an eclipse'.[12] Remorse too, like friendship, pride and the rest, is 'the effect upon us of physical sensitivity'.[13] 'As for the ability we have of comparing one object with another, it is easy to prove that this ability is nothing more than the advantage that we can derive from making the comparison, and if we further analyse this advantage it can itself be explained in terms of physical sensations'.[14] Helvétius' books are neither short of, nor sparing in, claims of this kind.

And since the human being's physical capacity to feel is thus the sole 'principle governing his needs, his passions, his sociability, his ideas, his judgements, his preferences and his actions',[15] he is a completely conditioned being. It is not possible to consider him as anything other than a purely passive being. He is nothing more than an insignificant component of the animal kingdom, lacking any freedom within 'the holy chain of being, father of the heavenly gods, of suns, of planets and of men'.[16] 'Man, he points out, is a machine which, once set in motion, *must* carry out the actions that ensue. He is the waterwheel ... moved by the stream'.[17] 'Man and the animals are merely machines made of flesh and blood and capable of feeling', agrees Diderot,[18] shortly after having read *De l'Homme* three times, 'an excellent work, full of intelligent thoughts', which 'will have effects as far-reaching as its reputation'.[19] A corollary of all this is the possibility of manipulating individuals as though they were puppets, by calculating the sense impressions to which they might be exposed and by triggering off the action of the decisive mainspring that is self-interest. 'In order to control the movements of the human doll', Helvétius says, it is sufficient to 'understand the strings that operate it'.[20] This, very largely, is the philosophy expounded by Helvétius and which, we should not forget, was destined to become almost the official view in France in the decade up to 1804.

His accomplice and friend,[21] baron d'Holbach (1723–89), is no less important a figure, far from it. If, despite the real interest they aroused, his writings were perhaps less sensational than those of Helvétius, it is because he preferred to hide behind a pseudonym or to publish anonymously. But the system of thought he developed, although in many ways analogous to the work of Helvétius, exhibits a far greater dialectical power than the latter, with his rather dilettante approach, was capable of – and d'Holbach made a point of honour of facing head on the reductionist implications of his work, which consequently makes them stand out all the more. His *Système de la Nature*, published in 1770,[22] insists upon these almost to the point of obsession. Hundreds of pages of talented prose are devoted to his attempts to prove that the moral sphere is in fact nothing more than the physical sphere,[23] and that *to think is merely to feel* [24] that *freedom is nothing but an illusion*, nothing but a dream and an absurd fairytale,[25] that nothing whatsoever can possibly escape the effects of inexorable *necessity*, which implacably determines, to the last detail, the workings of the cosmic theatre we inhabit as well as the destiny of each and every one of us as we are driven mechanically towards obeying the urgings of self-interest. 'All the failings of mankind are physical failings'.[26] 'Necessarily', 'necessary', 'necessity', 'necessitate' and 'determine' are words which punctuate his work at regular intervals, acting as the cement which helps him to build this monument to the triumph of reason, the cornerstone of which is the unshakeable certainty that the nature of mankind is one of pure and unmitigated passivity.

'Throughout his entire life, he likes to say, man is a *passive instrument* in the hands of necessity'.[27] 'Our life is a line that nature commands us to trace on the surface of the earth and which we have no power to waver from for a single instant'. And yet, he mocks, 'they claim we are free'.[28] 'The way we think' depends 'on our natural organisation and on the modifications which are worked upon our machine independently of our will',[29] we are constantly 'modified either by visible or by hidden causes which necessarily control the way we are, the way we think and the way we act'. 'From all of which we are obliged to conclude that our thoughts and our ideas, the way we see things, the way we feel, the judgements we make, the way we put our ideas together are none of them freely chosen or the result of our own will'.[30] 'Man is therefore not free for a single moment of his life',[31] 'no more free to think than to act'.[32]

Diderot, whose way of thinking is rather less rigorous and more volatile, nevertheless clearly tends towards the same reductionism. 'Consider it very closely', he recommends, 'and you will see that the word *freedom* is a word that has no meaning; that free beings do not exist and cannot exist; that we are merely what the general state of things would have us be, what organisation, education and circumstances demand. These are the things that make us willy nilly as we are'.[33] He maintains that anyone who views the world from a higher vantage point must accept that 'the man who prunes a tree ... the caterpillar which nibbles its leaves' are merely 'two different types of insect, each concerned with its own affairs',[34] and he scoffingly talks of 'all these two-legged mites that we call men'.[35] This is the same Diderot who reduces (or perhaps promotes) man and all other animals to the status of a musical instrument, to that of a 'harpsichord which is alive and capable of feeling'.[36] This type of metaphor is the order of the day. Helvétius uses it,[37] and d'Holbach compares 'human souls ... to musical instruments whose strings, already different from each other in type and in respect of the materials from which they are made, are also pitched differently', from whence comes the purely material diversity of what we call the 'moral realm'.[38]

We could quote d'Holbach for hours on end. The prisoner who escapes, he explains, is not free to not want to escape, and Socrates, who doesn't escape when condemned to death, is simply proving that he is the slave to a superior form of conditioning which allows him not to submit to the desire to escape[39]. And similarly: 'There is no difference whatsoever between a man who is thrown out of a window and a man who throws himself out of a window except that the force which acts upon the first comes from the outside and the force which provokes the fall of the second comes from within his own machine'.[40] All of which leads to a definition-*negation*, if we can coin such an expression, which has echoes of Spinoza. The latter wrote: 'That *thing* is said to be free which exists by virtue of the sole necessity of its own nature and which acts because itself alone determines that the action should occur'.[41] '*To be free*', d'Holbach teaches, 'is to yield to the necessary motives for action that we carry within ourselves'.[42] Or yet again: 'Human freedom is merely the necessity that man contains within himself',[43] an internal necessity that is itself affected (the debt due to sensualism) by the mechanistic interplay of impressions received from external sources:[44] man is 'purely passive in the impressions that he receives'.[45] Spinoza wrote, men 'are continually affected by external bodies'.[46] They 'also make the mistake', he said, 'of believing that they are free; and for them this belief consists solely of the fact that they are conscious of their actions, while remaining ignorant of the causes by which these are determined',⁴⁷ determined, we would conclude, *unbeknownst to themselves.*

Quite justifiably, a censor will sum up d'Holbach's thinking in the following words: 'According to this writer, man is not free. He is necessarily conditioned by the impressions he receives from the external world, by the ideas which come into being within his brain, *unbeknownst to him*'.⁴⁸ And we have no choice but to point out that this latter expression is frequently used by d'Holbach to underline the absolute passivity of the human machine. He assures us that man is conditioned 'often *unbeknownst to himself* and always in spite of himself'.⁴⁹ We are nothing but the playthings of our sense experiences, 'which mechanistically control all our actions *unbeknownst to ourselves*'.⁵⁰ Properly speaking therefore, there is no such thing as intellection. Our thoughts 'have arranged themselves in our brains *unbeknownst to* and in spite of ourselves'.⁵¹ And the brain is no more than a slave to 'the causes which in spite of itself and *unbeknownst to itself* continually act upon it'.⁵² The evidence would suggest that there is no such thing as will either. 'As we travel down the path that, *unbeknownst to us* and often in spite of us, nature has mapped out for us we are like swimmers who are forced to go along with the current that is carrying them off'.⁵³ Elsewhere, he says that it is a certain 'fermentation' of molecules 'which by gradually modifying man, often *unbeknownst to* and in spite of himself, make him think, wish and act in a determined and necessary way'⁵⁴. And from this he goes on to imagine that the rise of Islam can be invoked by way of illustration, a rise he imputes to 'a sensual, ambitious and deceitful Arab who was ruled by his passions', asking: 'What are the elements that need to be combined to produce a sensual, ambitious and deceitful man, ruled by his passions ...? They are the minute particles of his blood, the imperceptible fibres of his flesh, the more or less bitter mineral salts that stimulate his nerves, the greater or lesser amount of igneous matter that flows in his arteries' et cetera.⁵⁵ And it is all in the same vein: 'Man's ideas, thoughts, fleeting opinions' depending as they always do on the action exerted upon our organs 'by an infinity of causes which are either external to our being or are contained within our own machine' and which have an overall effect such that these 'organs are perpetually modified *unbeknownst to us*'.⁵⁶ In a word: 'The man who *believes himself to be free* is like a fly who believes he is in control of the movements of the whole machine of the universe, while it is merely being carried along by it *unbeknownst to itself*'.⁵⁷

Is it possible to imagine a surer way of reducing man to insignificance? Not a shred of freedom in evidence in any man, no active principle anywhere to be seen, no 'motivating principle independent of the machine itself',[58] but simply a complete and totally malleable passivity. As a consequence, man is a mere mechanism without responsibility for his actions. There is therefore no merit in claiming to be 'a virtuous man' if the latter is no more than 'a machine whose springs are adapted in such a way as to fulfil the functions of being pleasant to others'.[59] Men are no more than 'weak playthings in the hands of necessity', their least actions always depend upon 'a cause which sets them in motion unbeknownst to themselves and in spite of themselves'.[60] Now all this is of considerable importance, for the baron d'Holbach is far from being a marginal figure of the Enlightenment, some sort of obscure maverick. On the contrary, it is he who is the foremost figure in the financing of the *Encyclopédie*, to which he contributed almost four hundred and fifty articles. More generally, he is one of the most active and committed propagators of the new thinking. And this suggests that, as far as our own thesis is concerned, the *centre of gravity* of the Enlightenment is perhaps rather closer than we might previously have believed to such ways of thinking. This is a view that an appeal to Voltaire rather curiously corroborates and which the example of Rousseau, no less surprisingly, would seem to bear out. All of which leads us to suppose that, in so far as political anthropology is concerned, the Enlightenment could well be generally seen as a zone of rather lower axiological pressure than one might, in all sincerity, have thought it to be.

Notes

1. Claude-Adrien Helvétius, *De l'Esprit*, Paris, 1758, re-edited C.O.P.L.F., Paris, 1988. Helvétius, *De l'Homme, de ses facultés intellectuelles et de son éducation*, London, 1773, re-edited C.O.P.L.F., 2 vols., Paris, 1989. One month before his death, Helvétius gave a good summary of his system in a letter to V.-L. Dutens dated 26 November 1771: *Correspondance générale d'Helvétius*, 3 vols., (4th vol. in preparation), Toronto/Oxford, 1981, 1984 and 1991, vol. 3, 371–72.
2. Helvétius, *De l'Homme*, vol. 1, respectively 141 (and 194), and 179.
3. Helvétius, *Corr. gén.*, vol. 3, 371, 'since any imbecile has a soul'.
4. *De l'Homme*, vol. 1, 158 (w.u.o); *Corr, gén.*, vol. 3, 152, letter of 1765?
5. *De l'Homme*, vol. 1, 159.
6. Ibid. and 161 and164 (w.u.o); *Corr. gén.*, vol. 3, 371.
7. *De l'Homme*, vol. 1, 164.

8. Ibid., 171
9. Ibid., 194.
10. *Corr. gén.*, vol. 3, 36, letter of 15 April 1762 to the Abbé François Arnaud.
11. Helvétius, *De l'Esprit*, 323.
12. Ibid., 315, note b.
13. *De l'Homme*, vol. 1, 173.
14. *Corr. gén.*, vol. 3, 372.
15. *De l'Homme*, vol. 1, 194.
16. *Corr. gén.*, vol. 3, 274, letter to Voltaire, 3 January 1767.
17. *De l'Homme*, vol. 1, 'He is the waterwheel which is moved by the stream, which raises its pistons and thereafter the water which is destined to pour down into the pools which have been built to receive it' (194–95).
18. Denis Diderot, *Mémoires pour Catherine II* (1773–4), ed. P. Vernière, Paris, 1966, 245.
19. Diderot, letter to Mme d'Epinay, 22 July 1773, in *Correspondance Générale d'Helvétius*, vol. 3, 446 and 447.
20. Helvétius, *De l'Homme*, vol. 1, 45.
21. This complicity can also be traced through the correspondence of Helvétius: on 15 May 1764, for example, he writes to his wife: 'I am much inclined to rent another, somewhat cheaper house ... But I implore you not to have us move further away from the baron d'Olbac [sic]' (*Corr. gén.* vol. 3, 132).
22. P.H. d'Holbach, *Système de la Nature, ou des loix du monde physique et du monde moral*, 2 vols., supposedly by 'M. Mirabaud'; various re-editions, including that published in London, 1781, reprinted by C.O.P.L.F., Paris, 1990 (edition used here).
23. *Système de la Nature*, vol. 1, 40, 130–31, 152–53 et cetera.
24. 'What is to think ... if not to feel?' (ibid., 281). Likewise, 185: 'All those faculties to which we give the name intellectual, are explained by our capacity to feel' (w.u.o).
25. These are his own words: ibid., vol. 2, 216.
26. Ibid., vol. 1, 41.
27. Ibid., 107.
28. Ibid., 214.
29. Ibid., 225–26.
30. Ibid., 226.
31. Ibid., 229. 'Given that action is always a result of the power of vol.ition once this has been determined, and given that vol.ition cannot be determined by anything other than causes over which we have no control, it follows that we are never the masters to determine our own acts of volition and that, consequently, *we never act freely*' (223).
32. Ibid., 212.
33. Denis Diderot, *Correspondance*, ed.G. Roth, vol. 1, Paris, 1955, 213, letter to Landois, 29 June 1756 (w.u.o).
34. Diderot, *Le Neveu de Rameau* (1761), Paris, 1965, 107.
35. Diderot, *Correspondance*, vol. 4, Paris, 1958, to Sophie Volland, 25 July 1762.
36. Diderot, *Entretien entre d'Alembert et Diderot* (around 1770) Paris, 1965, 51; 50: 'We are musical instruments endowed with feeling and memory. Our senses are so many piano keys that are played by Nature around us and often by ourselves too'; 55: 'An animal is a musical instrument capable of feeling and perfectly similar to any other, endowed with the same structure, with the same strings that can be played in the same way when

touched by joy, by sorrow, by hunger, by thirst, by illness, by admiration, by fear...'
37. Helvétius, *Corr. gén.*, vol.1, 7, 2 July 1738: 'I have studied myself and I have detected a great capacity for *imagination*: the most insignificant images have an effect on my mind like someone hitting a harpsichord keyboard with a stick' (w.u.o).
38. D'Holbach, *Système de la Nature*, vol. 1, 150. 'Touched in the same way, each key gives off the sound which it is in its nature to make, that is the sound which depends on the material the key is made of, its tension, its size, its momentary state as determined by the surrounding atmosphere, etc.'
39. Ibid., p 231–32.
40. Ibid., 230 note.
41. Benedict de Spinoza, *L'Éthique* (1661–1675), First Part, I, in Spinoza, *Œuvres complètes*, Pléiade, 1 vol., Paris, 1967, 310. Cf. Second Part, proposition XLVIII: 'In the mind, then, there can be no free or absolute will; but the mind is conditioned to want this or that thing by a specific cause which is itself determined by another, this in its turn is determined by another, and so on to infinity' (ibid., 402); and *Traité de l'Autorité politique* (1673–77), chap. II,§ 11, ibid., 928.
42. D'Holbach, *Système de la Nature*, vol. 1, 244 (w.u.o).
43. Ibid., 246.
44. Ibid., 103–104: 'His life is merely a long succession of necessary and connected movements which have at their origins either causes internal to the body, such as its blood, its nerves, its fibres, its fleshy tissue, its bones, in a word the solid or liquid matter of which it is generally composed: or causes which are external to it and which by acting upon it modify it in various ways, such as the air surrounding it, the foodstuffs it takes in, and all the objects which constantly impinge upon its senses and which thereby continually effect changes upon it'.
45. Ibid., 226.
46. Spinoza, *L'Éthique*, Second Part, proposition XLVII, loc. cit., 402
47. Ibid., proposition XXXV, scolie, loc. cit., 389. See also First Part, appendix, 347: 'Men believe that they are free because they are conscious of their own will and of their appetites, and do not think ... about the causes which lead them to want these things, or because they are unaware of them'.
48. Prosecuting Counsel Séguier's speech to the Parlement de Paris (1770): in *Système de la Nature*, vol. 2, 415.
49. Ibid., vol. 1, 106.
50. Ibid., 198.
51. Ibid., 225. And, 231: 'You will say that because an idea originates in your mind you are acting freely if you do not come up against some sort of impediment to stop you. But what made this idea take shape in your mind? Were you in any way capable of preventing it from taking shape or recurring in your brain? Does this idea not really depend upon external objects which influence you in spite of yourself, or internal causes which act upon you *unbeknownst to you*, and thereby modify your brain?'
52. Ibid., 243.
53. Ibid., 245. He adds: 'We believe we are the masters of our destiny because we are forced to move our arms about for fear of sinking'.
54. Ibid., 272.
55. Ibid., 273.
56. Ibid., vol. 2, 299: cf. vol. 1, 331, where '*unbeknownst to us* and in spite of ourselves' also appears.

57. D'Holbach, *Le Bon Sens, ou idées naturelles opposées aux idées surnaturelles* (1772), Paris, Éditions Rationalistes, 1971, 74. This series of references to the use of the expression 'unbeknownst to' is by no means exhaustive: cf. for example *Système de la Nature*, vol.1, 87 and 203.
58. *Système de la Nature*, vol. 1, 108.
59. Ibid., 267.
60. Ibid., 322. The actions of man are merely 'the necessary effects of causes of which he is unaware and which determine his volition'. Cf. also, S. Zac, 'Spinoza', in Y. Belaval, (ed.) *Histoire de la Philosophie*, Pléiade, 3 vols., Paris, 1973, vol. 2, 469.

≈ CHAPTER 3 ≈

VOLTAIRE

'What a vain and feeble thing is man! and yet he claims to be free!' The author of this outburst was the baron d'Holbach.[1] But believe it or not, it might equally well have come from Voltaire. And yet, when we think of Voltaire we do not immediately think of materialism and the blunt rejection of the idea of free will, nor of the scornful attitude to human nature that accompanies these ideas. Whether they are aware of it or not, the vulgarisers of Voltaire's work would seem to have a tendency to refuse to allow any of this side of him to show through, preferring to keep the benefit of this knowledge to themselves, unbeknownst to us, the nonspecialists. In so doing they defer, as is only fitting, to a Voltairean principle: 'The common man is not worth the trouble involved in enlightening him'.[2] Or: 'Truth is not for the ears of everyone. The vast majority of mankind is unworthy of it.'[3] Now, although it is true that Voltaire was very slow indeed to fully assume reductionist views of such grave consequence as those we have just outlined, we must nevertheless accept that in the final analysis he did so unambiguously, and that the human archetype which takes shape in his writings over the years proves to be, for him too, very much 'a pitiful thing',[4] a derisory and passive toy offered up to whomsoever wishes and knows how to manoeuvre him. This aspect of Voltaire's thought needs to be carefully presented, partly because of its complexity but partly because Voltaire himself was seemingly so ambivalent about it. In any event, it would seem to deserve deeper analysis.

Voltaire, it must be said, had many reasons for hesitating on such matters. First of all, there is the fact that metaphysics was not his strong suit. For him, it was 'the domain of doubt and of fictions about the soul'.[5] He distrusts it and stops short of venturing into metaphysical speculation.[6] This is one of the numerous points he has in common with Rousseau, who makes his 'vicaire savoyard' say, 'General and abstract ideas are at the root of mankind's greatest mistakes; the jargon of metaphysics has never led to the discovery of a single truth'.[7] In Voltaire's eyes, Locke's greatest merit was that he 'restricted himself to *simply* showing the workings and the limits of human understanding'.[8] As for the rest, Voltaire advises: 'See, touch, measure, weigh, count, assemble, separate, and be sure that you will never do anything other than this'.[9] The disdain for metaphysics, associated with those who favoured the materialist tendency, is a well-known trait of the Enlightenment in France, and Morelly, for example, expressly forbids speculative activity beyond a very restricted field.[10] Nor should we forget the fact that it is possible to be genuinely confused as to the first origins of things. And furthermore, Voltaire considered an overly frank airing of one's convictions to be doubly inconvenient: firstly it might lay him open to censure, he who claimed 'to set greater store by the happiness life has to offer than by a single truth'.[11] This explains his decision, whenever matters of personal conviction were concerned, to frequently, if not constantly, muddy the waters, especially when such convictions lacked a solid foundation. Secondly, there is something inappropriate about openly expressing lines of thinking that it was socially preferable to keep from the commonalty of mankind. Indeed, the fear of a divine presence laying in wait for immortal souls somewhere in the great beyond and the notion that there is 'a God who avenges crimes and rewards virtue',[12] are the best methods yet found to prevent the 'riffraff'[13] from getting out of hand. 'I do not believe', he categorically states, 'that there exists in the whole world a civic leader or a local governor who has even so few as *four hundred of those horses which we call men* to govern, who does not clearly see that he must put some form of god in their mouths to act as a bridle and bit'. And this implies, he confided to the Duchesse de Choiseul, the wife of Louis XV's principal minister,[14] that it is useful that the common run of mankind should *imagine himself to be responsible* for his own actions and intentions. This is why, he says, 'the greater good of society demands that man should believe himself to be free'.[15] *Should believe himself to be free*: are the words he is already using as early as 1738, when his position on such matters was still far from having been decided.[16]

Nevertheless, the tendency is clear and gradually becomes clearer. Already, the simple fact that he does not have, from the very outset, an unshakeable faith in the *objective* dignity of the human being naturally prepares the ground for instances of axiological subsidence, against which the well-known deism of Voltaire is hardly sufficient to protect him: in fact, the consequence will be that his deism, and this is rarely mentioned, will gradually wane and then disappear entirely.[17] The clock of his famous god-clockmaker[18] may well show evidence of finality and presuppose what he calls 'design relationships',[19] but quite apart from the fact that such properties are not particularly exciting where clocks are concerned, they are certainly insufficient grounds for claiming there is a spiritual or immortal ingredient in the clock's make-up and that Voltaire's clock can be considered as possessing attributes that are not normally found in all clocks. The immortality of the soul may be a preoccupation which constantly haunts Voltaire but we never see him really believe in it. 'We are as nature has fashioned us', he says in 1751, 'thinking automata that are built to work for a certain time, *and then nothing more*'.[20] Or he evokes 'those fleeting moments we are left with and which are followed by no other moment'.[21] And elsewhere: 'When I say soul, it is in order to respect common linguistic usage, for we are perhaps no more than machines'.[22] Montesquieu in the *Lettres persanes* has a Frenchman say that the state of his beliefs is a function of his physical make-up, and that he believes in the immortality of the soul 'on a termly basis'.[23]

Uncertainty on these matters will lead Voltaire to readily adopt a scoffing tone. Hence he compliments the husband of a mother-to-be on 'the embryo of the immortal soul which has been lodged for two months between the rectum and the bladder of Madame d'Hornoy'.[24] To sum up, very briefly, his obsessions with nothingness and with annihilation provide good grounds for concluding that he no longer believes in an immortal soul at all.[25] Nevertheless, and for all that, he never ceased to consider it desirable that the common run of mankind should be encouraged to remain under the illusion that immortal souls exist, and this for the reasons we have already outlined. He explains elsewhere with even greater clarity, 'it is a very good thing to persuade men to believe that they have an immortal soul, and that there is an avenging God who will punish my peasants if they steal my wheat or my wine'.[26] In a Voltairean context, what this negation of the immortality of the soul implies is, in a quite obvious and logical way, the simultaneous obliteration of the nonmaterial dimension in the make-up of the human being. It would be a serious mistake to think that there is any attempt here to criticise Voltaire on this score: I would simply wish to underline the fact that coming to negative conclusions of this sort has certain logical consequences. It necessarily exposes mankind, in the opinion of the deist Voltaire just as much as in the opinion of the atheist d'Holbach, to the fate of pure passivity that is quite naturally and unavoidably present in the 'mechanicistic' way of thinking.

And this 'mechanicistic' way of thinking is very much a characteristic of Voltaire's thought. He is disappointed by La Mettrie's *L'Homme-Machine*, but he considers the title 'admirable',[27] and re-uses the expression on occasion.[28] 'We are clocks; we are machines', he has the habit of saying.[29] He also congratulates future parents on 'the little machine, as yet scarcely organised, that your two machines have produced without even knowing how'.[30] 'We are pitiful machines':[31] is a fairly common remark from him, one which he sometimes qualifies with an occasional 'perhaps'. Nor can there be any question that the supposed boundary separating man from the animals should be considered in any way significant: 'A repeater watch would need to be insolent indeed to think itself endowed with a completely different nature to that of the mechanical roasting-spit'.[32] He is quite taken with this graduated metaphor and had even employed it in a self-deprecatory way when comparing himself to an 'old roasting-spit' filled with envy by the vivacity of the two 'beautiful repeater watches' that are d'Alembert and Diderot.[33]

Voltaire was not one to theorise about sensualism, which can be considered as the eighteenth-century bridgehead of mechanicism in anthropology. But as a man of his times he professes himself to be a sensualist. He quietly sacrifices at the altar of sensualism, one might say, and he expressly gives his backing to Condillac, who is its theoretician *par excellence*, however much he seems to simultaneously profess a very ambiguous form of spiritualism. 'It seems to me that no-one thinks as deeply or as soundly as you', Voltaire tells Condillac[34] expressing the wish that he should agree to allow his work to be popularised for general consumption, 'in order to condense into a single volume everything that it is given to man to know about metaphysics', and offering him lodgings to allow him to carry out this worthy task.[35] Consequently, he himself, like his friend la marquise du Deffand, is always ready to explain the inner workings of the human being by nothing more complex than an appeal to the simple interplay of the five senses,[36] through formulations of this sort : 'The soul, poor thing, this sixth sense which depends entirely on the other five, suffers much from the decadence of the machine'.[37]

Someone like d'Holbach frequently uses the term 'machine' to refer to human beings. Voltaire often uses it to refer to himself, or to be more precise, to refer to his body. But if there is no such thing as a soul, what part of his being is there that is not mechanical? And if perhaps such a part exists, lodged somewhere within the machine, it only brings us back to the riddle posed by Cartesian anthropology, the very spiritualism of which advanced the cause of materialism, precisely because it was not viable. 'In vain can the privilege of freedom be claimed for mankind through appeals to the fact that he is a sentient being', concludes Jean Rostand.[38] 'If animals are merely machines it is quite clear that man too must be a machine. When modern science agrees with Descartes, it also agrees with La Mettrie'.[39] So when Voltaire says 'my machine', we understand that it is far more than a mere figure of speech, it has the value of a doctrinal nostrum. The frequency with which it is uttered and its mental context force us to this conclusion. It is also worth mentioning that on almost all occasions he qualifies it with a more or less pejorative adjective. The 'machine' is 'feeble', 'pitiful' or 'weak', not to say 'sickly' or 'lamentable'. References to the self involve denigration of the self, a pattern which echoes the quasi-automatic nature of the link between mechanicism and a certain tendency never to overestimate the dignity of man or the humble greatness of his calling.

This double tendency is quite clear in Voltaire's work. In his view, man is quite wrong to consider himself a free and deserving being because he has, in fact, no inherent value. In this respect, the capacity to think has little importance since both Voltaire and Diderot come to argue that matter itself is endowed with this capacity.[40] The man-machine will quite simply be 'a machine endowed with thought' that's all,[41] a 'machine which, I know not how, has the faculty of sneezing through the nose and of thinking with the brain'.[42] 'The gift of thinking with the brain and of feeling throughout the whole machine, are mechanisms'.[43] In other words, we are 'thinking automata',[44] we 'think with our heads in the same way that we walk with our feet'.[45] This is to say that thought is a result of purely mechanical processes, of which some belong to the realm of physiology, while certain others can be attributed to the astounding fertility of a secret structure of language. 'It is certain that every language in the world follows a secret logic which controls human ideas *without our realising it*' that is to say: unbeknownst to us.[46] Men are the playthings of destiny: tennis balls tossed in the air, he says on many occasions, or bowls that follow the incline of the bowling-alley. 'Poor automata that we are, we are not our own masters'.[47] So what of freedom? It is 'in any event a splendid illusion'.[48] And yet, it is not for lack of wanting to believe in it: 'I had a tremendous wish that we should be free. I did everything I could to believe that we are. Reason and experience convince me that we are machines built to work for a certain time, and as God sees fit'.[49] This God is also a very ambiguous notion, since Voltaire continues the letter, for the benefit of Frédéric to whom it is written: 'Thank *nature* for the way your machine has been built'.[50]

Certainly, in this respect, Voltaire does not have the self-assurance of someone like the baron d'Holbach and is far readier than he to add a qualifying 'almost' or a 'so to speak'. But the tendency certainly exists, and is articulated through phrases which are far too polished not to indicate something more than a mere tendency, even if the *Système de la Nature* of 1770, and even more so *De l'Homme* of 1773, cause Voltaire a certain amount of embarrassment. These publications certainly complicate matters somewhat. All the more so in that around this time Voltaire is quite willing to express inegalitarian ideas in his writings to various correspondents. But what is important here is that the reasons he articulates do not fundamentally address the reductionism to be found in the *Encyclopédistes*. They concern either corollaries of the arguments that their books propose, and which, as they stand, he is unable, perhaps wrongly, to accept, or they concern the untimeliness of such publications, which through their blatant lack of respect for the 'powers-that-be' (Voltaire makes this very complaint to the anonymous author – an anonymity behind which d'Holbach is sheltering), or which through their tremendous propensity for convincing the simple-minded that notions of individual responsibility are meaningless thereby threaten the whole cohesion of a society in which Voltaire, when all is said and done, had managed to carve out a comfortable niche: publications, then, which were liable in the very short term to agitate the authorities to the disadvantage of the *philosophes*.

As far as the *Système de la Nature* is concerned, first of all Voltaire is visibly embarrassed although his embarrassment is untainted by any suggestion of criticism,[51] then later to d'Alembert he confesses himself to be very largely in agreement with it,[52] as he does also to Mme du Deffand,[53] when he says of the author that 'although he makes terrible mistakes on some points, he is far superior to Spinosa [sic]',⁵⁴ a very great compliment indeed if we remember that Voltaire writes about the latter saying that as far as he is aware, Spinoza is the only person 'who has reasoned correctly'; but not without adding that he is, alas, unreadable.⁵⁵ But Voltaire is obviously in some confusion since at times he argues that d'Holbach (still unidentified) is inferior to Spinoza in so far as the latter, like Voltaire himself, allows for the existence and the workings of an 'intelligence' in nature.⁵⁶ The fact of the matter is that Voltaire's compass seems to be swinging wildly, and all the more so when he finds himself within the magnetic sphere of influence of the 'powers-that-be': when addressing Frédéric of Prussia or his nephew, the crown prince Frédéric-Guillaume, and when addressing Mme de Choiseul, Voltaire is much more critical of the *Système de la Nature*, adopting a position much closer to deism and spiritualism, fully aware that too strong a rebuffal of such views would not go down well with his royal correspondents.⁵⁷ 'The work is pernicious both in so far as principles and the good of the people are concerned', he concedes to the crown prince.⁵⁸

In spite of which, and this is the crucial point, Voltaire does not break completely with the reductionism of d'Holbach. The very hesitations which we have just outlined are a proof of this fact. And it is precisely 'around 1770', the year in which the *Système* was published, that he confides to an unknown correspondent: 'The notion of freedom, as many scholastic writers understand it, is in point of fact an *absurd illusion*',⁵⁹ but he does not take the trouble to tell us how the word might be understood so as not to be. To claim 'that man is free' is to do no more than to talk 'rubbish', as he has already said much earlier.⁶⁰ And then, in 1775, he expresses strong approval for *Le Bon Sens*, which he guesses to be by the same author as the *Système*, and even goes on to say that 'the author has made considerable progress'⁶¹ from one book to the other, even though *Le Bon Sens*, far from being less reductionist than the *Système*, is quite clearly a sort of *Défense et Illustration*. Indeed, one of the chapters announces: 'Free will is an *illusion*',⁶² an opinion which Voltaire would also have embraced, at least in private.

In all these respects, Voltaire's reaction to the publication of *De l'Homme* in 1773 is also very instructive. Without being able to bring himself to condemn the work outright, he confides to d'Alembert : 'This is perhaps *the gravest blow that could be struck against philosophy*'.⁶³ And why is this so? Because Helvétius, whose *De l'Esprit* (published some fifteen years earlier) had already provoked a storm of censure, had this time, after long rumination, published very similar arguments expressed in a far more powerful and audacious form. As a posthumous publication it exposed its author to no risk whatsoever but this was clearly not the case for his erstwhile colleagues who continued to labour on God's earth. To Voltaire's way of thinking in 1770, it was precisely because of its qualities and because of the fact that there were 'too many good things in it', that the *Système de la Nature* was destined to do 'such terrible harm to philosophy',[64] and, in fact, a short time afterwards, Voltaire claims that the increased police attention to his correspondence was a direct consequence of the book's publication.[65] And now this book, *De l'Homme*, comes along, written by an author who is himself well out of harm's way but whose very name cannot be dissociated from the terrible scandal provoked by his first book and who, furthermore, has the great generosity to compromise Voltaire by inflicting upon him the dubious honour of an epigraph.[66]

The fact is that, in the final analysis, the two 'friends' had little affection for each other. 'I had little to congratulate myself on as far as that innocent old Helvétius was concerned', Voltaire writes after his death,[67] at this point still ignorant of the great posthumous homage that the deceased had taken the trouble to pay him. And this is a sentiment he later reiterates: 'I had little to congratulate myself on as far as he was concerned'.[68] Maybe Voltaire was jealous of the financial and material prosperity of Helvétius. 'The posthumous work of poor old, or should I say, rich old, Helvétius' he lets slip to d'Alembert.[69] Perhaps too, he had not forgotten that Helvétius had once unremittingly demanded payment of the debts[70] owed to him by Mme du Châtelet, Voltaire's mistress. And Helvétius' functions as tax-collector were a source of annoyance to Voltaire, who paid his own taxes at Ferney.[71] Besides which, and perhaps more importantly, Helvétius had always maintained his distance from Voltaire and the latter had not found in Helvétius the docile and yet influential disciple that he had at first dreamed of.[72] And then there was Helvétius' annoying insistence on publishing his work openly, which was not a trait likely to endear him to Voltaire, who was tactically always more inclined to secrecy.[73] In addition, Voltaire would have preferred the younger man to work harder and more energetically[74] for the common cause, devote to it the considerable amount of leisure-time which his wealth afforded him, spend his time unleashing anonymous and painful barbs at the enemy rather than merely creating such a stink and then sinking into total inactivity.[75] 'Destroy the monster *but discreetly*', Voltaire advised him,[76] sometimes adding: 'and without compromising yourself',[77] which might well be interpreted to mean: without compromising *us*.

De l'Homme unashamedly contradicted this advice and exposed Voltaire at a time when he was growing old and hankering after the security of his own four walls – a security that he had won at such cost. 'If people in high station have the time and the patience to read this work', he noted, 'they will never forgive us for it',[78] and he meant that they would not fail to pick out the ten or so pages, among others, in which Voltaire is singled out for praise,[79] he whose extreme prudence was not unknown to Helvétius. This whole affair is so rich in hidden meanings and hidden messages that it seems to me to be a rather narrow interpretation of events to suggest, as one commentator does without offering any deeper analysis whatsoever, that here Helvétius 'was unstinting in the praise he lavished on the patriarch, as though he wished to repay a debt of gratitude'.[80] And he goes on : 'but this was not sufficient to satisfy the old master'.[81] It certainly was not, and for good reason. The person whom, not so long previously, Voltaire used to call antiphrastically that 'innocent old Helvétius' is treating him here in a very offhand way and exposing him without so much as a 'by your leave' to the risk of the thing he fears above all: the threat of being pestered.

What is sure is that in this moment of crisis, the master of Ferney can hardly see himself running off to beg shelter from that other 'friend' who must also be placed inside qualifying quotation marks, Frédéric II of Prussia. The latter, who, two decades earlier, when the honeymoon period of Potsdam was over, had proved himself as versatile as he was enlightened, by unstintingly pouring scorn on Voltaire for the vulgarity of his sycophantic behaviour, had pretended to keep him captive,[82] had told him he deserved to be chained up[83] and had delighted in the terrified squawking, the expressions of doleful repentance, the bleatings of faithful devotion and the various feeble, pleading protestations issuing from the mouth of his tutor in French prosody ('les plus désespérés sont les chants les plus beaux'). Afterwards, when Voltaire had finally set out to remove his person and his effects homeward towards the land of the 'Welches', the 'foreigners' whom he so despised – 'a nation of apes among which there have occasionally been found a few men',[84]– Frédéric had dispatched to Frankfurt yet more of his agents to inflict a few final, shameful humiliations on him.[85] This was the time when Voltaire was in such a state of disarray that he had taken to signing his name 'Goebbels' in order to fool the police of Frédéric, his Prussian hero,[86] whose 'big blue eyes', and 'soft smile', and 'sweet voice', and good taste in things literary, and whose simple good breeding[87] had on first meeting bewitched Voltaire ('all this turns my head'). Voltaire's infatuation with Frédéric had, at the time, made him proud to devote himself 'passionately, blindly and without questioning to his service',[88] and Voltaire had been thrilled, too, with the taste of 'the true freedom one enjoys at Potsdam...', and with the taste of 'strawberries, peaches, grapes, pineapples in the month of January'.[89]

But the fruits of early summer do not last forever. For Voltaire, Sans-Souci was to become something of an antiphrasis. Disgraced and unable to secure permission to leave, he soon comes to the bitter conclusion 'that it is harder to leave this place than Siberia',[90] a cold reality indeed for someone who henceforth has 'no other wish than to get away'.[91] 'I detest this country : my bag is ready packed', he confirms in mid-March 1753.[92] The time had now come when he would refer to the king as his 'mistress' only as a form of bitter derision,[93] and experience had taught him that an enlightened despot worth his salt knows how to handle the whip as a way of paying sycophants for their hypocrisy. Before leaving he was even obliged to repeatedly scrape and bow, and to offer numerous expressions of gratitude[94] and numerous assurances of his contrition towards his benevolent persecutor. 'I once again most humbly entreat his forgiveness for all my faults', he thus writes to the king's sister in June 1753.[95] Even at the age of fifty, it is still true that travel broadens the mind. Voltaire had learned his lesson and would never forget that he had worked for the king of Prussia. Some twenty years later he assures the party concerned that the 'pain' he suffered during that time 'will poison the remainder of [his] days'.[96] This painful episode, and the vagaries of royal censure in France, had made him more than prudent and resolved at any price to protect the privacy of his home, even convincing him, as a final precaution, of the wisdom of living close to the borders of several countries at once. It seems to us that this experience explains his strong reaction to the indiscretions of *De l'Homme*,[97] and that it is not wounded pride that motivates his disavowal of a reductionism of which he certainly had no wish to become the theoretician, but which, as we have seen, he was ready to accept more and more as the years go by.

It is probably very true that what Helvétius teaches about friendship (namely, that it involves a conjunction of common interests and is a purely technical matter), was deeply displeasing to Voltaire, who was in such matters much less coldly logical than the younger man.[98] Probably even more displeasing was the postulate that all men are born with the same intellectual potential, and that variations in the type and number of sense impressions alone suffice to explain the subsequent inequalities that can be observed between one man and the next;[99] not to speak of atheism, this 'sort of philosophy' of which Voltaire will repeatedly say that it 'can do no good and can do a lot of harm'.[100] But the fact remains that what Helvétius thinks of 'freedom' (in other words, his *denial of it*) can, to Voltaire's mind, be counted as one of those 'very good things',[101] which his final work is so full of, and which 'will be well received by all men who are either not stupid or not Jesuits'.[102] 'Essentially his reaction is negative', Roland Desné nevertheless concludes,[103] as if he were thereby pronouncing – could it be inadvertently? – that the existence or nonexistence of a human freedom is not an *essential* question. And it is true that the indifference to the historiographical, literary and political ramifications of this question can only be qualified as elephantesque. The same author goes on to say that, for Voltaire, Helvétius is 'a writer ... whose deepest convictions he could not share'.[104] It seems to me that it would be more correct to say that sharing *some* of his deepest convictions, he was unable to bring himself to *admit* the fact.

And why then, in a letter to d'Alembert of July 1775, does Voltaire appear to accept almost unreservedly baron d'Holbach's *Le Bon Sens*,[105] which is far more powerfully implacable than anything produced by Helvétius, whose dilettantism so often significantly weakened his powers of dialectic? It is because the ideological outlook seems to him to be much brighter. The relative storm provoked by *De l'Homme* has faded over the horizon. Turgot and Malesherbes are ministers.[106] In short, Voltaire's own tendency towards reductionism scares him less than before.

This tendency, to which so many of the quotations presented in the preceding pages seem to bear witness, was probably never so clearly and openly expressed as it was to Mme du Deffand, to whom rather than trumpet his confidences – 'let us fight', he said, 'without bugles and drums'[107] – he chose to address them in plain and measured prose,[108] 'Have you never really reflected on the idea that we might be nothing more than machines?' he wrote to her in March 1764, 'I have felt this to be true through a continuous experience of it'.[109] And once again, two months later, under the rather perverse pretext of trying to raise her spirits, which were flagging as result of her blindness and the emptiness of her day-to-day existence:

> I agree with you that nothingness is, generally speaking, of much greater worth than life, there is some good in nothingness; let us be consoled, we shall have a taste of it. It is quite clear that after our deaths we shall be what we were before we were born, but as far as the two or three minutes of our existence are concerned, what are we to do with them? We are *small cogs in the great machine*, little animals with two hands and two feet like the apes, less agile than them, but just as comical, and possessed with a larger *quantity of ideas* than they. We all follow the general impulsion given by nature, we give each other nothing, we receive everything, *we are no more the masters of our own ideas than we can control the circulation of the blood in our veins*. Every being, every form of life necessarily subscribes to the general laws of nature.[110]

And he continues, a little further on:

> All the privations you suffer, all your feelings, all your ideas are absolutely necessary things. You could not prevent yourself from writing the very philosophical and very sad letter that I received from you; and I am very necessarily writing to you that courage, resignation in respect of the laws of nature ... are true consolations. – This idea that I was destined to bring to your attention makes you necessarily reflect for your own part on your own philosophy. I become an instrument which, by this letter, gives strength to another, and through which I shall in turn be strengthened. *Happy are the machines* which can offer mutual help to each other!'.[111]

Such assertions are of very great importance. On the one hand, they attain a degree of insistence and explicatory value that bears comparison with the writings of the most out-and-out materialists of the whole century. And on the other hand, and this is a very remarkable thing, Voltaire had thought deeply about placing in the public domain an attenuated, asepticised version of his thinking, in which the deterministic content was prudently understated. In this version, the determinism tended to be reduced to a simple figure of speech, a sort of disillusioned fatalism,[112] such as each and every one of us might in our weaker moments succumb to without, for all that, having the slightest intention of seeking to adopt boldly reductionist doctrinal positions. This way of proceeding is certainly very instructive. Through this type of carefully calculated retrograde movement, what Voltaire is also simultaneously telling us is that he is haunted by a double fear: firstly, he is afraid of attracting attention to himself, and, secondly, he worries about disseminating theories which present the very grave threat to society of obliterating all notions of culpability. This was an idea the marquise did not fail to use as a sort of parasol in order to protect herself from any reproaches that might emanate from Ferney.[113]

There can hardly be any doubt, therefore, that, far more than is commonly supposed, Voltaire communes without too much difficulty with the spirit of the reductionist anthropology shared by his 'fellow' *Encyclopédistes*. And it is not difficult to predict that fundamental problems are likely to surface when we consider the question as to what sort of ideology such a seed-bed might produce where the rights of man are concerned. For, once he has set off down this road he will need to build his arguments on the writings of men whose *disdain for mankind* is in no way comparable to the sort of negative, throwaway remarks that drunkards make after some drinking session, but is rather the keystone, the central plank of a carefully thought-out doctrine. And quite logically, Voltaire, by the process of a sort of counterpoint, gradually comes to adopt a resolutely disparaging attitude to humankind both in himself and in respect of others: an attitude so cutting and so obsessive that at times there is something almost hallucinatory about it, an attitude too, which the experts are quite happy to treat as though it never existed: all of which may provide proof of their own intellectual piety but does little to assuage our curiosity. From quite the opposite angle, Mme de Staël's *De l'Allemagne*, is essentially a lively and intelligent counter-attack against the effects of the reductionist element of Enlightenment thinking,[114] and she takes Voltaire to task on this issue, immediately after blaming sensualism ('the philosophy of sense-impressions') for the deplorable decline of metaphysics in France. 'He adopted a curmudgeonly attitude', she writes, 'to final causes, to optimism, to *free will*, to all philosophical opinions which serve to dignify humankind'.[115]

But Mme de Staël was herself a woman of the Enlightenment, and she expresses admiration for Voltaire in other respects : for his work as a playwright, for example.[116] This serves only to increase the severity of her earlier, perceptively focused criticism, which has the added interest for us of being a hypothesis based on completely different sources than that provided by the inexhaustible flow of letters from Voltaire which has been the basis for my own arguments. It is worth noting, too, that, before Mme de Staël, another female enthusiast of the Enlightenment thinking had taken the exact measure of the man: had recognised both the affinity that existed between his deism and the atheistic ideas of his friends and also the disturbing internal contradictions that his narrow view of humanity had produced. And this woman, who is even more interesting in that she was a privileged witness to events and knew Voltaire very well, is Mme du Deffand, who has so often been quoted as the addressee of correspondence in the preceding pages. An event which caused something of a scandal at the time, provided her with an opportunity to discreetly convey to one of her intimate friends not only what she felt about all these questions but also what she felt about Voltaire, and these are feelings which are very relevant to our concerns. At Christmas 1773, a short time after the storm provoked by the publication of Helvétius' posthumous book had broken, two young soldiers committed suicide together in a hostelry near Paris and explained their action in a written note which placed the lion's share of the 'blame' at the door of the nihilistic doctrines which were then enjoying such a press.[117] This affair caught the public imagination and provoked two 'heat of the moment' reactions from Mme du Deffand, both of which came from a single impulse, which is itself highly revealing; but the two reactions were quite different and the gap between them, moreover, highlights the exact position she adopted. Writing to Voltaire on 3 January 1994, she is in a mood to cast blame, but she *only casts blame upon* 'all the pamphlet writers who poison our lives with their bland and boring cogitations',[118] boringness being the standard criticism she levels against Helvétius' books.[119] But only the day before in a letter to Walpole, in order to explain this fatal example of despair, she refers precisely to '*all the writings of Voltaire*, Helvétius and all those atheistic gentlemen',[120] ramming the point home by declaring that the two young suicides are 'the *first martyrs* to their systems'.[121] Coming from such a famous and well-informed follower of Enlightenment ideas – to such an extent that Voltaire can refer to her as 'in the whole of this century, the person closest to my heart and most in harmony with my tastes'[122] – the attack does not lack significance and gives food for thought. 'I find it more honest to know how to suffer', was the weak reply proffered by the visibly shaken Voltaire, to this incongruous attack[123] by which the Marquise soberly informs the writer that as 'pamphlet writers' go he could consider himself responsible for 'whole volumes'.[124] It was not many years before this that Rousseau, for his part, had tried to warn against 'an egoistic philosophy … *whose teachings are deadly*'.[125]

Notes

1. P. H. d'Holbach, *Système de la Nature, ou des loix du monde physique et du monde moral*, vol.1, 276.
2. Voltaire, *Correspondance*, vol. 3, 710; and vol. 8, 819. Given the breadth and quantity of Voltaire's writings I have deemed it sufficient for the purposes of the present study to draw solely upon references from his correspondence. This, I believe, offers a balanced view of his various positions on the matters under consideration. For practical reasons, the edition of his correspondence I have used is that published in the Pléiade collection (which is itself based on the Bestermann edition) with notes translated and adapted by Fr. Deloffre (13 vols, 1977–93).
3. Voltaire,*Corr.*, vol. 7, 877, to Damilaville, 1 October 1764.
4. 'Man is a pitiful thing' (14 November 1775, to André Morellet, *Corr.*, vol. 12, 305.)
5. *Corr.*, vol. 10, 315, to an unidentified person, around 1770.
6. *Corr.*, vol. 7, 586, 23 February 1764: 'True philosophy will take the place of ridiculous sophistry'. *Corr.*, vol. 10, 368, 8 August 1770, to Mme du Deffand: 'this deadly nature that I never stop talking about but about which I understand so little'. *Corr.*, vol. 11, 21 and 383 (1772 and 1773, to d'Alembert).
7. J.-J. Rousseau, *Émile* (1762), Book IV, Paris, 1966, 356.
8. Voltaire, *Corr.*, vol. 7, 586, 23 February 1764, where he goes on to write: 'Let those who would seek to go further beware'.
9. *Corr.*, vol. 9, 237, to Le Cat (1767–68?).
10. E.-G. Morelly, *Code de la Nature* (1755), Paris. 1970, 150–51: 'Laws governing types of study which would prevent erroneous reflections and all transcendant speculation'.
11. To Helvétius, around 11 November 1738: *Corr. gén. d'Helvétius*, vol. 1, Toronto/Oxford, 1981, 10. In 1766, he also writes to d'Argental that 'it would be madness to become a martyr to truth' (Voltaire, *Corr.*, vol. 8, 504).
12. Voltaire,*Corr.*, vol. 8, 699.
13. *Corr.*, vol. 7, 401: 'rewards and punishments after death', 'such a useful idea as far as the riffraff are concerned', vol. 8, 347, 774, Et cetera.
14. *Corr.*, vol. 10, 430.
15. To Helvétius, around 11 November 1738: *Corr. gén. d'Helvétius*, vol. 1, Toronto/Oxford, 1981, 10.
16. Ibid. ' Finally, I must admit that after wandering for a long time in this particular labyrinth and having lost my way a thousand times, I have *come back* to accepting that the well-being of society demands that man should believe himself to be free. All of us act according to this principle ... We all feel ourselves to be free. Might God not have fooled the lot of us? These arguments are mere women's prattle. I have come back to what I feel to be true after being led into error by reasoning'.
17. On the weak nature of the idea of 'God' as it is manifested in the works of the enlightened deists, Cf. G. Gusdorf, *L'Homme Romantique* ('Les Sciences Humaines et la Pensée occidentale', XI), Paris, 1984, 26–27.
18. Cf. his two celebrated verses which are so often quoted. On 15 December 1766 he declares to Mme de la Tour du Pin that it is 'just as ridiculous to say that the organisation which is apparent in the way the world is arranged does not prove the existence of a Supreme Creator, as it would

be impertinent to say that a clock does not prove the existence of a clock-maker' (*Corr.*, vol. 8, 774).
19. In the dictated letter of 1738, addressed to Helvétius but arguing against his views, he says: 'But as far as design relationships are concerned, I beg to differ. It seems to me that the existence of males and females, the blade of grass and the grass seed, are demonstrations of the fact that an intelligent being is organising things. Now, there are an infinity of examples of these design relationships' (*Corr. gén. d'Helvétius*, vol.1, 11).
20. To the Duc de Richelieu, 31 August: Voltaire, *Corr.*, vol. 3, 473.
21. To Mme du Deffand, 3 March 1754: *Corr.*, vol. 4, 83.
22. To the same, 3 February 1769: *Corr.*, vol. 9, 776.
23. Charles de Montesquieu, *Lettres persanes* (1721), Paris, 1949, L.LXXV, 110–11: and L.XXXIII, 51: a certain type of beverage is sufficient to restore life and movement to the 'machine' of the soul.
24. To Dompierre d'Hornoy, 5 July 1773: *Corr.*, vol. 11, 400. Likewise to Condillac, in 1756: 'If anyone is capable of inventing the spectacles that would allow us to see this imperceptible being [i.e. the soul] it is surely you' (*Corr.*, vol. 4, 850). To Frédéric II of Prussia, on 25 December 1772: 'our supposed soul', the illusion of whose existence 'seduces everyone, beginning with you … and ending with me'(vol. 11, 190).
25. To d'Alembert, 29 August 1757, on the subject of the 'thinking organs' of Rousseau who is suffering from 'the pineal gland': 'If there is a proof that the soul is not immaterial it is this sickness of the brain; it is possible to have soul-ache just as it is possible to have tooth-ache' (*Corr.*, vol. 4, 1079). Similar idea, vol. 9, 776.
26. To the same, 20 April 1769: *Corr.*, vol. 9, 873.
27. To Mme du Deffand, 7 August 1769: 'It is a pity that La Mettrie has written such a bad book on the 'man-machine': the title was excellent' (*Corr.*, vol. 9, 1027).
28. For example, twice in 1751, to Frédéric II: *Corr.*, vol. 3, 431 and 443.
29. To Mme du Deffand, 2 July 1754: *Corr.*, vol. 4, 201.
30. To Dompierre d'Hornoy, 5 July 1773: *Corr.*, vol. 11, 400.
31. To d'Alembert, 29 August 1757: *Corr.*, vol. 4, 1079.
32. To Mme du Deffand, 22 February 1769: *Corr.*, vol. 9, 792.
33. Reference to note 31.
34. 'In about September 1756': *Corr.*, vol. 4, 849. Voltaire says that he has taken the time to carefully read the *Essai sur les Origines des Connaissances humaines* (1746), the *Traité des Sensations* (1749) and the *Traité des Animaux*. 'I find that you are right in everything I understand you to be saying', he takes the trouble to point out. Favourable references to Condillac also, on the false rumour that he has died, in December 1764 and January 1765: *Corr.*, vol. 7, 951, 953, 981 ('it is a good thing to have one more Lockite in the world').
35. *Corr.*, vol. 4, 849.
36. From Mme du Deffand to Walpole, 20 December 1778: ' All my senses will give out before I die; we shall see what will become of my soul, which in my view ought to reside in the perfect harmony of our five senses' (*Correspondance complète de la Marquise du Deffand* by M. de Lescure, 2 vols., Paris, 1865, vol. 2, 671).
37. Voltaire, *Corr.*, vol. 4, 374, 9–10 February 1755. Likewise, to Delisle, 21 March 1774: 'I lose my five senses. They tell me I still have a soul. I would like to believe them but in truth it's not good enough' (vol.11,

644–45). The following year, he refers approvingly to these verses by Morton: 'He proved, though giving the Sorbonne offenses, / that *our thoughts are chiselled by our senses*' (vol. 12, 72).
38. J. Rostand, *Pensées d'un Biologiste* (1954), Paris, 1978, 30–31.
39. Ibid., 31.
40. To d'Alembert, summer 1757, on the subject of headings in the *Encyclopédie*: 'I beg the honourable gentleman who undertakes to write on *Matter* to prove that the unknown substance that we call *matter* is capable of thought just as much as the unknown substance that we call *mind*' (*Corr.*, vol. 4, 1059) (w.u.o).
41. To Frédéric II, 26 January 1749: *Corr.*, vol. 3, 20, 'the springs of the machine which is endowed with thought'.
42. To Frédéric II, 21 December 1775: *Corr.*, vol. 12, 347.
43. To Le Cat, 10 May 1765: *Corr.*, vol. 8, 50.
44. *Corr.*, vol. 3, 476.
45. To Mme du Deffand, 3 February 1769: *Corr.*, vol. 9, 776.
46. To the grammarian Nicolas Beauzée, 14 January 1768: *Corr.*, vol. 9, 263. Later: 'just as there is a geometry hidden within all the handicrafts, without the great majority of artists realising it'.
47. To the duchess of Saxe-Gotha, 25 May 1754: *Corr.*, vol. 4, 173.
48. To Cideville, 11 November 1753: *Corr.*, vol. 3, 1088.
49. Reference to note 41.
50. Ibid.
51. *Corr.*, vol. 10, 283, 10 June 1770, to Gabriel Cramer.
52. Ibid., 337–338, 10 July.
53. Ibid., 367–368, 8 August.
54. Ibid., 368.
55. To d'Alembert, 16 June 1773: *Corr.*, vol. 11, 383.
56. To Grimm, 23 July 1770: *Corr.*, vol. 10, 351; to Condorcet, 1 September 1772: vol. 11, 61.
57. 27 July 1770, letters to d'Alembert and to Frédéric II: *Corr.*, vol. 10, 355–57; 5 October, to the duchess: 430; 28 November to Frédéric-Guillaume: 499–500.
58. Ibid., 500.
59. Ibid., 314.
60. *Corr.*, vol. 4, 188. 12 June 1754.
61. To d'Alembert, 29 July 1775: *Corr.*, vol. 12, 192.
62. D'Holbach, *Le Bon Sens ou idées naturelles opposées aux idées surnaturelles* (1772), Paris, 1971, 70. Materialism, atheism, racism, the absence of any boundary between animals and humans, et cetera: everything is there, in this work.
63. *Corr.*, vol. 11, 382, 16 June 1773. The biggest criticism he makes of the book is to call it 'a hotchpotch' and 'generally boring'.
64. To d'Alembert, 16 July 1770: *Corr.*, vol. 10, 337.
65. Ibid., 371, 379 ('this *Système* has ruined everything') (w.u.o) and 430 ('It is my opinion that this book does great harm to philosophy').
66. Helvétius quotes a verse and a half from Voltaire: 'Ashamed, myself not to better know, // Within myself, my heart and soul, I try to go' (Discourse. 6 on the nature of man): title-page of the original edition, facsimile in *Corr. gén. d'Helvétius*, vol. 3, Toronto/Oxford, 1991, 440.
67. 6 January 1772: Voltaire, *Corr.*, vol. 10, 920.
68. 26 January: ibid., 935.

69. 26 June 1773:*Corr.*, vol. 11, 389.
70. R. Desné, 'Voltaire et Helvétius', in *Le Siècle de Voltaire. Hommage à René Pomeau*, 2 vols., Oxford, 1987, vol. 1, [403–415], 406.
71. A reference in 1767: *Corr.*, vol. 8, 1163.
72. Desné, op.cit., 404–407, passim, and 411.
73. To d'Argental, in 1766: 'Helvétius and Rousseau made a great mistake by putting their names to their books' (*Corr.*, vol. 8, 504).
74. Hence, Voltaire to Helvétius, 4 October 1763: 'How can you fail to spend every moment of your life seeking to avenge the whole of humanity, and in so doing avenge yourself? You betray yourself by not spending every one of your spare moments in trying to publicise the truth' (*Corr.*, vol. 7, 395).
75. 25 March 1765 (letter to d'Alembert), Voltaire suspects Helvétius of having contracted 'a paralysis of the three fingers that are used to hold the pen. Doesn't he realise that it is possible to kill off superstitious beliefs without engraving one's name on the murder weapon?' (*Corr.*, vol. 7, 1,110) (w.u.o).
76. *Corr. gén. d'Helvétius*, vol. 3, 12 (March 1761), 68 (1 May 1763: ' weed out erroneous thinking without ever showing by whose hand this is being done'), 82. Similarly, to Charles Bordes: 'Crush the monster quietly' (Voltaire, *Corr.*, vol.11, 395).
77. *Corr.gén. d'Helvétius*, vol. 3, 80 and 207 (1763 and 1765).
78. Reference to note 63. This phrase immediately follows the phrase quoted in the text here.
79. Desné, op. cit., 412. On the contrary, *De l'Esprit* had treated Voltaire in a very offhand manner: 408. In addition, an opinion on Voltaire taken from Helvétius' manuscripts and which is reproduced by Desné in an appendix, would appear to be equally dubious.
80. Ibid., 411.
81. Ibid., 412.
82. See, for example, the letter from Voltaire to d'Argental, 26 February 1753: *Corr.*, vol. 3, 912–13. Having arrived in Berlin in July 1750, Voltaire became the King of Prussia's chamberlain and grammar master. He left the country in March 1753 after numerous painful incidents arising out of the dramatic deterioration in the relationship between himself and the despotic monarch, who was so accustomed to adulation from all sides. On this whole question, see Christiane Mervaud, *Voltaire et Frédéric II: une dramaturgie des Lumières, 1736–1778*, Studies on Voltaire, 234, Oxford, 1985, 182–233. This very dense and well-written synthesis does not, however, quite give the full flavour of Voltaire's correspondence on the matter.
83. Note from Frédéric, around 5 December 1752: 'Your behaviour warrants you being put in chains' (Voltaire, *Corr.*, vol. 3, 1386).
84. *Corr.*, vol. 7, 794. Expressions of this type recur constantly in Voltaire's writings.
85. He found himself stuck there from 31 May to 7 July. Along with his niece, Mme Denis, who had joined him there, he experienced some terrible moments and suffered quite humiliating treatment. On this whole affair, which is far too complex for us to describe in detail here, see the very rich vol. 3 of Voltaire's *Correspondance* (Pléiade, Paris, 1975) and Mervaud, *Voltaire et Frédéric II*, 239–53.
86. Voltaire, *Corr.*, vol. 3, 991, 997 and 1433.
87. To the duc de Richelieu, 31 August 1751 : ibid., 471

88. Ibid., 472.
89. To Mme du Deffand, 20 July 1751: ibid., 446. In the euphoric phase, he readily speaks of the quality of 'freedom' that it is so 'agreeable'to find in a 'king's court'.
90. To his niece, Mme Denis, 16 January 1753: *Corr.*, vol. 3, 889. And he adds 'that it is exceedingly dangerous to have been a witness to the secret actions of a powerful man'. If the King of Prussia 'really knew me, he would not persecute me in such a horrible fashion'.
91. To d'Argental, 26 February: ibid., 913. His situation, as a man caught in a trap, is well analysed at the beginning of the letter, 912.
92. To Mme Denis, 15 March: ibid., 920.
93. To the duc de Richelieu, 20 March: ibid., 922.
94. For example, 11 March, to Frédéric II: 'I shall carry to my grave tender memories of all your past kindnesses, the respectful affection and the admiration I bear you.' (ibid., 917).
95. Ibid., 957; similarly, to von Freytag, 23 June, 961.
96. To Frédéric, 20 August 1770: *Corr.*, vol. 10, 390. Five years before, despite the renewal of good relationships, the King of Prussia had yet again made a stinging reference to these past events: *Corr.*, vol. 8, 1314–15.
97. In August 1773, Voltaire once again lays 'this rigorous treatment meted out to every book that appears nowadays' at the door of 'these atheistic gentlemen' : *Corr.*, vol. 11, 438.
98. To Saurin, 14 December 1772: 'But I was disgusted by what he says about friendship' (*Corr.*, vol 11, 179); to Prince Golitsin, 19 June 1773: 386. And already, on the subject of friendship in relation to *De l'Esprit*: *Corr.*, vol. 5, 290 and 300.
99. The first two references in the preceding note. Clearly, there are a lot of things to be said about all these themes.
100. To Mme du Deffand, 13 August 1773: *Corr.*, vol. 11, 438.
101. To d'Alembert, 3 July 1773: ibid., 398.
102. Ibid., 386; *Corr.gén. d'Helvétius*, vol. 3, 442, where 'fanatic' replaces the word 'jesuit'.
103. Desné, op. cit., 412.
104. Ibid., 413.
105. *Corr.*, vol 12, 192; See note 61.
106. There are several references to Voltaire's great satisfaction at this turn of events in vols. 11 and 12 of his *Correspondance*. On 27 May 1776, after the departure from office of the two ministers, he writes: 'Two great giants, in whose shadows I felt myself in safety, have been toppled and have crushed me in their fall' (*Corr.*, vol.12, 557).
107. To Morellet, 26 November 1766: *Corr.*, vol. 8, 740.
108. In addition to what follows, Cf. notes 21, 22, 27, 29, 32, 45 above.
109. *Corr.*, vol. 7, 634–35, 21 March 1764.
110. Ibid., 710–11, 22 May 1764, change of page between 'give each other' and 'nothing'.
111. Ibid., 711.
112. The details of these variants 'prepared with a view to publishing an edition which never saw the light of day' (Fr. Deloffre, in Voltaire, *Corr.*, vol. 7, 1380) are in this respect extremely interesting (1382–83).
113. From Mme du Deffand to Voltaire, 16 May 1764: 'Perhaps you will conclude from this that I haven't much of a brain, but do not tell me it is my fault unless you too wish to be accused of contradicting yourself; in one

of your recent letters you wrote that we were no more the masters of our affections, of our feelings, of our actions, of our behaviour, of the way we walk, than we are of our dreams' (in Voltaire, *Corr.*, vol. 7, 1382).

114. See my study 'Madame de Staël, Napoléon et les Idéologues' in *Himeji International Forum of Law and Politics*, no 1. (1993,) 39–62.
115. Mme de Staël, *De l'Allemagne* (1810), 2 vols, Paris, 1968, vol. 2, 115.
116. 'The greatest poet of the century', she writes ibid.
117. An extract from their 'will' is reported by Grimm, in January 1774: 'A few grains of gunpowder have just broken the springs of this mass of moving flesh that our proud countrymen call the king of creation' (*Correspondance littéraire, philosophique et critique de Grimm et Diderot ...*, Vol. 8, Paris,. 1830, 266).
118. *Correspondance complète de la Marquise du Deffand*, vol. 2, 388.
119. Thus *De l'Homme* would make her 'die of boredom' (letter to Voltaire of 24 October 1773; Voltaire, *Corr.*, vol. 11, 1,154). I'I admire the patience you display by reading the most boring books in the whole world', she tells him once again on 15 November (*Corr. gén. d'Helvétius*, vol. 3, 459/2).
120. *Correspondance complète de la Marquise du Deffand*, vol. 2, 384. This expression, 'these atheistic gentlemen', is the very one Voltaire uses when writing to her to mark the distance that separates him from them: Voltaire, *Corr.*, vol. 11, 438, 13 August 1773. Besides which, Mme du Deffand assures him that everything he admires in the work of Helvétius is like pure Voltaire: ibid., 1,161, 16 November 1773.
121. First reference of note 120. D'Holbach's *Système de la Nature* includes a logical legitimisation (or more precisely what one might call an absolute relativisation) of suicide: for example, vol. 1, 321f. It is also said that in her youth, Helvétius' eldest daughter 'had ingurgitated so much of her father's philosophy that she would occasionally tell her governess that she intended to kill herself'. Annoyed at this, the father is supposed to have 'coldly offered a pistol' to the governess (Baron de Frénilly, *Souvenirs*, Chuquet edition, 1908, 244–45, after the *Corr. gén. d'Helvétius*, vol. 3, 411/2). A song written to satirise *De l'Esprit* was so arranged that the author's daughters 'each in turn' should cry out: 'I have read your book, my father' (ibid., vol. 2, 303/2).
118. *Corr.*, vol. 12, 316, 26 November 1775. According to Benedetta Craveri, *Madame du Deffand et son monde* (1982), transl. Sibylle Zavriew, Paris, 1987, 331, 'it is impossible not to feel that there exists a deep, sincere, instinctive friendship and a fundamental affinity between the two of them'.
119. To Florian, 6 January 1774: *Corr.*, vol. 11, 577.
120. *Corr... de la Marquise du Deffand*, vol. 2, 387. She also wrote to him on this subject: 'We live in a very singular age; all our heads have been turned; such and such a person who is a complete scatterbrain believes himself to be a true Socrates. I do not include among that number the two soldiers, but all these "pamphlet writers" et cetera' (388). On 12 April 1779, writing on the plan to prepare a complete posthumous edition of the works of Voltaire, she predicts coldly that 'in a few years he will interest very few people and have only a limited reputation. As for the present time, the adoration that people show for anything that flows from his pen is excessive fanaticism' (to Walpole, ibid., 685).
121. J.-J. Rousseau, *Considérations sur le Gouvernement de la Pologne* (written in 1770–71), in Rousseau, *Œuvres complètes*, Pléiade, Paris, vol. 3 (1964), 1979, 969.

CHAPTER 4

ROUSSEAU

Rousseau (1712–78) has another name for this philosophy 'whose teachings are deadly' and which tells us that man's inner nature is inescapably bound up with the mechanistic laws of cosmic space, and it is a name which can be seen as a way of distancing himself from any such teachings. He calls it 'the philosophy of the privileged children of our age'.[1] The expression is doubly interesting. On the one hand, it makes the link that Mme de Staël will underline a short time later,[2] between this reductionist sensualism and the existential hedonism, effectively so ingrained, as Rousseau also points out,[3] in the 'pamphlet writers' and other 'fine scented philosophers' who are quite happy to leave others to deal with the menial tasks of feeling despair and angst. On the other hand, the expression gives every *appearance* of placing Rousseau at variance (and this on a question which in our view is of strategic significance) with the dominant trend of the century,[4] 'a century characterised by hatefulness and malevolence',[5] 'in which philosophy has only a destructive role',[6] and it also seems to place him at complete odds with what he very pertinently calls, 'the maelstrom of fashion'.[7]

'Nothing is more at variance with the philosophical mood of this century' he maintains, than his own ideas and his personal feelings.[8] This readiness to accept marginalisation is not at all unexpected. When the occasion demands, he is happy to stress it even further. And yet, the marginalisation is not so clearcut that Rousseau can avoid being seen as someone who also lends considerable weight to the argument which we are seeking to put forward in these pages, and certainly much more than one might have thought at first glance. Indeed he contributes to that argument substantially and substantively and not just on the rather negative grounds that he is the exception that proves the rule. To attempt to illustrate exactly how he contributes, however, is not such an easy matter.

It is well known that Rousseau's belief in deism and spiritualism was far more heart-felt than Voltaire's and that he preferred to see 'the infatuation with atheism' that he observed all around him as nothing more than 'a transitory fanaticism'.[9] For his own part and to the bitter end, he remains true to a belief in the principle that the human soul enjoys the exercise of free will. In writings as early as the *Discours sur l'origine de l'inégalité*, the 'quality of free agent' is the criterion by which man can be distinguished from animals,[10] and which allows him to 'recognise himself as being free to accept or to reject; and it is above all in the consciousness of this freedom that the spiritual nature of his soul is in evidence'.[11] He comes back to this in *La Nouvelle Héloïse*,[12] and afterwards particularly in *Émile*, where the 'profession of faith' of his famous 'vicaire savoyard' can be seen as something of a set piece in this respect, in that so many of the passages are quotable. 'No material being is *active of and by itself*, and yet I am'.[13] 'The principle of activity of any sort resides in an act of will by a free being; it is not possible to push the question any further than this. It is not the word freedom that has no meaning, it is the word necessity'. And elsewhere, 'Man, therefore, is a being who is free to act as he wishes, and as such is animated by an immaterial substance'.[14] Voltaire argues that the secret structure hidden within all languages exerts its control over all aspects of thought;[15] Rousseau's *Émile* tends to say much the same thing but without ever quite managing to do so, and instead it talks only in terms of influence : 'Young heads are formed by contact with language; thoughts adopt the colour of the idiom in which they are expressed'.[16] Et cetera. From time to time, Rousseau also comes back to the theme of freedom in his *Correspondance* and again in the *Dialogues*.[17]

Simultaneously, for it is the same battle, he persistently denounces the absurdity of materialism and its accompanying theories of blind mechanicism,[18] and he specifically criticises the reductionist conclusions that flow from the materialistic tendencies in the thinking of his time. He considers the tendency 'to attribute to the physical domain that which properly belongs to the moral domain' as 'one of the most frequent mistakes of philosophical thought in our century'.[19] To anyone who disputes the idea that there is a boundary separating man from the animals, he sharply retorts, and here he is implicitly targeting Helvétius' *De l'Esprit*:[20] 'Abject soul, it is your sad philosophy which makes you like the animals: or rather, it is in vain that you seek to vilify yourself, your very genius bears witness against your arguments'.[21] And he makes the following exclamation so well-attuned to the anthropology of his age : 'Oh philosophy! how much effort you put into demeaning the human heart and belittling humanity'.[22] The target here is sensualism, whose proponents (almost unanimously and, if nothing else, more or less consistently) 'cry "triumph", not because they have solved the question' of freedom, he says, 'but because they have replaced it with an illusion. They begin by supposing that all intelligent beings are purely passive, and then they deduce from this premise conclusions which allow them to prove they are not active'.[23] And the ageing author of the *Dialogues*, continues to rail against 'all those cruel doctrines which place man totally under the control of his five senses, and by reducing everything to the pleasure that can be gleaned from this short life, they make the age in which these doctrines hold sway as despicable as it is unhappy'.[24] Despite the fact that he is becoming increasingly obsessive about certain preoccupations of his own, he speaks out tirelessly against these doctrines and pleads movingly in defence of 'that inner voice that all these fine *philosophes* take such pains to stifle, and which they treat as though it were an illusion because it has nothing more to say to them'.[25]

Rousseau argues against this and to the very end, it would seem, postulates that, as far as the inner workings of the human being are concerned, there exists a clear distinction between the haphazard nature of feelings and the active principle, which is engaged in classifying these, weighing them up and certainly considering the implications they may have, but never allowing them to assume absolute mastery. 'Without being in a position to decide whether to feel or not to feel, I am nevertheless in a position to more or less examine what I do feel', we read in *Émile* in 1762. 'I am, therefore, not simply a being capable of feeling, but also an active and intelligent being, and whatever the *philosophes* may say on the matter, I shall continue to dare to claim the *honour of being capable of thought*'.[26] We know that to speak in such terms is not particularly excessive. But it is worth repeating that the real target here is Helvétius and his book, *De l'Esprit*, which caused such a scandal on its publication in 1758 and which Rousseau succinctly summarised in the laconic words 'to judge is to feel'[27] – clearly a view which Rousseau himself vigorously contested. 'Judging and feeling are not the same thing' we read in *Émile*[28] the chief objective of which is 'to crush underfoot a number of our new *philosophes*' and more precisely to combat 'that infernal book *De l'Esprit*, which, in line with the detestable principle enunciated by its author, claims that judging and feeling are one and the same thing, a claim which is clearly tantamount to establishing a philosophy of materialism'.[29] These are statements which led Voltaire to criticise Rousseau, saying that he only makes such boasts with a view to ingratiating himself with the reformed pastors in Geneva.[30]

But Rousseau understood the far-reaching implications of this debate very well, both in so far as individual human destiny was concerned as well as the way it touched upon the fate of society as a whole. He was not unaware that this modern brand of thinking and the philosophy of nihilism offered each other mutual support, comfort and legitimacy.[31] It is quite clear that to explain 'everything by reference to matter and movement' and thereby posit a view of humanity as pure passivity, is tantamount to doing away with 'the moral instinct',[32] de-moralising existence, divesting man and the citizen of any responsibility and emptying the concept of remorse of any meaning, all of which are ends towards which the authors in question are, in fact, more or less consciously working. And this is *convenient* for the 'privileged children of our age'. For Rousseau, as we have seen, never tires of making the connection between his adversaries' views and their lifestyle, just as he often makes the link between his own thinking and lifestyle. And, of course, we can understand the success of 'this convenient philosophy articulated by the privileged and the well-to-do, who create their paradise in this world'.[33] It is not difficult to explain 'the attraction that such a convenient doctrine exerts upon all young people'.[34] And some years on, Marat will expand on this theme, saying: 'The moral position of these gentlemen, is one as befits their corrupt hearts, and which holds tremendous attractions for the young; in truth, their disciples are legion'.[35]

It is therefore to be expected that many people were seduced by those whom Rousseau also calls 'this century's brilliant writers',[36] but who, when all is said and done, are not much more than 'a small group of *depraved souls* who find it in their own interests, and perhaps feel a particular need, to persuade people that their own corruption is shared by all'.[37] Certainly, these brilliant authors, these experts in matters relating to 'virtue', prided themselves on demonstrating 'that there is neither vice nor virtue in the heart of man, because there is neither any *freedom in his volition* nor morality in his actions, that everything, including even volition itself, is the result of the workings of blind necessity', and so on.[38] The well-to-do find this pathway well suited to them since it naturally leads those who follow it to conclude that virtues are 'vices in negative'.[39] By systematically accepting the sovereignty of self-interest it ultimately becomes possible to make a legitimate case for the overriding importance of self-interest in whatever form it happens to take. To this notion Rousseau replies: 'Personal interest will only ever be sufficient to explain the actions of vicious people',[40] those self-same people who, as if by chance, are exasperated by his principles and his personality: 'I have learned to question whether any man, whomsoever he may be, who disposes of a large fortune is capable of sincerely embracing my principles or feeling any warmth towards my own person'.[41] Their teachings are indeed 'cruel doctrines' full of dire social consequences, and 'which, while flattering the fortunate and the rich, oppress the unfortunate and the poor, since they allow the former to do away with all forms of restraint, all forms of fear and all checks on their behaviour, while depriving the latter of any hope and any consolation'.[42] This, by way of reaction, accounts for Rousseau's more or less latent propensity to consider religion from a socially utilitarian point of view,[43] a point of view, it must be said, which stands in direct contrast or contradiction to the emotional value that can be attached to the rather spineless form of deism he professed.

And this slight blemish on the picture points up something else. From the perspective which interests us, Rousseau is commonly considered as something of an exception among the great men of the Enlightenment. This would seem to undermine the argument being put forward, for how can we ignore the fact that Rousseau occupies a major position in the thought of his century? And yet I believe that the truth of the matter is quite different from what it would at first appear to be. Indeed, it seems to me that in a diffuse way Rousseau himself, through the general tenor of his work, the tremendous success it enjoyed and through the general tone and the great notoriety of his *moi*, substantially contributed to the construction of this archetype of a passive humanity cast hither and thither at the whim of fate, and which, if the need arose, it would be possible and legitimate to manipulate, and to orientate unbeknownst to itself, for good causes or at very least in the cause of good, however that might be defined by the manipulator. The references that might be adduced in support of this point of view are very numerous and very varied.

We should firstly remember that the model of humanity which acts as a starting point for Rousseau's thinking on social matters is an unsophisticated being, whose inner workings are devoid of intellectual and affective depth. His goodness can scarcely be distinguished from a clearly simplistic state of satiety. 'The only possessions he knows in the world', and there are three of these, are 'food, a female and rest'[44] (to which Diderot opposes his personal ideal, equally guilty of reifying women, which is, 'a carriage, comfortable lodgings, fine linen, a sweet-scented girl').[45] It would seem that these possessions, which are enjoyed by man in the state of nature, are provided for him as and when he needs them by a hospitable Nature, and he experiences no problems as far as fluctuations in supply are concerned.[46] Through the calming sensations it lavishes upon him, all-providing Nature also ensures that he remains in a state of 'delicious indolence'. Although Rousseau not infrequently tries to reject the charge of 'Epicureanism' laid against him, we are clearly caught up here in a *de facto* logic of pure sensualism and concomitant passivity. This is a pre-Epicurean Epicureanism, ataraxia experienced in an age that pre-dates the birth of the concept itself. 'His soul, untouched by any troublesome influence, is occupied solely with the sensation of its own present existence'.[47] 'All animals have ideas since they have senses; to a certain extent they even combine their ideas in sequences, and the difference between man and animals in this respect is merely a question of degree'.[48] The clarification is important. Similarly, Voltaire suggests that it is 'the *quantity* of [his] ideas' that alone distinguishes man from the apes,[49] and this gradation, in line with good sensualist orthodoxy, applies to the whole animal kingdom.

In other words, although Rousseau sees himself as disapproving of the reductionist line of argument that is demonstratively present in Enlightenment thinking and which is grafted onto a reactivated Epicurean rootstock, he nevertheless concentrates all the chief components of this type of thinking into the creation of his dull tree-dweller, whose prototype he offers to mankind. 'His desires do not outstrip his physical needs.':[50] this is precisely the point that Helvétius is at pains to make, in spite of appearances, in respect of the more complex men of his own times.[51] This ancestor of ours is a sleepy, contented being and Rousseau does not try to mislead us as to his abilities: this creature, he tells us, is 'a *stupid* and *limited* animal'.[52] This then, is the exact nature and condition of his state of contentment. It can also be seen as an expression of Rousseau's notorious distrust of man's innate faculty for reasoning and provides him with ammunition to deplore the fact that, at some point in history, use came to be made of these faculties, since, as everyone also knows: 'the state of reflection is an unnatural state, and the man who thinks about things is a depraved creature'.[53] It is quite clear that the words *stupid* and *limited* have a purely technical, descriptive function in this context and are in no way to be read as having any pejorative connotations. This is borne out by the fact that it is precisely these two adjectives which he chooses to describe the woman of his life, Thérèse Levasseur, 'so *limited*', 'so *stupid*' he says, and he will illustrate the point in the *Confessions*.[54] It is worth noting too that when the situation warrants it, Rousseau is not above applying the two attributes, shared by Thérèse and the noble savage, to himself. He refers to his own '*limited* intelligence' as an excuse for not actually reading Condorcet and for settling for the role of '*stupid* admirer'.[55]

This last reference is not merely anecdotal. It seems to us that introspection played its part in Rousseau's view of man, a view which grew ever more obsessive as the years went by and which tended, perhaps rather pathetically and almost asymptomatically, ever more towards the very reductionism that he made such a great show of refusing to accept – thereby setting himself up in opposition to the whole world, and, more particularly, to virtually every *philosophe* of his day. Tact might have led me to somehow avoid this subject if Rousseau himself had not written and published so much about it. He deplored the deficiencies in his own powers of reasoning and his lack of willpower with an insistence and with a degree of detail that would seem to suggest that he was far more acutely sensitive to this question than is generally the case for the common run of mortals, even though we can all derive benefit from the contemplation of our own personal weaknesses. Once the dubious good fortune of winning a competition organised by the academy had propelled him into a position where he had no choice but to defend and illustrate points of view that were full of internal paradoxes and confused speculation – a task for which his intellectual powers ill prepared him – Rousseau repeatedly expressed his discontent, especially in the *Confessions*, at the difficulty he experienced in coming to grips with concepts, in trying to bend words to his will and in structuring his ideas. He made no secret of his belief that the almost daily experience of a sense of chronic humiliation and his frequent bouts of snivelling self-pity were the result of the pressure he felt at having to play an intellectual role beyond his capabilities and which, it is certain, proved to be psychically draining for him.

'Continue to love me; but send me no more books; don't ask me to read any more of them', he begs Mirabeau the elder in 1756.[56] He goes on to admit that the task he has set himself in his political thinking is nothing less than that of 'squaring the circle',[57] which, of course, in no ways detracts from its merit. It seems clear therefore that he more than recognised how serious were the deficiencies and the logical shortcomings of the *Contrat Social*, and indeed of the rest of his work. Numerous semi-confidences attest to this fact, as does the distaste, which grew stronger with age, with which he reacts to talk of a 'system', whose contradictions, we could argue, tend to baffle critics rather than lend weight to their attempts at refuting it. It is almost as though Rousseau had behaved far too literally in adopting the advice offered to him in 1757 by an over-lucid friend: 'Build us some great system that we can neither follow nor refute'.[58] Rousseau will even go so far as to offer lessons in realism, and concede that 'the science of government is no more than a science of combinations, applications and exceptions, depending on the time, the place and the prevailing circumstances'.[59] He even confesses that he has 'always' had – and it is he who is speaking here – only 'a modest degree of confidence' in 'systems', 'my own included',[60] and this is a comment which does not seem to have been well-known among the Revolutionaries. Dare we conclude from all this that Rousseau was as loath to acknowledge fathering ideas as he was to admit to fathering children?

But to be fair, it has to be recognised that the special qualities we associate with Rousseau's great literary genius were not particularly well suited to the production of high level discursive thought. He is aware that 'the difficulties he has in understanding' scarcely predispose him to 'purely abstract meditations',[61] and alas, it is only belatedly that he seems to have realised that this constituted one of the great dramas of his personal destiny. He confides to a correspondent as early as 1757 that he no longer knows what he is writing to her about; having just re-read the long 'verbiage' he has written he no longer understands anything in it, 'my head has gone', he explains to her, 'my soul and my mind are exhausted'.[62] Later, he refers rather insistently to what, in his view, is the unnatural nature of cerebral work, which leads to 'these constant physical problems, this thinness, this paleness, this air of a man on his last legs that he wore for ten years of his life; that is to say, all the time that he was involved in writing, a craft that was as disastrous for his physical well-being as it was contrary to his taste'.[63] When considering such matters we should also bear in mind that as far as he was concerned everything that he published from *Émile* (1762) onwards should be considered as 'no longer belonging to his system'.[64]

So much for the power of reasoning. As for his total absence of will-power, this was something he himself complained about with such insistence that it is difficult to even allude to it without running the risk of seeming to be over-critical. This said, however, I must point out that the argument that man does not enjoy free will is a thesis which his own life paradoxically seems to illustrate while he personally argues against it, even though it was steadily gaining ground among his contemporaries. 'It is incredible the extent to which this *indolence of will* subdues his spirit', he says of himself.[65] And elsewhere he writes: 'all the strength of his will-power is used up in making resolutions; he has none left to put them into effect',[66] which is a more than ambiguous way of putting it and certainly marks a significant bipartite distinction, both elements of which were already present in embryo in *Émile*, in which, even while he considered himself to be taking up arms against the reductionist position, the 'vicaire savoyard' lets slip the following: 'I always have sufficient power to make my will known, but not to put it into effect'.[67] And it is true that Rousseau, in his twilight years, would have been 'the most virtuous of men if his physical strength had matched his will'.[68] But he was already complaining far too early, in the same year that saw the publication of *Émile* and the *Contrat Social*, of having lost 'the little strength of mind' that he 'still had; I am no more than a vegetating creature, a walking machine'.[69] Each one of us has the fundamental right to consider him- or herself completely dispirited, and to wish to proclaim it loud and clear so that there can be doubt about the matter. Nevertheless, there is food for thought in Rousseau's choice of words and the frequency with which he comes back to this subject, and this on the part of the only major Enlightenment figure to truly rebel against the theory of mankind as pure passivity.

This is undeniably a point on which his autobiographical writings serve to add grist to the mill of his adversaries.

Making no mystery of his 'almost permanently weak or pathetic' behaviour, of his 'feeble inertia', of the 'almost automaton-like' nature of his existence, and often of his downright 'laziness',[70] sometimes of his 'laziness in writing', and of his 'laziness in thinking', Rousseau makes it clear, still speaking of himself, that 'he appears absent-minded without really being so, and in actual fact he is only in a state of mental *sluggishness*'.[71] His 'natural state was, and always will be, one of mental inertia and mechanistic activity'.[72] 'Refusing to be imposed upon by any external will, neither does he know how to obey his own, or rather he finds it *so tiring even to exercise his will*, that he prefers in the normal course of daily life to follow purely mechanistic inclinations ... Never did a man more easily accept, from his youth onwards, the yoke under which labour the weak-spirited and aged, namely the burden of habit'.[73] 'With no other tasks before me than the very tiring ones of having simply to put myself to bed and to get up again, I find even these too much for me; in fact I am completely useless', he admits in 1768.[74] With the exception of the occasional fit of energetic activity, he claims to be wallowing, so to speak, 'in this primary vegetative state which places him completely at the mercy of force of habit, and this seems to him to be his natural and permanent state'.[75] This *natural dullard* obviously calls to mind someone else: the noble savage, since practically everything that Rousseau has to say about the latter is more or less interchangeable with what he has to tell us about himself. Rousseau's indolence, his obsessional fear of clocks and timetables, the distaste he feels at the prospect of having dealings with his fellow-man, his love of country solitude, and his belief that when we are face to face with nature '*without knowing why, we feel ourselves little by little opening up to its tender influence*',[76] all of this sits very easily with the characteristics he ascribes to the emblematic tree-dweller, who soberly illustrates so many features that make man human, and whom Rousseau brought to public consciousness under the brandname of 'noble savage'.[77] The '*promeneur solitaire*' admits 'I have never really belonged to civil society', and 'my naturally independent disposition always made it impossible for me to accept the restrictions on my freedom that any man who wishes to live in harmony with his fellow-man must accept'.[78]

This tendency of Rousseau's, which, he tells us, was present within him 'from his youth onwards', grew stronger with age and little by little led him to 'see' himself as nothing more than 'a purely passive being'.[79] The fact that this process seems to have become more acute with age would seem to confirm that it would be wise, for the purposes of my present argument, not to attach undue importance to such psychosomatic complaints. But it nevertheless seems to me that this chronic readiness to proclaim himself 'useless', that is to say asthenic and downcast, the mechanical plaything of habit, even if he does so for no other reason than to make himself interesting, is not unrelated to a set of philosophical doctrines that he considers perhaps alien to his own views but which in actual fact he, in some sense, shares. Indeed, Rousseau interposes nothing more than a porous membrane between himself and the surrounding reductionist philosophy. All things considered, the pages we have just examined might be thought proof enough that this is the case, but there are a good number of other symptoms too. The tendency to reason in the sensualist mode, which we have already come across in the context of the impoverished nature of the noble savage's inner life, is not uncommon in Rousseau's work as a whole. It is true that this is only a tendency, and, as Condillac himself shows, sensualism can easily coexist with a form of spiritualism, although it would be wrong to suggest that this particular combination of ideas was one that Rousseau himself favoured. And the fact remains that even if Rousseau admits the strong hold that 'physical sensitivity'[80] exerts upon him, to the point of describing himself as a 'slave to his senses',[81] he nevertheless sees this as being mitigated in his own case by the 'diversionary influence' of a 'moral sensitivity'.[82] The way he explains the latter seems to exclude materialism,[83] at least in so far as this is possible in the midst of the conceptual instability that typifies a philosophical context in which materialistic tendencies predominate.

And there is also the fact that Rousseau, like Voltaire, admired Condillac to such an extent that he could be considered his 'friend and disciple',[84] and boasted: 'I am perhaps the very first person to have recognised the significance of his work and judged him at his true worth'.[85] Rousseau even formed the very interesting project, which never came to fruition, of writing a treatise called *Morale sensitive [sic]*, which would have borne the co-title *Le Matérialisme du Sage*.[86] The outline plan of this treatise suggests quite overtly, but perhaps not very wisely, a tendency to take as self-evident the omnipotence of feelings, whether or not those who actually feel them and are therefore themselves fashioned by them, know anything whatsoever about the fact. Through pure observation, Rousseau believed that he had discovered 'that continually modified by our senses and by our organs, we carried over into our ideas, into our feelings and even into our actions, but without being aware of it, the effects of these modifications. ... Climates, seasons, sounds, colours, darkness, light, weather, food, noise, silence, movement, stillness, all these have effects upon our machines and consequently upon our souls'. As we can see, the soul, not without some difficulty, manages nevertheless to remain bobbing upon the surface. It is very weak and flickering when compared to the deep and invasive darkness of the 'physical principles' which are related to what the author calls 'the animal economy'.[87] It bobs about, tossed by the sea of feelings. And it is feelings which work their effects upon the soul much more than it is the soul which is capable of interpreting the messages to be read into feelings. Rousseau tells us that *Le Matérialisme du Sage* would not have been 'a real treatise on materialism',[88] but, whatever the case may be, we are nevertheless bound to recognise that he is not prepared to offer a less ambiguous comment than this on the whole matter.

Étienne Gilson suggests that 'In the absence of the lost work, we could make an attempt at an approximate reconstitution of the *Morale sensitive* by reassembling and classifying the various fragments scattered throughout Rousseau's writings'.[89] This is certainly a possibility, even if the size of such a task and the dangers it represents are so great that all we propose to offer here is an illustration of what such a reconstitution might entail. Rousseau never seems to allow the gap between himself and a totally reductionist sensualism to grow too wide. One would argue that Rousseau disagrees with the following succinctly expressed principle from Helvétius: 'We are *purely and simply* what the objects surrounding us make us into'.[90] But when he tells us: 'My ideas are practically nothing more than feelings, and the scope of my understanding goes no further than the objects which immediately surround me',[91] it is clear that he is running out of steam and is allowing himself to be dragged into the orbit of arguments with which he disagrees.[92] 'Insensitive to all major movements, he also writes, my soul can no longer be touched by anything other than physical objects; all that remains to me are feelings.'[93] It goes without saying that the fact he writes in this vein is not tantamount to conceding on matters of principle, but it is de facto tantamount to giving ground, and illustrates the tendency he had to relax his grip and to risk letting himself be overrun in the theoretical battle he was waging against reductionist ideas.[94]

And to take yet another example, we have no alternative but to recognise the fact that the new-born babies he repeatedly acknowledges as having planned to abandon, against the wishes of their mother, have no real, objective consistency in his eyes. He concludes the very sophisticated (not to say sophistry-ridden) pages of the *Confessions,* in which he affects to argue his innocence, by suggesting that 'the innards of a father have some difficulty in crying out very loudly in favour of children he has never seen'.[95] Does this not amount to, perversely but quite clearly, expressing both the concrete primacy of feelings and their fundamental axiological importance? In other words, without actually paying too much attention to the fact, is it not a way of deferring to the extreme demands of the sensualist views which hold sway everywhere and which in this instance are harmoniously wedded to philosophical idealism? In a context such as this, how can we avoid reflecting on the fact that in Rousseau's state of nature, maternal love is merely a product of a *"habit"* that mothers contract because of their physical need to breast-feed,[96] a fact which he considers to be a general truth applicable to 'females of all species'?[97] Similarly, how can we avoid meditating on the fact that the '*promeneur solitaire*' while once again congratulating himself on having abandoned his offspring, can speak of them as follows: 'I know full well that no father is kinder than I *would have been* to them had *habit* only been able to lend a hand to natural inclination'?[98]

In a similar and, in fact, connected way, since here we are dealing with a sort of universal corollary of sensualism, there is the widely-held belief that man's behaviour is totally subject to the dictates of naked self-interest. While Rousseau sought to counter this conviction and thought he had indeed succeeded in doing so, it is difficult to see how he himself could ever really fully escape its influence. He deplores the fact that in society, 'everyone thinks of their own interests and no-one thinks of the common good';[99] he also says that 'individual self-interest leads us astray', while castigating its 'vulgarity',[100] and although such remarks may help create a particular atmosphere, they do not even begin to constitute a refutation of the opposing argument. He also writes, 'That would be a truly abominable philosophy which taught us to feel embarrassment on account of our virtuous actions, and which left us no alternative but to try to explain such actions away by reference to dubious motives and ignoble intentions';[101] but here too the argument itself never really gets going. And the real problem is this: however much Rousseau may twist and turn he is incapable of breaking the chains that seem to bind him to a straightforward choice between good and bad forms of self-interest. 'I am well aware that you can only motivate men to act by bringing some form of self-interest to bear', he concedes; 'but the pecuniary interest is the worst form of all, it is the vilest, the one which most lends itself to corruption and even, and this I repeat with confidence and shall always maintain to be true, it is the least significant and the weakest in the eyes of anyone who claims to understand human beings'.[102] As far as self-interest is concerned therefore, there are forms of it that are less vile but also far stronger than mere pecuniary interest, and this good form of egoism is self-love ('amour de soi'), which is a harmless form of preoccupation with oneself, a sort of Epicurian tranquillity that consists of taking pleasure in peacefully enjoying one's own company[103] and of cultivating 'that pleasant indolence, that sweet nonchalance which is so attractive to all true seekers after solitude'.[104] This self-love, this 'good and absolute feeling',[105] can also be opposed to self-esteem ('amour-propre'), which involves a variety of forms of bitter and malevolent feelings towards one's fellow man, motivated in a variety of ways. Self-esteem also has the unfortunate consequence of producing harmful and distressing effects on the individuals who are concerned with it, since they are not seeking 'to gain a sense of satisfaction through pursuing what is advantageous to themselves, but through pursuing only what is detrimental to others'.[106]

Quite the opposite is true for those individuals who cultivate self-love. If 'they are less malevolent towards others', it is simply 'and solely because they know better how to love themselves'.[107] 'Forever preoccupied with himself or concerned with his own person', the self-lover is in fact 'too *busy thinking about his own affairs* to have the time to think of doing harm to anyone else'.[108] Described in this way it is difficult to see him as anything other than an egoist. But if Rousseau is to be believed, it would appear that such a person is not an egoist in the pejorative sense of the word – a word, by the way, which is quite new and indeed Rousseau was around when it was coined[109] – since, as he explains, ' if we take the word *egoism* in its true sense, [other people] are all egoists', and he, Jean-Jacques, 'is not',[110] simply because his make-up is such that it inspires him with a phobia for all the problems that self-esteem brings in its train. 'Lazy and sensuous as he is, how could he be spiteful and vindictive?'.[111] Indeed. But all the same: such dialectical virtuosity is enough to leave one speechless.

And that is not all. For this un-egoist, whose paradoxical nature is a result of his sensuous preoccupation with himself, is nevertheless capable, when he feels like it and if he thinks it suits his own interests, of reaching out to others and thereby cultivating a sort of altruism – which is, admittedly, rather strange in so far that in following his own natural inclination he is actually reaching out to no one other than himself. Rousseau saw this too: 'In this life, man's make-up is such that he can never really fully enjoy himself without the assistance of others'.[112] 'It is quite natural', he writes, 'that the person who loves himself should seek to extend himself and increase his pleasures, and *to appropriate to himself through attachment*, whatever he considers to be beneficial to his own person'.[113] We should make no mistake about this: 'Goodness, fellow-feeling, generosity, these first natural movements, which are nothing more than *emanations of self-love* ... are needs that he feels in his heart and which he will satisfy more in order to ensure his own happiness than through any principle of common humanity'.[114] Friendship is merely the sharing of *self-love*, 'all the favours' that one does for one's friend 'are favours that one does to oneself'.[115] It is obvious that Rousseau's intention to clearly illustrate what the good form of egoism involves leads him to quite simply set Jean-Jacques up as his model,[116] and time and time again it is the similarity between this model and the noble savage that leaps out at us from the page.

What is equally obvious is the fact that Rousseau, albeit after numerous diversions, detours and physical contorsions, finally arrives face to face with the very theme treated by all the authors he would like to denounce, and just as much as they do, he ends up deferring to the logical demands of arguments which can lead nowhere else but to a solemn consecration of naked self-interest. Although he claims to rail against 'the narrow prison of personal interest',[117] it is patently obvious that he aspires to little more than trying to make this prison a little less cramped, and indeed to paint false windows on its walls. He certainly is not in possession of the key to the prison, nor is he able to even conceive of the idea or have any presentiment of the fact that such a key might exist. And, as a result, his way of thinking on these matters comes at times to be barely distinguishable from the thinking of those he spends his time berating. 'There is absolutely no point in trying to understand men's characters, but only where their interests lie, in order to be able to guess what they will say on any issue. When a man speaks, it is in a sense the uniform he wears and not he himself that is doing the feeling; ... and men's apparent zeal for truth is never anything other than the mask worn by self-interest': this could be pure Helvétius[118] if it didn't come from the pages of *La Nouvelle Héloïse*.[119] 'The man of merit is the man whom true ideas have acted upon by showing him where his personal interest and happiness lie so that he acts in such a way that other people are *forced* to admire him and approve his actions for the sake of their own self-interest': this was written by d'Holbach,[120] but little would need to be changed for it to be from Rousseau's own pen. And why, for example, does Rousseau consider it right and proper that women should be in the front line as far as the education of children is concerned? A better answer couldn't have been dreamed up. It's because 'the success or failure of the enterprise affects them far more directly' in so far as 'the majority of widows find themselves almost at the mercy of their children'. Here we could once again be imagining ourselves reading *De l'Esprit*, or the authors of the Napoleonic Code, if it were not for the fact that we are in the first pages of *Émile*.[121] And the same thing could be said for any number of passages. For example: 'Pity is such a delicious feeling that it is hardly surprising that men should seek to experience it', which comment, in a letter of 1755,[122] prefigures the following, even stronger, remark taken also from the pages of *Émile*: 'Pity is sweet *because* even as we put ourselves in the shoes of the person who is actually suffering, we nevertheless feel the pleasure of not suffering as he does';[123] a remark which sees Rousseau's disconcerting 'innocence' mirroring and matching the cold cynicism of those of whom he overtly disapproves. 'The proud despotism of modern philosophy has pushed the egoism of self-interest to its utter limits', he is moved to complain.[124] But in reality such teachings posit a link that binds man to his personal interest which Rousseau can never untie or break. Even if he manages, overall, to loosen the chains by fiddling about with them, even if he manages to slacken the bridle somewhat, it is never more than a temporary relief and at any moment the binding can tighten up again.

Rousseau never had any ambitions to write 'a real treatise on materialism' *but* ... What he speaks out in favour of and recommends to us is not egoism 'in the true sense' *but* ... It is often the case, therefore, that he flirts with the boundary which delineates what is assumed to be reductionism: he approaches it, he puts his foot over the line or pretends to do so, he claims to be going in the opposite direction to it at the very moment when he supposedly inadvertently steps over it; and yet it would seem that he ultimately remains on this side of it. We can see to what extent the picture is fluid. The boundary-line in question bends and wavers, and, given that Rousseau is a specialist at splitting his personality, there comes a moment when we no longer know (when he no longer knows himself) whether the man on the other side of the line is himself or his double. As we have seen, the same thing is true for the theme of sensualism. And since sensualism can in many ways be seen as simply an extension of mechanicism as it is applied to the inner man, perhaps it is also possible to discern this tendency of Rousseau in respect of mechanicism itself and see whether there are traces of the same thing at work.

I have already been able to clearly identify precisely such traces here and there in certain forms of expression. But there are many more of them. Without being one of the leading lights in this respect, it is clear that Rousseau was at least contaminated by the mechanicism of his day which so powerfully, and almost by the simple force of ideas, contributes to the formation of a view of man as a purely passive being. Indeed, it is difficult to see how his view of the cosmos can be distinguished in any meaningful way from Voltaire's ideas about clocks and clockmakers. He tells us that the Universe is a 'mechanism', an 'immense machine'[125] whose very organisation proves the existence of a transcendent intelligence and a transcendent will at work. 'I am', he explains, 'like a man seeing an open timepiece for the first time and who cannot stop admiring the object even though he does not know what the thing is used for and he has not even seen the dial'.[126] Included within this cosmos-machine are animals, which are also machines, as, too, is man himself. 'All I can see in any animal is no more than an ingenious machine which Nature has endowed with senses so that it can wind itself up ... I observe exactly the same thing so far as the human machine is concerned'; it is true that he continues with a phrase that should suffice to alter the whole affair; 'with this difference, that Nature alone is responsible for all the actions that animals perform whereas man contributes to his own actions as a free agent'.[127] The ordinary difficulties that Rousseau encounters when he involves himself in dialectical reasoning are aggravated here by the fact that he too is obliged to steer a course within the impossible cul-de-sac of Cartesianism. Nor is it appropriate perhaps to quibble with him on that score. But since it is useful for my own argument here, I should simply record the fact that he does not seem to consider the status of 'free agent' as constituting such a 'difference' that it dispenses us from recognising that fundamentally 'the same things' can be observed as going on within man as within animals.

As far as man is concerned, Voltaire comes round to bluntly expressing a consistent mechanicism, that is to say, a mechanicism which negates any hypothesis concerning the possibility of freedom.[128] This is never the case where the man he habitually bullied is concerned, or rather, this is never the case to quite the same extent, for here as elsewhere, what we find in Rousseau is the asymptomatic tension that we have already identified. In his *Correspondance* and in his *Confessions*, like Voltaire and no doubt like many others, he often describes his health by way of references to 'his machine'. Once again, this merely indicates a tendency, but so many such indications all point in the same direction and give a clear general thrust to the case. And when Rousseau describes the beginnings of his persecution, in the *Rêveries*, does he not do so in terms which smack of a strict mechanicist orthodoxy applied to anthropology? 'And so ... I understood that in their relations to me my fellow men were nothing more than mechanical beings who behaved purely in response to the forces driving them, and whose actions I could only predict by invoking the laws of motion ... I came to see them as examples of mass set in motion in different ways'.[129] Such expressions give us much to think about in that they seem to break out of the confines of pure metaphor and would certainly not be out of place in d'Holbach's *Système de la Nature*. Nevertheless, we must also recognise that by setting himself apart in this way, and by claiming to be special, Rousseau is simultaneously undermining the absolute nature of the system. Rather like God, as it happens, he himself seems to escape from the closed world of mechanicism of which he is both a victim and a spectator. A 'worthless' and passive victim it is true, and one whom it is therefore difficult to consider *free*, caught up as he is in the meshes of the blind cogs of persecution.

According to the mechanicistic way of thinking, the human being, himself merely a particular example of the cosmic machine at work, eventually and in a mechanical sort of way comes to constitute society, which is itself entirely consistent with the mechanical nature of things. We can see that this is a process which is also ascribed to the political artificialism of the doctrines of the social contract. And it is true that it is another commonplace of the Enlightenment to describe society in mechanicistic terms. 'A people is an artificial body', Condillac explains. The 'magistrate' is 'the machine operator who must tighten up the springs and wind up the whole machine as often as the machine requires him to do so'.[130] 'Legislators', Diderot explains, seeing men as so many individual 'little springs isolated' in nature, decided to 'bring the little springs together and make them into a single great machine which they called society'.[131] Et cetera. Obviously, it is quite often a difficult thing to try to distinguish between that which should be read as a purely metaphorical expression and that which really implies some question of doctrinal belief. One thing is sure. Declaring too spontaneously or too explicitly that society is a machine serves at the very least to lessen the possibility of considering those who make up society as free and responsible beings. And in this respect too, Rousseau is among those who do not mind making such declarations, and this tips the balance yet a little further. Thus, in the *Contrat Social* we read that the great legislator 'is the mechanic who invents the machine', the prince 'is merely the workman who climbs aboard and makes it work'.[132] The words 'machine', 'springs', 'political machine' crop up time and again in his *Considérations sur le Gouvernement de Pologne*[133] and in those of his letters which deal with Geneva's institutional problems,[134] letters to which we should be thankful for this jewel of a precept, the true philosopher's stone of the art of politics: 'The workings of the machine should be as easy as they are simple, and they should always be as silent as possible'.[135]

These few words deserve a considerable amount of comment. There is much to say about them in their own right and for the utopian overtones they evoke, but there is much to say about them too (and perhaps this is much the same thing) in connection with the illusions that will hold sway in the early days of the Revolution and throughout the various attempts to produce a constitution. It is quite clear that if you consider politics as the easy and simple workings of a machine then you are accepting as a matter of principle that everything that is rough, complex, imperfect, individualistic, or a focus for reprehensible or legitimate autonomy in man, either as an individual or as a member of a group, is ipso facto a potential obstacle to the smooth working of that machine. By the same token, it is clear that the passive, standardised, mechanistically docile citizen is best suited to satisfying the demands of a 'programme' so well-intentioned in its vagueness. And we should also mention here Rousseau's political dig at Christianity: 'the strength of the spring driving politics is lessened by it, it complicates *the movements of the machine*'.[136] In what way? In that Christianity's ideal of universal love prevents the author of the *Contrat Social* from entertaining the hope that his ultimate aspiration of unwavering civic cohesion will ever be realised?[137] We know what meaning Voltaire attached to the word 'fanatic' and, around the same time, he confided to Helvétius that the *philosophes* 'inspire patriotic feelings whereas fanatics have the effect of agitating things'.[138] Rousseau deduces from the anti-civic potentiality of Christianity that 'it must degenerate completely or remain a troublesome and strange anomaly',[139] which remark is a rather timid version of Voltaire's more combative 'Écrasons l'infâme'. I should add that the case of Catholicism is doubly aggravated. On the one hand, Catholicism has the disadvantage of providing a very concretely institutional dimension to the separation of spiritual from temporal power, a yawning gap of huge significance from the point of view of politically-minded protestants and one which they would have liked to see reduced *manu militari* to a situation in which the adage *Cujus regio, ejus religio* prevailed. It constituted a yawning gap too in the eyes of a despot in the mould of Louis XIV, and of any *philosophe* slavishly defending the cause of 'enlightened' despots. On the other hand, by refusing to consider man as a simplistic and passive being and by preferring to see him rather as a free being who is responsible for his actions and is not predestined to act as a mere cog in the well-oiled wheels of some political system, by maintaining such views, Catholic anthropology stands out as an obstacle in the path of all utopian thinkers, Rousseau included.

In so far as the Napoleonic Code is concerned, (the document that was our point of departure and to which we shall in due course return) Rousseau is commonly seen as the man who inspired those who drafted it to adopt a reverential attitude (in our own view highly questionable) towards human volition. And French specialists in civil law refer, almost tropismatically, to the *Contrat Social*. But if this text is well known for the role it assigns to the notion of the *general will*, which to all intents and purposes appears to be an enormous and quite glorious role, it is nevertheless the case that this short treatise seems to me in reality to conform far more closely to the opposite impression, which has been outlined in the preceding pages. It is not even necessary to substantiate this assertion by referring to the doubts that are thrown up by the very enigmatic nature of the concept of general will, this key notion of the *Contrat Social*. It is enough to say that it has not been sufficiently recognised that Rousseau, remaining true in this respect to the concessions that he has reluctantly agreed to make to the reductionism of his day, exhibits the greatest possible scepticism when it comes to considering the question as to whether men are capable of arriving at a collective decision about what constitutes the public good. Will the 'people' have the 'necessary foresight' to organise society judiciously, or at least, will the people be the recipient of the grace of 'a sudden inspiration' directing them to this end? The answer is not affirmative. 'How can a blind multitude which *often* does not know *what it wants*, because it rarely knows what is good for it, put in place through its own efforts something so grand and so difficult as a legislative system?'[140]

Although it was Voltaire who said 'Man is a pitiful thing',[141] Rousseau thinks much the same, and in the light of this remark the general will can be seen to be too serious a thing to be left to the sum of individual wills to decide. It needs guidance and counselling. As early as the *Discours sur l'Économie politique*, Rousseau was of the opinion that the man who governs does not need to trouble himself with consulting the multitude in order to assume the role of faithful interpreter of the general will. It is sufficent that he be 'well intentioned'.[142] This is already saying a lot. The *Contrat* goes much further. The general will, although 'always right', needs to be manipulated. Or rather, one might almost say that it is because it is 'always right' that we must take the trouble to rectify it if we wish to be sure that it will continue to be so. This supposed adult citizenry is merely infantile and has to be hoodwinked. 'It has to be shown things ... sometimes in such a way that they appear *how they need to appear*',[143] and it is here that he even writes that such and such a citizen 'must be taught ... to recognise what he really wants'.[144] All of which goes some way to explaining the unexpected appearance at this point in the *Contrat Social* of that overwhelming figure, the great legislator-mechanic, to whom Rousseau devotes a whole *inspired* chapter which unambiguously describes his mission to mould the people, to model it into shape, and to undertake to modify mankind with a view to enhancing his social well-being. It is not at all a recent thing for Rousseau, this 'glimpsing of a secret opposition between the way man is made up and the constitution of human societies'.¹⁴⁵ And this élite being, the grand legislator, must also accept as part of his exorbitant mission, the task of changing human nature itself and of modifying the human constitution, if it should be so required.

It is no doubt worth being aware of this: 'He who dares to undertake to establish a people must be up to the task of changing, so to speak, human nature; of transforming each and every individual ...; of modifying the human constitution in such a way as to strengthen it'.¹⁴⁶ Has not present-day society, which is bad, already transformed natural man into an 'artificial and fantastical being'?¹⁴⁷ Since we are unable to go backwards, we must dare to go forwards and transform man even further in order to complete the process of socialisation and to better adapt him to the ideal society of the *Contrat*. The undertaking is by no means a small one and in its wake the notion that each individual-citizen can be seen as possessing the human quality of 'free agent' appears to have been forgotten, shunted off into some vague limbo, and in any case much diminished in terms of its influence on axiological principles. It seems to us that this decisive point of the *Contrat Social* provides a launching-pad for ideas which have extreme political consequences and express the anthropological reductionism of the age. Even the job description of the grand legislator himself is hardly an exception since precisely the function which identifies him 'has nothing in common with the world of mere mortals'.¹⁴⁸

Rousseau will also say of 'whomsoever seeks to establish a people', that he 'must know how to control opinion and to use it to hold men's passions in check'.¹⁴⁹ He thereby confirms the fact that what is involved is nothing at all to do with ensuring that individual free and sovereign wills realise their full expression, but rather the pure and simple exercising of control over men's minds. Once again we are bound to ask, can we consider this very far from d'Holbach's position when he says that rulers are 'the masters of the will of humanity'?¹⁵⁰ For we should note the fact that it is not just a question of knowing how to 'control opinion' but of *using* this control in order to govern, which necessarily suggests some form of manipulation of the inner man and demands of him a complete and unremitting allegiance to the omnipotence of the state. If the Spartans became the 'super-humans' so admired by Rousseau, it is partly because when Lycurgus 'undertook to establish a people', he did so 'by imposing a rule of iron upon it' but also because 'he made the people identify with this iron-rule', and never allowed them 'a moment's respite in which to be left to their own devices'.[151] Rousseau had just said as much: 'There can be no good and solid constitution except in circumstances where the law rules over the hearts of the citizens'; and with his usual candour, having realised that these remarks are not as harmless as they might seem, he rams the point home: the 'legislature' has to be prepared to go 'that far',[152] he insisted, and we know full well what sort of models of uniform totalitarianism such ideas are to be associated with and contribute towards setting up.

We can be quite sure that there is nothing accidental about these ideas, cropping up as they do in the midst of an argument of this sort. We are here at the very heart of Rousseau's political philosophy. And it is a philosophy that is explained and justified, or at least supported and reaffirmed, by the reductionist anthropology of the age which, whether or not Rousseau viewed it with misgivings and constantly wished to qualify with nuances that are ultimately insignificant (and in this respect he was less peculiar than he is generally considered to have been), he ultimately shared with the thinkers of his time. 'A true political body is a body composed of a multitude of men, but who are so united together that, possessing *a single will* and following one and the same direction, they form *a single unified force* to such an extent that they appear to constitute a single individual being'. This very well known extract from the *Contrat Social* could be both well known and from the *Contrat Social*, but in fact it is neither. It is from a physiocrat, Le Mercier de La Rivière.[153] Now physiocracy is not exactly the chamber occupied by Rousseau in the house of Enlightenment thinking,[154] but for all the vagabond tendencies he displays and likes to give the impression of possessing, he nevertheless occupies that house and shows all the characteristics one would expect of a tenant, especially the characteristics that I have accentuated in these pages.

It seems to me that what is of strategic importance in Rousseau is the relationship to others and in particular – but not solely – the relationship to authority seen as a form of *clever manipulation of the mind*, by which the will of the person concerned, and naturally unbeknownst to that person, is quietly superseded by the will of the manipulator. Rousseau may fear the consequences or he may be tempted by the advantages to be enjoyed by this process, but the negative effects are first and foremost something which he worries about, in so far as they may affect him personally. Isn't it just possible that he may have got wind of a little game played upon him by d'Holbach, who was convinced that one can *regulate* the will of men as one wishes, and who would amuse himself in company by contradicting Rousseau in order to fire his eloquence and then would lower the tone in order to bring the temperature of the discussion down again?[155] This particular Rousseau knows, in any event, that he is 'easy and pliable', and precisely the sort of man to let himself 'be subjugated, when one knows how to go about it, even by people that he has no time for'.[156] Which explains, finally, the strength of his obsession with conspiracies, with the intrigues that are supposedly woven around him, his fear of being constantly tricked and, unbeknownst to himself, manipulated, by virtue of this 'inviolable law that everything to do with him must be hidden from him',[157] the certainty that '*unbeknownst to himself* and behind his back' he is the object of calumny,[158] the fear too, which is so striking a feature of his personality, that he has become unwittingly *indebted* to others because of having supposedly received gifts in some roundabout way and without ever having known about it. Thus, he really believes that 'people have dreamed up the idea of giving him, *unbeknownst to himself,* lots of little but very public gifts' with the express intention of giving him a reputation for poverty,[159] or alternatively that '*unbeknownst to* and in spite of himself' his name has been wrongly included in certain subscription lists with the sole purpose of 'giving him airs of opulence and pretentiousness'.[160] Does he not also believe that in order to distort one or other of his writings they have had them 'printed *unbeknownst to himself*'?[161]

But if all these are reasons for Rousseau to seem fearful, he does so because he knows what a pliable thing opinion is; he knows its docile passivity, which is itself an effect of more general human passivity, in the hands of the calculating manipulators. 'You always say: we will; and yet you always submit to the will of others'.[162] Within social relationships, Rousseau has seen the proof that 'no one ever says what he thinks, but only what it is appropriate that others should be *made to think*', and that lovers of solitude themselves are merely 'machines which do not think, but which are moved to thought by a system of springs'.[163] This is what makes opinion so vulnerable to the intrigues and trickery of Rousseau's enemies the *philosophes*, by whom he notes, 'the public is enslaved *without realising it*',[164] because they are experts at taking advantage of the fact that 'the human mind, being naturally lazy, loves to spare itself trouble by thinking along lines laid down by others, especially when these flatter its own prejudices'.[165] This is why we see so many contemporaries '*unwittingly* treading the path of hatred whilst believing in all good faith that they are treading the path of pity'.[166]

Even if they are in reality less malicious than he believes them to be, Rousseau accuses these persecuting *philosophes* of organising public opinion against him by a system of insidious infiltration more carefully thought out than that of the Jesuits,[167] 'in that they know better how to act *in a covert manner*'.[168] A little while later Marat, too, speaks of 'the dark deeds of our *philosophes*', who '*without people knowing who they are*', infiltrate the very nerve centres of society.[169] It is the knowledge of the existence of such intrigues that leads Rousseau to raise the following objection to his interlocutor in the *Dialogues*: the ill-will you display towards Rousseau 'was not in any way a result of a reasoned judgement on your part but the effect of strongly felt emotions that took control of you *unbeknownst to yourself*',[170] so true is it that the brew of passions produced in this still 'can make men effectively unjust and malicious and this, so to speak, *unbeknownst to themselves*'.[171] He goes on to deplore the fact that 'the French are only capable of thinking and acting in groups'.[172] Of course, it is quite possible to see this as a passing remark, a hasty generalisation from the pen of a man who was at the time feeling disillusioned. But, given what we know, it seems clear to me that this remark flows naturally from a source that is to be located in doctrine, its anthropological underpinning is barely concealed and it is this which provides the main foundation for my argument. And, indeed, when Rousseau seeks to explain the unanimity of voices which are ranged against him, does he not come round to thinking that there might be some 'natural disposition within man', capable of producing '*a uniform effect by means that are cleverly organised* to this end'?[173]

Does he not come round to thinking? This formulation of the question leaves a lot to be desired. For in fact, Rousseau had for a long time been convinced of the technical as well as the moral possibility of conditioning human beings, by recourse to the methods identified by sensualism, with a view to manipulating men to accept other people's ideas as to what constitutes their own well-being. Far from being outraged by such an idea or expressing mistrust of it, he considers the implementation of such a procedure to be desirable for quite laudable reasons, and overall he only feared its effects to his own ultimate detriment. Did not 'the many striking observations' (which he had, incidentally, carried out upon himself) that provided the material in 1756 for the projected *Morale sensitive*,[174] appear to him to imply 'physical principles ... capable of providing an external regime which, when adapted to particular circumstances, would be able to dispose or maintain the soul in a position more favourable to virtue'? And he becomes quite excited by this idea: 'How often might we prevent reason from erring, how many vices might we prevent from seeing the light of day if we knew how to force the animal economy into working to support the moral order that it so often disturbs!'.[175] What is clearly taking shape here is the richly fertile possibility of a collective conditioning of humanity, which is itself seen as a collection of passive beings open to manipulation, provided that, (and I should underline this point) we know how *to force the animal economy*, with a view to inculcating in them appropriate behaviour patterns through the transmission of appropriate sensory messages dictated by a carefully controlled environment. That would have been 'a really useful book', he says, 'and one of the best that could have been given to mankind, if the composition of it had properly followed the plan that I had devised for myself'.[176] From the way the *Confessions* talk about the matter, it would not seem to be the case that Rousseau had initially envisaged acting without the knowledge of the supposed 'beneficiaries'. In his own mind at that time, it would seem to have been a question of including in the experiment only 'well-bred people who while sincerely loving virtue nevertheless feared their own weakness'.[177]

But at various points in his writings, the method to which we see him aspiring and which we see him recommending, or at very least implying in contexts which are quite unambiguous, is a method which quite straightforwardly involves imposing behaviour patterns or even modifying men's behaviour by bringing influence to bear on them so that their happiness is programmed for them without their knowing. Thus *La Nouvelle Héloïse* offers the example of a model in which those employed in the household are 'united so to speak *in spite of themselves* through the help they are in a way *forced* to offer each other'.[178] Through a series of subtle calculations, which afford him pleasure of almost divine proportions, the head of the family treats his servant as 'his possession, his own offspring, he *appropriates* him. He had control over his actions alone, but he now takes control of his *will*'.[179] It is through this type of seizure of control that he has become a past master in the art of 'fully enjoying his possessions, his family and himself',[180] 'he is the master of his own happiness because he is happy in much the same way as God himself is happy'.[181] Not everyone can say as much. Incidentally, it is worth noting once again that, in the final analysis, on matters such as this, the orthodox atheistic materialist (a title which has become a synonym for a member of the 'd'Holbach group', those opponents of Rousseau) scarcely differs in his thinking.[182]

If need be, *Émile ou de l'Éducation* should finally convince us that this tendency to encourage the covert exercising of a remote-control over 'individual wills' is in no way accidental. It is impossible not to call to mind here the famous advice given to the 'tutor' concerning the 'ruse' he should employ. The tutor, having 'at his mercy' the pupil, who 'knows nothing, who can do nothing, who understands nothing', is in a position which allows him to create *the illusion of freedom* whereas he systematically conditions his pupil by the sovereign arrangement of 'all that surrounds him'. Here once again we are in the presence of a total acceptance of the sensualist way of thinking and its concomitant reductionism.[183] 'Let him always believe himself to be the master, Rousseau explains, and let it always be you who is really in command. There is no form of subjection so absolute as that which preserves the illusion of freedom; the will itself thus becomes subjected ... No doubt he should only do what he wants to do; but he should only want to do what you want him to do'.[184] These are significant words indeed.

And finally, what is said about the education of young women, although coming from a quite different perspective, nevertheless foregrounds the same sort of thinking. On the one hand, women have a 'machine' which in its human dimension, 'is constructed in the same way, its pieces are the same, the workings of the one are the same as the workings of the other'.[185] On the other hand, women as women have only one advantage in life which is their ability to subtly lead men along without the latter realising it, and it is to this end that they must be trained from childhood onwards. 'The mechanism of a woman is stronger than ours, all its levers are designed to set the human body in motion. She must acquire *the art of making us want* all the things that her sex cannot provide for itself, and which are necessary and agreeable to it'. Thus, very early on, she must study the 'way men around her think ... Through her speech, her actions, her looks, her gestures, she must learn how to make them feel what she wants them to feel, without ever appearing to give the matter a moment's thought', which is another way of saying, yet again: unbeknownst to them.[186] Condillac, we are told, 'praised *Émile*'.[187]

As we can see, children do not have the monopoly over the pure and simple vocation of pure passivity – a passivity that believes itself to be capable of activity simply because it is capable of being activated. Such is the fate of human beings in general, as is reflected in the doctrines of the anthropology of the period. This was an anthropology which had nothing at all specifically Rousseauist about it and one with which, in fact, Rousseau would most likely have considered himself to be at odds, even though intermittently he proved himself to be one of its staunchest defenders. The audacious legislative transformation of man, the unashamed *modifying* of 'the human constitution' which is envisaged in the *Contrat Social*,[188] a book exactly contemporaneous with *Émile* (which is itself concerned with changing man's nature,[189] and which as we have already said has to be read alongside the former text as if they formed a single entity) – this daring undertaking has no other means at its disposal than those identified by the omnipresent sensualism which is an all powerful component in the thinking of the entire century. It is worth betting too that the self-same methods are those envisaged in order to deal with would-be dissenters, namely, the paradoxical proposal *of forcing them to be free*.[190] Once it is considered legitimate to exercise a controlling influence over human beings, it is a small step to considering it licit to reprogramme them.

Even though he had only managed a perfunctory and 'exceedingly rapid' reading of *Émile*, one young correspondant of Rousseau's nevertheless immediately grasped the fact that what is at stake beneath all its dialectics and argument is the fascinating prospect of an 'art more potent than the methods ordinarily employed' and which, by 'persuasion' would lead men, who are far too reticent to follow it of their own accord, down the path to virtue. 'If, for example, we knew how to place men in circumstances that were of interest to them and to create for them situations that cajoled them along'. What is ultimately at stake actually comes to the surface at a number of points in the book: 'I was struck by several illuminating passages in which you allowed the reader to glimpse some of the mechanisms involved', and we might suppose that these are the very passages we ourselves have been considering. He goes on to ask, 'does not some simple, unknown and commonly neglected principle underlie this sublime art of moving men and persuading them to action?'.[191] The fact that he asks this question would tend to indicate that the young man is not yet very well informed as to the existence of the rising tide of sensualism of a materialistic tendency, even though he has accurately predicted and enthusiastically welcomes the rich potential it holds for the psychic, individual and collective conditioning of mankind. And this to such an extent that he has quite purely and simply sketched out an entire plan for Rousseau's abandoned treatise on *Morale sensitive*.[192]

Perhaps too, he has at least noticed the passage in *Émile* where Rousseau, with his usual brilliance, once more articulates his belief in man's constant inertia, the fact that he is permanently enslaved to his habits and that, consequently, whatever age he may have reached, he remains vulnerable and in need of guidance: 'Every period of man's life has its own *springs* that *trigger off* his actions', he says, 'but man himself is always the same. At ten years of age he is motivated by sweetmeats, at twenty by his mistress, at thirty by pleasure, at forty by ambition, at fifty by avarice: when does he pursue wisdom? Happy is the man who is led to do so *in spite of himself*'.[193] But it is also the case that the subject has to be open to the possibility of being manoeuvred. A man's character defects can provide such an opening because they allow him to be influenced. Ten years later, replying to a letter from a woman whose husband has decided to leave her, Rousseau can offer her no hope because he can see no way of acting upon this 'nonentity of a man' who sadly 'possesses neither vices nor virtues'. He has 'no springs of any kind',[194] and Rousseau goes on to explain: 'If he were a man with many vices and possessing passions that could be *channelled in other directions*, the problem would probably not be insoluble'.[195] The way he expresses this idea is very significant: there is no suggestion here that he is supporting some active principle of an autonomous nature by making the man more aware of his responsibilities or urging him to make greater efforts, rather he is suggesting that, if the man's character were such as to allow it, he could become the object of a form of conditioning that is subject to almost exactly the same laws as the laws of physics.

Seeking to use man's vices in order to control him and to lead him where one would, instead of urging him to reform and helping him to rid himself of his vices, is very much an eighteenth-century idea, and it is one that Mandeville, whom Rousseau had read, turned into something of a personal preoccupation at the beginning of the century.[196] It is also an idea that the writers of the *Code Napoléon* would admit to seeing as particularly timely. It is in complete harmony with the utilitarianism of the age and with that materialistically orientated anthropology which more or less directly and overtly, or surreptitiously, considers man as a mere mechanism. All of which seems to support the argument that I have been making: namely, that in spite of the tendency of so many commentators to classify Rousseau's work as being inspired by purely affective considerations, and in spite of his own oft-repeated declaration that man is a 'free agent', Rousseau's thinking, in actual fact, follows much the same lines as those who deny that freedom, and is close, for example, to a thinker like d'Holbach who also stresses the fact, as does Voltaire, that men who really enjoy the power to reason are rare indeed. Should we see Rousseau as a defender of the view that freedom is a defining characteristic of mankind, in an age that professed the contrary view? He was far too inclined towards sensualist orthodoxy to deserve such an epithet, and the way he is prepared to *force* citizens to be free does little to help dispel our suspicions on the matter. Freedom? 'Rousseau is rather odd on that subject', remarks one of his correspondants, 'he not only wants to be free himself, he wants everyone else to be free with him, *even his dog*, which he won't ever call so that it only comes to him out of friendship and loyalty'.[197] 'There is no point in demanding the privilege of freedom for mankind for reasons of sentiment', says Jean Rostand,[198] but he says it as a materialist and as a not ungrateful, indeed as an admiring, successor to the materialists of the Enlightenment. And, in fact, Rousseau, who thoroughly disapproved of the latter, was nevertheless far closer to their way of thinking than is usually supposed and than he himself ever supposed himself to be.

Notes

1. J.-J. Rousseau, *Rousseau juge de Jean-Jacques. Dialogues* (1772–75), *Premier Dialogue*, in *Œuvres complètes*, vol. 1, Paris, 1959, 727.
2. See my study 'Madame de Staël, Napoléon et les Idéologues' in *Himeji International Forum of Law and Politics*, no 1. (1993,) 39–62.
3. Letter to Tronchin, 27 February 1757 : *Correspondance complète de Jean Jacques Rousseau*, ed. R.A. Leigh, 50 vols, Geneva, then Oxford, 1965–91, vol. 4, 162.
4. 'I have never adopted the philosophy of the privileged children of our age; it is not for me' (reference to note 1).
5. Rousseau,*Troisième Dialogue*, (see note 1) 890.
6. *Premier Dialogue*, 728.

7. To Paul-Claude Moultou, whom he accuses of allowing himself to be caught up in it, 14 February 1769: Rousseau, *Corr.*, vol 37, 56.
8. *Troisième Dialogue*, 934. The words *'philosophe'* or 'philosophy' when used without further qualification, usually have pejorative connotations in Rousseau's writings.
9. *Troisième Dialogue*, 971.
10. J.-J. Rousseau, *Discours sur les fondemens et l'origine de l'inégalité parmi les hommes* (1755), in *Œuvres complètes*, vol. 3, 141.
11. Ibid., 142.
12. J.-J. Rousseau, *Julie ou la Nouvelle Héloïse* (1761), Paris, 1988, 671–72. To what extent are we justified in assuming that the fictional correspondence in this novel reflects Rousseau's own thinking? I have decided to refer to passages in the novel when they are corroborated by Rousseau's other writings.
13. J.-J. Rousseau, *Émile ou de l'Éducation*, (1762). Book IV, Paris, 1966, 364. He attacks those who are readier to 'grant that stones are capable of feeling rather than that man has a soul' (363).
14. Ibid., 365.
15. See above, 28.
16. Quoted by J-M. Carbasse, «Langue de la nation et «idiomes grossiers»: le pluralisme linguistique sous le niveau jacobin», paper presented at the Journées Internationales d'Histoire du Droit, Anvers, 1993, publication in preparation, to which note 43 provides a reference.
17. *Deuxième* and *Troisième Dialogue*, 342, 967, respectively.
18. For example, *Émile*, Book IV, 356–57; *Premier Dialogue*, 687,*Troisième Dialogue*, 968.
19. *Émile*, Book IV, 279.
20. R.A. Leigh, in *Corr.*, vol. 17, 115/2.
21. *Émile*, Book IV, 361.
22. Preface to *La Nouvelle Héloïse*, 739.
23. *Nouvelle Héloïse*, 672.
24. *Troisième Dialogue*, 972.
25. *Premier Dialogue*, 687.
26. *Émile*, Book IV, (the 'vicaire savoyard') 352. Cf. the anonymous author of *L'Élève de la Raison et de la Religion*, Paris, 1773, 245, who writes: 'Whatever certain *philosophes* may say, I dare to claim the honour of being capable of thought'.
27. To Paul-Claude Moultou, 1 August 1763: Rousseau, *Corr.*, vol. 17, 114 (w.u.o).
28. *Émile*, Book IV, 351.
29. Letter of 25 September 1762 to Montmollin which the latter refers to in a letter to d'Ivernois on 27 November (Rousseau, *Corr.*, vol. 14, 123) before publishing it in August 1765 (*Corr. gén. d'Helvétius* vol. 3, 233/1). Another fundamental reason for Jean-Jacques' disagreement (as well as that of Voltaire and many others): Helvétius' suggestion that all men are born equal in terms of ability (on this point, see also *La Nouvelle Héloïse*, 550–52, a passage which was added after Rousseau had read *De l'Esprit*).
30. A criticism addressed in particular in letters written to d'Alembert, Damilaville and Hume: references to his correspondence in *Corr. gén. d'Helvétius*, vol. 3, 234/2, to which we should add Voltaire, *Corr.*, vol. 8, 218.
31. Rousseau, *Corr.*, vol. 37, 243, 19 February 1770.
32. Reference to note 7, 56 and 57.
33. *Troisième Dialogue*, 971.

34. *Deuxième Dialogue*, 890.
35. Letter to Roume de Saint Laurent, 20 November 1783, in *Correspondance de Marat*, ed. Charles Vellay, Paris, 1908, 38.
36. *Deuxième Dialogue*, 841.
37. From Belloy, one of Rousseau's correspondents, in 1770: *Corr.*, vol. 37, 245/2. Jean-Jacques wrote to him: 'The only path that is open to your nation [France] is to seek consolation for the fact that it has forgotten what virtue is, by denying that it ever existed and by attacking those who still possess it' (243).
38. *Deuxième Dialogue*, 842.
39. *Troisième Dialogue*, 971, footnote.
40. *Émile*, Book IV, 377. These words are spoken by the 'vicaire savoyard' who goes so far as to speak of 'the abjection of human self-absorption' (409, footnote) (w.u.o).
41. Rousseau, *Les Confessions* (1766–71), Paris, 1980, 713.
42. *Deuxième Dialogue*, 842.
43. For example *Émile*, Book IV, 411; *Troisième Dialogue*, 967–972, passim.
44. *Discours sur l'inégalité*, 143.
45. Letter from Diderot to l'abbé Le Monnier, around the 15 September 1755: *Corr. compl. de Rousseau*, vol. 3, 1966, 174.
46. 'His modest needs are so readily available within his reach' et cetera. (*Discours* 144). See also, with regard to food and rest, 135 and, for the 'mate', 147: 'Males and females came together haphazardly, through chance encounter or when circumstances and desire coincided'.
47. Ibid., 144. 'His imagination has nothing to show him; his heart makes no demands of him'.
48. Ibid., 141.
49. See above, 37–38.
50. *Discours*, 143.
51. Likewise, Jean-Jacques' friend and fellow-spiritualist, Bernardin de Saint-Pierre, is not averse to writing that all 'friendship originates first and foremost in physical need' (*Harmonies de la Nature*, vol. 1, Paris, 1815, 143), which is precisely one of the most provocative claims made by the materialist Helvétius.
52. Rousseau,*Contrat social*, Book I, chap. 8, 364.
53. *Discours*, 138. At least this is what the writer 'almost dares to say' if nature 'intended us to be healthy'.
54. *Confessions*, 390. And yet, very often, 'she saw things that I was unable to see myself'.
55. From Rousseau to Condorcet, 16 February 1770: *Corr.*, vol. 37, 240. Condorcet's *Essais d'Analyse* is the text in question here.
56. 26 July 1767 : *Corr.*, vol. 33, 241.
57. Ibid., 240; then *Considérations sur le Gouvernement de Pologne*, O.C., vol. 3, 955.
58. Letter to Alexandre Deleyre (1726–96, *philosophe* and future member of the Convention): Rousseau, *Corr.*, vol. 4, 255.
59. Same letter to Mirabeau, 239. He goes on to defend the 'descendants of Adam', against the 'Utopian people' (240).
60. To Pierre-Alexandre Du Peyrou, 10 June 1768 : *Corr.*, vol. 35, 304.
61. *Deuxième Dialogue*, 816.
62. To Mme d'Houdetot, 17 December : *Corr.*, vol. 4, 398.
63. *Deuxième Dialogue*, 865.
64. *Troisième Dialogue*, 933.

65. *Deuxième Dialogue*, 846.
66. Ibid., 817
67. *Émile*, Book IV, 364.
68. *Deuxième Dialogue*, 897. He is also able to define himself as 'a man ... who adores virtue without practising it' (774).
69. To Tscharner, 27 July 1762 : *Corr.*, vol. 12, 111.
70. *Deuxième Dialogue*, 812, 847, 849, 846.
71. Ibid., 806.
72. Ibid., 850.
73. Ibid., 846. There are other similar passages. For example, 811, or 812: 'Never did a man base his behaviour less on principles and rules, nor more blindly follow his instincts. Prudence, reason, precaution, foresight: all these are merely empty words to him. When he is tempted, he succumbs, when he is not tempted, he remains in his state of torpor'.
74. To Mirabeau the elder, 9 March : *Corr.*, vol. 35, 192. It's better, he continues, for 'my laziness' and 'my mind', not to 'fight against what can't be avoided' and not 'to put up any resistance against those who are in charge of me here'.
75. *Deuxième Dialogue*, 804.
76. *Nouvelle Héloïse*, 589. On reading Bernardin de Saint-Pierre we also have the feeling that Paul and Virginie's sweet benevolence is entirely consistent with the psychic conditioning that they have undergone through their closeness to nature.
77. Just like his noble savage, reduced to 'the pure feeling of his own present existence' (*Discours sur l'Inégalité*, 144), Rousseau can write later in life: 'The pain that I am not feeling at the present moment has no effect on me whatsoever' (Rousseau, *Les Rêveries du Promeneur solitaire* (1778), Paris, 1960, 115).
78. *Rêveries*, 86, 1777.
79. Ibid., 111.
80. *Deuxième Dialogue*, 807.
81. Ibid., 808. But the fact that he is 'too much a slave of his senses' is an advantage from a literary and aesthetic point of view.
82. Ibid., 807.
83. Ibid., 807–808.
84. According to J. Voisine, Introduction to the *Confessions*, Paris, 1980, lvii. Condillac's *Traité des Sensations* 'had a great influence on Rousseau', writes R. Osmont (in Rousseau, *Œuvres complètes*, Paris, vol. 1, 1959, 1752).
85. *Confessions*, Book VII, 409.
86. Ibid., Book IX, 485. The project dates from 1756 (Rousseau, *Corr.*, vol. 4, 111/2).
87. *Confessions*, ibid.
88. Ibid., Book XII, 720.
89. É. Gilson, 'La méthode de M. de Wolmar', in *Les Idées et les Lettres*, Paris, 1932, 275–98, quoted by B. Gagnebin and M. Raymond in Rousseau, *Œuvres complètes*, vol.1, Paris, 1959, 1469.
90. Helvétius, *De l'Esprit*, 539; also, d'Holbach, *Système de la Nature*, vol. 1, 103–04.
91. *Rêveries*, 95
92. Superficially similar (but nothing more) formulations are to be found in *La Nouvelle Héloïse*, 484, and *Le Persiffleur* (1749): 'Even more so: the return of the same objects normally provokes within me the same reactions, the

same states of mind, as those I experienced when I perceived the objects for the first time' (*Œuvres complètes*, vol.1, 1109); and from the pen of Mme du Deffand, letter to Voltaire, 28 February 1766, Bestermann, D. 13188, vol. 114 of the *Œuvres* of Voltaire, vol. 30 of the *Correspondance*, 117.
93. *Rêveries*, 97
94. Likewise, ibid., 115: 'Dominated as I am by my senses, whatever I may do, I have never known how to resist their impressions, and for so long as an object is acting upon them my heart continues to feel their effects.'
95. *Confessions*, 425.
96. *Discours sur l'Inégalité*, 147. 'In the first instance, the mother breast-fed her children to satisfy her own needs; then when habit had endeared them to her, she then fed them to satisfy theirs.'
97. Letter to Charles Bonnet, October 1755: *Corr.*, vol. 3, 191.
98. *Rêveries*, 122. Beginning of the phrase: 'I would do it again with less misgivings if it were to be done again, and I know full well...' et cetera.
99. *Nouvelle Héloïse*, 210
100. *Émile*, Book IV (from the 'vicaire savoyard'), 409.
101. Ibid., 377.
102. *Gouvernement de Pologne*, 1,005.
103. *Deuxième Dialogue*, 852, concerning the self-lover: 'All his reflections are sweet ones because he loves to take pleasure in them'. On the primordial nature of self-love, see *Discours sur l'Inégalité*, n. XV, 219; and on its decisive importance, see *Émile*, Book IV, 275–77.
104. *Deuxième Dialogue*, 852.
105. *Premier Dialogue*, 669.
106. Ibid., see also *Rêveries*, 114–15.
107. *Premier Dialogue*, 671.
108. *Deuxième Dialogue*, 851.
109. The word *égoïsme* seems to appear for the first time in 1755, in the *Encyclopédie*, and in 1762 in the *Dictionnaire* of the Academy. In 1756, Alexandre Deleyre, one of Rousseau's correspondents, tries the word 'égoïté' in order, it would seem, to designate the fact of being oneself and to persist in being so (23 September, Rousseau, *Corr.*, vol. 4, 113).
110. *Deuxième Dialogue*, 851–52 (w.u.o).
111. Ibid., 852.
112. *Deuxième Dialogue*, 813.
113. Ibid., 805–06.
114. Ibid., 864.
115. Letter to Mme d'Houdetot, 17 December 1757: Rousseau, *Corr.*, vol. 4, 394.
116. We should not forget the general title Rousseau gave to these *Dialogues* from which we have so often quoted: *Rousseau juge de Jean-Jacques* [Rousseau the judge of Jean-Jacques].
117. *Deuxième Dialogue*, 815.
118. Or indeed from La Rochefoucauld, as Voltaire, for example, never ceases to point out when arguing against Helvétius' censors.
119. *Nouvelle Héloïse*, 209.
120. D'Holbach, *Système de la Nature*, vol. 1, 334.
121. *Émile*, 36, footnote (beginning of Book I).
122. Letter to Charles Bonnet, 15 October 1755: Rousseau, *Corr.*, vol. 3, 191. This is from a *doctrinal* letter which was never sent and which was a response to published criticisms of the Genevan *philosophe*.
123. *Émile*, Book IV, 287.

124. *Deuxième Dialogue*, 890.
125. *Émile*, Book IV (from the 'vicaire savoyard'), 348.
126. Ibid., 357.
127. *Discours sur l'Inégalité*, 141.
128. Bluntly, at least in private: in this respect, see above 37–38.
129. *Rêveries* (1770s), 110.
130. Condillac, *Traité des Systèmes* (1749) (1798 edition), C.O.P.L.F., Paris, 1991, 254.
131. Diderot, *Mémoires pour Catherine II* (1773–74), Paris, 1966, 173.
132. Rousseau, *Contrat Social* (1762), Book II, chapter 7, in *Œuvres complètes*, vol. 3, 381.
133. *Gouvernement de Pologne* (1770), 1,005, 1,036 ('If the king died ... we should barely notice that the machine has a piece missing so little is this piece essential to the solidity of the whole'), 1,040, 1,041.
134. For example the letter of 1768 : Rousseau, *Corr.*, vol. 35, 93, 102, 109.
135. Letter to François-Henri d'Ivernois, 9 February 1768 : ibid., 104 and 111.
136. Rousseau, *Lettres écrites de la montagne* (1764), in *Œuvres complètes*, vol. 3, 705.
137. Ibid., 706.
138. *Corr. gén. d'Helvétius*, vol. 3, 82, letter of 15 September 1763.
139. Reference to note 136.
140. *Contrat Social*, Book II, chapter 6, 380.
141. See Chapter Three above, note 4.
142. Rousseau, *Discours sur l'Économie politique* (1755), in *Œuvres complètes*, vol 3, 251.
143. Reference to note 140. The first version of the *Contrat Social* added: 'show the multitude the right path that it wishes to follow' (311).
144. *Contrat Social*, 380.
145. This quotation is probably from the *Dialogues*.
146. *Contrat Social*, Book II, chapter 7, 'Du Législateur', 381.
147. *Premier Dialogue*, 728.
148. *Contrat Social*, 382. It should also be said that it is difficult to unreservedly accept the point made by Jean Starobinski, when he claims that 'Jean-Jacques works for the destruction of any form of authority imposed from the outside' (1789. *Les Emblèmes de la Raison*, Paris, 1979, 41).
149. *Gouvernement de Pologne*, 965–966.
150. D'Holbach, *Système de la Nature*, vol. 1, 242.
151. *Gouvernement de Pologne*, 957.
152. Ibid., 955.
153. Le Mercier de La Rivière, *De l'Instruction publique; ou Considérations morales et politiques sur la nécessité, la nature et la source de cette instruction. Ouvrage demandé pour le roi de Suède*, Stockholm, 1775, 34.
154. This is self-evident, and Rousseau's unfavourable reaction to *L'Ordre naturel et essentiel des Sociétés politiques*, by the same Le Mercier de La Rivière, provides a further proof: letter to Mirabeau the elder, 26 July 1767, *Corr.*, vol.33, 238–41.
155. Cérutti, a friend of Mirabeau and d'Holbach, gives an account of remarks made by the latter: 'Nothing was more uninteresting than the everyday conversation of Jean-Jacques; but it became truly sublime or extraordinary as soon as he was annoyed. I'm afraid I must confess to having multiplied these sources of annoyance in order to increase the moments of sparkling and vivacious eloquence. However, when I saw that he was becoming over-excited, I took pains to calm him down

again and he would once more fall back into a state of torpor' (*Corr. compl. de Rousseau*, vol 3. Appendix A 140, 347).
156. *Deuxième Dialogue*, 793; same idea, 847.
157. *Premier Dialogue*, 719.
158. Ibid., 739, where he also mentions 'the tortuous and ill-lit paths by which he has been gradually led to that point, *without realising what was happening*'.
159. Ibid., 721; 'so that to the horror felt at his misdeeds can be added scorn for his poverty and a feeling of respect for his benefactors' (in reality, his 'persecutors').
160. *Troisième Dialogue*, 961.
161. Ibid., 962.
162. *Émile*, Book I, 99.
163. *Nouvelle Héloïse*, 209.
164. *Troisième Dialogue*, 965.
165. *Deuxième Dialogue*, 880. See, also, 841, concerning the public: 'But today, completely subjugated, it no longer thinks, it no longer reasons, in its own right it is worthless and merely follows the impressions that its guides give it. Henceforth, the only doctrine that it can accept is one which gives full reign to its passions and paints over its moral shortcomings with a varnish of wisdom'. On this theme, see above, 46–47.
166. *Troisième Dialogue*, 970.
167. *Deuxième Dialogue*, 889–890.
168. Ibid., 890.
169. Reference to note 35.
170. *Deuxième Dialogue*, 881.
171. Ibid., 883.
172. *Troisième Dialogue*, 965, footnote. We also read in *Émile*, Book III: 'There are some men who are so similar to each other that there is no point in studying them separately. If you have seen ten Frenchmen you've seen them all'.
173. *Premier Dialogue*, 760.
174. See above, 55–56.
175. *Confessions*, Book IX, 409.
176. Ibid., 408.
177. Ibid., 409.
178. *Nouvelle Héloïse*, 445. 'We do more than that, we get them to mutually help each other in secret, without ostentation, without drawing attention to the fact; a thing which is all the easier to achieve because they know very well that the master, who sees all of this, values them all the more on account of it' (sic). Et cetera.
179. Ibid., 449
180. Ibid., 450.
181. Ibid., 449.
182. D'Holbach, *Système de la Nature*, vol.1, 336–37. The head of the family thus 'becomes an object of interest for all those who come near him; it is a constant source of pleasure to him ... he is loved, respected, esteemed by others, *everything brings him back to himself*; he knows the rights that he has assumed over the hearts of men; he is pleased to be at the source of the happiness which *binds everyone to his personal destiny*. The feelings of love that we have for ourselves become a hundred times more satisfying when we see that they are shared by all those whose fate is linked to ours.' (337).

183. *Émile*, 150. 'In your relation to him, are you not in control of everything that surrounds him? Are you not in a position to influence him as you see fit? When he is at work or at play, in his moments of pleasure or pain, is he not entirely in your hands, *without his knowing it?*' (unbeknownst to him).
184. Ibid., 'he must not take a single step that you have not already foreseen; he must not open his mouth without you knowing what he is about to say'.
185. Ibid., 465.
186. Ibid., 507.
187. R. Osmont in Rousseau, *Œuvres Complètes*, vol. 1, 1,752.
188. See above, 68.
189. *Émile*, Book I, 39: good social institutions are those which 'best know how to change man's nature'.
190. *Contrat Social*, Book I, chapter 7, 364.
191. Letter from Niklaus Anton Kirchberger (1739–59, who came from a patrician family in Berne and was an officer at the time), to Rousseau, 17 November 1762: Rousseau, *Corr.*, vol. 14, 61–62.
192. See above, 55–56 and 73.
193. *Émile*, Book V, 566.
194. Letter to Mme Guyenet, née d'Ivernois, end of August beginning of September 1772: Rousseau, *Corr.*, vol. 39, 102.
195. Ibid., 101.
196. Bernard Mandeville, *La Fable des Abeilles, ou les vices privés font le bien public* (1714), trans. and ed. by L. and P. Carrive, Paris, 1985.
197. Letter from Fr. Favre to Paul-Claude Moultou, 11 December 1759: Rousseau, *Corr.*, vol. 6, 227.
198. See above, 27.

Chapter 5

Pedagogy and Politics

When Rousseau himself acknowledges the existence of an organic link between *Émile* and the *Contrat Social*, books which 'taken together form a complete whole',[1] he is offering more than a hint that, in the eighteenth-century, political realignment and pedagogical reform are part and parcel of the same struggle. Perhaps they are even more tightly bound together than we might think at first glance. However important Rousseau's reputation as a theoretician of pedagogical matters may be, it would seem to be quite justifiable to claim that his reputation as a political thinker nevertheless takes precedence. But it is useful to remember that as far as he himself was concerned the order is reversed. It is the *Contrat Social* that he sees as 'a sort of appendix' to *Émile*, and not the other way round.[2] Rousseau even considers his treatise on education to be not only 'his greatest and best work',[3] but the one that contains the first principles 'of his system'[4] and this clearly suggests the fundamental importance we should assign to education when considering the political aspects of the Enlightenment. Even those *philosophes* who are furthest removed from Rousseau's own way of thinking agree on this point. Helvétius writes in *De l'Esprit*, 'In all countries, the art of educating men is so closely linked to the country's form of government that it is probably impossible to make any real changes in the system of public education without also making changes in the very constitution of the State'.[5] And the full title of *De l'Homme* includes a reference to 'education'.[6] As for d'Holbach and his *Système de la Nature*, in the very chapter which contains a resolute denial that there is any such thing as freedom, he writes: 'Education is nothing more than necessity made evident to children. Legislation is nothing more than necessity made evident to the members of the body politic'.[7]

When Rousseau turns his attention to the 'government of Poland' he declares that education is 'the important section'. Indeed, it is education 'that must instil into the souls of the people a sense of nationhood, and *so direct* their opinions and their tastes that they become patriots by inclination, through passionate conviction, *through necessity*'.[8] This is the logic of human conditioning and of *socialisation* through coercive action. Nor is this likely to surprise us, given what we already know of the 'tutor's' virtuosity in the praiseworthy art of invading Émile's psychic space, while never appearing to do so. It is also important to recognise that this is not a characteristic which is peculiar to the pedagogical writings of Rousseau alone. It overwhelmingly represents the whole, or very nearly the whole, of the pedagogical thinking of the entire age which, by simply applying the anthropological views current at the time, tended to consider children as purely passive entities, as objects to be manipulated and *modified* in accordance with the particular programme which the theoretician considers it fitting to implement and whose methodology he usually analyses in depth. It is quite normal, then, that, in this respect, the pedagogical thinking of the Enlightenment should ignore the Thomist doctrine that 'in any discipline and in any form of teaching the master merely offers external assistance to the principle of immanent activity that is present within the pupil';[9] according to this doctrine teaching is, like medicine, *ars cooperativa naturae*, dealing with corporal nature in the case of the latter and spiritual nature in the case of the former.[10] 'These arts are only effective in so far as they furnish the internal principle which is present within the subject with the wherewithal and the help needed for it to produce its effect. It is the *internal principle*, it is the light of intellect present in the pupil, which is the *cause* or *principal agent* in the acquisition of knowledge and skill'.[11]

A recent thesis[12] has clearly demonstrated how the Enlightenment marks the triumph of the opposite viewpoint, which openly seeks to '*take control of the minds of children* thanks to the great increase in scientific activity'. For almost all the theoreticians of this *pedagogical* age, children are a raw material in the hands of the tutor, a mechanism to be programmed, or whatever other rhetorical figure we care to draw on, so long as it expresses the notion of the passive and artificial nature of inner man and a view of this as an object susceptible of being constructed or kneaded into shape. 'The moral being is a completely artificial being',[13] Le Mercier de La Rivière claims, and thereby ensures that we are clearly operating from the usual materialistically orientated perspective. Louis de la Caze considers that what is decisive in education is the way we act upon the 'animal economy' of children,[14] an expression which Rousseau also uses when talking about the conditioning of adults.[15] The Parisian professor of medicine, Le Camus, who proves that 'the functions of understanding and the springs that activate the will are mechanical',[16] would also like to persuade us that we can 'use purely mechanical means to correct defects in understanding and vices associated with the will'. He would even have us believe that we can 'uproot those defects we think of as belonging to the soul in the same way that doctors cure an inflammation'.[17] In short, he is prepared to claim that by intervening intelligently to modify a man's organs, it is possible 'to make a clever man out of a stupid one'.[18]

Charles Bonnet, the famous Genevan sensualist, who undertook 'to study man' just as he 'studied insects and plants',[19] although he believes that 'the soul contains an active principle within it',[20] nevertheless talks about the human 'machine', and about the 'mechanism' of the heart and mind.[21] For him, education is little more than a process of priming a machine which is capable of feeling. It is like 'a second birth which imprints new forms of determination upon the brain'.[22] Writing about childhood, he says, 'I shall never forget that if we are machines it is especially the case at this age, and the springs of this machine that we are constructing are the senses'.[23] He also writes, 'the perfection of education' consists for him 'in increasing as far as possible the number of movements in the sensorium'.[24] Even without wishing to do so, therefore, Bonnet establishes 'a system which can only lead to materialism. In addition, he leaves the path wide open for those pedagogues who seek to fashion their pupils into a particular mould, by creating a "physical" basis for their theories. He thus further distances education from an end-product by reducing it to a functional process'.[25] Michel, who studied Bonnet in some depth, considered the child to be 'a block of marble in which we must find the citizen, just as the artist tries to find a human shape'.[26] And the sculpture metaphor is precisely the one that Maritain uses to express the idea of what education, in a Thomist perspective, can never be.[27]

Another, (this time more specifically sensualist,) metaphor frequently occurs in the pedagogical discourse of the period, namely the image of soft wax awaiting the imprint of the seal, or alternatively, of the malleable clay awaiting the potter's hand. These metaphors very clearly express what Marcel Grandière has called 'pedagogical totalitarianism',[28] the child's complete subjection to the power of the person educating him. The former tutor, La Fare, speaks of his pupils thus: 'As you know I had complete control in deciding how to influence their faculties, their young minds were like soft, pliable wax in my hands to be shaped, so to speak, as I saw fit'.[29] For the child, finally, is nothing more than 'a small piece of organised matter' and it is the task of his master to endow him 'so to speak, with a soul':[30] the tone here is far more anodine than the task envisaged. 'His mind as well as his heart are in your hands, they are a blank surface on which all sorts of impressions can be stamped'.[31] And thus, it is the task of the 'generous hands' of the tutor (how telling are all these expressions) 'to knead his soul into shape'.[32] As for Vauréal, good sensualist that he is, he believes that 'it is *external objects* that should prepare children for citizenship'.[33] He expresses the view that 'intelligently exercised guardianship and a knowledgeable chemist'[34] are essential elements of an educational policy. He would prefer that things were so arranged that at three years of age children should be ready to 'be offered up, on the altars of the nation, to the national education system, like lumps of clay that are ready and waiting for the soft and beneficent hands of the potter'.[35]

Such views are published a mere ten years before 1793. They confirm that there is an organic link between the pedagogical and the political on the eve of the Revolution. And what they have in common, what they share as a result of having the same anthropological roots, is an acceptance of the fundamental principle that the human being can be viewed as a purely passive entity. And furthermore, that it is the job of those who bear responsibility in the pedagogical or the political spheres, provided they are enlightened people – which they alone are capable of judging – to shape men for their own individual and collective good, and this without their knowing anything about it rather than at their own request. Such a vocation allows them a completely free rein, it affords them an exorbitant degree of power. As we have seen, d'Holbach spontaneously gives those who are entrusted with authority over others the title: 'the masters of the will of mankind'.[36] The power that they have is nothing less than the power to produce men in accordance with the particular view of man that the reformers themselves may hold. This presupposes, ipso facto, that there exists a gulf between, on the one hand, the masses who provide the brute raw material and, on the other, the enlightened élite who are self-appointed to fulfil their mission, the audacious blacksmiths who will forge the new humanity and who are simultaneously the clockmakers of the ideal society. 'Education can do anything', Helvétius says,[37] and it should be remembered that this omnipotence is just as much moral as it is technical, although the question never even arises. 'Man is really nothing more than the product of his education', he writes elsewhere.[38] Phlipon de la Madeleine echoes this view: 'It is education alone that makes a man what he is, he is never anything more than his education would have him be'.[39] For education is merely the 'art of modifying and of pressing into shape',[40] it is a a matter of drills, and of habit-formation, and our habits are 'controlled by those who teach us to contract them'.[41] Now, as 'luck' would have it, the sensorial apparatus at man's disposal is so richly endowed that it makes him susceptible to even more acute forms of conditioning. Michel writes that there is a 'propensity within man to become anything that his instructor would have him become'.[42] 'There is no animal easier to train than man', said one of his colleagues.[43] 'We can do exactly what we will with a man', writes d'Holbach,[44] in a phrase that makes us once again think of Helvétius. 'Nothing is impossible for education: it can teach a bear to dance'.[45]

We know that Rousseau, who sought to refashion the child's nature unbeknownst to itself,[46] is by no means out of place in this survey of pedagogical thinking in the age of Enlightenment. In his *Émile*, the book that talks about changing human nature, there are no second thoughts whatsoever about the high degree of manipulation which it is both possible and necessary to inflict upon the pupil.[47] We only raise this issue again in order to point out once more the extent to which Rousseau is remarkably close to opponents whose thinking, in the context of the age, we quite happily imagine to be diametrically opposed to his own, as indeed did those concerned. In fact, they are much closer to Rousseau's thought than they, or he himself, ever imagined. 'Education is nothing more than *the agriculture of the mind*', pronounces d'Holbach, in both an accent and a context which we might define as hyper-materialist.[48] But did Rousseau really express himself so differently? 'We give plants the form we want by the way we grow them, and men by the way we educate them', we read at the beginning of *Émile*.⁴⁹ 'The education of children consists of nothing more than forming good habits', he writes to a mother,⁵⁰ and this *nothing more* indicates the reductionist climate in which we are operating. To another mother (his advice on educational matters was much sought after), he recommended for her child, who was barely seven years old at the time, a subtle, not to say perhaps perverse, interplay of scheming and blackmail which was intended to give her 'an ascendancy over him which it would be difficult for him to break down thereafter'. The general aim was to create, in an almost geometrical way, a form of synthetic and yet durable subservience.⁵¹ I must emphasise yet again that this manipulation of the inner man, which is fundamental to Rousseau's thinking in matters pedagogical, is also a feature of his political thinking, and the two aspects are organically linked. Hence, we read in his *Discours sur l'Économie politique*: 'If it is a good thing to know how to take men as you find them, it is much better to know how to make them into what you need them to be; the most absolute form of authority is that which penetrates *the inner man*, and has as much influence on his will as on his actions'.⁵²

We do not usually associate Rousseau with the practice of taking full advantage of the supposed malleability located within individuals, nor of boldly breaking down the rigid partition in order to assume 'the most absolute form of authority'. Neither are such practices usually associated with his contemporaries, the *philosophes*, at least in the version of their thinking that is usually disseminated. However, in the light of what has just been said, it is difficult to claim that Georges Gusdorf is entirely wrong when he posits a strong connection between sensualist philosophy and the impulse towards reform present in the thinking of the age of Enlightenment. He writes: 'This remodelling, which begins on the outside and works inwards, results in the creation of a new man, fully consistent with the preoccupations and the methods of a totalitarian pedagogy whose main features are discernible in the Treatises of Helvétius, of d'Holbach, of Condorcet, of Bentham and in the reforming activity of the lawmakers of the Revolution. The whole impulse of the Enlightenment was directed towards producing a series of citizens, all created in the same mould, and would result in the general depersonalisation of mankind'.⁵³ On the eve of the Revolution which, according to Michelet, was to usher in 'the adulthood of humanity' we are suddenly, on the contrary, faced with the overriding impression of a view of mankind, argued on the basis of scientific reasoning, as an infantilised mass. Much less than this would already be worrying. So, despite whatever Gusdorf may have to say on the matter, is it not rather overdoing things a little to claim, as I have rather abruptly done, that there exists a continuous link between the Enlightenment and the Revolution? Is the Revolution, which is renowned for having done so much for mankind, really the child of a philosophy which takes such trouble to *reduce* man to almost insignificant proportions, to 'disparage the human heart' and to 'belittle man'? as Rousseau himself complained,[54] even though it is perfectly clear that for his own part he never ceased to contribute to these efforts.

Notes

1. Letter to N. Duchesne, 23 May 1762: Rousseau, *Corr.*, vol.10, 282.
2. Ibid.
3. J.-J. Rousseau, *Premier Dialogue*, 687.
4. *Troisième Dialogue*, 933.
5. C.-A. Helvétius, *De l'Esprit* (1758), Paris, 1988, 553.
6. Helvétius, *De l'Homme, de ses Facultés intellectuelles, de son Éducation* (1773), Paris, 1989.
7. P.H. d'Holbach, *Système de la Nature* (1770), 2 vols, Paris, 1990, vol. 1, 241.
8. J.-J. Rousseau, *Considérations sur leGouvernement de la Pologne*, in Rousseau, *Oeuvres complètes*, vol. 3, 966.
9. J. Maritain, *Art et Scolastique*, Paris, 1927, 72.
10. Saint Thomas Aquinas, *Summa Theologica*, I, q. 117, a. 1; ibid., ad 1 et ad 3. 'Ad primum ergo dicendum, quod ... homo docens solummodo exterius ministerium adhibet, sicut medicus sanans. Sed sicut natura interior est principalis causa sanationis, ita et interius lumen intellectus est principalis causa scientiœ'.
11. Maritain, *Art et Scolastique*, 73, (w.u.o).
12. Marcel Grandière, 'L'Idéal pédagogique en France au XVIIIe siècle (1715–1789)', (Thesis, Doct. État, University of Lille III, dir. by Pr. Jean de Viguerie, 1991, 1,031 typed pp. in 4 vols). The phrase we quote is from p. 538, where the author points out that the reforming zeal really comes into its own after 1762. The majority of quotations in this paragraph and in the next two paragraphs are second-hand and are taken from this thesis, which provides a wealth of information.
13. P. Le Mercier de la Rivière, *De l'Instruction publique; ou Considérations morales et politiques sur la nécessité, la nature et la source de cette instruction*, Stockholm, 1775; M. Grandière, 734.
14. A. de la Caze, *Lettre sur le meilleur moyen d'assurer le succès de l'éducation*, Paris, 1764; M. Grandière, 568 and 569.
15. See above, 56.
16. A. Le Camus, *Médecine de l'Esprit, où l'on cherche 1° Le Méchanisme du corps qui influe sur les fonctions de l'âme, 2° Les causes physiques qui rendent ce méchanisme ou défectueux ou plus parfait, 3° etc.*, 2 vols, Paris, 1753, the very subject of the original title: 'Let there be no mistake about it', he writes, 'the will is no less mechanical than the understanding.' (109); M. Grandière, 776 and 777.

17. Le Camus, *Médecine de l'Esprit*, 8; M. Grandière, 776. Voltaire remarked in 1757: 'the soul can ache just as a tooth can' (*Corr.*, vol. 4, 1,079).
18. According to the presentation that appeared in the *Mercure de France* in April 1769, 2nd edn; M. Grandière, 537.
19. Charles Bonnet, *Essai analytique des facultés de l'âme*, Copenhagen, 1760, beginning of the preface; M. Grandière, 308.
20. Charles Bonnet, *Contemplation de la Nature*, 1770, preface; M. Grandière, 277.
21. Charles Bonnet, *Essai de Psychologie, ou Considérations sur les opérations de l'âme, sur l'habitude et sur l'éducation...*, London, 1755, 341.
22. Ibid., 217.
23. Ibid., 257; M. Grandière, 281, footnote 3.
24. Bonnet, *Essai de Psychologie*, 219; M. Grandière, 280, footnote 5.
25. According to M. Grandière, 282.
26. Michel, *Essai sur les moyens d'améliorer les études actuelles des collèges*, Nancy and Paris, 1769, 3; M. Grandière, 538.
27. Maritain, *Art et Scolastique*, 72–73.
28. M. Grandière, 538. 'We get the impression of manufactured children. What we have here is a type of education that is completely controlled and totally supervised' (726). 'Children were probably never subjected to as much supervision or as many constraints as during this period when everyone is busy proclaiming the benefits of natural education' (general conclusion, 981).
29. M. de la Fare, *Le Gouverneur, ou Essai sur l'Éducation*, London, 1768, 'letter to a friend' epigraph; M. Grandière, 619, who comments: 'the natural personality of the child, its powers of reasoning and its freedom are thus denied'.
30. De la Fare, *Le Gouverneur*, 99; M. Grandière, 619.
31. De la Fare, *Le Gouverneur*, 85; M. Grandière, 619.
32. Reference to note 30.
33. Comte de Vauréal, *Plan ou Essai d'Éducation général et national, ou la meilleure éducation à donner aux hommes de toutes les nations*, Bouillon, 1783, 69; M. Grandière, 812, footnote 5.
34. Vauréal, *Plan ou Essai d'Éducation*, 93; M. Grandière, 814.
35. Vauréal, *Plan ou Essai d'Éducation*, 65; M. Grandière, 812.
36. D'Holbach, *Système de la Nature*, vol. 1, 242; 241, speaking about men, he calmly talks of 'those who rule over their wills'.
37. Helvétius, *De l'Homme*, vol. 2, 879; This is the actual title of the first chapter of section X. 'Education makes us everything that we are'(881).
38. Ibid., vol. 1, 45.
39. Phlipon de la Madeleine, *Vues patriotiques sur l'Éducation du Peuple tant des villes que des campagnes...*, Lyon, 1783, 69.
40. D'Holbach, *La Morale universelle, ou les Devoirs de l'Homme fondés sur sa nature*, 3 vols, Amsterdam, 1776, Part III, chapter: 'De l'Éducation', 53.
41. D'Holbach, *Système de la Nature*, vol. 1, 214.
42. Michel, *Essai sur les moyens*, 3; 'Education makes man everything that he is'.
43. H.-C. Picardet, *Essai sur l'Éducation des petits enfans*, Dijon, 1756, 3.
44. D'Holbach, *Système social, ou principes naturels de la morale et de la politique, avec un examen de l'influence du gouvernement sur les mœurs par l'Auteur du Système de la Nature*, London, 1773, 12.
45. Helvétius, *De l'Homme*, vol. 1, 334.
46. M. Grandière, op. cit., for example, 344, 559, 615 (where the expression 'unbeknownst to' is used twice).

47. See above, 75
48. D'Holbach, *Système de la Nature*, vol. 1, 236 (w.u.o).
49. Rousseau, *Émile ou de l'Education* (1762), Book I, Paris, 1966, 36.
50. To Mme Delessert, née Boy de la Tour, 23 August 1774 : Rousseau, *Corr.*, vol. 39, 264.
51. To Mme Thellusson, née Girardot de Vermenoux, 6 April 1771: *Corr.*, vol. 38, 210–11.
52. Rousseau, *Discours sur l'Économie politique* (1755), in *Œuvres complètes*, Paris, 1959, vol.3, 251.
53. G. Gusdorf, *L'Homme Romantique* ('Les Sciences humaines et la Pensée occidentale', vol. XI), Paris, 1984, 27.
54. See above, 44.

Chapter 6

Mirabeau and Sieyès

No one seems to have pilloried Jean Starobinski for openly declaring: 'The whole century had set itself the task of going back to first principles and formulating them clearly. The language of principles was in existence long before 1789'.[1] If therefore, as it seems fair to suppose, the conception of man I have outlined in the previous pages, and in particular the conviction that he is somehow fundamentally incapable of being free or being held responsible, if these may be counted among such *principles*, it should be possible to find traces of them throughout the decade that begins in 1789. But since this is the decade which, on the contrary, is ordinarily understood to have made much of man's freedom and the grandness of his various attributes, there would seem to be good grounds to be somewhat perplexed. If the Revolution proved to be consistent with the 'principles' outlined above, the very fact of doing so would have the unquestionable inconvenience of demolishing too many of the myths which the Revolution has spawned; it would have the further, perhaps even more serious inconvenience of illuminating a great many other things besides. It is too late to retreat. We must take a closer look at the matter.

D'Holbach can be considered the most pugnacious and hardest-hitting determinist in the whole of the eighteenth century. I have already pointed out that his conception of man's lack of freedom could be understood as a clear echo of Spinoza.[2] However, we find the following in the writings of a well known scholar of Spinozism:

In the Revolutionary period, we can see no indications that Spinoza's political thinking had any direct influence on the people whom we might have expected to acknowledge such an influence. We can see only Mirabeau and Sieyès whose thinking appears to offer strange parallels with his, to the extent that we are obliged to talk in terms of influence but without being able to establish the fact with any certainty.[3]

Whether it is a matter of direct influence or not, the reference to 'strange parallels' is hardly likely to leave me indifferent, as readers may well imagine. Likewise, my interest is aroused by the equally remarkable 'we can see only' which can only pass muster as a restrictive phrase if it is read as an antiphrasis. For Mirabeau and Sieyès are not characters of secondary importance. Both men could unquestionably stake a claim to a place of honour in any roll call of the dominant personalities involved in the early phases and the first few years of the Revolution. Indeed they might well head such a list of names. Even supposing then that *we can see only these two* philosophically refusing to recognise man's freedom (and this restrictive formulation still needs to be checked out), the fact would have tremendous significance in my view. All the more so when we consider the fact that the style and the character of the men are rightly famous for offering so many stark contrasts.

Mirabeau is technically a sensualist by persuasion. Moreover, we find in his case an example of the marriage of two tendencies: sensualist views and the practice of Epicureanism, a marriage which is quite normal without being automatic, and which Rousseau identified as typical of the 'privileged children of our age'. His own life is, in fact, one huge example of irresponsibility, one might almost say: of fully accepted insolvency. The first article of his creed, including his political beliefs, is that the human machine has a tendency to seek pleasure. This naturally implies an interplay of corollaries to which we have by now grown accustomed. 'To live is literally to seek pleasure', said Condillac. 'It is the attraction to physical pleasure that should guide us in all things', thought Voltaire,[4] who consequently confided thus to Frédéric II: 'It is quite clear that we must seek out physical pleasure and all the rest is mere madness'.[5] And d'Holbach in 1770 began his *Système de la Nature* with the following exhortation: 'Seek out pleasure, that is what nature commands you to do, allow others to seek out pleasure, that is what equity demands of you, make yourself available to experience pleasure, that is the advice that sacred humanity gives you'.[6] As everyone knows, the evidence would appear to be conclusive that Mirabeau was not slow to take up the offer. And he even combined the theory with the practice. Thus, in his *Essai sur le Despotisme* in 1776, he defines man as 'a good and just animal who seeks physical pleasure'.[7] There are clear overtones in this definition to suggest that there exists a certain natural 'goodness' in man which is no more distinguishable here than it is in Rousseau from a sense of basically animal satisfaction. For the groundswell of materialistic thinking confers an obviously physical slant upon this ideal of pursuing physical pleasure, which in reality is nothing more than a recognition, after mature reflection, of the existence of a form of necessity.

Mirabeau's *Essai* includes these unequivocal and very important words (since he develops in quite an unambiguous way a number of the sociopolitical possibilities inherent in the sensualist position):

> The duty of all men consists in fulfilling the law. The law, that is to say order, is wholly *based on physical feelings* and the physical needs of man, to whom nature has granted as many faculties for enjoying pleasure as she allows him forms of pleasure: it is therefore in the midst of these forms of physical pleasure, it is in their distribution, the way they are arranged, the way they reproduce themselves, that we should *look for the 'code social'*...[8]

In Mirabeau's scheme of things social life is seen as a coordination of appetites. These appetites, which mechanically condition men, are organised by a handful of manipulating reformers who, in their Olympian remoteness, have inexplicably been self-selected for this task and whose role, according to Rousseau, 'has nothing in common with the world of mere mortals'.[9] This is far more in line with the thinking of the age than the images of explosive liberation which we normally associate with the name of the great revolutionary, Mirabeau. To be more precise, the quest will not be to liberate man by helping him to loosen the hold which the appetites exert over him, but quite to the contrary, to free up his appetites, to liberate the different forms of pleasure-seeking by harmonising them as far as it is possible within the social context, in other words to push them to their limit. It will also involve, if necessary, revealing all this to men themselves, and in any case liberating the pleasure-seekers instead of imprisoning them on the orders of the king, which is precisely what happened to Mirabeau and which is a sure sign of the ineptitude of the 'code social'.

Condorcet offers a good illustration of the logic behind this regulated, and ultimately self-regulated, coordination of the pleasure-seeking appetites into a form of collective harmony when he considers the possibility of contraception and the possibility of being able to pre-select the sex of unborn babies. He counters the demographic argument that this would lead to one of the two sexes becoming much rarer than the other by assigning to the sexual partners a subtly selfish motivation which would have long-term effects. He asks himself: 'Is it not in the interest of each of the sexes to increase the numbers of those belonging to the opposite sex? Men, so that when they grow old they may find it easier to have relationships with younger women; women, so that when men are faced with a more limited choice they will be forced to be less choosy on the question of the age of their partners'.[10] Beneath this rather complex formulation of the argument, the meaning is quite clear. There will never be a shortage of girls because young men, keen to build up a stock of young women for later life, will always keep this selfish objective in mind and seek to achieve their aim by collectively producing girls for one another. But there will never be a shortage of boys either, because women, for their part, will take good care to prevent any likely infidelity on the part of their husbands as they grow older by restricting the market. Men, 'faced with a more limited choice', will be obliged to 'be less choosy on the question of the age of their partners'. In other words, to put it bluntly, they will have to make do with partners who, like themselves, are getting on in years. The free interplay of selfish motives leads to a self-regulation which benefits the whole of society, in this case in the interests of demographic equilibrium. It goes without saying that this astonishing line of reasoning and the underlying value which it is perceived as having, are extremely valuable to my present argument.

'Baudelaire makes a good point when he writes that the revolutionaries were voluptuous men', says Starobinski, who himself never tires of evoking Mirabeau.[11] It would be wrong to suppose that this reminder contains any suggestion of a desire to apportion blame (however naïve and incongruous) – we can leave that to Robespierre. My point is a purely technical one and my only interest is in tracing the continuity of doctrinal positions and the profusion of corollaries that they entail. The link between sensualism of a materialistic tendency and the diffusion of a sort of demagogic hedonism was a link that was made very early on. In any event, it is mentioned for example just after the appearance of Helvétius' first book, *De l'Esprit* (1758), in a light-hearted way in a satirical song:

> A lawmaker who's no fool
> Combines, at his own leisure
> What's useful for his rule
> With whatever gives him pleasure.
> Yes, the surest path to tread
> To keep the people quiet
> Is let nature have its head
> And Man's senses all run riot.[12]

In other words, allow full sway to the pursuit of pleasure but as a means of *keeping the people quiet*. We seem to be getting very warm here; we appear to be very close to the key which will lead us to recognise something that is sham about the whole Revolution, and on a question that is by no means of secondary importance. We would appear to have little choice but to accept that the Revolution in some way involved liberation, given the extent to which this view of the Revolution is generally accepted and given also the extent of the urge to see it as an explosion, a fireworks display of liberating activity, to which Mirabeau in no small measure contributed. But this fireworks display is also a bonfire of vanities. In the context of my own argument, and what is absolutely crucial to the thesis I am proposing, is that we seem to remain firmly positioned in a logic that is exactly the opposite to a logic of liberation. In Mirabeau's way of seeing things, his fellow citizens are cogs or machines (the rather approximate nature of this terminology may appear problematic but it is familiar to mechanicistic socioanthropologists), their kinetic autonomy has nothing to do with freedom, nor does it prevent them from being subject to manipulation or modification at the whim of the enlightened lawmaker, whom Mirabeau for his own part partially embodies. What is sure is that if he had really thought differently it would have meant his making a clean break with the main current of doctrinal thought of the time, and that, rather than anything else, would have been the truly surprising thing.

Anyone who continues to have doubts about this casting of Mirabeau as lawmaker and sensualist, a man who sees himself as a legitimate and all-powerful manipulator of his compatriots, would probably do well to consult a few paragraphs of his posthumous speeches, piously edited by Cabanis,[13] and to which we shall return later. 'Man, as a being capable of experiencing sensations', wrote Mirabeau, tends to follow his feelings, it is therefore easy 'by making use of imposing objects, striking images, grand spectacles, deep emotions' to lead him along. He stresses the fact that, by such means, man is so easily manipulated that it would be possible to make 'completely absurd, unjust and even cruel forms of social organisation' attractive to him, and even make him feel 'happy' in such conditions.[14] 'Man ... more readily responds to his impressions than his reasoning',[15] so in order to make men collectively docile and contented it is necessary to '*fire ... their imaginations*. It is therefore less a question of convincing a man than of moving him; less a matter of proving that the laws by which he is governed are excellent laws than of making him develop strong and affectionate feelings towards them, feelings that he would *vainly seek* to eradicate and which accompanying him *wherever he may go* would *constantly* call to his mind the beloved and venerable image of his native land'.[16] This line of argument, which contains echoes of virtually *all* the great writers of the century (Rousseau included), was intended to justify the creation of *fêtes nationales*[17] which, as everyone knows, was a constant concern throughout the revolutionary period. The very persistent sensualist underpinning given to this preoccupation, in so far as it treats citizens as passive beings that can be manipulated and remanipulated, could hardly be more explicitly linked to the purposes of my argument. Mirabeau is a total sensualist for whom the philosophical possibility of human freedom is, at the outset, more than doubtful, and for whom therefore, at the end of the day, the possibility of political freedom remains, at the very least, more than doubtful. Like so many others, in the name of a 'freedom' that deserves closer scrutiny, Mirabeau is a philanthropically totalitarian thinker. To achieve his goal of political contentment, he seeks to stamp indelible marks upon man's inner being, and so on. If I continued to offer commentary on this passage, I might well weary my readers with repetition.

In many ways very similar to Mirabeau was the marquis d'Antonelle, another revolutionary aristocrat from Provence, whose own reputation has only recently been reassessed. The marquis was a very assiduous reader of Mirabeau.[18] In 1788 he published a widely acclaimed *Catéchisme du Tiers État*, and went on to become a deputy in the Legislative Assembly and an active member of the Jacobin Club. As a member of the Revolutionary Tribunal he was particularly concerned to ensure that the Girondins' rights to a defence should not work against the interests of the Mountain. Under the Directory he was a combative journalist and became involved in the Babeuf conspiracy. In short, his *curriculum vitae* describes a life lived in the service of progressive ideas[19] and a man who even had first-hand knowledge of prison at the time of the Terror. The notes he took while reading have never been published but they are very interesting indeed. He is a dyed-in-the-wool materialist who attacks the notion of 'our supposed superiority over the animals',[20] and who refuses, after so many others and along with so many others, the idea that man could be free. 'All the movements of his body', he writes, 'all the feelings his soul is capable of, everything that makes him capable of thought, of speech, and of action, is thanks to a mechanism that will forever remain a mystery to him'.[21] Whether he gives in to his inclinations or whether he resists them, he is still inexorably a slave. A derisory, easily-manipulated plaything, 'he is always seduced ... often *unbeknownst to himself,* by the man who has the most strength or the most ability to *ensnare* him, ... and he *believes himself a free man*'.[22] Having come to this conclusion, Antonelle has no hesitation in denouncing the notion of free will 'as a philosophic con-trick'.[23] 'I am merely an instrument', he says, 'which has been built according to a design I know nothing of and which is used for purposes which are equally unknown to me',[24] all of which seems to suggest not so much a strong dose of individual responsibility as man's innate aptitude to be manipulated: 'It is because man is not free that education, morality and laws modify him, subjugate him and rule over him. It is because he is not free that one can guide or misguide his imagination, move him, interest him, fire his enthusiasm, ... take control of his mind by enlightening him or by deceiving him' and so on.[25]

It must be said, however, that the critic to whom we are indebted for this useful presentation of Antonelle's ideas nevertheless leaves us somewhat perplexed when he describes Antonelle's very detailed negation of freedom as a 'critical re-reading' of the Enlightenment.[26] For it is quite clear, give or take a slight shift in emphasis here or there, that Antonelle simply *pursues* the general line of thinking that was commonplace at that time. He shares the same major ideas as the thinkers who preceded him, and he was also a wealthy man,[27] as so many of them were. Nor, for sure, can it be argued that he is undertaking a particularly 'critical re-reading' of the theme of freedom during the Enlightenment, to *consistently* present Helvétius 'in a positive light',[28] or to simultaneously adopt and repeat what the most important of the *Ency*-

clopédistes and Voltaire, and even Rousseau, to a large extent, had to say about freedom. The basic problem, which almost instinctively tends to be ducked, is that the doctrinal negation of free will obliges us to view the Revolution in a far more derogatory light than it is customary or comfortable to do.

And yet, the case of Sieyès might also have made us aware of this fact. His celebrated *Qu'est-ce que le Tiers État?* of January 1789, is very largely the programme which the States-General will implement from June onwards, spurred on by the author himself. Now, anyone who undertakes a close reading of this text after having been told by others what it contains, and even after having believed themselves to have been teaching its contents on the basis of summaries and commentaries, will be mildly surprised to discover that it implicitly excludes any notion of the freedom of citizens, since it clearly supports a mechanistic view of society: 'We shall never understand the mechanism of society if we do not take the decision to analyse it as if it were a simple machine'.[29] 'The mechanism of society', 'simple machine': if these words have any meaning it has to be that the men who compose this 'society' are nothing more than cogs, in other words that they are endowed with neither reason, nor will, nor responsibility for their actions. It is of course true that someone like Morelly, for example, can talk in his *Code de la Nature* of 'the marvellous *automaton* of society, its pistons, its counterweights, its springs' and go on to concede that this 'machine' is 'made up of intelligent parts', a fact which still doesn't prevent it from 'generally' operating 'independently of the way these parts reason':[30] this odd way of expressing things once again serves to illustrate not only the fact that absolute mechanicism constitutes a complete dead-end but also, that partial mechanicism is itself a very strange beast indeed.

But the very fact of adopting such a mechanicist position, whether its absoluteness or its partiality is nothing other than mere fantasy, inevitably places those concerned at the top of the slippery slope that leads to a denial of freedom – a denial which is, in unequal measure, conscious and light-hearted or unavoidable. This is an important point for a character as significant as someone like Sieyès, who, while expressing himself in a tone which differs only very slightly from that of Mirabeau, favours ideas that are very similar indeed to those we have been considering. In deciding to view society as a machine, Sieyès and his friends deeply implicate themselves in the exorbitant role of organising their fellow men as they see fit – fellow men who from this point onwards cease to be their fellow men because ipso facto a gulf is created between the mechanic himself and the pieces of the machine that he is working upon. This is exactly the situation encountered by Diderot's 'legislators' as soon as they take it into their heads (touched by the fingers of which fairy godmother?) 'to bring together all the little individual springs and create the wonderful machine called society'.[31] Before Diderot, the *Contrat Social* had already said that the great legislator 'is the mechanic who invents the machine', and the grand prince (let us say: the man who wields power) 'is merely the workman who climbs aboard and makes it work'.[32] In the first flush of Revolution it is quite conceivable that Sieyès and the more passionate of his colleagues vaguely considered themselves as combining both roles, a fact which could have the very serious disadvantage of adding to the executive powers of government, the powers that Rousseau reserved for the legislative arm and which he had already described in excessive terms as having: 'nothing in common with the world of mere mortals'. In any event, the mechanicising propensity of Sieyès is by no means a spasmodic affair. Again in 1793, when presenting the plan of the Convention's Committee for Public Instruction, he compares (and these are his own terms) the 'teaching machine' to a 'hydraulic machine' and 'the legislator to an architect-mechanic'.[33]

Whatever margin we allow for in terms of accepting that there should be some play between the literal intention contained in such expressions and the purely rhetorical effects to be achieved, it goes without saying that at the very least the omnipresence of this imagery, in the climate of opinion we are now familiar with, illustrates a clear tendency to deny the existence of human freedom. And since, nevertheless, there is freedom, even in the remarks uttered by the very people who refuse to acknowledge its existence, we have no alternative but to accept or at least to assume that this must be a rather special kind of freedom which probably doesn't involve free will at all. It is worth noting that the great *Encyclopédie* offers several entries under the word 'freedom'. One of the shortest and most marginal of these is nonetheless worthy of our consideration here. It claims to belong to the world of clockmaking, and refers to the easy movement of the works when the mechanism is in good order.[34] Thus, one might say of a wheel that it 'is very free, or that it has a good deal of freedom, when the slightest force is capable of setting it in motion'.[35] This sort of freedom is therefore something quite different from what is generally understood by the word freedom, in the sense that it seems to refer us back to an ideal of society conceived of as a well-oiled interplay of individual mechanical parts, whose wills are purposely conditioned for the precise behaviour that is expected of them. D'Holbach, you will remember, in a reference to the governed, spoke of 'those who *regulated* their wills':[36] the verb used here also has its place in the vocabulary of clockmaking. And many of the features of the whole case presented here lead me to believe that, in effect, the model for this purely mechanical type of freedom would have figured in the mind-set of those people who, in June 1789, set about systematically organising a programme that would result in public happiness. For them, it was a logical necessity to go, at least mentally, as far as this, or to be very much inclined to do so.

I will probably be accused of overstating my case. And some people may even believe that I am doing so. But if it is true, it is simply because it is difficult to get people to understand. Certainly, views such as those presented here have something very unreal about them. But the fact that they seem very ill-suited to the fabric of human society does not mean that they were never entertained. The painful treatment that this very fabric of society suffered proves that these views had a proportionate influence on what ensued. Slaughter and butchery attest to the fact that the mechanic's precision was brought to bear upon matters of flesh and blood. Indeed, how very disconcerting it is when a machine that you are doing your utmost to perfect starts bleeding. Did Sieyès ever forgive men for having demonstrated the shortcomings of the plans he had laid for them? 'He dislikes the human race', Mme de Staël said later, 'and he doesn't know how to handle men: it's as though he would prefer to be dealing with *other things* entirely'.[37] This not unfelicitous expression illustrates some of the dangers and some of the miscalculations of the Enlightenment and of some of those who were its inspiration. Spinoza held that 'men, like *other things*, act out of natural necessity'.[38] With Mme de Staël's words, is there not a feeling that somehow a wheel has come full circle?

Whether or not that is the case, the idea of man that Sieyès and so many others in 1789 had a *tendency* to cultivate, was not without a good deal of important and quite diverse implications. In a first phase, this idea of man awaited the simple or complex, but in any case sure and infallible, formulae and methods of a social mathematics that the sharpest brains of the period were putting together. We shall come back to this point. Then, this idea entered into a marriage with the belief that was so perceptibly in the air of the times, and the source of so much later disillusionment, namely that private happiness and public happiness would appear on the scene *effortlessly*. The cogs of a machine are pure passivity and sensualism convinces everyone that simply erecting around men the new scenery that everyone is dreaming about will suffice to make them better. Men 'will always be *good without even trying*',[39] the 'vicaire savoyard' is well-known for saying. In fact, we are just as likely to find in Rousseau the idea that human beings, since they are not very well adapted to working at things, really wouldn't know how to be good *except* without trying: this was the declared logic behind that very sensualist project of his, the *Traité de Morale sensitive*,[40] just as it is the reasoning behind the revolutionary holidays (*fêtes nationales*). As is more usually the case than is commonly thought, Rousseau holds no monopoly in such matters. For it is at this point that, in a diffuse way, the idea that one can somehow get away without having to make an effort (although not going so far as to exclude the idea entirely since this would have been too obviously at odds with common sense), is denied in theory by the doctrines on which I have been commenting. If I were to remind readers what they are, I should once more need to quote Helvétius and d'Holbach at great length. Voltaire, lecturing Mme du Deffand wrote: 'We shall never be as contented as fools are. But let us try to be, in our own way'. Voltaire immediately corrects himself: '*Try to be* – what an expression! What we want is not important. We are clocks, machines'.[41] The revolutionary utopian view of a world where everything is guaranteed to happen effortlessly is not simply a quirk of the imagination of a group of dreamers, or the nonsensical idea of demagogues: it follows directly on from the logic of mechanicism and sensualism. These make it inevitable, one might say, in the name of science.

Finally, like so many of the witnesses who have been called to testify already in these pages, the views professed by Sieyès tend towards a refusal to accept that man can be held responsible for any of his actions. 'The rewards and the punishments which are meted out to us are always a result of chemistry or luck', was the logical conclusion of Jean Rostand, whom we have already quoted in this study as a pious continuator of Enlightenment scientism.[42] And indeed 'if there is no such thing as freedom' were not people like Diderot, who shared this conviction, quite right to conclude that 'there are no deeds that deserve praise or censure';[43] a fortiori, we might add, nor any of our thoughts or our feelings, and besides, we know that *to think is nothing more than to experience feelings*. In such a context as this, it is interesting to note that in the summer of 1789 the projected Declaration of Rights, which Sieyès proposed, contained as one of its many variants and rewordings, the following: 'no one is responsible for his thoughts or his feelings'.[44] It is probably quite right to suggest that I would be misguided if I sought to give this phrase its widest possible interpretation when all that is really being excluded here is quite simply juridical responsibility. But given what we already know, and the climate we have become used to working in, it is difficult to argue that such a wording does not lend itself, even if only marginally, to an anthropological reading which has a close organic link to the obvious meaning and which provides a basis for the latter, or at least supports it. For it is natural and quite elementary to consider as a zone entirely free from responsibility an inner space which is seen as a place where physical sensations combine in a very mechanistic way so as to mechanically produce only thoughts, feelings and impulses of diverse sorts. Willy nilly (but more often willingly than reluctantly), the principal writers of the century agree on this point with so many of the lesser-known authors, and it is difficult to see why Sieyès, who was their faithful disciple, should have seen things any differently.

If, in fact, as Voltaire so remarkably put it, 'we are no more in control of our ideas than we are of the circulation of the blood in our veins', and if, as a result, 'all our feelings, all our ideas are *absolutely necessary* things',[45] then of course we have no choice but to conclude that no one is *morally* 'responsible for what he thinks or feels'. 'Feelings, passions ... ways of thinking, ways of speaking', he also declares, 'they all come to us I know not how, they are all like ideas that we have in a dream, they all come without us doing anything about it'.[46] And d'Holbach: 'I am not the master of the thoughts that come into my head and determine what I want'. If, as this same author repeatedly says of man, 'the more or less abundant quantities and degree of heatedness of his blood, the more or less tense or relaxed state of his nerves and fibres ... decide ... his ideas and his thoughts at every moment', if these latter ' come to us involuntarily', if they have organised themselves 'in spite of us and *unbeknownst to us* in our brains', if the thinking man 'is not in control of his ideas or of the modifications to his brain which are due to causes that in spite of himself and *unbeknownst to him* continually act upon him',[47] if 'thoughts present themselves to him involuntarily',[48] we are, quite clearly 'obliged to conclude that our thoughts, our ideas, our way of seeing, of feeling, of judging, of combining ideas cannot be either voluntary or freely chosen'.[49] In which case, does not a man like Sieyès, who is correlatively inclined to believe that everything is mechanical, have all the more grounds to declare that all men are fundamentally free from any responsibility for the thoughts and feelings they may have? D'Holbach had only spoken of 'the freedom to *produce* one's ideas', and the expression is worth noting, but this was a freedom which he did not think of as limitless.[50]

And did Rousseau express himself so very differently? He writes to Mme d'Épinay that 'we are not the masters of our own thoughts',[51] and elsewhere he chooses to forestall possible recriminations on the part of those close to him by protesting: 'It was never open to me to organise my brain in some other way'.[52] Antonelle, the revolutionary mentioned above, spoke in much the same way: 'Whoever examines himself in detail soon realises that the real tyrant that rules over him is the way his own particular constitution is organised: an organisation that he has not chosen for himself, that he is not fully aware of, and which is nevertheless the real and unique source of his mind's ideas, his heart's feelings, and whatever his will hesitates about and finally fixes upon'.[53] Antonelle and d'Holbach are materialists, Rousseau cannot be taken for one, Voltaire hesitates to let anyone know that he is becoming one: and yet all of them manage somehow in their different ways to share a point of view that reminds us that the atmosphere in which Sieyès has just expressed himself confers upon what he has said a presupposition that there exists an anthropological foundation to his words that implies a much more fundamental absence of responsibility in the human make-up. So if I may be allowed to repeat the point, Mirabeau and Sieyès were not men who counted for little in the last years of the Revolution – a Revolution that, at least in its first passionate impulsion, one would have tended to think of as being far more solidly concerned with exalting mankind, freedom and all that the latter implied.

And the case of Antonelle would suggest that there is no great discrepancy between the way the understudies saw matters and the way the leading actors did. This will hardly be a surprise to anyone who accepts as true what I have been so carefully arguing, namely, that the Enlightenment played its part in shaping revolutionary thought. Lequinio, for example, provides a good illustration of this. A deputy in the Legislative Assembly, where he made his mark by proposals of a somewhat avant-garde nature, then later a member of the Convention, a regicide and a particularly pugnacious *représentant en mission* (including time spent in the hotbed of rebellions in the West of France), this Breton was considered by many in Paris to be an overzealous supporter of dechristianisation. He spared neither time nor effort in the cause of the Revolution and also earned the gratitude of the nation by devoting his intellectual abilities to it as well: indeed, in 1792 Lequinio gave France a book of doctrine entitled *Les Préjugés détruits*.[54] The book opens with a 'preliminary question' where he robustly argues that man is not made for thinking[55] – by this we should understand not made for thinking *actively*. A passive being, man can only think by allowing his inner space to become a battleground for the unique interplay of sensations. 'Man', he says, echoing so many others before him, 'is not put on earth to think but to feel'.[56] The best proof that he can offer, apart from the fact that people who think are very rare indeed,[57] is that thinking is difficult and tiring, and dangerous for one's health, 'that nothing is more alien to man's temperament',[58] and it is therefore an activity which goes 'against nature',[59] and which he sees as requiring training and conditioning, 'just as one can train a hunting dog to be useful on a battlefield'.[60] 'The best proof that man is not made to think, is that the difficult training that is required in order that he may eventually do so, damages his physical constitution and often destroys him'.[61] And let there be no mistake about it:

> We should no more conclude from the fact that some men have learned to think and to reflect, by dint of very hard work and great dedication, that this is the lot of all men in general, than we should conclude from a handful of exceedingly rare examples which can be explained by years of training, that a horse is designed to count the hours by stamping his hooves, or that a hare is intended to beat a drum, simply because we have seen such animals, as a result of long hours of training manage to perform these tasks quite well *against all their instincts* and their natural habits.[62]

To anyone who might object that Lequinio is overdoing things and that this exaggeration undermines his point of view, it should be pointed out that words such as the ones he utters are not very far removed from what was said by a good many of his contemporaries, the *philosophes*. At one point, Rousseau, speaking through the mouth of the 'vicaire savoyard', claimed that he had 'the honour to think'.[63] And yet anyone who takes the trouble to read him carefully will realise that the human being's basic unfittedness for reflective and directed thought must, in the long run, be considered as one of the founding notions of Rousseau's anthropological outlook. Rousseau 'can only think with *great effort*, thinking tires him, he becomes alarmed at anything that makes him think even in small measure',[64] unless it's a question of 'thinking' effortlessly (as in the passive meaning of the word associated with sensualism), which is not really anything more than 'dreamy meditation' in which 'we are not active at all. Pictures take shape in the brain, and combine there *as they do in sleep* without the will being involved: we let all of that follow its own path and we enjoy it without actually doing anything'.[65] Hence Rousseau clearly prefers to think only 'freely and without hindrance, letting his ideas wander as they will and without controlling them in any way',[66] he prefers 'letting a happy imagination rule over him rather than *through effort* have reason rule his head'.[67] He can't bring himself to do 'any work that requires his mind to act, in however small a degree'.[68] This view goes back a long way and led him to oppose thought (which is passive) to reflection (which is active), which requires an effort which is not usually found in the normal faculties of man's nature. Man, as Rousseau said, is born 'to act and to think, and not to reflect'[69] – that is exactly what Lequinio meant. Rousseau expanded the idea further: 'Study corrupts man's morals, spoils his health, destroys his temperament and often weakens his reason'.[70] So it is not at all inadvertantly that Rousseau decides to place in a more recognised setting his famous precept (which has often been subjected to interpretations that have not done it justice), according to which reflection depraves the human animal,[71] because it does violence to his natural tendencies, in much the same way that drum-beating is inappropriate in a rabbit-hutch or dancing for a horse.

Or, as is equally true, dancing for a plantigrade. 'Education can do anything: it can teach a bear to dance'. Repeating this quotation from Helvétius[72] calls to mind the fact that he too contributes, with a slight difference in emphasis, to this cultural breeding ground to which the work of the Conventionnel Lequinio, *Les Préjugés détruits*, also contributes. And Diderot himself concedes in an aside that 'we are not made for reading, for meditation, for literature, for philosophy'.[73] Like Rousseau, he tends to see in all this simply 'a form of depravity that we pay for more or less with our health. We must never break entirely with our animal *condition*'.[74] This remark is far from devoid of interest. The extreme scarcity of examples of men using their reason is also a theme of d'Holbach's, and in Voltaire's writings[75] the idea that there are only a minutely small number of thinking beings among the ranks of men is something of a commonplace, not to say an obsession.

All of which seems to confirm that, in expressing himself as he does, Lequinio is much less of a marginal figure and much more of a conformist. He is nothing more than a product of, or a mere follower of, ideas that were in the air at the time, much as Antonelle was, and Sieyès or Mirabeau. He too would argue that man's highest sentiments are the result of 'a few vibrations more or a few vibrations less in the arteries, a few oscillations more or a few oscillations less in the fibres of the brain'.[76] He too tends to see children, those educational objects, as nothing more than 'as a wild animal who gradually adapts, becomes tame and learns through good treatment, instruction and kindness'.[77] He too believes that it would be a good thing to convince man 'that it is in his interest to seek pleasure' 'from a very early age'.[78] And while deferring, as more or less everyone around him is doing, to the categories of the all-pervading mechanicism, he tends to be rather less extreme than many others and opts for a less hardline version of it. The reason is that he more clearly distinguishes between the manipulated human mechanisms that form the masses and the intelligence, which is not necessarily mechanical, of the small group of those who do the manipulating. When he makes the claim that 'men are no more than real machines', it is quite clear that he despises them for it, a view which is not particularly in harmony with the doctrines of scientism.[79] Likewise, when he divulges the techniques that are used to handle meetings he mentions the way men are employed to 'plant themselves here and there among the assembly in order to clap their hands and force into applause a large number of machines who clap without knowing why' (in other words: unbeknownst to them).[80] It goes without saying that the mechanicism on show here involves a pejorative metaphor rather than a considered doctrinal judgement. When he speaks thus, Lequinio, this reductionist theoretician and disdainful philosopher on matters concerning 'sad and unthinking humanity',[81] is far from being an extremist or some sort of aberration. It is certainly true that he is not a major figure. But when he decrees *ex cathedra* that thinking does violence to human nature, he is not in some backwater on the margins of the Enlightenment but at the very heart and in the mainstream of its concerns. It is true that his book, from which he diligently undertook public readings while on his various missions (that is, when servile subalterns did not do it for him), did not provoke any intellectual scandal. It is equally true, and I remain firmly convinced of this, that in the mental universe of his times it would have been strange indeed had it done so.

Notes

1. J. Starobinski, *1789. Les Emblèmes de la Raison*, 'Principes et volonté', Paris, 39.
2. See above, 18.
3. J.-P. Deschepper, 'Le Spinozisme', in Y. Belaval, ed., *Histoire de la Philosophie*, Pléiade, vol. 2, Paris, 1973, 495–96.
4. Voltaire, *Corr.*, vol. 7, 703.
5. Letter of 22 December 1772: Voltaire, *Corr.*, vol. 11, 190.
6. D'Holbach, *Système de la Nature* (1770), Paris, 1990, vol. 1, 33, end of the 'Discours préliminaire'.
7. H. Mirabeau, *Essai sur le Despotisme*, 2nd edn., London, 1776, 63.
8. Ibid., 60 The words *order* and *social* are underlined in the original.
9. See above, 68.
10. M. Condorcet, Notes for his *Esquisse d'un Tableau historique des progrès de l'esprit humain*; quoted by A. Béjin, 'Condorcet, précurseur du néo-malthusianisme et de l'eugénisme républicain', in *Histoire, Économies, Sociétés*, 1988/3, 351 and footnote 7.
11. J. Starobinski, *Les Emblèmes de la Raison*, 27.
12. Un législateur habile
    Joindra selon ses désirs,
    Un gouvernement utile
    Avec l'amour des plaisirs.
    Oui, la règle la plus sûre
    Pour rendre un peuple soumis,
    C'est qu'en suivant la nature
    À ses sens tout soit permis.
    Anonymous song published in *Corr. gén. d'Helvétius*, vol. 2, Toronto/Oxford, 1984, 305. Many of the twenty couplets would merit being quoted here.
13. *Travail sur l'Éducation publique, trouvé dans les papiers de Mirabeau l'aîné; publié par P.J.G.Cabanis*,Paris 1791, three speeches. I consulted long extracts from the edition mentioned in the next note.
14. Br. Baczko, *Une Éducation pour la Démocratie. Textes et projets de l'époque révolutionnaire*, Paris, 1982, Second Discourse, 96. Mirabeau alludes here to monastic life.
15. Ibid. On 17 August 1789, at the Assembly, Mirabeau spoke of 'a people prepared for freedom by the impression events had upon them rather than by reasoning' (*Archives parlementaires.*, 1/8/438).

16. In Baczko, *Une Éducation pour la Démocratie*, 97.
17. This speech is on 'les Fêtes publiques, civiles et militaires'.
18. P. Serna, 'Aux origines culturelles d'un engagement politique: les notes de lecture d'Antonelle', in *Annales historiques de la Révolution française*, n° 292, 1993/2, 169–202. From 1787 onwards, 'Antonelle systematically asks his bookseller to provide him with any wrtings from the pen of Mirabeau' (202).
19. In addition, he was the first elected Maire of Arles, campaigned for the annexation of the Comtat-Venaissin to France, took part in the Queen's trial, was twice deposed as a member of the 'Conseil des Cinq-Cents', being 'one of the most important personalities in the neo-Jacobin party', and, finally, was considered an object of suspicion in the early days of the Consulat.
20. Quoted by Serna, 'Aux origines culturelles d'un engagement politique', 173.
21. Ibid., 182.
22. Ibid., 183. The suspension points may contain the expression ('or unbudgeable'/'ou enraciné') but the accuracy of its transcription from the manuscript remains uncertain.
23. From Serna, 'Aux origines culturelles d'un engagement politique', 183, who adds: 'Choice, if it exists at all, is nothing more than the fulfilling of a potential, which we do *unbeknownst to ourselves* without chance ever being involved and without any trace of independent will ever being detectable. Thus, man is a prisoner of an implacable determinism'.
24. Quoted by Serna, ibid., 185.
25. Ibid., 191. The quotation has the word 'embrasser' for 'embraser'.
26. Ibid., 182. Here is the phrase in question: 'Antonelle offers more than a reading, he offers a critical re-reading of one of the bases of Enlightenment thinking: he questions the very essence of freedom' [*sic*]. Likewise, 175, where, rather strangely, some of the most basic themes of the Enlightenment are presented as though they were somehow peculiar to Antonelle's thinking, and that he is therefore at odds with the views of the age.
27. Ibid., 173 and 191.
28. Helvétius is 'consistently presented in a positive light', in the analysis that these two works propose (Serna, 201; but on 188, footnote 55, the same author tells us that only *De l'Esprit* is quoted). We should remember that d'Holbach wrote under a pseudonym or anonymously.
29. E. Sieyès, *Qu'est-ce que le Tiers État?* (1789), Paris, 1982, 65.
30. Morelly, *Code de la Nature* (1755) Paris, 1970, 45.
31. See above, 64.
32. See above, 65.
33. Article by Sieyès in the *Journal d'Instruction sociale*, end of June beginning of July 1793, concerning the plan for a national system of schooling presented by Lakanal to the Convention, on behalf of the Committee (of which Sieyès was a member), on 26 June: *Archives parlementaires*, 1/68/213/1. Article published by J. Guillaume, *Procès-verbaux du Comité d'Instruction publique*, 6 vols, Paris, 1891–1907, vol. 1, [567–78], 569. Lakanal unreservedly offers his endorsement, and that of the Committee, to this article (567).
34. D. Diderot and J. d'Alembert, eds., *Encyclopédie, ou Dictionnaire raisonné des Sciences, des Arts et des Métiers, par une Société de Gens de Lettres*, vol. 9, Paris, 1765, 476/1: 'FREEDOM, *for clockmakers*, refers to the ease with which the works move', (w.u.o).
35. Ibid., (w.u.o).
36. D'Holbach, *Système de la Nature*, vol. 1, 241.

37. Mme de Staël, *Considérations sur la Révolution française* (1818), Paris, 1983, 363.
38. B. Spinoza, *L'Éthique* (1677), in *Œuvres complètes*, Pléiade, Paris, 1967, 573; on the freedom of 'things', see above, 18.
39. J.-J. Rousseau, *Émile*, Book IV, 381.
40. See above, 55–56.
41. Letter of 2 July 1754: Voltaire, *Corr.*, vol 4, 201.
42. J. Rostand, *Pensées d'un Biologiste*, (1954), Paris, 1978, 27. 'When society ... thinks it is punishing a man ... it is never doing anything other than punishing an ovum or a set of circumstances' (28). Et cetera.
43. Letter to Landois, a minor contributor to the *Encyclopédie*, 29 June 1756: D. Diderot, *Correspondance*, ed. G. Roth, vol. 1, Paris, 1955, 214. The satirical song (we have already quoted) against *De l'Esprit* (which was published two years later) constantly comes back to the convenience of this whole doctrine and its refusal to acknowledge human responsibility.: *Corr gén. d'Helvétius*, vol. 2, 1984, 304 and 305.
44. These words are in the article first numbered 5 then 6, then 11: *Archives parlementaires*, 1/8/260/2 (21 July 1789), 422/2 and 428/2 (12 August).
45. Letter to Mme du Deffand, 22 May 1764: Voltaire, *Corr.*, vol. 7, 711.
46. Idem., 21 March, ibid., 635. See also, for example, vol. 9, 236–38, letter to Le Cat (1767–68?).
47. D'Holbach, *Système de la Nature*, vol. 1, 230, 107, 214, 225 and 243.
48. D'Holbach, *Le Bon Sens*, (1772), Paris, 1971, 71.
49. D'Holbach, *Système de la Nature*, vol. 1, 226. 'The ways we think are necessarily determined by ... the way we are naturally organised and the modifications that are effected upon our machines independently of our will' (225–26).
50. D'Holbach, *Éthocratie ou le Gouvernement fondé sur la Morale*, (1776), Paris, 1967, 160.
51. Letter of 29 October 1757: Rousseau, *Corr.*, vol.4, 316.
52. J.-J. Rousseau, *Considérations sur le Gouvernement de Pologne*, (1770), in *Œuvres complètes*, 1,041.
53. Quoted by Serna, 'Aux origines culturelles d'un engagement politique', 184–85.
54. M.-J. Lequinio, *Les Préjugés détruits*, Paris, 1792, a work he says was written before 10 August: 67.
55. Ibid., 9: 'Was man made in order to think? I had the stupidity to believe so; but for a long time now I have realised I was wrong and I very firmly answer: *no*' (w.u.o.).
56. Ibid., 97.
57. Ibid., 10 and 11.
58. Ibid., 11 or again, 92, concerning the fact 'that men do not think; it is because they were not made in order to think; it is because the thing that causes them the most pain is having to think'.
59. Ibid., 13: 'It is not a natural thing for man to think, and nature does not suffer being violated with impunity'.
60. Ibid., 9.
61. Ibid., 10.
62. Ibid., 11.
63. Rousseau, *Émile*, Book IV, 352.
64. J.-J. Rousseau, *Rousseau juge de Jean-Jacques, Deuxième Dialogue*, in *Œuvres complètes*, 845. 'For me thinking is a very painful task which tires me, plagues me and displeases me' (839).

65. Ibid., 845.
66. Ibid., 839.
67. Ibid., 865.
68. Ibid., 845.
69. Rousseau, Preface to *Narcisse* (written at the end of 1752, beginning of 1753), in *Œuvres complètes*, Pléiade, vol. 2, Paris, 1964, 970.
70. Ibid., and he adds: 'If it ever taught him anything at all, I would consider him badly paid for his efforts'.
71. See above, 50, *Deuxième Dialogue*, 845: 'As soon as thinking and reflection are involved, meditation is no longer a restful activity; it is a very tiresome thing to do' et cetera.
72. See above, 85.
73. Letter to Sophie Volland, 7 November 1762: Diderot, *Corr.*, vol.2, Paris, 1958, 212–13.
74. Ibid., 213. Likewise to the abbé Le Monnier, 15 September 1755, letter from Diderot published in *Corr. compl. de Rousseau*, vol. 3, 174.
75. For example, to d'Alembert, 5 April 1766: Voltaire, *Corr.*, vol. 8, 426.
76. Lequinio, *Les Préjugés détruits*, 30.
77 Ibid., 57.
78. Ibid., 162.
79. Ibid., 178; Cf. also 10, 16 and 163. Similar thing to be found, for example, in Collet d'Herbois, who rails against 'these citizen-automata that our cities are so full of' (*Archives parlementaires*, 1/74/382/2).
80. Lequinio, *Les Préjugés détruits*, 272.
81. Ibid., 68.

≈ *Chapter 7* ≈

The Audacity of the Philanthropists

With Lequinio we enter the period 1792–94 in which it becomes clear that the golden age is rather reluctant to return to the earth – a period which will subsequently be marked out as the Jacobin upheaval. In so far as this period is concerned, my sole aim is to consider the events of these years while following, if that is at all possible, the same line of enquiry as before: the theme of man's inner space seen, above all, as something passive, and therefore capable of manipulation and reorganisation. Will this line of enquiry prove to be an Ariadne's thread? If it is possible to continue to trace the theme's presence through this period the conclusion must be that we have to exclude the idea that there was any rupture or 'break' between the initial impulse of the Revolution and these two controversial years, and indeed that the very continuity is a determining factor. There is a view, not uncommonly held, that somewhere along its journey, the Revolution unfortunately misplaced a whole set of luggage crammed with deferential attitudes and precious guarantees for the grandeur of humanity and its attendant dignity. Such a view is not an option for us, given everything that has gone before and which, if we consider the ground we have already covered, can clearly be seen as following on directly from the Enlightenment. It may not be saying very much, but we should be cautious about the contents of this luggage, a fact that seems to be confirmed by what emerges when, under the Terror, it falls open up and its contents spill out. Intending as I do to forego the comfort to be enjoyed from following well-trodden paths, I may at least take consolation in the fact that there is a surprising sense of coherence in the picture that is emerging as I re-examine the original evidence.

What is interesting about the point at which we now arrive in the history of value systems, which is more or less the history that I am tracing, is that the reformers in charge of legislation at this moment in history are remarkably self-confident and uninhibited, and this at a time when the field of possibilities has widened to infinity (so they would like to believe), by virtue of the fact that what had previously existed has been destroyed, and because of the urgency of the situation in which they find themselves. The impulse that had been at the *foundation* of the burgeoning Revolution, and the concomitant belief that the slate had been wiped clean, were undoubtedly renewed in a still more radical form from the end of the summer of 1792 onwards, the moment that symbolically marks the end of the first phase of the Republic. Those theoreticians in clubs and assemblies, moved by the sort of convictions mentioned above concerning human malleability (at the time, the word 'perfectibility' was often used), saw the biological mass of Frenchmen, their psyches included, as crying out for a far-reaching reorganisation, the sovereign principle of which was the exercising of total power by the State over children. The inheritors of a pedagogical century (and pedagogical for political reasons[1]) are now in power, and they are not handicapped by scruples, since, as good sensualists, they tend to see in the stuff of childhood merely something that is available to receive their influence, something that is completely docile in the hands of the educators, something that is completely subject to their beliefs. The tone had been set by the Enlightenment. 'Children were probably never supervised and controlled as much as during this period in which people everywhere are proclaiming the benefits of natural education'.[2] This is, without exaggeration, an admission that the intention is a *totalitarian* one. The word totalitarian is used here only in a technical sense. And if some people insist on considering it as polemical, I am happy to adopt any alternative, but necessarily less precise word, they may see fit to suggest, providing it serves as a means of describing what I am actually talking about.

In order to see an educational project of such a huge scale to a conclusion, the demiurgic State is obliged to perpetrate two acts of violation, to break through two screens of which it ipso facto denies the existence: that of the privacy of the family and that of man's inner space. As for the latter, we know enough about the theories in fashion at the time to realise that in the opinion of the philanthropists, worked up into a state of high excitement as they were, there is no problem here, neither on a technical nor on an axiological level. When the Conventionnel, Portiez, wants to subject future citizens to 'a sort of violence in order to make them learn', or when Chénier, his colleague, wants 'to squeeze the souls of children and surround them with a triple rampart of patriotism',[3] both of them are expressing quite normal ideas, given what has preceded throughout the century and has been exacerbated by the imperatives of the moment – ideas that are just as easy to find in the reports and speeches of numerous authors and expressed in the vivid language of which we know them to be capable. And we shall turn our attention first of all to the violation of the privacy of family life. A very clear and concrete example of this, and one that we cannot avoid mentioning, is the quite legal use of home visits, carried out at night if this was thought necessary. It was not an essential but it was nevertheless an important element in the philanthropists' armoury.

Seeing the family as an obstacle to the programming of social harmony, seeing parents as intruders, as overstepping the limits and competing with the State in the training of children: these are ideas of the times and they are entirely consistent with the nominalist bases of modern thought. Louis XIV, in his attitude to Protestants, was in a way the proto-revolutionary investigator into what might be considered appropriate techniques in this field.[4] We find more than traces of these same ideas in authors who are renowned for being as different from each other as Helvétius and Rousseau. The latter strongly argued that the fatherland should exert a necessary and unalloyed control over the citizen, who consequently becomes far more important in his status as citizen, than he ever could be as a mere human being. 'It is education that must instil national strength into people's hearts and orientate their opinions and their tastes in such a way that they are patriots by inclination, by passionate commitment, out of necessity. A child opening his eyes should see the fatherland, and until the day he dies he must see nothing else'. Love of one's country 'is his whole life, he sees nothing except the fatherland, it is all he lives for'.[5] Previously, and in its own quiet way, *Émile* had warned of this: 'The man who seeks to maintain the primacy of natural feelings while living in civil society, doesn't know what he wants'.⁶ We should not be surprised that Saint-Just, in the very heart of the volcano, should express exactly what Rousseau had written in some solitary retreat or other: love of the fatherland 'is so exclusive' that it sacrifices everything, including 'private affections' 'to the public interest' and this 'without a second thought'.⁷ As for Helvétius, he believed that the best education was the one that put the greatest distance between parents and child, and he did not even think it advisable that the latter should see the former 'during the holidays and on days off'.⁸ To support his argument, he sought to demonstrate the superiority of 'public education ... over that conducted at home'.⁹ On the very eve of the Revolution, the abbé Grégoire, seeking in a philanthropic and utilitarian manner to further the regeneration of the Jewish people, argued that their children, if they could be withdrawn from the educational influence of their parents, 'would, *without even wishing to do so*, pick up healthy ideas that are the antidote to the absurdities which they are fed upon within the family'.¹⁰

The tone had been set. Hostility to the family, in the context of education, was more akin to open warfare at the climax of the Revolution. Lequinio is not afraid to publish 'that he would feel happy for the whole human race if children never knew their fathers'.¹¹ Here, once again, I should remind anyone who prefers to think that Lequinio is exaggerating that, in this respect, Rousseau himself had led by example and given a *doctrinal* underpinning to the neo-natal desertion of his own children. In his own writings he considers this desertion in terms of a pure and simple *handing over to the public education system*: 'Suffice it to say ... that in handing over my children to the public education system ..., I thought I was acting as a citizen and a father; and I considered myself as a member of Plato's Republic',¹² having already previously qualified this work as 'the finest educational treatise that has ever been written'.¹³ Robespierre and Danton are united in denouncing the *restricting* effect that the family has on the mental universe of the child,¹⁴ and like almost everyone else, they would like to extract children from this emotional cocoon and replace it with a collectivist type of training in line with the views of Le Peletier de Saint-Fargeau, whose famous project, inspired by egalitarian principles, demanded the education in common of children between the ages of five and twelve. Because, concurred Robespierre, we have 'to get hold of children at the moment when they are receptive to decisive impressions if we are to make them into men worthy of the Republic'.¹⁵ This is purely and simply a matter of technical engineering by impressions whose effects are precalculated. And he reminds us: '*The fatherland alone* has the right to raise its children',[16] whereas Danton had said, 'My son doesn't belong to me, he belongs to the Republic',[17] which is just one particular application of the same principle, also formulated by him and according to which 'children belong to the Republic before they belong to their parents'.[18] One would possibly be right in thinking that what we have here, for very many people during these decades, is a stereotyped view; there were lots of people, like Danton and Robespierre, and in this instance like Barère, who were ready to defend the view that 'children belong to their general family, the Republic, before they belong to their individual families'.[19] 'By means of education in common', argued his colleague, Jean-Baptiste Leclerc, 'you rescue the hearts of children from the counter-revolutionary influences of their parents'.[20]

The decision to settle on five years as the age at which future citizens begin to be taken in hand by the authorities of the Republic could be seen, arguing *a contrario*, as a recognition that during the years leading up to the age of five parental prerogative nevertheless exists. We should not assume this to be the case, however. Vauréal, an Enlightenment theoretician on pedagogical matters who arrived rather late on the scene, calculated, as we have already said, three years to be the age at which children could 'be offered up to the national education system … like lumps of clay that are ready and waiting for the soft and beneficent hands of the potter'.[21] But isn't three a little too old? In his famous speech of 21st December 1792, Rabaut Saint-Étienne, makes a distinction between 'public instruction', intended to train men's minds, and 'national education system' whose real, and much deeper objective is 'to train [men's] hearts'.[22] He was not afraid to develop this idea by conferring on this *national education system* the status of a monopoly of a fundamental and exorbitant nature: 'Its whole doctrine consists therefore in taking charge of a person from the cradle onwards, and even from before he is born; for the as-yet-unborn baby already belongs to the fatherland'.[23] In exactly the same way, Michel-Edme Petit explained that education 'should go seek man out in the embryo of the species'.[24] Through force of circumstances, since perinatal technologies had not yet made anything else feasible, such words could have little influence on the reality of the matter; but they already tell us a great deal indeed and beg a number of very serious questions, among them the whole question of the Enlightenment's interest in eugenics and selective breeding, which such words forbid us from simply dismissing out of hand. And Rousseau, once again, goes a long way down a similar path in his *Contrat Social* when, clearly without any ulterior motives, he professes that the life of a citizen in the state of society 'is no longer simply an example of nature's beneficence, it is a conditional gift from the State'.[25] At the height of its power, the revolutionary State is very close to Rousseau's conception of the State and certainly, in those moments when it denies that the family has certain privileges by natural right, and in those moments, too, when there are those among its orators who will claim that it is justified in meddling with the relationship which many consider to be the strongest and most sacrosanct of all natural relationships: that between the mother-to-be and the as-yet-unborn child.

Taking charge of children even before they are born; 'we are taking charge of the generation that is just being born', Rabaut Saint-Étienne is alleged to have said.[26] 'Let's take charge of the generation that has just been born, the generation that is rapidly heading towards puberty', Grégoire said, talking of the Jews.[27] And Constant complains: 'What arguments will people not put forward when it comes to defending the need to allow the government to take charge of future generations in order to shape them as it sees fit!'[28] The repeated use of the same verb says a great deal. It clearly expresses the absolute power over individuals that the legislator believes that he can arrogate to himself, through a convenient appeal to some fictitious notion of the general will, in order to model and reshape men, moulding them into a contented society. The same word, or analogous ones, are not at all rare in the discourse of the age. 'Taking charge' of Émile was the task that Rousseau specifically identified for his tutor.[29] Robespierre tells us that it is at the age of five that the State should 'take hold of children',[30] that is to say, he goes on, 'at the age at which we begin to form habits', and should only loosen its grip 'at the age when these habits have become sufficiently strong as to form the definitive character of the adult when he enters society'.[31] Given that the latter age was, in principle, considered to be twelve years, it is with a certain degree of surprise that we learn that some nine months later Barère suggests that the age of sixteen (and above) is the most propitious moment of all for the collectivity to lay hold of the individual: 'It is at the age when his intelligence begins to combine with his physical strength that the nation should take charge of the individual'.³² Clearly, the atmosphere of the age is a *captivating* one, and all individuals run the risk of being captivated at some time or other in their lives, and probably two or three times rather than on a single occasion, and that in all likelihood when they have already reached adulthood and beyond. Moreover, it is true to say that it is this very process of repeatedly taking charge of the individual which Rabaut Saint-Etienne considers (perhaps with a hint of jealousy) that he has to condemn Catholic priests for having dreamed up, in their usual diabolical fashion – virtuosi in the art of manipulation that they are: 'They took charge of people from birth onwards; they took control of them in their early youth, during their adolescence, in their maturity, at the moment when they come to wed, at the birth of their children ... in their moments of sickness and on their deathbeds'.³³

This is the minimum that is required in fighting the good fight. When Mirabeau wishes the ruler to 'take control' of the citizen's imagination, he is quite clearly thinking of all adults.³⁴ Mona Ozouf includes as one of the objectives of those who seek to create new man, the necessity of 'taking control of his most insignificant thoughts'.³⁵ And we would suggest that time does little to alter matters. Even if you are an honest citizen of one hundred and twenty years of age, living in secluded retirement, you would still run the risk that some overzealous philanthropist or some insatiable lover of humanity might decide to take you in hand. And this actually happened. A gentleman who had reached the august age of six score years and who had been honoured with an invitation to the Constituent Assembly in October 1789, had the great misfortune to suddenly excite the enthusiasm of the 'author of a plan for a national education system' who, seizing the opportunity thus presented to him, 'sought *to take charge* of the venerable old man' no less. The latter would have enjoyed all the benefits of a happy incarceration in a 'patriotic school', with the express design of better inculcating in the youth of the day a healthy respect for aged people. The old man 'whom nature had spared so that he could witness the regeneration of France and live to see his fatherland enjoy freedom', apparently owed the preservation of his own freedom only to the humanitarian intervention of a monarchist representative of the Assembly: 'Do whatever you see fit for this old man, but allow him his freedom'.³⁶ All the same, citizen Jacob, born in the Mont-Jura in 1669, had had a narrow escape. And his little mishap illustrates perfectly the spirit that underpins what, to take another example, Rabaut Saint-Etienne has to say about a 'national education system': 'It takes charge of the whole man and never lets go of him, so that the national education system is not an institution for childhood but for one's whole life',[37] even if, in stubbornly refusing to die, you end up being used as a human teaching aid.

'It takes charge of the whole man and never lets go of him'. The immediate reason for such an approach is quite obvious. Those who nurture the rather exorbitant ambition of building a new world by conditioning new-born babes through subjecting them to an appropriate programme, are obliged temporarily to turn a blind eye to one unavoidable fact, a fact whose existence even the purest idealists have to acknowledge, that for the time being, and for a long time to come, the possibility of social perfection is somewhat undermined by the very patent imperfection of those men who already actually exist and who have already 'adopted certain habits', as Grégoire points out.[38] Not only is it fair to think of these men as *badly educated,* it is possible to think of them as a living explanation why the Revolution, although inspired by good intentions, has for many years now been finding it difficult to deliver the human happiness it promises. This explains why, during this whole period, youth is a relatively valued commodity, relatively only in so far as youth itself is relative. Dulaure says of mature men that they are made of 'hard stuff', and Mona Ozouf translates this by saying they are 'all stiffened up with habits'.[39] Still in December 1792, Rabaut Saint-Étienne announces as 'a certainty' that at the same time as we prepare for the new man yet to come, 'we absolutely must, we absolutely must', he says twice, 'renew the present generation of men', that is to say, change the stuff it is made of.[40]

An urgent task maybe, but also a pious hope, it would seem, at least if we are to believe what someone like Lanthenas says a few months later, when he exposes in rather vivid language this whole problem of these men who are already fully formed, and therefore need to be re-formed, because they are not capable of accepting and making the most of what the last four years have offered them: 'No one, especially among those in the Convention, has shown the slightest interest in that part of the Public Instruction system which should be devoted to dealing with *fully grown men*. In the wake of a Revolution as all-encompassing as ours, most such men have become comparable to *big children*, who have no real understanding of what is going on all around them'.[41]

A short time later, Sieyès, acting as a mouthpiece for the views of the Committee for Public Instruction, admits with some embarrassment that instruction on a national scale should be available to 'people of all ages'.[42] This is less daring and seems pointlessly circumspect when compared to what Fouché has to say on the matter: 'the French people *no longer wants* to receive half an education any more than it wants to be half free; *it wants* to be completely regenerated like a new being freshly delivered up from the hands of nature'.[43] At the beginning of Book I of *Émile*, Rousseau already felt he could offer the diagnosis that 'our species *does not want* to be half formed'.[44] This is a mammoth undertaking which is justified by the immediate political need to regenerate human kind, but which, once it has been brought to fruition, finds itself having to go on in a 'continuing education' mode, to such an extent that, as Rabaut says, ' the national education system is not an institution for childhood but for one's whole life'.[45] 'A child', Rousseau warned, 'opening his eyes should see the fatherland, and *until the day he dies* he must see nothing else'.[46]

This is a form of 'continuing education', Mona Ozouf comments, 'that they have to remember to make available to future generations'. And she goes on to observe, 'The school takes on an extraordinarily dilated form here: it can be confused with the Revolution itself'.[47] Indeed, it is for want of a better term that I have gone along with the impression that I am talking about some form of extended schooling. This was in order to avoid confusing the categories, but my care in the use of terminology was merely for the sake of clarity of exposition, and I am finally obliged to agree that in concrete terms the categories I have outlined fuse together. I have merely been putting off the moment when I must use the key word, itself clearly of major significance, which is the word *propaganda*. Because this, of course, is what it is really all about. From 1792 onwards there is no question as to the know-how that was demonstrated by the technicians who massaged 'the views of the public'. Their ability in such matters is public knowledge, and it is not my concern to consider in detail the sorts of techniques they used, any more than it was my aim to look at actual methods employed in respect of education. The thing that interests me is the way the doctrinal legacy of the Enlightenment introduces patterns of behaviour that are totalitarian in nature.[48] Similarly, I shall confine myself now to the observation that, however ingenious were the methods dreamed up or actually employed, in all practical respects they can be seen as following on directly from the belief that human beings are purely passive entities waiting to be manipulated into the desired shape. The liberal outpourings of propaganda that accompanied the hardening of the Revolutionary line should not be seen as the mere by-product of a rather extraordinary set of circumstances at a particular moment in history. It should rather be seen as one feature in a succession of moments that together make up a whole reductionist way of thinking the social anthropology of the day. The outpouring of propaganda stands out as a very clearly defined example of the implementation of a process that flows from that way of thinking. It is not the culmination of that way of thinking, nor is it even the high-point of it: it is simply one moment in the process, possibly the most dramatic moment, but nevertheless merely one moment; and in spite of appearances it is not necessarily the most technically important moment at that.

The politicians and various purveyors of doctrine who had sufficient innocence of spirit to believe that the task of looking after the common well being had been devolved to them, were faced with a problem: the fact that the individual machines they were expected to deal with showed no innate propensity to social harmony when left to their own devices. They had to be twisted into shape and re-educated to the purpose. It is to this end that the genius of Jacobin propaganda was employed and the breadth and audacity of the propaganda machine can only be really understood in the context of *sensualist* thinking. It is sensualism that offers justification for its use on the double grounds that it makes it technically achievable and gives it a moral legitimacy. It is easily achieved technically in that it can be considered as nothing more difficult than exchanging one set of habits for another. What could be easier when human beings are considered in terms of pure passivity? Not only do they say that 'habit is everything',[49] we also know that 'our habits are controlled by the person who makes us acquire them',[50] and we therefore think accordingly,[51] and, as one mishap is piled upon the next, the post-Thermidorians come to interpret the French political equation in terms of a simple conflict of habits which was inexplicably more difficult to resolve than they had ever expected. As for the matter of moral legitimacy, there is less reason to call this into question once one remembers that the whole undertaking is concerned with bringing about 'the happiness of all' which the first article of the Declaration of Rights of Year 1, identifies as the aim to which society aspires.

The Audacity of the Philanthropists

Breadth and audacity: these two characteristics of Jacobin propaganda are consequently given free rein. Henceforth, it is a question of 'making a Revolution *in men's hearts and minds just as it has been made in living conditions and in government*'.[52] It is worth pointing out that *it has been made* in the socio-institutional domain but it has *yet to be made* in men's hearts and minds. The order of the day therefore is nothing less than the total control of the inner man, which presupposes this inner space to be both transparent and susceptible of being penetrated. Such a notion calls to mind Thomas More's *Utopia*, where, for the sake of the happiness of the collectivity, each individual is 'constantly exposed to the view of everyone else'.[53] 'In a free country, no one can or should disguise the inside of his house'. These words, uttered by a member of the Convention[54] during one of his missions, are revealing and say a great deal. But they still do not say quite enough, because what they should say is: in a free country no one should hide his own conscience, his inner self, from view. And if this is the case, this 'free country' could easily be mistaken for the seraglio of the *Lettres persanes*, where nothing remains hidden, neither 'the most secret deeds' nor 'the most secret words', and where, in so far as the occupants are concerned, it is above all a matter of 'taming their spirits' and 'subduing their hearts'.[55] Rousseau, in keeping with what we have learned to expect from him, simply argues: 'If it is a good thing to know how to use men as they are, it is a much better thing still to make them into what we need them to be; the most absolute power is that which *penetrates the inner man*, and exerts its influence as much *upon his will* as upon his actions'.[56] And as far as the child to be educated is concerned, Rousseau warns the educator: 'He must not take a single step that you have not foreseen, he must not open his mouth without you knowing what he is going to say'.[57]

On reading which, it is difficult not to agree with the view that, in this particular context, which is one where it is assumed by the charismatic reformers that the normal state of existence for all mankind is one in which the active principle is totally absent (except, strangely enough, in the case of the reformers themselves), '*the very core of man's inner space is by nature criminal*'. These are very strong words indeed from Mona Ozouf. For my own part, I would say that it is *predelinquent* rather than criminal. In any event, the words are so suggestive that I would have written the present book solely in order to provide them with a commentary. The author goes on: 'This ideal of complete social and psychological visibility is at the very root of Jacobinism',[58] whose world, she also writes, 'is the world of the declaration',[59] by which we should understand: the world of the civically necessary confession of everything confessable; she might also have said: the world of denunciation, since it went as far as making a virtue out of the act of anonymous delation.[60] She also tells us that the Jacobin model involves, 'a project of absolute visibility where indeterminacy cannot be tolerated', and where 'war is declared on man's inner space'.[61] What is involved is total warfare and the Jacobins will stop at nothing. It is against this yardstick and set against this example that we should understand the glare of publicity under which debates and ballots take place.[62] Once again, it is a question of manipulating men, it is not a question of persuading them but of proceeding by sleight of hand. The education that is proposed to the people should be 'enchanting',[63] it involves exercising 'a magic control over the human consciousness',[64] they want to electrify, to 'republicanise' each and every member of the human herd; the word 'electrify' recurs frequently,[65] and expresses their anxiety to bring to speedy fruition the processes they have imagined and set in train.

Nothing more needs to be said about the extraordinary stubbornness of the propagandists of the age in meticulously tracking down psychic states and processes, in dissecting them under the metaphorical microscope, in learning how to manipulate them, in mobilising or inventing, and orchestrating the sources from which the most diverse range of sensations originate. Everything has been explained, and in great detail, or almost everything, and almost explained. When an analyst as penetrating as Mona Ozouf talks, in passing, of 'the sensualist illusion' which inspired these indefatigable friends of humankind,[66] we almost have the impression that this 'illusion' only exists, suspended in the atmosphere, by virtue of some obscure stroke of meteorological good fortune, and that it is some sort of marginal phenomenon, a left-over from a world that is completely alien to politics, that has come from elsewhere or from nowhere at all. This is to refuse to give sufficient emphasis to the organic relationship between Revolution and Enlightenment thinking. All the great writers of the Enlightenment, and not only the fully accredited technicians of sensualism, not only the *Encyclopédistes*, but also Rousseau, unanimously based their politics on a philosophy of sensations. And they did not do so for reasons of historical serendipity, which are not open to the scrutiny of reason, but purely and simply because it is natural that any carefully thought-out political stance should be founded upon an anthropological basis. If the underpinning anthropological view is a sensualist one it is unavoidable that the politics which result from it should reflect this fact both in terms of the policies pursued and the methods used to pursue them. By way of example, Rousseau refers to our classical forebears and assures us that they tended to show things far more than actually explain them. 'The object that is placed before us fires our imagination ... and frequently it is the object alone which tells us all there is to tell ... What great care the Romans gave to the language of signs! ... For them, everything was adornment, representation, ceremonial, and everything was meant to make an impression upon the hearts of citizens'.[67]

It is true, as it happens, that many people consider what actually came out of the Revolution as doing some sort of an injustice to the doctrines that gave rise to it, but if we allow ourselves to be sidetracked by such a trivial consideration we run the risk of turning our backs on the richness that actual experience has to offer us. For when Rabaut de Saint-Étienne speaks on 21st December 1792, the aspirations he expresses mirror the whole viewpoint of the eighteenth-century on man and on society, a viewpoint that has simply been brought to a state of incandescence by the turn events had taken in the first few years of the Revolutionary period: he hopes to have 'soon, an *infallible* means of immediately communicating a set of common and *uniform impressions* to *all* Frenchmen *at once*, the effect of which would be to make them all, *all together*, worthy of the Revolution ...'. This 'means' does exist: the great civic liturgies of Antiquity provide a model for it. These liturgies, which are so well suited to the techniques that find concrete form in *fêtes nationales*, 'ensured that on the *same* day, at the *same* moment, *all* citizens at *all* times and in *all* places, were *all* subjected to the *same* set of impressions acting upon their senses, their imagination, their memory, their reason, upon *every* faculty that man possesses'.[68] These few lines speak volumes. The repetitive allusions to notions of totality, uniformity, immediacy, simultaneity betray an obsession that underscores the grandiose breadth and infinite audacity characterising the Jacobin propaganda machine. What legitimises both the breadth and the audacity displayed here is the supposition that human nature is purely passive and thoroughly prone to manipulation and re-formation. The stakes too are incredibly high and involve 'man in his *entirety*, the *whole* society of French people, the *whole* of humankind'.⁶⁹ Rousseau tells us so and I have already quoted him on the matter: 'Good social institutions are those which best know how to change man's nature'.⁷⁰ And what he has in mind as far as the child to be educated is concerned, is thus applicable once more to the citizen who is to be conditioned by the *fête nationale*: 'I shall begin by firing his imagination; I shall choose the most favourable time and place and the objects best suited to making the impressions that I wish to make'.⁷¹ 'Men are nothing more than *old children*', Diderot agreed, adding for his own part: 'Men in great numbers moved by a common spirit always make a great impression on me'.⁷²

Those who are familiar with the documents of the Revolutionary period will no doubt readily agree with me when I claim that I could string together a hundred or more quotations very similar to that given from Rabaut de Saint-Étienne (whom I shall again use as a source later on), or that I could easily reel off lists of measures that had been decided upon, lists of such length and containing such a degree of detail⁷³ (sometimes specifying even 'the cut of the garments to be worn by citizens') that they illustrate the attention to minutiae shown by these would-be programmers of civic transparency, as well as their feverish desire to 'fill the social space and to control it in its entirety'.⁷⁴ But what I am simply seeking to do in these pages is to suggest the existence of a certain continuity, and to follow, if at all possible, the logic of a particular drift. If I decided to analyse, in detail, the conception of the Revolutionary *fête nationale*, used as a means of producing in spectators a rush of sensations and impressions intended to favour their *republicanisation*, this would not lead me very far away from my point, but it would slow down my progress without adding a great deal to my argument. Similarly, despite the very interesting nature of the topic, I shall only touch upon the question of the Revolutionary calendar,⁷⁵ even though it is essential. This was the calendar which sought to speak 'at one and the same time, to the senses, to the heart and to the mind',⁷⁶ and was particularly intended as a way of modifying hearts and minds by a repeated play of messages, providing a subtly insistent echoing of an appeal to or by Mother Nature. Rousseau had written that at the sight of nature, 'we feel ourselves *insensibly* moved without realising it', and that 'the voice of nature tames our wild hearts'.⁷⁷ This was the express aim of Fabre d'Églantine, the chief architect of the new calendar, in precisely this respect. If he is to be believed, what this is all about is 'as far as institutions are concerned, allowing nothing to filter through to the conscious understanding of the masses, other than things which are of great usefulness to the public as a whole', keeping the individual under pressure 'every minute of the year, the month, the [ten-day] week, and the day', exploiting 'the control exerted by images over human intelligence'; as a result, it is a question of 'making a striking impact on man's reason' and 'striking his imagination'.[78] Thus, it is unbeknownst to them that his fellow citizens are to be subjected to conditioning, it is 'insensibly and without realising it'.[79]

What is really remarkable about this whole affair is not that Fabre d'Églantine was guillotined shortly afterwards. It is true that he was dead before his system had been in place for six months, but at that time a miscalculation of this sort was not at all out of the ordinary. What is really remarkable is that Saint-Just and Robespierre saw fit to *reproach* him with having been something of a specialist in the whole area of the manipulation of men's minds (when we might have expected them rather to have congratulated him for this). Saint-Just says that he knew how to deceive others 'by leading them in the direction of their natural inclinations'.[80] According to Robespierre his cleverness consisted in 'putting forward a few men whom he thereafter controlled'.[81] Robespierre also says – and it would be very wrong of me not to draw attention to this particular reproach – that he possessed 'the art of making others accept his own ideas and his own views *unbeknownst to them*'.[82] This is really the icing on the cake when the manipulative powers of the republican calendar are paradoxically subjected to such severe criticism on the part of the man who was probably the best-known among the architects of the Reign of Terror!

Notes

1. Cf.supra, 79–80.
2. In the conclusion of M. Grandière's thesis, from which I have already had occasion to quote (including this phrase), 'L'Idéal pédagogique en France au XVIIIe siècle (1715–1789)', vol. 4, 981.
3. Quoted by M. Ozouf, *L'Homme régénéré*, Paris, 1989, 144 and 145.
4. Apart from the *dragonnades*, which also give the whole question a very concrete form, there is the policy of withdrawing any children between the ages of five and sixteen from recalcitrant families so as to enforce a Catholic education upon them. On the idea that the 1680s was a decade in which there occurred an axiological break which prefigured many of the distinctive features of the Enlightenment, see the very profound study by Jean de Viguerie,

'Quelques réflexions critiques à propos de l'ouvrage de Paul Hazard *La Crise de la conscience européenne*', in *Études d'Histoire européenne. Mélanges offerts à René et Suzanne Pillorget*, published by the Société française d'Histoire des Idées et d'Histoire religieuse, Presses de l'Université d'Angers, 1990, 37–54.
5. J.-J. Rousseau, *Considérations sur le Gouvernement de Pologne* (1770), in *Œuvres complètes*, 966.
6. J.-J. Rousseau, *Émile ou de l'Éducation*, Paris, 1966, Book I, 40.
7. *Archives parlementaires*, 1/87/629–630, 11th germinal Year II, 31 March 1794.
8. C.-A. Helvétius, *De l'Homme, de ses facultés intellectuelles et de son Éducation* (1773), Paris, 1989, vol.2, 887.
9. Ibid., 887 ff.
10. Abbé Grégoire, *Essai sur la Régénération physique, morale et politique des Juifs* (1788), Metz, 1789, 167. Since children are 'susceptible to all sorts of impressions'.
11. Lequinio, *Les Préjugés détruits*, Paris, 1792, 144. It is quite clear that the author wishes to affirm that it is desirable that *no* child should ever see its father.
12. J.-J. Rousseau, *Les Confessions*, Book VIII, Paris, 1980, 423.
13. Rousseau, *Émile*, Book I, 40.'Do you want to have some idea of the system of public education, then read Plato's *Republic*'.
14. Robespierre speaks of a 'domestic federalism that has a *restricting* effect on souls by isolating them' (18th floréal Year II, 7 May 1794: *Archives parlementaires*, 1/82/138/2). And Danton: 'Everything is subject to *restrictions* in education that takes place in the home' (13 August 1793, *Archives parlementaires*, 1/72/126/2).
15. 13 August 1793, *Archives parlementaires*, 1/72/126/1.
16. 18th floréal Year II, *Archives parlementaires*, 1/82/138/2.
17. 13 August 1793, *Archives parlementaires*, 1/72/126/2.
18. 22nd frimaire Year II, 12 December 1793: *Moniteur* no. 84, 24th frimaire, 14 December, 339/2.
19. Barère to the Convention, 13th prairial Year II, 1 June 1794, published in Br. Baczko, *Une Éducation pour la Démocratie*, Paris, 1982, 442.
20. To the Convention, 18 December 1792: J. Guillaume, *Procès-verbaux du Comité d'Instruction publique*, Paris, vol. 1, 196.
21. In 1783; see above, 84.
22. *Archives parlementaires*, 1/55/346/1.
23. Ibid., 346/2. A rather strange similarity is to be found with an expression used by Rousseau when he denounces a vast project to seek control of education in all its forms envisaged by the *philosophes* (*Deuxième Dialogue*, 889). He says of those involved: 'The whole of the generation just being born is devoted to them from the cradle onwards' (890).
24. *Archives parlementaires*, 1/55/133/2, 18 December 1792.
25. J.-J. Rousseau, *Contrat Social*, vol. II, chapter 5, 376.
26. Quoted by M. Garaud and R. Szramkiewicz, *La Révolution française et la famille*, Paris, 1978, 142.
27. Grégoire, *Essai sur la Régénération*, 166.
28. Benjamin Constant, 'De la liberté des anciens comparée à celle des modernes', Speech made at the Athénée royale in Paris, February 1819, in B. Constant, *De l'Esprit de Conquête et de l'Usurpation*, Paris, 1986, 284.
29. Quoted by J. de la Viguerie, 'Le mouvement des idées pédagogiques aux XVIIe et XVIIIe siècles', in *Histoire mondiale de l'Éducation*, Paris, 1981, [273–99], 293.

30. See above, 112.
31. *Archives parlementaires*, 1/72/126/1, 13 August 1793.
32. Reference to note 19.
33. *Archives parlementaires*, 1/55/346/1.
34. Speech written between 1789 and 1791: Baczko, *Une Éducation pour la Démocratie*, 97
35. Ozouf, *L'Homme régénéré*, 120.
36. 23 October 1789, *Archives parlementaires*, 1/9/484/1. It is Mirabeau's younger brother who pleads on behalf of 'the venerable old man'.
37. 21 December 1792, *Archives parlementaires*, 1/55/346/2.
38. Grégoire, *Essai sur la Régénération*, 165.
39. Ozouf, *L'Homme régénéré*, 142.
40. *Archives parlementaires*, 1/55/346/2. 'We have to make the French people into a new nation, instil in them habits that are in harmony with their laws, give them an education system which is pleasant, charming, seductive, make them love ... freedom, equality, fraternity, especially this latter sweet and gentle quality.'
41. 10 May 1793, *Archives parlementaires*, 1/64/424/2. The logic upon which the Republic is *founded* places adults in a position exactly similar to that which was imagined by Destutt de Tracy some years later when he was developing the following argument: 'Even if a man was born with all his strengths fully developed, he would nevertheless be as imbecilic as a child; likewise, in the very first moments of his life he would be in complete ignorance with regard to everything around him and with regard to himself' (Destutt de Tracy, *Mémoire sur la Faculté de penser*, III/1, read to the Institute on 27th vendémiaire Year V, 18 October 1796, C.O.P.L.F., Paris, 1992, 137).
42. Reference given in Chapter Six, note 33.
43. Fouché, 'Réflexions sur l'Instruction publique', end of May 1793. Ibid, appendix II, 616.
44. Rousseau, *Émile*, Book I, 35.
45. *Archives parlementaires*, 1/55/346/2.
46. Rousseau, *Gouvernement de Pologne*, 966.
47. Ozouf, *L'Homme régénéré*, 9.
48. It is indeed quite true that one could write a book 'about the philosophy of education around the time of the revolution' without ever going in to 'the actual teaching methods envisaged' (ibid., 8), since the intentions behind such thinking and the principles that inspired it already offer sufficient food for thought.
49. Lequinio, *Les Préjugés détruits*, 166.
50. D'Holbach, *Système de la Nature*, vol. 1, 214.
51. Cf. for example, the way Robespierre expresses himself on the subject of education, above, 114. A grass-roots revolutionary observes: 'Aristocracy or indifference to virtue is often a matter of habit or of the organic make-up of the individual concerned' (quoted by Ch.-L.Chassin, *La Vendée patriote, 1793–1795*, vol. 4 (1895), Mayenne, 1973, 173).
52. Rabaut Saint-Étienne, December 1792, *Archives parlementaires*, 1/55/346/1.
53. Thomas More, *L'Utopie* (1516), ed. A. Prévost, Paris, 1978, 94. Cf. the very fine study by Monica Papazu, 'L'Utopie face à ses habitants', in *Bulletin de la Société française d'Histoire des Idées et d'Histoire religieuse*, no. 9 bis, (1993): 33–72.
54. Fayau, 14th nivôse Year II, 3 January 1794: Chassin, *La Vendée patriote*, vol. 4, 14.

55. C.-L. Montesquieu, *Les Lettres persanes*, Letter LXIV, 94.
56. Rousseau, *Discours sur l'Économie politique*, 251.
57. Rousseau, *Émile*, Book II, 150. Whence my reservations when J. Starobinski thinks he is justified in saying that 'Jean-Jacques works towards overthrowing any form of authority which is externally imposed'.
58. M. Ozouf, *L'École de la France. Essais sur la Révolution, l'Utopie et l'Enseignement*, Paris, 1984, 83.
59. Ibid.,
60. L. Jaume, *Le Discours jacobin et la Démocratie*, Paris, 1989, 203.
61. Ozouf, *L'Homme régénéré*, 120.
62. Robespierre insisted on the idea that the architecture should be such as to ensure that sessions of the parliamentary assembly could be held in the presence of 12,000 spectators (10 May 1793,*Archives parlementaires*, 1/64/431–432), adding : 'Leave obscurity and secret ballots to criminals and to slaves: free men wish to have the nation to witness what they think. This way of doing things educates the people in republican virtues' (433/1).
63. Rabaut de Saint-Étienne, see above, note 40.
64. J. Starobinski, *1789. Les Emblèmes de la Raison*, 45.
65. Several examples are to be found in Chassin, *La Vendée patriote*, vol. 3, 255; 274, and vol. 4, 230, 234 and 319.
66. Ozouf, *L'Homme régénéré*, 9; and 144.
67. Rousseau, *Émile*, Book I, 422. See also, on the importance of civic liturgies in classical times, Rousseau, *Gouvernement de Pologne*, 958.
68. *Archives parlementaires*, 1/55/346/1. Rabaut goes on: 'This secret was well known among the priests', who had the gift of extracting the maximum advantage out of 'everything that nature and art placed within their reach' and he goes on to catalogue these as if they were part of some vast attempt at sensualist conditioniong.
69. Ibid.
70. Rousseau, *Émile*, Book I, 39.
71. Ibid., Book IV, ('vicaire savoyard'), 423.
72. D. Diderot, *Mémoires pour Catherine II* (1773–74), Paris, 1966, 245.
73. Examples of lists are given in Ozouf, *L'Homme régénéré*, 10 and 144; or *Archives parlementaires*, 1/64/427 et circa.
74. M.Ozouf,*L'Homme régénéré*, 8.
75. I refer readers to my study of 'Le calendrier révolutionnaire', a paper originally given at the colloquium *Le Droit entre laïcisation et néo-sacralisation*, Université de Picardie, November 1993, published Paris, 1997, 215–27.
76. *Archives parlementaires*, 1/76/695/2.
77. J.-J. Rousseau, *La Nouvelle Héloïse* (1761), Part V, Letter VII, Paris, 1988, 589.
78. These quotations are from the speech made by Fabre d'Églantine on 24 October 1793: *Archives parlementaires*, 1/77/500 to 502.
79. *Archives parlementaires*, 1/77/503/1.
80. Report on behalf of the Committee for Public Safety to the Convention, 11th germinal Year II, 31 March 1794: *Archives parlementaires*, 1/87/632/1. Fabre was executed on 6 April.
81. Ibid., 654/2, on the same 11th germinal.
82. This quotation is given in J. Tulard, J.-F. Fayard, and A.Fierro, *Histoire et Dictionnaire de la Révolution française*, Paris, 1987, 811. A more precise reference is not available.

Chapter 8

ROBESPIERRE

We mustn't be too hard on Maximilien Robespierre. It is no easy matter for a son of the Enlightenment and, morever, a disciple of Rousseau – a man already difficult enough to understand in the abstract – to find himself in hands-on control of a country like France at such a thankless time. It was enough to make anyone lose their bearings. And it is quite clear that the reproach which Robespierre levelled against Fabre d'Églantine is one that could equally well be levelled against Rousseau himself. In just as striking a manner, though it is perhaps less generally recognised, Robespierre's criticism can be seen as going to the very heart of Rousseau's pedagogical theories as well as his politics,[1] which, as has already been said, are indissociable the one from the other in that the author himself maintained 'both together form a complete whole'.[2] It is equally clear that Robespierre himself has recourse to the methods he denounces, and his own power base seeks to make good use of them. But he finds himself somewhat disorientated by certain false divisions in eighteenth-century thinking: he is caught in the jaws of a pair of pincers representing the two terms of a contradiction. On the one hand, he feels duty bound to reject the militant reductionism associated with the principles on which this type of manipulation is based. On the other hand, he believes he is able to counter these principles with another set of principles which in fact imply the same reductionist ideas but in a far more insidious form. Despite appearances to the contrary, Robespierre's principles lead him to justify the same sort of practices as those he attacks, but which he more or less comes to adopt as his own, or which, at the very least, are adopted by his government. The least one can say is that the situation is not very clear.

The basic problem is that the dramatic and critical nature of the situation in which Robespierre found himself led him to overstress qualities of abnegation and self-sacrifice, and as a result to demand from his fellow-citizens something that the anthropology of the age has decreed them to be technically incapable of providing, to the extent that it had even banished it from its list of mental categories, namely, they are asked to make an *effort*. What is more, he was asking this of a people that, for several years, had been driven either into the dead-end of constant protestation or the dead-end of unobstructed, facile thinking. Obviously, this sudden about-turn could only expose him to the full brunt of a counter-offensive from the theoreticians of a mechanically legitimised self-interest, which they considered as the only possible foundation for public or private life. In the 'corridors of power' what he saw prospering was precisely the cynicism and the corruption that manage to shield themselves behind the façade of self-legitimising anthropological principles.[3] 'The treacherous friend, the disloyal debtor, the anonymous sneak, the dishonest judge', all find themselves conveniently justified by the moral nihilism that is omnipresent in the theories of the day.[4] Contrary to what had commonly been believed, unleashing the free play of the powers of self-interest had not spontaneously led to a state of social harmony, but rather to dissension, to the declaration of unforgiving hatreds, and to the mutual destruction of the philanthropists themselves. The latter, however, had been warned. As early as 1759, the Faculty of Theology in Paris had sounded the alarm bells, saying of the followers of Helvétius and company: 'Above all, they should be wary of one day being obliged to actually create this republic for which they are so keen to draw up the plans, and in which men, solely driven by self-interest, lawless, without religion and without any means of checking the fires of passion, will *mutually destroy* each other, ... and will thus rid the earth of an inhuman breed which does it nothing but dishonour'.[5]

In a word, Robespierre is too well placed not to see the practical and the theoretical links between the weight of the materialistic tendencies in Enlightenment thinking and the immorality, or amorality, underpinning patterns of behaviour. As far as the construction of society is concerned, materialism and atheism are concepts with which he has little truck, and for good reason. Rousseau was well aware of the fact: there is no such thing as a 'man who reasons correctly', who does not see 'immediately, that when he rejects the idea of a prime cause and explains everything by reference to matter and to movement he is undermining any notion of morality in human life'.[6] For this very reason, just as Robespierre himself disavowed it, Voltaire would have frowned upon Fouché's indiscretion in having inscribed over the entrance to the cemetery at Nevers, in October 1793: 'Death is an eternal sleep'. What if the simple-minded took it into their heads to actually believe such a thing? And so we see Robespierre decide to take a daring initiative and have *atheism and materialism outlawed by law* through the decree of 18th floréal Year II (7 May 1794). The first article of this decree does not involve itself in metaphysical debate but states quite coldly and simply: 'The French nation acknowledges the existence of a Supreme Being and that the soul is immortal'.[7] This is a famous decree and it was accompanied, on the same day, by a famous speech[8] which deserves our full attention because it has been cited, unwisely in my view, but in a quite understandable if ill-judged attempt to offer a definitive proof that the materialistic and therefore reductionist nature of the doctrines that inspired the Revolution were not as deep-rooted as I have been arguing.

On the contrary, however, not only do Robespierre's efforts in this respect confirm the very importance of what he is seeking to outlaw, but the way he goes about it also proves that his 'spiritualism' is tainted with the same basic weaknesses as that of his master, Rousseau, on whose memory a whole section of the speech heaps praise.[9] It is interesting to see the principal actor in the Revolution, at this its most climactic point, attacking what seem to be the most distinctive features of Enlightenment thinking – a current of thought in which materialism was so strong an element that even the spiritualists of the day were attracted to it, including Rousseau himself who valiantly and indignantly threw down the gauntlet to the materialists while simultaneously and rather indecisively, turning out the quite ambiguous *Matérialisme du Sage*.[10] Following in these very footsteps, Robespierre in turn speaks of the link that exists between, on the one hand, the hedonistic lifestyle of these men who, he also reminds us, cluttered up the corridors of power under the monarchy and went bowing and scraping at the feet of tyrants,[11] and on the other hand, the substance of their doctrines – arguments deriving from their own corruption and which were used in turn to legitimise it,[12] in a never-ending vicious circle. In particular he attacks the sect 'known under the name of *Encyclopédiste*', many of whose 'leaders had become important figures within the State'.[13] Nor should we forget that Robespierre himself had been present some eighteen months earlier in a session of the Jacobin Club when the bust of the Epicurean Mirabeau stoically allowed itself to be smashed to pieces by the assembly. It was Robespierre himself who personally saw to it that the bust of Helvétius underwent the same fate on the very spot by whipping the meeting up into a sort of rabid frenzy that had disastrous consequences for the unsuspecting work of art.[14] The standing enjoyed by 'libertines' and the 'privileged children of the age' was clearly in a downward spiral.[15] Almost thirty years earlier, one of Helvétius' correspondents had warned him that, as a wealthy man, he would have a great deal to lose by the Revolution that his theories were ushering in.[16]

As we have said, what the speech and the decree both specifically reject are atheism[17] and any refusal to accept that the soul is immortal. And it is important to understand that the battle being waged around these two themes has a very precise objective. It is not, as we might easily be led to imagine, in order to create a more social atmosphere by propagating fine sentiments among men, but rather in order to keep alive a conviction that is vital, and can be considered indispensable, to the very existence and well-being of the sociopolitical fabric: namely, the belief in the personal *responsibility* of each and every individual. This is quite logical. Suppressing any view of man's inner being that is at odds with the view that it consists of a purely passive substance has clear consequences: it encourages a nihilistic outlook and it tends to strip mankind of any sense of responsibility for his actions. Of course, it goes without saying that this tendency was too far removed from practical reality to lead on directly to the absolute results that logically follow from it: in this respect, things were not quite as bad as all that. But the tendency was nevertheless sufficiently strong and sufficiently in evidence for it to have disturbing effects on the finely tuned mechanism of the individual consciences of men, and to have effects too on public attitudes at a time when, day by day, the boundaries of what was possible and what was impossible seemed to be subject to constant upheaval. It is probably enough to turn our attention to a single case in point, but one whose seriousness makes it an especially revealing example. The numerous, quite incredible, atrocities that were perpetrated in Vendée lose some of their edge, in a subjective sense at least, when they are set against the anthropological system of values which the perpetrators had been led to adopt by the spirit of the times in which they were living.

I have had occasion to examine the Vendée question elsewhere.[18] Suffice it to say here that General Turreau, shortly before sending his deadly columns into action, and worried at the seeming unwillingness of the Convention and the Committee to clearly authorise this purifying mission, reacts by stating that, in this campaign, he is nothing more than 'the passive agent of the legislature'.[19] Passive agent: the collocation of these two words is very interesting indeed. If due philosophic rigour is applied, there is no alternative but to see them as mutually exclusive, and for this very reason they seem to me to take on a very special symbolic value. The serious ambiguity of Enlightenment thinking, with its tendency to go against all the dictates of common sense and stubbornly deny that there exists any active principle within man – this whole ambiguity seems to come to a head, one might say, in the incongruous juxtaposition of these two words. And what bestows an exceptional degree of significance on the symbolism at work here is the fact that this combination of two theoretically incompatible words – *passive agent* – should occur on the eve of a military campaign, above the signature of the man who organised and carried out what must be considered the most atrocious massacres and the worst devastation of the whole century, because they were coldly and calculatedly planned for reasons of political advantage. Scarcely two months later, representatives travelling on a mission write to the General saying, 'everything, except victory, exposes you to being held responsible, and this will be no illusory responsibility'.[20] What is quite clear is that if I attempted to undertake a detailed exegesis of this expression it would shed little light on the case. But at least it has the merit of highlighting all the equivocal elements involved.

The idea of individual responsibility is thus dangerously threatened in a way that would seem to presage a state of increasing anarchy, as far as individual attitudes are concerned, and this at the very moment when assuming complete control of men's attitudes has been identified as the most pressing political problem. And it is in support of this urgent undertaking that appeal is made to the two invaluable dogmas of the immortality of the soul and the existence of God, dogmas which are politically irreplaceable. The objective which has to be achieved – the complete transparency of man's inner being – is an unrealisable aim in the particular circumstances of the time and given the scientific knowledge that was available. There is some corner of the human consciousness that always escapes the probing of those who would like to know everything, in the hope of being able to control everything. And it would be wrong for individuals to assume that this partial opacity offers them some sort of immunity, it would be wrong for anybody to end up convincing themselves 'that their destiny is controlled by a blind force that lashes out indiscriminately at vice and at virtue alike',[21] and that consequently they run no risk at all if they choose to please themselves in everything they do. Rousseau rebuked the 'century's brilliant authors' for having given credence to the idea that 'conscience and remorse are mere illusions and prejudice, since one can no more congratulate oneself on a good deed that one has been obliged to carry out, than one can reproach oneself for a misdeed that one did not have the power to prevent oneself from committing'.[22] The *philosophes*, he said again and again, have demolished morality, 'they have undermined its very bases by destroying all religion, any notion of free-will, any sense of remorse',[23] and indeed this was true. In 1760, Palissot's play *Les Philosophes*, which was considered so distasteful by those whom it attacked, gave a comic twist to these very criticisms:

> When I cheated Cydalise I confess I felt quite awful:
> But I feel a good deal better now I know that cheating's lawful,[24]

as did a satiric couplet which targeted *De l'Esprit*:

> What an incomparable book
> Is the book, *De l'Esprit*!
> It lets us all off the hook.
> No regrets. We're not free![25]

As we know, in his second book, Helvétius goes even further. 'Remorse', he writes, 'is *nothing more* than an advance awareness of the physical suffering to which vice exposes us. Consequently, remorse is an effect of our own physical sensitivity'.[26] This explains the rebuke that the King's counsel at the Parlement de Paris was to address to him at the beginning of 1774, trying to establish that 'if a man finds it useful to commit a crime without any fear of being punished, he will be wicked without feeling any remorse, and without being a criminal'.²⁷ It is certainly very interesting to see Robespierre's battle in the month of floréal Year II, slotting quite neatly into a long line of opposition to the *philosophes*, that had been undertaken by, among others, the royal censors.

Such a phenomenon is really quite easy to explain. It was a result of the very Rousseauist colouring that Robespierre's thinking had taken on, but also, and more importantly, it was a result of a need to respond to the imperatives of that particular moment of history. In September 1793, the Committee for Public Safety was questioning the principle which argued that 'that thing is honest which is useful'.²⁸ By the following spring the internal political situation had hardened to such an extent that it came to be seen by Robespierre as of paramount importance that no one should succumb to the laxity of 'a system which, bundling together the destinies of good and wicked people, allows no difference to be made between men except that established by pure chance, and allows no other form of arbitration than the law of the strongest or the most cunning'.²⁹ On the contrary, what is needed is that each individual should feel in his heart of hearts that 'a sanction has been given to moral precepts by a power superior to Man',³⁰ that he should know himself to be, or think himself to be, watched over by a potentially vengeful Being, that he should know, or think, that the part of himself which he can hide away from the eyes of his fellow-men is naked beneath the gaze of a Supreme Being who *punishes* and *rewards* mankind in the great beyond. 'Leave all that behind', said the 'vicaire savoyard', 'I can see nothing more than injustice, hypocrisy and deceit in the company of men', and free rein accorded 'to self-interest'.³¹ Clearly, such pressure cannot be exerted if the soul believes itself to be 'a mere puff of wind that dies away at the entrance to the tomb'. The dual dogma that is promulgated in the floréal decree is therefore quite specifically intended 'to compensate for the inadequacy of an authority founded in man alone',³² it is intended to go some way towards making up for the persistent inability of the governors (an inability which it is hoped is only temporary) to unreservedly conquer the psychic apparatus of those whom they govern.

And in this whole affair there is a clear sense that it is probably much less a matter of defending some philosophical conviction that human responsibility exists, than it is of preserving, among those who are governed, the very useful concept of *feeling*. Which is far from being the same thing. This way of looking at things is not at all that of a realist. The

Rousseauist view that religion is simply a comforting illusion which it would be too cruel not to allow human beings to indulge themselves in, is a view that re-emerges in the month of floréal Year II. Rousseau railed against the 'sad doctrines' of amoral materialism because they 'deprive the afflicted of the last source of consolation in their misery',[33] 'cruel doctrines' he writes elsewhere, 'which oppress the poor and the unfortunate', by stripping them of 'any hope, any consolation'.[34] In his floréal speech, Robespierre once more took up this argument in the very same terms: he offsets against these 'sad doctrines'[35] the 'consoling dogmas' that Rousseau had used all his eloquence to defend.[36] And a few days later, when Jullien from the Drôme was offering thanks on behalf of the Jacobin Club to his colleagues in the Convention for the floréal decree, he once again speaks of the need not to 'reduce poor unfortunate virtue to a state of distress or despair by exposing it to these horrible ideas', that are propagated everywhere by the general tendency to nihilism.[37]

It seems to me that this theme of religion as an illusion that has powers to console men, is really of only secondary importance. But where it is very useful indeed is in underlining the fact that the outbreak of religiosity that occurs in floréal (May 1794) has a clearly *utilitarian* purpose. In my opinion, the decree is less concerned with recognising the existence of a vengeful or rewarding God than it is with 'the *need* to recognise the existence of a God who avenges crime and rewards virtue', and these are the words of Voltaire.[38] So the real purpose of this outbreak of religiosity, over and above that of providing solace to humanity, is to force each and every individual to take cognisance of the fact that there exists an effective system of transcendent repression operated by the Supreme Being. As Rousseau said, and as we have to fully recognise, 'the moral order ... is ultimately located in a different system that we can never seek out on this earth, but to which we shall all, one day, be held accountable'.[39] It is socially desirable that people believe this to be true,[40] to such an extent that Rousseau would have liked to have written a treatise on the subject, *De l'Utilité de la Religion*.[41] And in the long run it is not really important whether the spiritual and transcendent worlds exist or not, providing at least that the belief in their existence produces the desired effect. Robespierre says, 'I cannot understand how nature could have suggested to men fictions that are of greater use than real truths; and if the existence of God and the immortality of the soul were mere imaginary notions, they would still have to be counted among the noblest products of the human mind'.[42] This rather contrived and embarrassed line of reasoning reveals a great deal, and occasionally the ambiguity it contains is expressed in the form of a confession: 'As far as the Legislator is concerned, everything that is *useful* and good on a practical level can be deemed to be *true*. The idea that the Supreme Being exists and that the soul is immortal is a constant reminder of the need for justice: it is therefore a social and republican idea. (*Applause*)'.[43] One may well castigate utilitarianism,[44] but it is difficult to avoid it. In the event, it is this that determines metaphysical truth. Diderot was quite right when he said: 'Usefulness is the criterion that encompasses everything'.[45]

In spite of all this, it is not my belief that Robespierre was insincere in matters concerning religion, but it is clear that such subjective views offer only a fragile and uncertain foundation for questions touching faith and dogma. Someone like Lequinio argued that man had the right to 'freely worship the god that he finds *depicted in his own imagination*',[46] this expression too is worth its weight in gold. The sensational legalisation of these profound metaphysical matters which is embodied in the floréal decree can be seen as counterbalancing the ontological uncertainty as to what is deemed useful for people to believe. But it is also the price to be paid for this subjectivism, because if inner feeling is everything in such matters, it is essential, for reasons of public order, that something be done about those who refuse to accept the norm, for example, beginning with quite simply making such behaviour an offence. This may seem surprising but it is the way things are. It is exactly the same trick as is used in respect of the arguments concerning the collective will. The notion of a collective will can only have any real effect once it has been accepted that less importance is to be accorded to the will of any single individual.[47] Individual consciences may be seen as sovereign but they are also seen as passive, and there is no way of avoiding the urgent need to act on their behalf, precisely because their very passivity makes their sovereign status a dangerous thing. It is important that the people should be clear as to what 'the French people accepts' in respect of religious dogma and metaphysical beliefs, even if it means legislating so that there is no misunderstanding. There is no easy way out of this. Despite his real desire to respond to the concrete problems which he faces, Robespierre is ill-equipped to cope with the doctrinal jousting to which he is here exposing himself. Just like Rousseau himself, deep down he has too much sympathy for the point of view of the very people whose arguments he opposes and so he ends up trapped, going round in circles.

The theme of egoism, which appears in the speech, provides another significant example of this fact. Indeed, in attacking these doctrines, Robespierre particularly criticises the fact that they invoke self-interest as the sole motive behind human behaviour in far too crude a way. He simply states the case here rather than seeking to enter into a debate on the matter. But it is worth noting that, in the face of cynical arguments justifying self-interest, he does not respond by brandishing the flag of generosity. His opposition is a little more subtle. Against what he calls 'vile' self-interest he simply opposes a type of self-interest that is 'generous' and 'beneficent'.[48] When placed on the spot like this, his pathetic inability to offer a better counter-argument illustrates the fact that he is very much a man of his time and that deep down he accepts the logic behind the arguments, which, with a sort of heavy fatalism, dominate the scene. As a man whose business it is to govern the people, he may find some of the consequences of this logic repulsive, but he nevertheless shares it, because at that time self-interest, in all things, was the only reason that could be imagined as an explanation for the way men act.

It is simply that Robespierre shared these views in their Rousseauist version, which recommends cultivating, and expects each and every one of us to cultivate, only the 'good' form of self-interest called *self-love*. It is this form of self-interest that takes the trouble to be deserving of the benevolence of others (since in order to 'fully enjoy oneself', 'the help of others' is essential),[49] and thus constantly seeks to make social life and the company of others a pleasant thing. In 1793, Volney asked the question: 'Is self-interest not incompatible with life in society?' And he offered this reply to himself: 'No: because ... *self-love* is not only compatible with society it is one of its *firmest foundations*, through the need to avoid harming others for fear that they might repay us by harming us in return'.[50] It is clearly this particular form of 'generous' self-interest that Robespierre had in mind and wished to glorify when, on the same day, he proposed that there should be an annual *fête nationale* dedicated to Disinterestedness.[51] And after denouncing Epicurianism,[52] the force behind all the 'sad doctrines' of wasteful self-interest,[53] he also proposed an annual *fête nationale* dedicated to Stoicism, in memory of 'that sublime sect of Stoics who held the dignity of man in such high esteem'.[54] Not that the height of their esteem was so great that it could prevent even Stoicism from being congenitally imprisoned within a logic that defended the sovereignty of egoism. It is clear, therefore, that, despite the 'generous' impulses discernible in his rhetoric and in line with contemporary thinking and its Hellenistic models,[55] Robespierre remains embroiled in a view of the individual as necessarily and inexorably wrapped up in himself and as having a single aim, which is to satisfy his own self-interest.

To give a little more substance to these arguments it is worth pointing out that, during this period, it is not uncommon that the word 'egoist' appears to be insufficiently charged with pejorative connotations and very often it is felt that the word has to be qualified with a specifically uncomplimentary adjective, the resulting expression in no way being seen as a linguistic redundancy. Thus people speak of 'vile egoists', or 'cowardly egoists', or 'foul self-interest', or 'selfish egoists', 'base egoists', or 'arid self-interest', and so on.[56] In the *Encyclopédie*, the word was still considered a neologism, and Rousseau had claimed to be using it 'in its true meaning' (which for him was pejorative), which seems to indicate that usage was slow to become fixed.[57] This lack of certainty can also be illustrated by reference to sources in Vendée. Thus, at the end of 1793, when Bréard, a member of the Convention, was castigating certain 'vile egoists' in the west, he suggested that he might bring them round to a more civically-minded way of seeing things by speaking to them 'in terms of their own self-interest'.[58] And then again, only three weeks before the floréal Year II decree, his colleague Hentz uses some surprising expressions in a speech he does the honour of making to the society of the people at Fontenay-le-Comte. He 'said that they had to put up with everything without complaining: that anyone who complained was an egoist, a friend of Charette, because the Nation would reward them generously'.[59] As it stands, this phrase is meaningless: it is absurd to say, enemies of the nation are egoists *because* the Nation rewards generously. But we can guess what it means. Lukewarm patriots (immediately promoted to the status of friends of Charette, the leader of the anti-revolutionary rebels) are egoists, they are not happy with the sacrifices that the situation calls for; but above all they are *ill-advised* egoists, they cultivate precisely what Rousseau calls 'ill-understood self-interest',[60] because if they wholeheartedly supported the Nation, *they would benefit* from it because the Nation would reward them generously (the 'generosity' of the Nation is itself not disinterested here). They would still be egoists but all of a sudden they would have become *intelligent* egoists, and we should take that to mean, egoists who meet the approval of those who govern. This is indeed straight talking. But what he says literally is something quite different, and absurd, because the way of thinking about these matters at the time was bogged down in two completely contradictory notions: that of *self-interested altruism* and that of *generous egoism*, in much the same way that there are contradictory notions co-present in the term *passive agent*.

Similarly, we might be justified in presuming that Robespierre's opinions on the nature of man's inner being and the rights that the great reformer might exercise over it, are not very far removed from the sort of views that we have encountered thus far and which I have adopted as the basis of my central argument. This presumption seems justified in the first place, in that the doctrinal importance that Rousseau takes on, tends to make it very unlikely that the opposite view can be entertained as a serious prospect. Secondly, there is the fact that the power that Robespierre and a few others wielded is precisely the sort of power that involves the large-scale deployment of a range of methods consistent with the supposition that man's inner being is an essentially passive space which it is important that the legislator should occupy in so far as this is possible. This is why the 'spiritualist' content of the floréal sermon seems to me to be based on such shaky ground. Its weakest point, and the one which in my view is enough to bring the whole argument crashing down, is undoubtedly the passage in which Robespierre confesses that the ideal thing, from the point of view of the doctrinaire who finds himself in a position of power, would be to achieve a situation in which the citizen was *dispensed from exercising his reason*. 'The masterpiece, for society, in matters relating to morality would be to create a very *rapid instinctive reaction* within man, such that he was led to choose to do good and to avoid evil without his reason ever being consulted for its advice'.[61] Robespierre is, in fact, saying here that if man were to act as if he were a perfect automaton he would be *the masterpiece, for society*. This would be the perfectly regulated society, the absolute utopia (for what is utopia if it is not the 'masterpiece, for society?'), and extremely convenient for the statesman, who would find himself with practically nothing to do. Rousseau had remarked, 'If he could ensure in some way that everybody behaved well, he himself would have nothing more to do, and *the masterpiece of* his work would be to be in a position where he could idle away his time'. This ideal situation presupposes, and here we encounter one of the leitmotifs of Rousseau's thinking, a control *'over men's wills* even more than over their actions'.[62]

It is difficult to overestimate the importance of the wish that Robespierre is expressing here. Couched in the way it is, it also reiterates Rousseau's deep distrust of the power of reason which Rousseau called 'this ample vehicle for all stupidities'[63] – the same power of reason which Saint Thomas Aquinas, who arrived on the scene too early to have been in a position to enjoy the advantages of the Enlightenment, had recognised as 'the first principle of human actions'.[64] 'I have more confidence in my *instinct* than in my reason', Julie, the new Héloïse, had confided.[65] Rousseau also said, 'Sensual man is the creation of nature; thinking man is the creation of opinion; the latter is the dangerous one'.[66] And he goes on to ask:'Why create difficulties for oneself when one can enjoy life? ... And yet this choice, which is so reasonable, is made neither by the reason nor by the will; it is the work of *pure instinct'*, the author is, in the event, drawing on the authority of his own experience and taking pride in the fact of his having 'for sixty years ... followed the impulses of nature alone'.[67] And we already know to what extent this particular theme is of absolutely central importance in his work.

What is equally clear, but possibly less commonly recognised, is that when Robespierre talks in this way he is not very far removed from many other writers of the eighteenth-century, in relation to whom Rousseau's perceived marginality, although real, is partially, but nevertheless broadly, based on superficial differences. Rousseau would agree with Montesquieu's assessment that, 'It is much better to treat man as a being who feels rather than treat him as a being that thinks'.[68] And as for Voltaire, who was uneasy with anything to do with metaphysics, is it not the case that he congratulates himself on having 'returned to the fold of feelings after having strayed into the realm of reasoning'?[69] And does he not also claim that 'instinct is a far surer thing than virtue'?[70] He was also proud to consider himself as one of the select club of thinking people. Indeed, he was convinced that 'when the populace at large gets involved in reasoning, nothing is safe'.[71] Is Robespierre saying anything very different, albeit in a different way and a little less bluntly? Not only Rousseau but the whole of the Enlightenment tend to think in much the same way on this point: fundamentally, man is especially good when considered as an animal. He is 'a good and fair-minded animal who seeks enjoyment', and Diderot says, as often as Rousseau does, that the use of the intellectual function does damage to 'the animal condition'.[72] And this is why, according to Grégoire, 'if Jews were mere savages, it would be easy to regenerate them'.[73] With a subtle cynicism, Helvétius waxes lyrical on a similar theme. In substance, he writes that we should be thankful that calculating 'prudence' is so rare among men, who are dominated by their impulses for the greater good of the species and of society: if the scheming prompted by the prudent side of man's nature were ever to spread widely, who would ever decide to get married, for example? The supposed virtue of prudence would be 'the most disastrous gift' possible for the nation, since on the contrary, it is 'to man's thoughtlessness that future generations will owe their existence'.[74] And he concludes by saying that 'prudence is a desirable thing in only a very small number of citizens'.[75] Here, once again, we come across the recurrent theme of the small, knowledgable, manipulating élite which enjoys the benefits of its position, and the herd which is closely observed and which is controlled from a distance, without being aware of it: a group that was used so often during the Revolution, especially in Paris, as a manoeuvrable mob. Voltaire speaks of 'thinking people who, in the long run, rule over the rest',[76] whereas Robespierre, who is a democrat, but one undermined by troubles of all kinds, praises 'the unsullied and courageous minority' to the real detriment of 'the corrupt and imbecilic majority'.[77] Voltaire, once again, judges it to be 'appropriate that the people should be guided and not that they be instructed. They are not worthy of being instructed'.[78]

It is quite clear that the tremendous effort towards providing instruction that the Jacobin upheaval conceived and planned for citizens of all ages does not contradict this remark of Voltaire's, in the sense that what the Jacobins intended was not a form of education designed to strengthen man's talents or to reinvigorate an active principle present in each and every one of us, but rather a complete process of moulding and standardising man's inner being. Rabaut Saint-Étienne prided himself on the fact that, in order to achieve this aim, and by the method used to achieve it, appeal would be made to 'the magic of reason'.[79] This is yet another confession. Whatever one may choose to think about magic and reason, it is difficult to accept in this way that reason could operate through magic channels, or at the very least could operate in the same way as magic. As far as the theme that interests us is concerned it is quite clear that, throughout this paroxysmal period, the perspective has in no way changed from what it previously was. For the main part, the viewpoint is one that holds man to be a purely passive being, totally open to manipulating influences, and, in a way, more so than ever, we might almost say, because of the prevailing circumstances. The spiritualism of a Robespierre or a Saint-Just, following on from, and developing upon, that of someone like Rousseau provides an obvious proof of this, in so far as it does nothing whatsoever to make a break with the reductionism of the age. At best it simply tugs at the shackles a little. 'Our aim is to create an order of things such that a universal tendency towards good should be established'. A *tendency towards good*, and which will be established: the expression is Saint-Just's, and Rousseau too used it, more or less.[80] It confirms that we should expect nothing at all from human initiative and that men's good behaviour can only result from a programmed environment, in exactly the same way that the opposite, the 'antisocial vice' of the Vendée rebels, can be analysed by Merlin from Thionville in terms of their being purely a product of the landscape they inhabit.[81] As for Robespierre, he also believed that 'in order to try to make oneself accomplished in the arts, all one has to do is follow one's passions'.[82] A confidence such as this is also significant. It too comes from the floréal speech which it would have been a pity not to examine. This speech, by the way, was not afraid to announce the fact that 'it contained deep truths of great importance for human happiness'.[83] Exceptional arrangements for its diffusion and even for its translation 'into every language',[84] should this be deemed necessary, were put in place.

The nations which received news of events in Paris probably learned of Robespierre's tragic demise even before they could have guessed at the contents of this speech, which was intended to communicate 'deep truths' to them – truths which they had to forego as best they could. During these eventful years, they had an opportunity to ponder on all that was being perpetrated, both in France and coming out of France, in the name of freedom. But it is extremely doubtful that anybody has paid sufficient attention to this strange fact: that the freedom that was being demanded (or imposed on people) was to be achieved through the efforts of an, admittedly, diverse intellectual movement, whose followers essentially shared this common characteristic that they believed or presumed man to be devoid of free will, or they tended to act as though this were the case. This 'freedom' without 'freedom' is a strange thing indeed. I am well aware that pointing this out does not dispense me from undertaking the more detailed sorts of analysis that this fact and this problem call for, and in comparison to which the theme we are considering in these pages pales somewhat in significance. All I am seeking to do here is to point out the fact that this anomaly actually existed and to suggest that if we fail to recognise its existence we may be depriving ourselves of tasting the full flavour of the revolutionary epic.

The campaign in Vendée offers one final example of this. In March 1794, Ripault de la Cathelinière, a rebel who had been taken prisoner and who had been rebuked for having 'wreaked havoc and mayhem in the name of religion and the King', replied to his captors, 'You deserve exactly the same rebuke, since you sacrifice the people in the name of freedom, which is a mere illusion'.[85] There is nothing very interesting about all this, one might suppose. And indeed, if we simply apply the categories of the various types of academic historiography, there is nothing unusual about a nobleman from Vendée, who has been captured in battle, describing as a mere 'illusion' the idea of freedom held by the Revolution and, we might suppose, by the Enlightenment. But this is precisely the point. If we remind ourselves, for example, that for Voltaire freedom is 'in any event, a beautiful illusion', that in his opinion it is even 'in fact, an absurd illusion',[86] that for d'Holbach 'free will is an illusion', and that later he says 'the feeling' that man has 'of his own freedom is an illusion',[87] that for Manon Lescaut's turbulent father, 'everything that they say about freedom at the church of Saint-Sulpice is an illusion',[88] that if we are to believe Diderot, 'the word freedom is a word that has no meaning',[89] does it not then become obvious that the captive nobleman's reply suddenly demands to be viewed in quite a different light? Either – at very least –he is aware of the fact that he is catching his accusers in their own doctrinal trap, or, quite simply, their doctrinal position is also his own position, since so many noblemen of all ranks, and including those in the army fighting for the Catholic and royalist cause, were, as we all know, familiar with Enlightenment thinking. The views people held concerning human nature perhaps provide a thread which is insufficiently valued as a way of guiding us through the labyrinth of the Revolutionary period.

Notes

1. See above, 67 and thereafter, and 75 and thereafter.
2. See above, 79.
3. J. Starobinski, *1789. Les Emblèmes de la Raison*, Paris, 47.
4. B. Constant, *Des Effets de la Terreur*, Year V, quoted by J. Starobinski, ibid.
5. In *Corr. gén. d'Helvétius*, vol. 2, Toronto/Oxford, 1984, Appendix 14, 403. This was concerning the censorship of *De l'Esprit*.
6. Letter to Paul-Claude Moultou, 14 February 1769: Rousseau, *Corr.*, vol. 37, 57.
7. This text has been subjected to an intelligent analysis: Fr.-X. Testu, 'Un texte méconnu: l'article premier du décret du 1er floréal an II', Conference given in the Première Chambre civile at the Court of Appeal, 13 January 1987, Order of lawyers at the *Conseil d'état* and the Court of Appeal.
8. *Archives parlementaires*, 1/90/132–40 (the speech), and 140–41 (the decree).
9. Ibid., 137/1.
10. See above, 55–56.
11. *Archives parlementaires*, 1/90/137/1. 'In their writings they showed great pride but they went crawling on all fours in the antechambers of the powerful'. This was true, and Rousseau wrote as much at the time.
12. Ibid., 134/1–2
13. Ibid., 137/1.
14. Session of 5 December 1792: F.-A. Aulard, ed., *La Société des Jacobins. Recueil de Documents pour l'Histoire du Club des Jacobins de Paris*, vol. 4, Paris, 1892, 550: 'Helvétius was a schemer, a miserable dilletante, an immoral man, one of the most cruel persecutors of dear Jean-Jacques Rousseau, to whom we pay homage. If Helvétius had been alive today, do not make the mistake of thinking that he would have been on the side of freedom'; and 551: 'The enthusiastic response that this speech provokes forestalls any decision being taken by the Society .... The meeting rises and demands at once that the busts of Mirabeau and Helvétius be taken down . While everyone *was glaring threateningly* at them, two ladders were brought into the room amidst great applause and Mirabeau and Helvétius were brought down. These two busts are quickly broken, people rush forward and everyone wants to share in the honour of trampling them underfoot. – After this civic ceremony, the Society turned its attention to the day's agenda' et cetera.
15. See above, 42, 46 and 91.
16. A. Sabatier de Castres, 15 July 1766, speaking of 'the dangers of the dominant ideas of the century, which, unless a miracle happens, will bring about, before the end of the century, the fall of the clergy, and as a consequence of that, the fall of the monarchy, and as a consequence of this, the fall of all great landowners; and, reflect for a moment, Sir, that you are counted among these latter', *Corr. gén. d'Helvétius*, vol. 3, Toronto/Oxford, 1991, 260. Turgot frequently expressed his annoyance at the way Helvétius criticised a system from which he so richly benefited: letter to Condorcet, around the 8 December 1773: ibid., 464–65.
17. On this theme, see especially *Archives parlementaires*, 1/90/135/1 and 137/2.
18. See my publication *Sur les Droits de l'Homme et la Vendée*, ed. Dominique Martin Morin, Bouère, France, 1995, which develops a paper given at the Colloquium *Les Déclarations des Droits de l'an I*, (Poitiers, December 1993).

19. 26th nivôse Year II, 15 January 1794: Ch.-L. Chassin, *La Vendée patriote 1793–1795*, Mayenne, 1973, vol. 4, 249.
20. 20th ventôse Year II, 10 March 1794: ibid., 364.
21. Robespierre, *Archives parlementaires*, 1/90/135/2.
22. J.-J. Rousseau, *Deuxième Dialogue*, in *Œuvres complètes*, Pléiade, Paris, 1959, 842.
23. Rousseau, *Troisième Dialogue*, 967.
24. Palissot de Montenoy, *Les Philosophes, comédie*, Paris, 1760, 37. The original lines are:

> J'avais quelque regret à tromper Cydalise;
> Mais je vois clairement que la chose est permise.

25. *Corr. gén. d'Helvétius*, vol. 2, 304, beginning of the first of twenty verses. The original lines are:

> O l'incomparable livre
> Que le livre *De l'Esprit*!
> Des remords il nous délivre
> Par le code qu'il prescrit.

26. Helvétius, *De l'Homme* (1773), Paris, 1989, vol. 1, 173.
27. *Corr. gén. d'Helvétius*, vol. 3, 477.
28. Quoted by Chassin, *La Vendée patriote*, vol. 3,254.
29. *Archives parlementaires*, 1/90/137/2.
30. Ibid., 136/1.
31. J.-J. Rousseau, *Émile ou de l'Éducation*, Paris, 1966, Book IV, 411; and 412: 'Philosophe, your moral laws are very fine; but I beg you, show me where *punishments and rewards* are mentioned'.
32. *Archives parlementaires*, 1/90/136/1.
33. Rousseau, *Émile*, Book IV ('Vicaire savoyard') 408.
34. Rousseau, *Deuxième Dialogue*, 842 (and 814). 'This convenient philosophy of the fortunate and the wealthy' is not at all suitable for 'the masses' who 'not having experienced happiness in this life, need to have at least the hope and the consolations that this barbaric teaching robs them of' (*Troisième Dialogue*, 971).
35. *Archives parlementaires*, 1/90/140/1.
36. Ibid., 137/1.
37. Ibid., 389/1, 27th floréal Year II, 16 May 1794. As for Saint-Just, if he was outraged at the fact (11th germinal, 31 March) that anyone should attack the notion of 'the immortality of the soul', it was because this notion 'consoled Socrates on his death-bed' (*Archives parlementaires*., 1/87/632/2).
38. To the Duc de Richelieu, 28 October 1766, Voltaire, *Corr.*, vol. 8, 699.
39. Rousseau, *Troisième Dialogue*, 972.
40. On this point, see how Rousseau develops the idea, *Émile*, Book IV, 411, footnote, and *Troisième Dialogue*, 969.
41. Rousseau, *Troisième Dialogue*, 972, footnote.
42. *Archives parlementaires*, 1/90/135/2.
43. Ibid., 136/1.
44. See above, 132.
45. D. Diderot, *Pensées sur l'Interprétation de la nature*, 1753, second-hand quotation.
46. At Saintes, 1st nivôse Year II, 21 December 1793 : Chassin, *La Vendée patriote*, vol 3, 548.
47. See above, 67–68.

48. *Archives parlementaires*, 1/90/133/1.
49. See above, 58 ff. 'All forms of attachment are a sign of inadequacy: if each one of us had no need of other people we would see no reason to seek their company' (Rousseau, *Émile*, Book IV, 286–87).
50. C.-F. Volney, *La Loi naturelle, ou Principes physiques de la Morale* (1793), Paris, 1980, 48.
51. *Archives parlementaires*, 1/90/140/2, article 7 of the decree.
52. Ibid., 136/2.
53. Ibid., 137/2. On D'Holbach's admiration for Epicurus, see for example his book *Le Bon Sens*, Paris, 1971, 233.
54. *Archives parlementaires*, 1/90/136/2. 'Cato never hesitated between Epicurus and Zeno'. 'Stoicism saved the honour of human nature when it had fallen into a state of degradation' et cetera.
55. In January 1759, in Fréron's *L'Année Littéraire* (55–56) the abbé Arnaud reproached Helvétius with never having done anything except 'serving up re-hashed systems that would have been successful two thousand years ago if they were ever going to be successful at all' (quoted in *Corr. gén. d'Helvétius*, vol. 3, 35/2).
56. Several references: *Archives parlementaires*, 1/62/2/2, and 1/78/604/2; Lequinio, *Les Préjugés détruits*, Paris, 1792, 80; Chassin, *La Vendée patriote*, vol. 4, 106, footnote.
57. See above, 59.
58. Quoted in J. Crétineau-Joly, *Histoire de la Vendée militaire*, Paris, (1840–42), re-edited, 4 vols, 1979, vol. 1, 313.
59. Quoted in Chassin, *La Vendée patriote*, vol. 4, 454, 27th germinal Year II, 16 April 1794.
60. J.-J. Rousseau, *Considérations sur le Gouvernement de Pologne*, in *Œuvres complètes*, Pléiade, Paris, 1959, vol. 3, 974.
61. *Archives parlementaires*, 1/90/136/1.
62. J.-J. Rousseau, *Discours sur l'Économie politique*, in *Œuvres complètes*, Pléiade, Paris, vol. 3, 250.
63. Letter from Rousseau to Charles Bonnet, around 15 October 1755: Rousseau, *Corr.*, vol. 3, 186. Also from him: 'Reason, far from enlightening us, blinds us' (quoted by J. Maritain, *Trois Réformateurs. Luther, Descartes, Rousseau*, Paris, 1925, 213).
64. Saint Thomas Aquinas, *Summa Theologica*, Ia–IIæ, 58, 2.
65. Rousseau, *La Nouvelle Héloïse*, Part 2, Letter XVIII, 235.
66. Rousseau, *Deuxième Dialogue*, 808. Likewise: 'I possess an inner feeling which does not operate by syllogisms but which is far more persuasive than reason' (Rousseau, 'The art of enjoying and other fragments', in *Œuvres complètes*, Pléiade, vol. 1, Paris, 1959, 1,175).
67. Rousseau, *Deuxième Dialogue*, 854.
68. C.-L. Montesquieu, *Les Lettres persanes*, Paris, 1949, Letter XXXIII, 51.
69. Letter to Helvétius around 11 September 1738: *Corr. gén. d'Helvétius*, vol. 1, 10.
70. Letter to Mme Denis, 7 May 1754: Voltaire, *Corr.*, vol 4, 157.
71. Letter to Damilaville, 1 April 1766, ibid., vol. 8, 422. From a social point of view, it is 'essential that there should be ignorant beggars. If you were trying to exploit a piece of land like me, and if you owned a few ploughs, you would think the way I do'.
72. See above, 89 and 106.
73. Abbé Grégoire, *Essai sur le Régénération physique, morale et politique des Juifs*, (1788), Metz, 1789, 171. And he continues in this way: 'but they possess *acquired ignorance* which has sapped their intellectual faculties'.

74. C.-A. Helvétius, *De l'Esprit* (1758), Paris, 1988, 512.
75. Ibid., 513.
76. To d'Argental, 20 April 1769: Voltaire, *Corr.*, vol. 9, 872. We also read in *La Nouvelle Héloïse*, 210: 'Thus there is a small number of men and women who think for all the others, and on behalf of whom everyone else speaks and acts.'
77. Quoted by Jean-Marie Carbasse, 'Les responsables de la Terreur en Vendée: les hommes et le système', in *La Vendée dans l'Histoire*, published papers from the colloquium held at La Roche-sur-Yon, April 1993, Paris 1994, [341–57], 355, footnote 18. Laignelot, member of the Convention, held that it was for 'the minority to make the law', and says, boastingly, that it was a small minority that imposed the Republic on the rest (Chassin, *La Vendée patriote*, vol.4, 59).
78. To Damilaville, 19 March 1766: Voltaire, *Corr.*, vol 8, 409.
79. Speech, already quoted, made on 21 December 1792 :*Archives parlementaires*, 1/55/346/1.
80. *Archives parlementaires*, 1/85/518/1, 8th ventôse Year II, 26 February 1794. See above, 78.
81. *Archives parlementaires*, 1/78/604/1, 18th brumaire Year II, 8 November 1793.
82. *Archives parlementaires*, 1/90/132/2.
83. Ibid., 132/1
84. Ibid., 141/1
85. Report by Hentz and Francastel, of vendémiaire Year III, quoted in Chassin, *La Vendée patriote*, vol. 4, 338.
86. Voltaire, *Corr.*, vol. 3, 1,088 (1753, to Cideville), and vol. 10, 314 (1770; see above, 30).
87. D'Holbach, *Le Bon Sens*, 70, the title of Chapter LXXX; *Système de la Nature*, vol. 1, 234. See above, 15 and afterwards.
88. Abbé Prévost, *Manon Lescaut* (1731), Paris, 1990, 59.
89. Diderot, *Corr.*, vol.1, 255, letter of 1756. See above, 16–17.

≈ *Chapter 9* ≈

Making an Impression

After the 9th thermidor, and throughout the years that followed, it would be wrong to think that everything began to wind down. It is certainly true that, during this period, nothing like the dictatorship that went under the name of the Terror exists any more, and that the frequency of violent political acts diminishes. However, it would be far from the truth to suggest that such acts disappear entirely. Either they take on new forms or they flare up from time to time spasmodically. And yet it is true to say that, in hindsight, one is left with a distinct impression that such acts were on the decrease. But this is not at all the important point. What is important, in our view, is that in the minds of the people who had lived through the Revolution, there was, as the years went by, first of all an ever *more acute* sense of despair that they would ever break out of the chaotic and cruel chain of events that had been triggered off in 1789, and, secondly, at least in respect of those who govern or prided themselves that this was what they were doing, an increasingly *acute* sense of the urgent need to put to good advantage their influence over the innate pliability of men's psyches with a view to quickly establishing a stable society. It would be very worthwhile to follow in some detail the course taken, from the very beginning of the Revolution to the supposed end point that it is generally agreed should be assigned to it, by the very real obsession with 'finishing the Revolution'. But we shall restrict ourselves to investigating the extent to which the main theme we have been considering in these pages takes on a greater topical interest, and indeed a hitherto unprecedented degree of importance, in the years after thermidor.

In a France that has been through the mill of revolution and has finally emerged battered and bruised on the other side, who would not yearn for the tender care and attention, the soothing balms of a tutelary authority? Yes indeed, but there is this to consider: if the Terror was a form of 'anarchy' – and it is worth noting that this above all is the reproach levelled against it by those who managed to survive it – it nevertheless also deserved the name tyranny, another name by which people used to describe it and whose accuracy no one can seriously challenge. And this fact, until the very end of the maturation period that gave birth to the events of brumaire and their aftermath, works to prohibit not only all forms of authoritarianism but also anything that vaguely resembles it, including measures designed even for the protection of citizens. Hence the constitution of 1795, called the Constitution of Year III, which ushered in the Directory,[1] seems to be completely devoted to finding new ways of countering and rendering impotent any attempt at exercising power of any sort. Rendering power impotent: the paradox is discernible in the language used here because it exists in reality. Now, the new constitution comes into effect at the very moment when the individualism underpinning the doctrines on which the social contract is based, – an individualism which tends to promote a view of society as a particular arrangement of individual units – has, as a result of recent events, taken on a more pessimistic colouring. Men are not good, men are asocial. When we try to bring them back closer to nature they go berserk, they attack each other and show themselves for the 'ignoble savages' that they are. When the desire to establish politics as an agreement between contracting parties finds itself pushed into a dead-end of this sort, it automatically takes on a Hobbesian flavour and tends to hanker longingly after some vigorous form of authoritarianism, which is an option that the contemporary reaction to the Terror firmly rules out. In other words, the historical moment is such that it has the singular misfortune of having produced at one and the same time, a strong tendency towards authoritarianism and its exact opposite. This in-built tension contributes to the general sense of *malaise* that is characteristic of the period. 'I am annoyed that Hobbes is right' says Voltaire,[2] and the people who, like him, realised as much at the time were hardly in a position to proclaim the fact in public.

As a result, anyone who was toying with the idea of devoting his talents to the considerable task of social reconstruction that was called for (and the need for which is both suggested by, and exaggerated by, the habitually simplistic responses associated with the pessimistic version of political contractualism referred to above) – any such person had little choice but to envisage other means of achieving his ends than simply that of exercising authority. In a large country from which, for the time being, authority had been outlawed as something that was associated with blood-letting and with wounds which had not yet had the time to heal, creating a society out of its citizens necessarily meant adopting the very procedures that continued to be offered by Enlightenment anthropology, namely, they must start from the assumption that man's inner being is pure passivity, undertake to socialise men and turn them into social beings by conditioning individuals unbeknownst to themselves. The Directory, which was entering into its functions at this time, expressly adopted, as part of its stated programme, the ambitious task of 'regenerating morals'.[3] This was tantamount to saying that nothing had changed and it was increasingly the case that a *totalitarian* programme was the order of the day, because the people who were responsible for drawing it up were incapable of proposing anything different, even if it had ever occurred to them to wish to do so. The desire to exercise a pernickety control over every aspect of human life grew stronger and began to assume the proportions of a monomania for the social theoreticians of the Directory. Indeed, one of the minor figures of the age went as far as to claim that it was necessary 'to keep a close eye on the air we breathe'.[4] And this should not surprise us. Mona Ozouf writes, 'The most surprising thing' (she should perhaps have written 'the least surprising thing') 'is to track this ambition as it makes its way through the various upheavals of the Revolutionary period, as it gets the better of the fatigue which its heroes eventually succumb to, and not only as it survives the reign of Terror but even provides the most obvious substitute for it'.[5] We would prefer to say that this is what is least surprising about it, because in point of fact, it is difficult to claim that there were any alternative substitutes available at all. Moreover, the more the régime became bogged down, the more its social engineers took it upon themselves to persist in working in the same vein. This is most patently the case after the republican *coup d'état* of fructidor, namely on the 18th fructidor Year V (4 September 1797), which, following (and overturning) a resounding royalist victory in the May elections, set about once again radicalising the Republic, and gave a fresh impetus to the 'republicanising' project of remodelling society.

So it is by no means an exaggeration to suggest that the pressure exerted by sensualism, far from diminishing, actually increases under the Directory. One should say, in passing, that this fact would tend to add weight to my own bold claim that Enlightenment thinking connived with the spirit of Revolution. It also contradicts the view that, post-thermidor, there was any real solution based on continuity, in the sense that the doctrinal substratum, identifiable beneath the methods which were still used, was unchanged. In the post-thermidor period, there is hardly a single project for the reform of man or society – and God knows this type of project continued to proliferate – that did not bear visible signs, either diffusely or in a very technically pronounced way, of the decision to make use of the means and the methods proposed by sensualism. And this is especially true of those who drafted the laws and feverishly took it upon themselves to set about mapping out the social organisation of the twenty-five million asocial beings planted on French soil.

Thus, the practice of using *fêtes nationales* and celebrations as a way of acting upon man's inner consciousness through resorting in a calculated fashion to the influence of a whole range of sensory interventions, is more than ever the order of the day. This is the case even when the reluctance of citizens to participate in such events is equalled only by the enthusiasm of the organisers to organise them, which is saying quite a lot. The detail of these festive occasions is so fascinating that a certain amount of self-discipline is called for if we are to restrict ourselves to considering only one or two examples. In any event, it would be difficult to justify doing less. The decree issued by the Directory, on 8 June 1796, sets the conditions in which the Agricultural festival will take place firmly within the following solemn context: 'The failure to pay to Agriculture the public respect that it fully deserves is a sure sign of a corrupt and enslaved nation'.[6] It goes on to organise in minute detail a parade, drums and fanfares and, among other things, arranges that 'a plough bedecked with branches and flowers' will, on the one hand, be followed by a cart 'on which will be mounted a statue of Liberty, holding in one hand a cornucopia, and with the other pointing to the implements used in ploughing which will be stacked up at the front of the cart', and which will, on the other hand, be preceded by a group of twenty-four ploughmen ... chosen for their dedication and skill in ploughing; they will be preceded by their wives and children. All will hold in one hand one of the implements used in ploughing and in the other a mixed sheaf of corn and flowers. Their hats will be decorated with twigs and with tricolour ribbons'. Article 8: 'To the sound of instrumental music, interspersed with hymns, the parade will make its way through the countryside...' Article 9: 'The ploughmen will mingle with the armed citizens and, at a given signal, will temporarily exchange the ploughing implements for the firearms'. Article 10: 'To the sound of a fanfare and singing, the president will plunge the ploughshare into the earth, and will begin a furrow'. Article 11: 'The ploughmen will give back the firearms bedecked with sheaves of corn and flowers, and will take back the implements, at the top of which will flutter tricolour ribbons' and so on. As we can see, the industrious men who thought up these directives are far from lacking in didactic intention or in good will.

The Freedom festivals, set for the 9th and 10th thermidor, are also an occasion for a similar ritual defined in astonishing detail. Indeed we find ourselves wondering, at first, whether the symbolic richness of what is envisaged does not far exceed the capacity for assimilation that one might reasonably expect of a normal and well-disposed brain. But then it could be the case that even if they didn't succeed in inculcating republican reflexes in all cases, at least they might be seen as offering a degree of relaxation to a citizenry that has had its fill of hard times. Certainly it is difficult to imagine, in any commune across the whole of France, how the various participants acting out these little scenes and duly bedecked with garlands, could keep a straight face as, on the 9th thermidor, they crossed the village square 'to the sound of martial music' in order to storm a throne bearing 'a sceptre, a crown, an armorial coat of arms, and a book on which figures the title: *Constitution of 1791*';[7] any more than it is possible to imagine them remaining impassive when they are expected, the following day, to cross the same square, still 'to the sound of martial music' and this time to witness the carefully programmed setting on fire of 'a new throne built from the wreckage of the first one, covered in a tricolour robe', and bearing 'a mask, a blindfold, daggers and torches, and a book on which figures the title: *Constitution of 1793*'.[8] And these are only fleeting glimpses of the level of creativity exhibited by these specialists in the art of making impressions count.

Throughout this period, these same specialists also set great store by the costumes which are designated for those filling each category of the various offices of public, political, administrative and judicial life. This, likewise, must be understood in relation to the avowed intention of making an impression, of provoking reactions which, once again, in accordance with the notion that they are *acting* upon human passivity, are supposed to train individuals to automatically respect hierarchies and organisations, and therefore the republican régime itself. 'No other form of superiority exists among citizens than the grades of public officialdom' lays down article 351, at the beginning of the last section – clearly designed as a mopping-up section – of the year III Constitution. The fact that this form of superiority is the only one that is acknowledged means that the legislator is all the more duty-bound to make sure that everyone is aware of it, and it is this objective that the dress law of 24 October 1795 seeks to fulfil, betraying, by the wealth of detail it contains, the deep-seated concern for visual conditioning.[9]

Many hopes are also pinned on the theatre, which was the object of a number of finicky and feverish measures: songs that were banned, songs that were insisted upon and programmes that were imposed by the authorities.[10] As early as April 1795, Daunou signalled the importance of the arts, 'whose power touches all the faculties of man, his senses, his imagination and his intellect', in any attempt to work towards a nation's 'political regeneration'. This is a very familiar refrain, and one which nonetheless, in a rather mysterious way, seeks to derive maximum benefit from the 'increases in freedom'.[11] But this is a double-edged sword. For those republicans whose job it was to jealously watch over the fate of the Directory, how could they avoid wanting to neutralise such people as 'by a dangerous misuse of the principles' of freedom, might conceive the cunning plan 'of using the prestige of the declamatory arts to influence a great mass of citizens', who would thus be infected with 'the poison of the most anti-republican maxims'?[12] On the contrary, is not the whole point of theatre, and its 'essential objective', to 'contribute, *through the very attraction of a pleasurable experience,* to the purification of morals and to the dissemination of republican principles'? We should, of course, be aware of the fact that the formula can be reversed: in the event, counter-revolutionaries are just as likely to misuse 'the attraction of a pleasurable experience', and republicans hope to make the most of the 'prestige of the declamatory arts', since both parties are supposed to be vying for control of that purely passive entity that is the 'great mass of citizens', according to official thinking. Authority for this political policing of the theatre is drawn, in particular, from the Conventional legislation of August 1793 on the matter, and especially from the law of 14 August, bestowing the right and the duty on the administrations of communes, 'to take over control of theatres, and to make sure that the plays that are shown in them are those best fitted to educate the audience and to develop republican zeal'. It draws also on article 356 of the Year III Constitution: 'The law is particularly watchful of those professions which concern themselves with public morality, and the security and health of citizens'. Something very similar to this preoccupation with a sensualist control over the lives of citizens is to be seen in the intensive medication applied at the bedside of the new revolutionary calendar, the neonatal senility of which nevertheless constitutes a hopeless case. Shortly after Fructidor, a whole series of coercive measures is supposed to ensure that the calendar is adopted.

Notes

1. Robespierre fell on 9th thermidor Year II (27 July 1794). The Convention, hence called the Thermidorean Convention, remained in place until the end of October 1795, when the Constitution of Year III, which it had had the task of drafting, came into effect.
2. To Palissot (who became an opponent of the *philosophes*), 11 August 1764: Voltaire, *Corr*, vol. 7, 813.
3. Proclamation of 14th brumaire Year IV, 5 November 1795: *Bull. Lois* of Year IV, no. 1, 5.
4. Quoted by M. Ozouf, *L'Homme régénéré*, Paris, 1989, 10.
5. Ibid.
6. Decree of 20th prairial Year IV, for the *fête* arranged for 10th messidor (28 June 1796): *Bull. Lois* no. 52, p. 9. The quotations which follow are from pp. 10 and 11.
7. Decree from the Directory, 17th messidor Year IV, 5 July 1796: *Bull. Lois* no. 56, p. 14 (w.u.o) ; 'and the throne will collapse beneath their repeated blows in order to remind everyone that the abolition of the monarchy is due to the courage of the entire people'.
8. Ibid., 15 (w.u.o.); this time, it is 'the president of the administration' who 'will set fire to the throne, to remind everyone that the abolition of the tyranny of the triumvirate is particularly due to the courage of those in authority'.
9. Law of 3rd brumaire Year IV 'on the dress code of legislators and other public functionaries': *Bull. Lois* no. 202, pp. 1–5.
10. Decrees from the Directory of 18th and 27th nivôse Year IV (8 and 17 Januray 1796): *Bull. Lois* no. 18, pp. 5–6 and 15. 'Every day before the curtain is raised, all directors, producers and owners of shows are expected, as a matter of personal responsibility, to ensure that their orchestra plays tunes dear to the hearts of all Republicans, such as *la Marseillaise, Ça ira, Veillons au salut de l'empire* and *le Chant du Départ*. – In the interval between two plays, *la Marseillaise* or some other patriotic song will always be sung' (5), et cetera, et cetera.

11. To the Convention, in the name of the Committee for Public Instruction, 27th germinal Year III, 16 April: *Moniteur* no. 209, of two days later, 852/2.
12. Decree from the Directory, 25th pluviôse Year IV, 14 February 1796: *Bull. Lois* no. 27, 3. The quotations which follow are from 2.

≈ *Chapter 10* ≈

CABANIS AND DESTUTT DE TRACY

Fundamentally, the calendar is a *scientistic* undertaking, and the confirmed predilection for sensualism among the influential figures in the Directory is in the long run merely one aspect of this never-questioned ambition to gain scientific control (which it was hoped was imminently achievable) over all men and the whole of society, even if this implied a complete remodelling of both of them. The ascendancy enjoyed by this particular point of view, during these years, is reflected in the prestige that attached itself to a group of people who, without having a monopoly over such ideas, nevertheless gave them a clear expression and systematised them with great energy and to great effect. This group naturally deserves our full attention and it is probably easy to deduce that I am referring to the *idéologues*, members of the sect devoted to the study of 'ideology', in its original sense of *science of ideas*. The tone was set: the inner being of animals, including men, could be completely accounted for by the procedures and the formulations normally associated with the exact sciences. Did not Maupertuis, naturalist, Enlightenment thinker and one-time president of the Berlin Academy, entertain the hope of discovering the exact mechanisms that went into the act of thinking, by dissecting the brain of a living man?[1] When Destutt de Tracy coined this word 'idéo-logie', in order to refer to what he specifically calls 'the science of thought', he expressly sought to banish from the cultural landscape the overly spiritualist and metaphysical connotations of the word 'psychology'.[2]

In their work of bringing together, reorganising and revitalising the forces of Enlightenment rationalism after the mishaps and the miscalculations of the Terror, which one of them modestly sought to minimise as 'minor details',[3] the *idéologues* look on the reconstruction that will be necessary without any trace of obscurantist reticence, but rather with the sort of zeal that is inspired by their confidence in scientific progress and with the sense of urgency that is dictated by the pressing needs of the moment. Destutt de Tracy and Cabanis can be considered the leaders of the movement. The movement itself, which might be better thought of as a small nebula of thinkers, also included, besides Daunou, for whom 'the genius of the sciences' was 'the precursor of the Revolution',[4] Volney, Garat, Sieyès, and a number of others among whom it should be noted, figured Bonaparte himself, who frequented the group when he was not otherwise engaged. The *idéologues* were well established and their thinking is never very far removed from the official thinking of those who wielded power. They had a strong base at the *Institut national*, a politico-cultural body to which article 298 of the Year III Constitution assigned the duty of 'recording discoveries, perfecting the arts and sciences', by which we should understand: imposing on 'the whole Republic' a sort of State scientism which seems to imply an even more concentrated version of the anthropological inheritance of the Enlightenment.[5] It is the *idéologues* who are the driving force behind the huge plan for Public Instruction, both in its broad outlines as well as in its detail, which is elaborated in the aftermath of thermidor and which resulted in the setting up of the famous *écoles centrales* in each department. And it was they who largely formed the teaching body of these institutions. As the recent past would lead us to expect, this project bore all the hallmarks of reductionist thinking and reflected totalitarian political concerns. October 1794 marked the creation of the École 'normale', that is to say, an institution intended to define the norm (something we tend to forget), with the express mission, according to Lakanal and Garat, who were the *rapporteurs* for this project, of training 'a large number of teachers capable of becoming the implementers of a plan which aimed to regenerate human understanding in a Republic of twenty-five million people on whom democracy has conferred equality of status'.[6] '*To regenerate human understanding*', or, as it is put elsewhere (and this is the same thing), 'to perfect the way humans are organised':[7] for anyone to judge such a programme as lacking in ambition they would need to be foolish or ill-intentioned, especially when we realise that the project is less concerned with the content of knowledge than with a complete restructuring of intelligence itself with the almost express aims of standardising and conditioning the population.

The chief *idéologues* owned up to key beliefs which were no less ambitious than a project of the magnitude just outlined. They were committed believers in atheism and worshipped at the altar of a materialism which they had the good grace to try to follow through to its logical conclusions. They even made a point of honour out of this. In other words, as far as man was concerned, reductionism was the order of the day. Georges Gusdorf said as much: 'The decline of theology goes hand in hand with the decline of anthropology, a fact which is borne out by the pale colours in which man according to Locke, Condillac and Destutt de Tracy is sketched out. ... The age of Enlightenment might well have been the age of the euthanasia of divinity, but it was also the age of the euthanasia of individuality';[8] the range of the references he makes and the impressive density of his work lead me to believe that this author read and thought a great deal before arriving at such a conclusion. Indeed, the *idéologues* simply take their place in the tradition of reductionist thinkers as it was elaborated throughout the eighteenth-century, even if a factual and purely fortuitous detail seems to suggests that they were apparently more especially linked with one of these latter, who happens to have been the first to be considered in this study: Helvétius. Helvétius had died in 1771,[9] and it was at the house of his widow, in Auteuil, that Cabanis had taken lodgings. This then was where the group generally convened, earning themselves the name, 'the Auteuil circle'.

It is indeed perfectly logical that Helvétius' reputation should be held in such high esteem under the Directory. There are at least four different reasons why this should be the case. Firstly, the veil of optimism that the anthropology of the Enlightenment and of 1789 had drawn across men's eyes had come to be seen as illusory and this had served to expose the underlying reductionism it concealed. This conferred even greater credit on those writers who had expressed its basic premises in the most unashamed fashion and had been prepared to accept its consequences, among them the unambiguous declaration that egoism is the absolutely sovereign power behind human behaviour. It is probably no chance thing that Helvétius' complete works were published in 1795 and those of La Mettrie in 1796. D'Holbach, who died in 1789, was a thinker of greater substance, and the major *idéologues* certainly more than dipped into his works, but the fact that they had been published anonymously somewhat hampered the spread of his fame. Helvétius, however, whose work was much more that of a dilettante – Voltaire occasionally complained as much and Condorcet quite rightly, in my view, could not 'bring himself to consider Helvétius as a great mind'[10] – had managed to associate his name with resounding scandals and been the object of stinging criticism on the publication of each of his books. Paradoxically enough, this had sufficed to make him a martyr in the name of the very freedom whose existence he had, in essence, been at such pains to philosophically deny.

Secondly, there is the fact that rationalism, refusing to be contradicted by the facts (in a word, by the nightmare of the Terror which had been a direct result of the rationalist principles which promised easy happiness for all), had less a tendency to soften in the face of these disavowals than a tendency to harden its stance. It seemed to be persuaded that it had only sinned by default and that the men and society it saw as the object of its experiments should be subjected to even greater scientific rigour. 'It was the *philosophes* who made the Revolution, it is they who will finish it': this belief, formulated by Mme de Staël in 1798, seems to have been adopted as their own by the *idéologues*.[11] It could almost be argued that rationalism was still at the stage of seeking to realise throughout France the wish expressed by Voltaire that reason should be tried out with a view to 'seeing if it is as harmful as all that'.[12] Such a desire to re-shape the mould was stimulated by the general state of the country, in which institutional, material, moral and mental disarray, perhaps somewhat exaggerated in the minds of the people at the time, seemed to offer endless possibilities for assuaging the zeal of reformers, who were encouraged by the simplistic doctrines that were all around and reflected the general mood of mechanistic materialism. The *École polytechnique,* created in October 1794, was very quick to recognise the need to provide classes in human anatomy for 'engineers who have to determine the effect that *animated motors* have upon machines'.[13] And, believe it or not, Rousseau had already poured scorn on 'stupid professions including workmen' who are 'almost automata'. He disapproved of the fact that 'men of good sense' should be employed in such jobs, on the grounds that 'it's a case of one machine being led by another'.[14]

Thirdly, the very reaction against Robespierre was itself a contributing factor in the rehabilitation of the writings of

Helvétius. No doubt many Thermidoreans had shared Robespierre's opinions while he was in power, but once he had been cast in the role of scapegoat, his campaigns against materialism, against cynical self-interest, against Helvétius himself and the smashing of his bust in the Jacobin club,[15] all these, paradoxically but quite logically, suddenly assumed a negative value. And in fact this reversal of opinion is all the easier to understand if we bear in mind that Robespierre, like Rousseau, was far closer to those things he thought he was pillorying than he ever realised himself.

Finally, the political and moral justification for various forms of egoism, which is at the heart of Helvétius' thinking, was completely in tune with the historical moment. Moralists writing at the time readily admit that the horrors of the Terror led citizens to adopt an attitude of 'every man for himself'.[16] As far as the life of the nation was concerned, it is probably the case that it had never before been so openly and absolutely the plaything of groups with vested interests: for example, the interests of those who were buying up the nation's assets, and the interests of the regicides, whose personal survival depended on transforming public life, particularly electoral processes, into one gigantic fraud. We shall return to this point later. Those who had grown rich during the Revolution enjoyed power and associated with the powerful. They seem to reflect, therefore, the image projected by Helvétius himself: a man grown immensely rich under the monarchy, a tax-collector on behalf of the king, a great nobleman who was excessively particular about his lordly rights and privileges,[17] and an archetype, if one were needed, for what Rousseau had called the 'privileged children of the age', a man, finally, who counted among his many worries the potentially disastrous effects a safe crammed full of coins was having on the floors of one of the rooms in his *château*.[18] We should stress the fact that Helvétius was a perfect example of a particular type which exists and can be recognised in other periods of history: he works to disseminate (and profits from the dissemination of) a hyper-egalitarian ideology which he combines with political and economic views that are insolently élitist. When we learn that, shortly after his death, the marriage contract of his youngest daughter was signed by four kings of France, we have some grounds for wondering about his credentials.[19] And in 1818, when Ballanche is arguing in defence of the dignity of 'moral and intellectual ideas', he identifies Helvétius by name and proposes him as the archetypal champion of the 'vulgar interests of fortune and material subsistence.

I would like us to finally shake off the yoke of these political Helvétius figures'.[20] To sum up in a word, in the public and private life of post-Thermidorean France egoism is the consecrated value touching the lives of all men. We only have to listen to what Bonaparte says to his eldest son, Joseph, in summer 1798: 'At the age of 29 I have exhausted all possibilities, all that remains for me is to become a true egoist'.[21] This way of thinking, that claimed the prestige of science as subject to its dominion and decreed that whatever man may do he is always completely and necessarily determined by his appetites, was destined to have tremendous appeal for the political classes. Hence the semi-official status of the *idéologues* who, in the way I have just described, come to take their rightful place following in the footsteps of the author of *De l'Homme*.

Destutt de Tracy (1754–1836) was more the general theoretician of *idéologie*, Cabanis (1757–1808), who was a medical doctor, was much more the anthropologist of the group. The main thrust of the present study leads me to give rather greater emphasis to the role of the latter while from time to time shedding light on what he has to say by referring to comments from Destutt, who consistently expressed his agreement with his friend's thinking. 'If we consulted our experience instead of our prejudices', wrote d'Holbach, 'medicine would provide the moral sciences with the key to understanding the human heart'.[22] It seems to us that this very aptly sums up the position of Cabanis who articulated his ideas, above all, in a famous series of very heavy-weight discussions that took place at the *Institut* in autumn 1796 and which were published in the collected proceedings of that body in 1798–99. In 1802 they were brought together in a single volume and then published in an expanded form as the famous book entitled *Rapports du Physique et du Moral de l'Homme*, re-edited in 1803, 1805 and 1844.[23] Turgot, d'Holbach, d'Alembert, Diderot and Mirabeau were all well known by Cabanis, as was Condorcet, whose posthumous brother-in-law he became and whose papers he collected. Cabanis also collected together the papers of Helvétius and lodged in rooms at the house of his widow.[24] It is not surprising, therefore, to find that Cabanis echoes the major themes and convictions expressed in the reductionist thinking of the chief materialists of the Enlightenment, and echoes them with all the added assurance that he feels his professional competence as a doctor allows him to display. It would be monotonous and no doubt unnecessary to systematically draw attention to the connections between Cabanis and the materialists. On the other hand, it would seem useful to point out here and there some of the ways in which this exceedingly reductionist thinking has affinities with tendencies in the work of Voltaire and Rousseau. It is important to understand that, in spite of appearances and in spite of certain views routinely trotted out by many academics, such affinities underline the fact that there exists what is in reality a very close relationship between these spiritualists (to a greater or lesser extent) and the leaders of opinion in the opposite camp.

Cabanis considers it as axiomatic that the moral side of man is merely one facet of his physical make-up, that it 'is merely the physical side of man considered from certain particular points of view'.[25] This is merely orthodox materialist thinking, and any variations on the theme that Cabanis comes up with seem to us to be on a par with those produced by d'Holbach. Destutt de Tracy said that 'everything that we think, everything that we are, derives from our physical needs in all their simplicity and solely from the way we are organised'.[26] 'Organisation of the machine', 'movements of the machine', 'animal economy' – these expressions, applied to humankind in general, are equally common in the works of both d'Holbach and Cabanis, both of whom simply inherited this line of thinking, as we well know. Cabanis considered it to be a truth that he himself had demonstrated 'that ideas, instinctive tendencies, reasoned decisions and all the various feelings are formed by a mechanism which is perfectly analogous to that which determines the simplest organic operations and movements'.[27]

This 'mechanism' is, obviously, sensualist. The inner nature of any animal, and therefore any human being, can be reduced to a chemistry of the sensations. Cabanis is simply concerned that we should not forget the role of cenesthetic sensations within this chemistry. Thinking is merely feeling: both Destutt and he adopt and make this idea their own. It was, of course, the first article in the credo of Helvétius. 'Thinking', Destutt wrote, 'is *always feeling, and is nothing more than feeling*',[28] to such an extent that the collocation 'thinking and feeling', as he clearly states, involves a form of linguistic redundancy; perceptions or ideas: 'these two words' are 'absolutely synonymous',[29] he explains. What logically follows from this is an equality of status 'between our basest appetites and our most refined sentiments'.[30] It also follows that in no circumstances can such a thing as true disinterestedness exist; what seems to pass as such is, like everything else, a mere offshoot of self-interest. Cabanis assures us that the moralist 'could also prove to us and make us feel in an unequivocal way that carrying out the strictest of duties and acts of the most generous devotion towards others are, when they are imposed by reason, closely and directly linked to the sense of self-interest and the personal happiness of the person who accomplishes them'.[31] The same idea is expressed in Helvétius and d'Holbach.[32] In short, and once again, what in the final analysis is at issue here is the radical impossibility of any form of freedom: 'Living is nothing other than receiving impressions, and carrying out the movements that these impressions call for'.[33]

Cabanis wanted his readers and those who listened to him speak not to have the slightest doubt as to the reality of this out-and-out reductionism. He candidly described its essence and argued that its moment had come.[34] He hypothesised on the exact equivalence between, on the one hand, 'the operations of the intelligence and the will', and, on the other hand, 'other vital movements'. This equivalence, once posited, justified the annexing of the 'moral sciences' to 'the domain of physics'.[35] In order that no one should be left in any doubt, he took the trouble to furnish an explanation of the processes involved in thinking as being strictly analogous to the digestive function. The conclusion of this could only be to turn feelings, ideas and all the rest into what we could very exactly describe as cerebral waste matter. And this way of putting it very accurately reflects what he himself said. He explained,

> We see items of food enter into these viscera [the stomach] with the qualities that are peculiar to them; we see them come out with different qualities: and we conclude that the viscera have truly made them undergo this transformation. We also see impressions arriving in the brain by the intermediary of the nerves: at this point they are isolated and lacking in coherence. The viscera go into action and work upon them: and soon they are sent back out metamorphosed into ideas that the language of physiognomy or whatever or the signs of speech and writing make externally manifest. We conclude with equal certainty that the brain in some way digests impressions; that it *organically brings about the secretion of thought*.[36]

These words are clear and calculated. Cabanis will say later, 'The laws which govern the abdominal viscera, for example, are clearly the same laws as those governing the organs of thought; these latter are equally subject to them and this without restriction',[37] he insists. Voltaire, who did not display quite the same degree of *scientistic* rigour as Cabanis, had nonetheless expressed a similar idea, emphasising 'how insignificant a thing man is, and that *we no more control our ideas than we do our digestive system*'.[38]

Another notable corollary of the sensualism of the *idéologues*, as it is of any consistent form of sensualism, is that there is no difference in nature between animals and human beings and therefore no axiological boundary between the two. Humans and animals function essentially in an identical way. Plants too, moreover, and we might dare to suggest that even women do as well, since it happens that Cabanis, good nominalist that he is, deals with women as a separate 'species'[39] – a species, by the way, that he scientifically demonstrates to be fundamentally ill equipped for any tasks of an intellectual nature (as well as for tasks involving gymnastic prowess).[40] Rousseau had ventured down this road before him,[41] and we know that Rousseau would have agreed with Cabanis' precept that 'women's happiness will always depend on the impression they make on men'.[42] Voltaire, referring to Mme du Châtelet's extensive knowledge, declares her to be 'a great fellow whose only defect was that she was a woman'.[43] Setting misogyny on one side, it is nevertheless true that sensualism always puts all animate beings on an equal footing. According to Cabanis, the foetus, even though it is 'merely an organised mucus',[44] is capable of 'will', the proof being simply the fact that it moves,[45] which would seem to confirm, if it were at all necessary, that 'will' of this sort is in any event a pretty feeble thing, and that if we applied the same criteria it would quite clearly be necessary to assign 'will' to animals too. How interesting it is to hear Cabanis speak of 'the *voluntary* and proud isolation of the wild boar' in illustration of the fact that each species, through the mechanicising nature of things, is endowed with its own 'instinctive determinations'.[46]

The complete interchangeability of animals and humans is consequently one of the dialectical bases of the *Rapports* which, in the various arguments it proposes, makes a point of moving without differentiation between man and the animals, when it is not in the opposite direction. What is more to the point, it draws conclusions about animals by reference to premises identified in the human sphere, or vice versa.[47] Helvétius used this strategy quite happily and referred to the behaviour of eagles, negroes and wild boar in order to argue against the strength of the 'bond which exists between children and their fathers'.[48] And it so happens that Rousseau himself adopted a similar argument.[49] For his own part, Destutt de Tracy explained: 'We have only an incomplete understanding of an animal if we know nothing about its intellectual faculties. *"Idéologie" is a branch of Zoology*, and it is in man above all that this part of his make-up is important and deserves to be studied in greater depth'.[50] And he immediately exclaims, 'How many people drive horses all their lives without reflecting anywhere near as much about what they are doing in order to drive the horse as the horse itself does in order to obey them!'.[51] This way of arguing is typical both of himself and of Cabanis, who, for his own part, turns his attention to speaking about 'maternal love' and 'fatherly tenderness' among winged creatures,[52] which is exactly what Rousseau himself had already done,[53] as well as Diderot. Speaking of birds, the latter had explained, 'They complain, they suffer, they love, they take pleasure; they have *all the affections you have*'.[54]

Insects have their share of them too. And Cabanis refers to 'the strong and sweet leaning towards social life to be found in men, bees and ants'.[55] As far as humans are concerned, we notice his pen betray a moment of abandon and of mellow optimism that the context scarcely warrants. And he is fully aware of the fact since his work as a man of science has the express aim of providing therapy that applies to the realm of politics. The moment of history seems to have arrived when specialists in the study of human nature have plenty to say indeed on the sorts of conditioning that man will need to undergo in order that the social mix may gel. The science of ideas, to which Destutt de Tracy devotes himself, presupposes the elaboration of a science of grammar, which is necessary 'in order to really understand the way human intelligence operates',[56] and which, in his view, constitutes 'the only solid basis for the moral and political sciences':[57] these words too are heavy with meaning. Cabanis as well, although in a more general way, sees anthropology as the foundation upon which politics is based. And, given the circumstances in which France was languishing, it appears that the time seemed to him to be ripe to think about putting to good use the maxims voiced by Helvétius: 'The science of man is part of the art of government ... Therefore, let the *philosophes* delve ever deeper into the abyss of the human heart: let them there seek out *all the principles which govern its movements* and let the Minister, benefiting from their discoveries, put them to good use in ways that befit the times, the place and the circumstances'.[58] We should perhaps be aware of the fact that Cabanis may well have believed himself to be the ideal link between 'the science of man' and the 'Minister'. After all, he is not only a man given to study, a pure intellectual, he is also a politician. We have already mentioned that Sieyès and Bonaparte frequented the meetings of the Auteuil circle of which he was a leading light; Volney, Garat, Daunou (who were also politicians) were there too, and in April 1798 Cabanis became a legislator himself when he joined the *Conseil des Cinq Cents* in which he was a *rapporteur* and where he intervened on matters relating to medicine and hygiene, on prisons and on medical education.

In concrete terms and as far as the mission to remodel his fellow citizens is concerned, Cabanis probably has not much more to propose than all those techniques that have already been tried out and which continued to find favour as methods of government. These are inspired by a corpus of ideas which at best he could be considered as having arranged into a system, although his profession led people to believe that he had some special competence in the matter and was intellectually better equipped than most to carry out such a task. But at bottom it is still a matter of programming people so they adopt different habits, exploiting the malleability of the human mind as a way of bringing people to change their behaviour: 'We are nothing more than what the objects around us make us become' said Helvétius.[59] Animals, said Cabanis, including man, 'are, in a way, the living picture of their locale', (we would now say: their environment).[60] But remaining within this same logical framework Cabanis will claim – as *scientism* demands – to be doing far more than merely ploddingly following the standard routine. On the one hand, he personally will seek to be far more ambitious in the conditioning of men and the control of their minds, and will seek to work much more deeply upon their inner natures. He speaks of *'learning* to govern the habits of the mind and the will by the habits of the physical organs and the temperament'.[61] He sets himself the objective of 'modifying and perfecting the operations of the intelligence and the habits of the will'.[62] This is exactly the same project as the one we heard described elsewhere as *regenerating human understanding.*[63]

On the other hand, his self-confidence as a man of science, his fervent belief in progress and the parlous state in which France found herself and from which she seemed incapable of breaking out, all these led him, on occasion, to entertain an even more daring fantasy, the scope and implications of which cannot be underestimated. We are, of course, thinking here of the tremendously striking conclusion to the sixth *mémoire* of the *Rapports*, in which the philanthropic demiurge suddenly rises up, shows his true nature and prophesies in words that are heavy with significance:

> It is no doubt possible, through a well thought-out life style assiduously followed to quite markedly influence the very habits of one's constitution;[64] as a result, it is possible to improve the particular nature of each and every individual; and this objective, which is so deserving of the attention of moralists and philanthropists, merits further research by physiologists and by medical practicioners. But if one can usefully modify individual temperaments taken separately, one can exert a far greater and a far deeper influence on the species as a whole, by intervening in a systematically uniform and uninterrupted way upon successive generations. It would be unambitious now if hygiene were merely to limit itself to defining the rules that should apply to any given circumstances in which a particular man might find himself; it should have the ambition to do much more than that; it should consider the whole of humankind as a single individual whose physical education has been placed in its care; and consider the indeterminate length of the species' existence as allowing it to get constantly ever nearer to *a perfect type of human*, which could never have been imagined starting from the original; in a word, hygiene must seek to perfect human nature in general.
>
> After having busied ourselves to such an extent in order to find ways of making different species of useful and agreeable animals and plants more beautiful and improving them; after having altered species of dogs and horses a hundred times, after having transplanted, grafted and worked fruits and flowers in every conceivable manner, is it not all the more shameful that we have totally neglected the human race as if it were somehow less dear to us! as if it were more important to have big strong oxen rather than healthy, vigorous men; sweet-smelling peaches and beautifully-coloured tulips rather than wise and fair-minded citizens!
>
> The time has come, in this respect as in so many others, to follow a system of ideas more worthy of a period of regeneration: it is time to dare to practise upon ourselves what we have practised with such success upon many of our fellow creatures; that is we must *dare to revise and correct the work of nature*. What a daring undertaking! which truly deserves all our attention ... It is in this way, in the long run, that for groups of men consid-

ered *en masse*, it could be possible to produce a sort of equality of capability which does not exist in their original make-up, and which, like equality before the law, would therefore be a direct product of enlightened thinking and perfected reasoning.

And within this state of things itself, it would be mistaken to think that it would not be possible to discern quite distinct differences, either in respect of the nature and types of living physical strength on display, or in respect of the habits of the understanding and the will. The equality would only exist as a general rule, in individual cases it would be purely approximate in nature.

Consider those stud farms where a breed of selected horses is reared with equal care and according to a uniform set of rules: they do not all end up equally capable of undergoing the same training or of carrying out the same kind of movement. It is true, they are all good and well-mannered; they all have many common characteristics which indicate that they are issued from the same stock: but each, however, has its own particular physiognomy; each has its predominant qualities ... Likewise, in the human race perfected by a long period of physical and moral training, particular characteristics would probably distinguish individual members.[65]

It would denote a somewhat cavalier attitude if we were not to pause a while to reflect on this passage, if only to make a number of comments which often confirm various points already broached in the course of this study, and with regard to which many *philosophes* whom I have already quoted might be invited to return to the witness box. And, first of all, it has to be pointed out that in this passage man is seen as a purely passive substance, completely available to be remodelled at the hands of the great reformer who considers himself as having the right to undertake, in accordance with his own personal view of things, the task of reshaping 'groups of men considered *en masse*' – the expression is worth noting. One of the texts by Mirabeau which Cabanis had collected into a volume springs to mind here. It is a text which argues that if the technique of conditioning men's minds 'is rigorously applicable to individuals, it is even more so to nations considered collectively, especially the French nation on account of its mobility'.[66] When Mirabeau or Cabanis reason in this way, what remains a total mystery is what distinguishes them from the common herd and furnishes them with a mandate to hold forth in this way, unless we are mindful, once again, of the fact that enlightened men in the tradition of the Enlightenment formed a very restricted élite which was ipso facto accredited with the right to make firm plans involving the fate of their fellow citizens and to take it upon themselves to look after their interests for them. As we have seen, Voltaire talks of 'thinking people' but, even when he includes himself among their number, he has to admit that they are very thin on the ground, although he is delighted to add that they 'end up governing the rest'.[67] And Rousseau considered that if someone wished to really make significant decisions without bothering to consult the people, it was enough that they be 'well-intentioned'.[68] Quite clearly, the tendencies which are apparent in the passage from Cabanis betray the sort of audacity that puts us in mind of the 'philanthropists' – they are inspired by only the best of intentions, namely that of manufacturing 'good and wise citizens' who are happy into the bargain. But they presuppose a point of view which tends to treat the citizen as a permanent infant, a mere minor: this too is a constant feature of Enlightenment thinking to which we have had to accustom ourselves and which is evident too throughout the Revolutionary period. Turning 'good judgements' into habits, that is what 'all education, that of adults as well as that of children'[69] ultimately boils down to, wrote Destutt de Tracy. And he subsequently suggests that 'legislation is nothing other than *the education of grown men*',[70] a theme which also recurs throughout this study.

The collective happiness that is envisaged for these big children required that they be standardised, and Cabanis, who did not want this aspect to be over-dramatised, consequently reassures us that it only need be (and indeed it only could be) an approximate form of standardisation. As proof of this he points to the residual, but oh so welcome, diversity that is still to be seen among our equine cousins that are produced through standardised methods in stud farms. At very least this 'equality of capability' which brings man ever closer to the 'perfect type of human being' will need to be sufficiently serious to be able to give some consistency to the 'equality before the law' which, it is our impression, Cabanis, Destutt and company consider as having failed hitherto only because it was ushered in before the time was ripe for it. This passage or its author, like so many others, is therefore typical of the enormous paradox at the heart of egalitarian ideology. Those who promote such views, by virtue of the very fact that they have the pretention of disseminating them, thereby excavate a huge axiological abyss between, on the one hand, the people, whom they wish to consider as an undifferentiated mass, and, on the other hand, their good selves: a small group of men who have quietly arrogated to themselves the right to set up a totally immodest programme that they assume they have the authority to inflict upon those 'groups of men considered *en masse*' mentioned by Cabanis.

What is also noticeable in this text – and this fact is hardly likely to come as a surprise – is that the whole of humanity is seen as falling under the sway of the knowledge and the know-how of the 'physiologists': 'physical education', 'physical and moral training' are equivalent expressions; 'moralists' and 'physiologists' are not only on an equal footing, they are literally interchangeable, since what is moral is physical and, as we have already seen, the process of thinking is exactly analogous to what happens in the intestinal tract. As a result, science and its exact methods are seen as capable of providing the answers to all man's problems. Man, concomitantly, is not substantially different from other living things, animals or plants. If the last paragraph is eloquent in this respect,[71] the second paragraph is even more so. He is not very far from quoting what Rousseau or d'Holbach have to say on education as 'the agriculture of the mind'. 'Men are like plants who never grow happily if they are not well tended: among people living in misery, the species loses vigour and sometimes even degenerates': this phrase was written by Montesquieu,[72] which, if such proof were needed, seems to confirm that the theories put forward by Cabanis are consonant with the general mood of the century. Moreover, this same paragraph provides a faint echo of the retort made by Lakanal who, when faced with members of the Convention who were wondering what exactly was this *fête* planned in honour of the animals by the Committee for Public Instruction, replied to their faces 'My friends, it is in *your* honour',[73] and the context would seem to suggest that he wasn't joking. And really, the paradoxical 'advantage' that man enjoys over his cousins in the animal kingdom is that he is endowed with a greater degree of 'perfectibilty', and is therefore able to undergo a more advanced, more perfect form of training. This is the reason why he has the honour of topping the hierarchy in the menagerie. But it is an ambiguous honour: man is 'the most flexible of all the animals, of all the species he is the most peculiarly gifted with the faculty of imitation and is the most likely to receive the imprint of any impression imaginable'.[74] He is, therefore, and to sum up, the most open to manipulation. As one theorist of education had said in the past, 'there is no animal easier to train than man'.[75]

Whatever the case may be in this respect, what is clear is that this reduction of humanity to the status of merely one particular example of an animate being – a type of reductionism that is at the very least clearly discernible in this passage – rids the drive towards eugenics that is also present in these lines of the *Rapports* (and by no means in a marginal way), of any ethical scruples that might have weighed it down. In this respect too, Cabanis remains true to the high traditions of the Enlightenment, which are clearly recognisable here as in so many other instances, just as they are present throughout the Revolutionary period too, if we are only willing to recognise them rather than shut them out. After having improved 'species of useful... animals and plants', Cabanis indignantly argues, 'how shameful [it is] that we have totally neglected the human race!' Some forty years earlier the *Encyclopédiste*, Faiguet de Villeneuve, had deplored the fact that, unlike what happens in the case of animal husbandry, where man is concerned we allow 'the weakest, the ugliest and the most inept couples to marry each other day in and day out' and the result for human kind is a weakening, an uglification and a mongrelisation of the species.[76] La Chalotais put the question this way, 'There is an art of modifying breeds of animals. Does none such exist for the perfecting of men?'.[77] In 1793, Sieyès had written, not without the endorsement of the Committee for Public Instruction, that 'after having sought to perfect the individual' it was necessary to set about 'improving the species'.[78] 'The perfecting of breeds is one of the aims most deserving of the attention of a true legislator', he adds almost immediately, speaking about domestic animals,[79] but this in a context where no real differentiation is made between men and animals. All this is merely a glimpse at the overall picture. The theme of physical regeneration with purificatory connotations is inexplicably underexploited by historiographers who are by no means averse to value judgements and who find themselves preparing to celebrate the bicentenary of these events in a world threatened on all sides by racism. And yet this very theme is at the heart of the revolutionary spirit which, in this respect, is the obedient child of Enlightenment thinking. Nor can its importance be ignored in the case of the repression in Vendée, where, for example, one of Carrier's agents clearly speaks of wishing 'to regenerate the human species by ridding it of old blood'.[80] The pages quoted from Cabanis, although demonstrating greater technical control and an equal amount of philanthropy, and although expressed in a rather less exalted tone, seem to deal with exactly the same theme as we have been touching upon here.

As a result, this text, which is so rich in axiological implications, can be considered as a turning-point in modern and contemporary history. Within it we see converging, like a web of railway lines converging on a turntable, the major axes of thought of the whole eighteenth-century, or at least a good number of them, and by no means those of least importance. Outlined here, we see the prospect of the manipulation of men's minds, more or less painful, more or less painless, by all the state propaganda machines of our own century. Outlined here, too, are all the later collectivist totalitarian systems, and obviously the eugenics of national socialism but also their current extension into the genetic manipulations of our own day and of which the eighteenth-century version was merely the forerunner and the foremost experimental example.[81] As Destutt de Tracy was to say, 'where can we not go when we set out from a clear starting point and we are following a good road'?[82] And in identical terms Cabanis congratulated himself on the fact that humanity was taking 'this road to improvement that has no end'.[83] In his reconstitution of the very suggestive history of the *Mythe Aryen*, Léon Poliakov did not fail to emphasise the role played by the *scientism* of Cabanis as a staging-post in this whole affair. Neither did he omit to remind us, while about it, that the *idéologues* 'deeply influenced a number of French intellectual traditions, especially that of lay militancy'.[84] He goes on to observe in his *Mémoires*: 'The idea that racial ideology was a child of the Enlightenment comes as no great surprise to experts on the period ... But despite the many books that have been devoted to the subject since, the average intellectual continues to know nothing about it'.[85] *The average intellectual continues to know nothing about it.* Today this phrase is already nearly twenty years old.[86]

And Rousseau himself too – that uncontested prophet of contemporary democracy – is not very distant in spirit from these exceedingly reductionist pages from Cabanis. We know how vigorously he argued for a daring transmutation of human nature through legislative means. He wished it to be *altered* and made clear his conviction that it needed to be completely refashioned. We find this above all in the *Contrat Social*, but, as we have emphasised,[87] it is also in *Émile*. It could be argued that it is also present in the words of Saint-Preux in *La Nouvelle Héloïse*: 'Is it not infinitely better to create a *perfect model* of the reasonable man and the honest man and then *bring each child closer* to this model by the *force* of education ... by repressing the passions, by perfecting reason and by *correcting nature*?'[88] Cabanis, for his part, speaks of 'getting ever nearer ... to a perfect type'. He says that in order to achieve this we must 'dare to revise and correct the work of nature'. The rhetoric is exactly similar to Rousseau's even if the idea is not, and even if the idea is, in the event, less radical in Rousseau's version of it. It could equally well have come from another work by Rousseau, the aborted *Traité de Morale sensitive*, where it was to be a question of 'making us better' by using techniques inspired by sensualism which, he tells us, would have 'force[d] the animal economy'.[89] An expression such as this would not have been out of place in the *Rapports* of Cabanis, and nor should we forget, by the way, all that is implied when Rousseau uses the words 'the force of education'.[90] Immediately after his death he was praised for having devoted 'his talents to *pushing back the moral boundaries of the soul*, and for having made men better and happier'.[91]

We also know, by the way (but do we make the connection?), that, in a more general sense, manipulating men's inner natures, substituting one's own will for that of others in order to bend them to one's own ends, these are at the very heart of Rousseau's work, whether it is a matter of his private relationships or his views on education or politics.[92] Now Destutt de Tracy, that close friend of Cabanis, taught that the mainspring operating in society is the 'need *to take possession of the will* of one's fellow man'. He even suggests that this is 'the source of all morality'.[93] In reality, this 'will' does not amount to a great deal, as we have already pointed out.[94] It is indistinguishable from the drive towards pleasure or the repulsion we feel for pain,[95] and it is sufficent that we use it cleverly as far as other people are concerned, in order to ensure that we gain some advantage from it and make them 'favourable to our views', as they say. A great many things, Destutt teaches us, 'happen within us, so to speak, *unbeknownst to ourselves*, or at least in such a quick and fleeting fashion' that we need to pay great attention if we are to notice them at all.[96] This is the great trump card in the hands of those who aspire to manipulate others. He underlines the point. Man is the architect of his own life 'without realising it'. This happens through the interplay of his own perceptions and 'what seems to us most natural in ourselves is *totally artificial* and is the work of our own hands even if it is *unbeknownst to us*'.[97] The really subtle thing that has to be achieved is to discreetly meddle in this process of self-construction in such a way as to turn it imperceptibly into a process of 'construction by the other'. From the spiritualist Rousseau to the materialist *idéologues*, by way of so very many others, along this whole path we never stray from a dialectical position that is reductionist by nature and manipulative in intent. Consequently, it seems to me that it lies at the very heart of the Enlightenment and is central to an understanding of the Revolution. Condorcet, another friend of Cabanis, spoke of 'this multitude of weak and insignificant men without virtue and without vices, whose behaviour depends on circumstances more than on themselves, and whose *will belongs to whomsoever chooses to control it*'.[98] Without virtue and without vices, they are not endowed with responsibility and controlling them from a distance can take nothing away from them. This is all the more true, it would seem, if it is with the intention of perfecting them.

Notes

1. L. Poliakov, *Le Mythe aryen*, Paris, 1971,160 ('L'anthropologie des Lumières').
2. A. Destutt de Tracy, *Mémoire sur la Faculté de penser* (read at the *Institut* on 2nd floréal Year IV, 21 April 1796, then on 20 June and 18 October 1796 and finally on 10 and 15 February 1798; published in Year VI), re-ed., C.O.P.L.F., Paris, 1992, 71.
3. P. Cabanis, in *La Décade philosophique*, 30th germinal Year VII, 19 April 1799, 150.
4. Reference to Chapter Nine, note 11.
5. We would argue that there is, of course, a connection between the logic underpinning state scientism in the post-thermidorean period and which leads to the creation of the *Institut*, and this provision in Morelly's *Code de la Nature* (1755): 'There will be a sort of public codification of all the branches of knowledge, in which nothing will ever be added to metaphysics or moral science beyond certain bounds which are defined by law: all that will be added to it are physical, mathematical or mechanical discoveries which have been confirmed by experiment or by reasoning' (re-edited, Paris, 1970, by a member of the Academy of Sciences of the U.S.S.R., 151.). See above, 22.
6. Quoted in J. Dhombres, ed. *L'École normale de l'an III, Leçons de mathématiques. Édition annotée des cours de Laplace, Lagrange, Monge*, Paris, 1992, 125.
7. According to a comment from one of Garat's students, who says that he 'has rather lofty ideas: he speaks of nothing less than perfecting the way humans are organised' (quoted by J.-R. Armogathe, 'L'École normale de l'an III et le cours de Garat' in *Corpus, Revue de Philosophie*, no. 14–15, 1990, [143–54] 1)
8. G. Gusdorf, *L'Homme Romantique*, ('Les Sciences humaines et la Pensée occidentale', vol. XI), Paris, 1984, 26 and 27. We would prefer 'humanity'

to 'individuality', on account of the philosophical individualism which remains a basic element of this whole doctrinal position. It would even seem to us that what is beginning to emerge here is a correlation between the individualisation of the point of view, and the dehumanisation of what is being individualised.
9. See Chapter Two.
10. Letter from Condorcet to Turgot, 1 October 1772, quoted in *Corr. gén. d'Helvétius*, vol. 3, Toronto/Oxford, 1991, 422/2.
11. Mme. de Staël, *Des Circonstances actuelles qui peuvent terminer la Révolution*, (1798), Paris/Geneva, 1979, 273. She maintains that in a Revolution, as in everything else, a return to basic principles is the only way of modifying and correcting matters (but here she is thinking about freedom rather than reason).
12. Letter to Marmontel, 20 December 1766: 'I cannot see what harm can ever be done by reason. Up to now, it has never been tried. We should at least give it a try to see if it is as harmful as all that' (Voltaire, *Corr.*, vol.8, 785).
13. From the Conseil du Perfectionnement de l'École, nivôse Year III, January 1795: quoted by A. Fourcy, *Histoire de l'École Polytechnique* (1828), reprint, Paris, 1987 (J. Dhombres), 70. The École's course bears the heading 'De l'homme et des animaux considérés comme moteurs': Laplace, *Rapport sur la situation de l'École Polytechnique*, 3rd nivôse Year IX, 24 December 1800, Paris, floréal Year IX (April–May) 1801), 51.
14. J.-J. Rousseau, *Émile ou de l'Éducation*, Book III, 261.
15. See above, 128.
16. On this point, see the quotations proposed in my study which has already been mentioned: 'Madame de Staël, Napoléon and the *Idéologues*', in *Himeji International Forum of Law and Politics*, no. 1, 1993, 41–42, footnote 9.
17. For example, *Corr. gén. d'Helvétius*, vol. 3, 200–01 and 329.
18. Hence, he writes to his wife in September 1762: 'You know that I have a great deal of money in my safe ... All this money has accumulated there little by little .... It is absolutely essential that I live in the same place as my safe. Now, laden as it is, this safe could not be placed on the first floor without breaking through the floorboards. On the ground-floor, where it is at the moment, it is resting on a supporting vault' et cetera. (ibid., 52). A little later on: 'If it's weight does not cause it to break through the floor, there would be no harm in leaving it in the salon', et cetera. (60) On his death, his estate was valued at 3,350,000 Touraine pounds.
19. Marriage to the Comte d'Andlau; the contract was signed by Louis XV and the future kings Louis XVI, Louis XVIII and Charles X, 27 September 1772: ibid., 418/2.
20. P.-S. Ballanche, *Essai sur les institutions sociales dans leur rapport avec les idées nouvelles* (1818), re-edition, C.O.P.L.F., Paris, 131.
21. Letter published in J. Massin, ed. *Napoléon, Bonaparte. L'Œuvre et l'Histoire* (large selection of public and private writings, and the testimony of various collaborators), 12 vols, Paris, 1969–71, vol.1, 420 (abbreviation: N.B.O.H.).
22. D'Holbach, *Système de la Nature*, 2 vols, Paris, 1990, vol.1, 153.
23. We refer to the reprint of the 1844 edition, Paris /Genève, 1980.
24. At her death in 1800 she bequeathed the usufruct of the house to him.
25. Cabanis, *Rapports*, 78.
26. A. Destutt de Tracy, *Mémoire sur la Faculté de penser* (1796–98), C.O.P.L.F., Paris, 1992, 140.

27. Cabanis, *Rapports*, 583.
28. Destutt de Tracy, *Élémens d'Idéologie, Première Partie. Idéologie proprement dite* (1801, 1804), re-edition of the edition of 1817, Paris, 1970, 24 (w.u.o). See also 225 et circa.
29. Ibid., 25.
30. Destutt, *Mémoire*, 95: 'All are equally the result of the way we are organised, and are products of the same operations of our thinking combined in different ways'.
31. Cabanis, *Rapports*, 337–38
32. Hence d'Holbach, *Système de la Nature*, vol. 1, 332–33: 'This having been said, no man can be called disinterested; this word can only be used for those whose motives we are not aware of or whose interests we agree with'.
33. Cabanis, *Rapports*, 399.
34. Ibid., 261, where, speaking about his own thesis, he remarks: 'As we simplify the human system, these opinions and these conclusions cast much light upon it'.
35. Ibid., 47.
36. Ibid., 138.
37. Ibid., 581.
38. Letter to Tronchin, 20 May 1765: Voltaire,*Corr.*, vol. 8, 62. The affinity between the digestive function and the the act of thinking is a recurring theme in Voltaire: *Corr*, vol. 7, 518; vol. 9, 391, 873, and 1,027; vol. 11, 326–27.
39. Cabanis, *Rapports*, 244.
40. Ibid., 242–44.
41. Rousseau, *Émile*, Book V, 507: 'The search for abstract and speculative truths, principles and axioms in the sciences, everything which involves a tendency to generalise ideas is not for women' and so on.
42. Cabanis, *Rapports*, 244. As for Rousseau, see above, 75–76.
43. Letter to Frédéric II, 15 October 1749: Voltaire *Corr*, vol. 3, 122. Voltaire's misogyny (with its general tendency to reduce women to the sexual function, 'the job they all know how to do well': *Corr*, vol. 9, 477) is commonly expressed in a vulgar and ribald tone.
44. Cabanis, *Rapports*, 234. On the child as a 'small portion of organised matter', See above, 83.
45. Cabanis, *Rapports*, 516.
46 Ibid., 538.
47. Hence, see ibid., 120–21, 127, 417–18.
48. C.-A. Helvétius, *De l'Homme*, 2 vols, Paris, 1989, vol.1, 182–83.
49. Hence, above, 57–58.
50. Destutt de Tracy, *Élemens d'Idéologie*, preface of 1801, xiii.
51. Ibid., 12.
52. Cabanis, *Rapports*, 127 and 128.
53. Letter of October 1755 to Charles Bonnet: *Corr, compl. de Rousseau*, vol. 3, 191; J.-J. Rousseau, *La Nouvelle Héloïse* (1761), Paris, 1988, 460.
54. D. Diderot, *Entretien entre d'Alembert et Diderot* (around 1770) Paris, 1965, 52.
55. Cabanis, *Rapports*, 538.
56. Destutt de Tracy, *Élemens d'Idéologie*, preface of 1801, xxiii.
57. Ibid., xxiii–xxiv.
58. Helvétius, *De l'Homme*, vol. 1, 46.
59. C.-A. Helvétius, *De l'Esprit*, Paris, 1988, 539.

60. Cabanis, *Rapports*, 411.
61. Ibid., 300.
62. This expression, which could have been lifted from the *Rapports*, is quoted by J. Fiévée, *Correspondance et relations avec Bonaparte 1802–1813*, 3 vols, Paris, 1836, vol. 1, 113.
63. See above, 153.
64. That is to say man's physical constitution, of which his moral constitution forms a part.
65. Cabanis, *Rapports*, 298–99.
66. H. Mirabeau, *Deuxième discours sur l'Éducation publique* (between 1789 and 1791), already quoted (see above 92–93) 97.
67. To d'Argental, 20 April 1769: Voltaire, *Corr.*, vol. 9, 872.
68. See above, 67.
69. Destutt de Tracy, *Mémoire*, 171.
70. Destutt de Tracy, *Élemens d'Idéologie*, vol.1, 213. On this theme, see above, especially 116–17.
71. The connection he makes is very much in the style of Helvétius, who writes, for example: 'The skill of the groom consists in knowing exactly what movements he can make the animal he is training perform; and the skill of the Minister in knowing what he can make the peoples he governs do' (*De l'Homme*, vol.1, 46).
72. C.-L. Montesquieu, *Les Lettres persanes* (1721), Paris, 1949, Letter CXXII, 174.
73. 26 June 1793; reported by Sieyès in the *Journal d'Instruction sociale*, end of June/ beginning of July 1793; J. Guillaume, *Procès-verbaux du Comité d'Instruction Publique*, vol.1, Paris, 1891, 573, and *Archives parlementaires*, 1/68/218/2.
74. Cabanis, *Rapports*, 411. See also, for example, 219: 'Man as well as the most perfected among the animals, at the head of which he is placed by virtue of his structure and his great sensitivity...'
75. See above, 85.
76. Faiguet de Villeneuve, *L'Économie politique. Projet pour enrichir et pour perfectionner l'espèce humaine*, London, 1763, 115–20, quoted second-hand.
77. Caradeuc de la Chalotais, *Essai d'Éducation nationale, ou Plan d'Études pour la jeunesse*, 1763, 6, second-hand quotation.
78. Document quoted above, 97, note 33; J. Guillaume, *Procès-verbaux du Comité d'Instruction Publique*, 569. Lakanal, reporter to the Committee, sees in the Sieyès text 'a faithful and illuminating exposition of the principles that had guided the Committee for Public Instruction' (567).
79. Ibid., 573.
80. I refer to my study, already quoted, 'Sur les Droits de l'Homme et la Vendée', Bouère, 1995, as well as to my study 'Sur l'Homme de la Déclaration des Droits', in *Droits, Revue française de Théorie juridique*, no. 8, (1988), 83–89.
81. See the very important article by Benno Müller-Hill, 'La génétique après Auschwitz', in *Les Temps Modernes*, no. 511, (February 1989), 52–85 (translated from the German by A.-D. Balmès).
82. Destutt de Tracy, *Élemens d'Idéologie. Deuxième Partie. Grammaire*, 14.
83. Cabanis, *Rapports*, 300.
84. L. Poliakov, *Le Mythe Aryen*, Paris, 1971, 222–24 (the quotation is from p. 222; re-edition 1987, 248–50). Once again this calls to mind so many of the deeply 'eugenicist' quotations from J. Rostand.
85. L. Poliakov, *L'Auberge des Musiciens. Mémoires*, Paris, 1981, 220.

86. See on this subject an important article, which will no doubt become a classic reference, and which seems to have a bearing on many of our own comments: J. de Viguerie, 'Les 'lumières' et les peuples. Conclusions d'un séminaire', in *Revue Historique*, no. 287/1, (1993), 161–89.
87. See above, 68 and 76.
88. Rousseau, *La Nouvelle Héloïse*, 550.
89. Rousseau, *Les Confessions*, 408–09; see above, 73.
90. See above, 75.
91. From 12 July 1778, letter from one of his friends to the *Journal de Paris*, in *Corr. complète de Rousseau*, vol. 40, appendix 682, 359.
92. See above, 70 and thereafter.
93. Destutt de Tracy, *Mémoire*, 139. Sexual need plays a primordial role in this respect. And the author explains: 'all our moral feelings and all the means we possess for disseminating our thoughts stem from the sole need we have to reproduce ourselves, because by giving us the need to take control of the will of our fellow human beings, it gives us the need to communicate with them' (140).
94. See above, for example 162.
95. Destutt de Tracy, *Élemens d'Idéologie*, vol. 1, 67.
96. Destutt de Tracy, *Mémoire*, 136.
97. Ibid., 173.
98. M. Condorcet, 'Rapport sur les Prisons' (1780–84), in Condorcet, *Arithmétique politique. Textes rares ou inédits (1767–89)*, Paris, 1994, 151–52.

Chapter 11

La Révellière-Lépeaux and Leclerc

My aim in examining the *idéologues* was to underline the extent to which the materialist tendency was such an important element of post-Thermidor thinking, but with a view to enquiring afterwards as to whether the anti-Christian spiritualist faction, which was also very solidly represented in the Directory, offered, after all, a noticeably different way of looking at man, that is to say, a more deferent way of looking at him. Now it would seem that by the very nature of things I have already begun that enquiry. The clear affinity between the most out-and-out spiritualists and the anthropology of the least timorous among the materialists was one of the lessons to be learned from the journey through the Enlightenment we have just taken. And in the front line among these spiritualists was Rousseau, whom I have once again just identified as bearing an astonishing but distinct family resemblance (to say the very least) with some of the pages in which Cabanis is at his least discreet. I should add that the group formed by the *idéologues*, however tight-knit it may, quite justifiably perhaps, appear to have been, was nevertheless far from being impenetrable or set in stone. One of its members, Maine de Biran, was soon to follow a resolutely spiritualist line of development and, more generally, the whole group was in visible osmosis with a variety of external influences. Within the cultural melting-pot of the age, which by its very nature was less homogeneous, *idéologie* served precisely the function of adding greater power and influence to the more diffuse reductionist elements.

Under the rule of Bonaparte, and under Napoléon even more so, the materialism of Cabanis tends to pull in its horns: whether this is a case of reining in or caving in is not really important. The important thing is to understand that the passage from a hard-line materialism to a wishy-washy version of spiritualism, or from defiant atheism to vague and ever more utilitarian forms of deism, is an easy passage to make and it can be made in either direction. Return trips are not unheard of, and this is a realm where hesitations and realignments can be seen as merely revealing an underlying sense of perplexity which is often present beneath even what appear to be the most outspokenly dogmatic positions.

I have already mentioned the Directory's very real obsession with propaganda, and the totalitarian ambitions it entertained in this respect could have seemed to be necessitated, if I may be allowed to use such an expression, by the coming together of historical circumstances of particular delicacy and tension and a particular range of socioanthropological ideas. Now it could hardly be more obvious that among the proudest proselytisers for a republicanisation of minds, in accordance with the reductionist procedures of sensualism that were classic procedures at the time, there were those who were keen to develop the line of thinking proposed by the *Contrat Social* and by Robespierre, and experiment at inventing religions that would meet the needs of their political objectives. This provides a clear illustration of the point I have just been making. The religiosity of these spiritualists is clearly compatible with a simplified vision of humanity. As has so often been the case, I am simply touching upon this point in order to check whether the archetype of humanity underpinning it continues to involve the version we have become used to and which consists of a purely passive being, lacking volition, lacking free will, completely open to manipulation, to remodelling and to external control, as 'the whim of social engineers' dictates.

Only two of these latter will retain our attention because they seem to be exemplary in many respects. Both offer the interesting case of being men who were, at one and the same time, active politicians at a very high level, regicides, and theoreticians with a particular interest in propaganda and republican cults. The first is La Révellière-Lépeaux (1753–1824), a member of the Constituent Assembly and the Convention, a member in the post-Thermidor years of the Committee for Public Safety, first president of the *Conseil des Anciens* and thereafter, from October 1795 to June 1799, permanently one of its five directors. While holding this position he conspired in the *coup d'état* of fructidor (September 1797), which, as we know, marked an acceleration in the drive towards republicanisation in France, and which came as a violent reaction to the increasing favour that the monarchist movement was finding among the electorate. The second example is his companion, Jean-Baptiste Leclerc (1756–1826), whose career was possibly less impressive but who was a member of the Constituent Assembly, then the Convention, a member of the *Conseil des Cinq Cents* of which he was also president for a while, just as under the Consulate he held the same honour in the *Corps législatif*. He spent more of his time on theoretical matters than did La Révellière, who nevertheless devoted a fair amount of time to such questions, like Leclerc, often in speeches and pamphlets. For that matter, La Révellière was not one to hide the fact that he agreed entirely with the more audacious aspects of what Leclerc had to say. The latter conceived, and twice vainly presented (once in August and once in November 1797), a fully-developed plan for a civil cult, while La Révellière is well-known for the active support he offered to the theophilanthropic religion.

Just like Robespierre in floréal, therefore, and like Rousseau in earlier times, La Révellière was exposed to the risks of the very same ambiguous positions. In May 1797 at the *Institut* he tried his best to adopt a vehement tone in his attack on Enlightenment rationalism. He sought to criticise its dryness, the feeling of an absence of responsibility it tended to awaken in men and the deplorable social side-effects that flowed from this. In fact, the comments are couched in a fair amount of discretion. One must conclude that this is because of the power exercised at the *Institut* at this time by the *idéologues*, but there can be no doubt as to the underlying message,[1] and the closing words of the speech express a fierce condemnation of 'the persecution meeted out in the name of proud philosophy'.[2] In the event, La Révellière even goes so far as to speak of ways of thinking which 'passing from one abstraction to another ... lead us ... to conclusions which are completely destructive of all social virtues'.[3] And these latter, as a result, can be seen as nothing more than 'pure convention; all these virtues are complete illusions, miserable prejudices, which are incapable of putting a brake on the man intent on pleasure or halting the ambitions of a clever man or the *philosophe* currently in vogue',[4] (or should we simply say the ambitions of the intellectual dogmatist).

There is still a tendency for self-interest to enjoy an unfounded legitimacy. La Révellière is saddened by this[5] as Robespierre before him had been. But was his distatste for the notion of self-interest as such really stronger than that which Robespierre had felt, or, like Robespierre was his distaste not simply targeted against *the vile form of self-interest*?[6] A few months later a proclamation issued by the Directory, of which he was a member, complains of the absence of enthusiasm shown by the French for providing the wherewithal to ensure road repairs are carried out. The proclamation does not condemn egoists but precisely those *vile egoists* who don't even know how to *work out that their self-interest is served* by donating the share they are called upon to contribute with a view to raising 'the sum for the general good of all'.[7] The charge levelled is an interesting one: in the style of the floréal sermon, the Directory here places in opposition the vile form of self-interest, that works to the detriment of society, and a better, well-informed type of egoism, that works in the interest of the egoist through the mediating process of serving the 'general good of all' which through calculated self-interest he has helped to advance. Once more we come into contact with the very basis on which the social contractualism of the day is founded. Under the Terror, La Révellière was obliged to go into hiding, but that does not mean that his spiritualist outlook and the battles he waged against Enlightenment reductionism do not themselves run the risk of being predicated on the same weaknesses or contain the same ambiguities as the position adopted and the battles waged by Robespierre. These fraternal enemies were both men of their times, just as those against whom they fought were also men of their times.

And this affinity between them is also perceptible in matters relating to religion. The dogmas in favour of which La Révellière militates may recall those defended by Robespierre, in that the commitment felt to them does not stem so much from any conviction that certain metaphysical notions may be held to be objectively true, but rather from the belief that they are *socially useful* in a unique way. This is perhaps saying rather a lot. I am not seeking to cast doubt upon the sincerity of anyone's beliefs here (any more than I was in the case of Robespierre, and even less in the case of Rousseau, and, in any event, that is not the question), but the assurance on which they are founded. I am not going so far as to say that the social usefulness of the idea of a God who metes out punishment and reward in some great beyond[8] was a first principle, but I am indeed saying that very little was required for that very notion of social usefulness to come to be thought of as a first principle. All of which tends to call into question somewhat this particular article of faith, and tends to confer relatively more importance than would seem appropriate on the desirability of God's rule over individuals. And, naturally, much the same can be said of the notion of the immortality of the soul, in the absence of which any anxiety about sanctions in an after life loses a considerable amount of its effectiveness, and above all, and this is the important point, loses its beneficial consequences for society. The way La Révellière expresses himself leaves us in no doubt as to the mental logic within which he himself is operating on such matters: 'The existence of a God who rewards virtue and avenges crimes, the immortality of the soul, which is a natural *consequence*, so to speak, of this first proposition, these provide the bases for a cult that is *useful* for a nation; without them the whole moral edifice will crumble to the ground'.[9] As before, the concern of those promoting civil religion is to provoke a feeling of moral responsibility in the consciousness of men, whereas in fact, this same consciousness is neither conceived of nor treated as though they were really capable of responsibility, since, on the contrary, the claim that is made is that they can be profoundly influenced and even modified by multiple 'impressions'. As Voltaire says (and his religious sincerity becomes an object of greater suspicion as a result): 'it is very good to *make men believe* that they have an immortal soul, and that there exists a vengeful God who will punish my peasants if they steal my corn and my wine'.[10]

Let us therefore perhaps caricaturise matters a little. Materialists, since they presume that man's inner nature can be completely accounted for in terms of scientific methods and procedures and that it is therefore totally open and transparent to the investigations that the scientist undertakes or advises for political purposes, not to say for purposes to do with *policing* mankind, have, for these very reasons, *no need* for additional support based on arguments of a religious nature. The spiritualists, on the other hand, are convinced that there exist pockets of man's inner nature which are hidden in inaccessible corners and which manage to escape the control of those who seek to govern, just as an irreducible residue of men's actions also escapes their scrutiny. They consider it politically necessary that everyone should at least believe himself accountable in the eyes of a transcendent authority from which no corner of man's psyche, any more than a single one of his actions even his most secret ones, can escape observation.[11] As one of their number writes: 'A religion is a necessary thing. It supplements the laws of mankind which cannot have access into man's inner being'.[12] Judged by this standard, the 'spiritualist' can sometimes be considered as nothing more than an indecisive materialist, sceptical of the capability of reason to master one day, or at least in a not-too-distant future, all the mechanisms and all the secrets of man's inner life. As you will have guessed, Voltaire's 'spiritualism' would be very much of this variety, but it also finds a very vigorous expression in the person of Bonaparte as he was around the time of the Concordat, whereas Robespierre and La Révellière move much closer to it when they appear to place emphasis on the social usefulness of religion. If this paragraph is rather schematic it is with the sole purpose of bringing certain ideas into sharper focus. I should repeat that what is at issue here is not drawing attention to questions concerning moral sincerity but the whole problem of intellectual consistency.

For indeed, deferential reservations about the mystery surrounding what it is to be human, which might be seen as implying belief in the immortality of the soul, would hardly be appropriate in reality if such a belief were seen as emanating from concerns relating to matters of mere social convenience. La Révellière deplores the fact that civil ceremonies, which had been laicised beyond all recognition by the Revolution, no longer inculcated in the citizens the feelings of natural piety that should be associated with the important moments of their existence.[13] He indignantly exclaims, with respect to burials, that: 'we are being made to become accustomed to considering the remains of a spouse, a father, a child, a brother, a sister, a friend, like those of any other animal whatsoever'.[14] *Any other animal whatsoever*: once again, the expression is extremely interesting: at the very moment when the speaker is claiming to make a clear demarcation between the human and the animal kingdoms, the network of reductionist postulates that provide a framework for the mental atmosphere with which he is impregnated drag him back into line and confine him inexorably within a mode of expression which, it has to be pointed out, contradicts his intended message.

And the exorbitant power with which he considers himself to be invested, following on from so many others before him, and which he wields with a view to remodelling his fellow-citizens, this also testifies to an absence of deferential reservations with regard to the humanity that resides within the breasts of his fellow-men. Like so many others during these decades, La Révellière holds dear the philanthropic ambition of 'contributing to the improvement of the human species'.[15] He even goes so far as to talk of 'modifying, so to speak, the substance of humanity'.[16] It says a great deal that when we read such words we are no longer surprised. We have become desensitised to such expressions, which would not be out of place in a certain page of the *Contrat Social* with which we have by now become familiar, and in another such page in Cabanis where it is said that we should 'dare to revise and correct the work of nature'[17] and in so many others still which tend to proliferate during these years.[18] Under the Directory La Révellière is an ardent and zealous supporter of Revolutionary *fêtes*, which were presumed to have an immense, and therefore extremely precious, capacity for conditioning men. He is among those who explain and re-explain and seek to maximise the use of this electrifying power (he uses the verb 'to electrify'), that assemblies of citizens and the atmosphere of massed crowds, offer to representatives of government. It is far more effective to make an impression on souls collectively than it is to do so on individuals. 'The mere fact of bringing together large numbers of men, moved by the same feeling, all expressing themselves at the same time and in the same way, has an irresistible power over men's souls, the result it produces is incalculable',[19] he is happy to point out. Like Robespierre, and in the spirit of Rousseau, he has far more confidence in feelings than in reason when it comes to manipulating crowds.[20] In this respect, all things must be calculated in advance. The 'unctuousness of the speeches', a 'sweet and penetrating moral message', a 'sense of tender harmony' will all have the automatic effect of creating a happy frame of mind and fraternal instincts.[21] But it is also intended that, if necessary, the *fête* should be able to 'fire the imagination'.[22]

These *Réflexions sur le culte* were read in May 1797. At this time the Royalists were on the crest of a wave. The April elections had been a total success for them, a fact which confirmed the urgency of having recourse to the sort of techniques that La Révellière talks about so favourably. The *coup d'état* of fructidor Year V, led by him and two fellow members of the Directory, aimed to set an obstacle in the path of any legal return of the monarchy – an aim in which it succeeded. This strong-arm intervention occurred on 4 September. On 9 September the purged Directory, presided over by La Révellière, addressed a proclamation to the French people.[23] What seems to us to be particularly interesting about this proclamation is that political dissension in France is therein presented, in a sense, as a truncated form of a mere *conflict of habits*. And indeed, one of the corollaries of this is that the mass of citizens are reduced to being considered as the equivalent of a passive substance over which Royalists and Republicans can be seen to be fighting for technical control. For Rousseau, education is merely the inculcation of habits;[24] re-education, therefore, is merely a question of replacing one set of habits with another, which habits, said d'Holbach, are 'within the power of those who make us contract them'.[25] Rousseau also spoke of those '*voluntary* practices that it is always easy for the government to set up'[26] – the internal ambiguities in the terminology here will no longer surprise us.

Apparently the words 'always easy' rather overstate the case. As far as the Republicans are concerned has not everything already been done to try to make sure that new habits have been adopted? If, under the Directory, that still hasn't produced the desired results among the population at large, it is because, on the one hand, mental routines would appear to be more deeply ingrained than was thought – the new city, as it will be termed a little later on, has stumbled upon resistances 'on the part of all those men tied to old prejudices by the force of habit'.[27] On the other hand, it is because enemies of the Republic can only be conceived of as necessarily working upon this self-same patch where the focus is on man's habits. All those 'friends of royalty', working in the Royalist cause, are accused of having 'omitted nothing ... in their efforts to bring institutions, *fêtes,* customs and practices back into *the fold of despotism.* They knew very well that man is a creature of habit and that by changing his habits you change the man himself'.[28] Although one would not wish to waste time by going too deeply into the wording of this accusation, in which the theme of the modification of mankind once again surfaces, it is worth noting in passing how significant it is that the Republican propagandists can only explain their own lack of success by accusing the Royalists of having subtly used the very methods that they themselves have theorised and sought to practice. Of course, all this is mere illusion, it reveals the narrow system of categories within which the social anthropology inherited from the Enlightenment has imprisoned the most committed supporters of the Revolution. Those who combat the Revolution are accused by La Révellière as having 'remodelled the mass of the nation *according to a Royalist design*'[29] – a wonderful expression, especially in so far as it serves to reveal *a contrario* the primordial concern of the Republican élites: to remodel *according to a Republican design*, so to speak, the mass of the nation. As a result of which, there can be no grounds for surprise, a month later, when we hear La Révellière talking to the *Institut* about 'ways of forcing the universality of spectators to participate fully in all that is organised on the occasion of *fêtes nationales*'.[30] The delirious utopianism of this speech is most impressive: moreover, the author confesses to having taken 'a holiday' from problems of a more concrete nature[31] when developing his ideas in this speech, ideas which he would nonetheless like to see put into practice. In such a context the idea of freedom can only have connotations of a utopian sort, and such a notion of freedom is, in reality, the negation of true freedom: in this scheme, the free citizen is the one who is willing to allow himself to be led into happiness in a state of mind such as the reformer imagines him to be in, or in which the reformer intends to put him. In fact, we can speak of the text concerned in terms of a pathological desire for unanimity and for the standardised, for the complete control of men's minds and their behaviour. It envisages, incidentally, a communal council of elderly people to safeguard the moral purity of young girls.[32] Civic beatitude must be realised and, if necessary, enforced upon the citizens: it even envisages measures to avoid a situation in which 'spectators *deprive themselves* of their enjoyment'[33] through their failure to follow the programme, that is to say, to respect what has been organised with them in mind. To this end they are called upon to have the goodness to remain patiently in place so that the festivities may work their full civic effect on the minds of each and every citizen. Uniforms (and carefully conceived ones at that), are needed, since 'a sense of pomp cannot be created ... by the ridiculous cut of our angular and ill-fitting clothes, and from the clash of colours from individual to individual'.[34] A little while later, the same theoretician writes, 'creating a sense of public-spiritedness' is merely 'putting citizens in harmony with the laws'.[35] Consequently, we have here the same totalitarian perspective which has now become so familiar to us. On many occasions when La Révellière deals with the techniques to be used and the advantages to be had in mounting civic festivities, he calls to mind, although secretly we may be reluctant to admit as much, more recent liturgies that have been recited at Nuremburg, Peking or elsewhere. Henri Grange said of this exemplary philanthropist, who was not the inheritor of Enlightenment materialism but rather of a very ambiguous form of Enlightenment spiritualism: 'It was through his drive and his initiative that the manipulation of mentalities and the republicanisation of public opinion under the Directory took on a new dimension, and both the methods he used and the projects he imagined make him a *true forebear of the ministers of propaganda we find in totalitarian states*, and of their most elaborate techniques'.[36]

An equally flattering view could have been advanced in respect of his friend Jean-Baptiste Leclerc, whose total communion of ideas with La Révellière is well-attested: 'Same principles, same views, same feelings...' So runs the anonymous epigraph to a combined collection of *Opuscules politiques et moraux*, dated during their lifetimes and drawing on work by both authors.[37] Even if the epigraph did not say this, however, it would be sufficient to read through the work of either of them to understand that on the frontispiece of their brochures their names are almost interchangeable. Less constantly solicited by the demands of high-level political activity,[38] Leclerc simply appears to have published a slightly greater number of plans for reform.[39] And running through these, like an obsession, there is always the same concern to work upon man's inner nature for the good of the cause, with a view to 'insinuating Republicanism everywhere', 'quietly infiltrating the public mind'. There is also the constant desire to achieve absolute control of the slightest action and the slightest thought of each and every citizen. If it is necessary to extirpate all traces of Royalism it is, as he himself puts it, '*even in men's thoughts*'.[40]

In this respect, Leclerc proved himself to be hypersensitive to the value of music, whether it was instrumental or vocal, as a method of working transformations on men's minds. This particular sensualist championed the auditory mode. He even interpreted the rebellion by the inhabitants of Vendée as a pathological reaction to being too suddenly plunged into a state of deprivation – these rough country folk had been too abruptly deprived of their usual Sunday melodies. This, he insisted, is 'the most concrete reason' for the uprising.[41] Once again we come face to face with the idea that was, as we know, current everywhere at the time, and according to which man's inner life was a purely mechanical reaction to to his environment. Leclerc explains the brutishness of the rebels by reference to the roughness of their natural milieu, which he caricatures because this is necessary for the purposes of his own mental logic.[42] In doing so he reasons in exactly the same way as Cabanis, who, in these same post-Thermidor years, when it suited him to have a pejorative human archetype at his disposal in order that his thinking should remain attuned to the pessimism that was then the order of the day, arbitrarily places his natural man in a wildly inhospitable setting, which he, too, copiously caricaturises so that the mind of the savage cannot avoid but be influenced by it in a very negative way.[43] This is how we can move from a 'noble savage' to a 'brutish savage' without, in reality, ever abandoning the Rousseauist view of man's total and entirely passive permeability to his milieu.[44] And, once again, this similarity in the methods of Cabanis and Leclerc is highly revealing. Cabanis is a materialist and reduces man to the status of an animal. Leclerc, on the contrary, is a spiritualist and when he hears a rumour that 'a famous naturalist' claimed to identify in the inhabitants of Vendée 'the link in the chain that joins apes to men', he is outraged as though this is an 'insult to the whole of humanity'.[45] But this does not mean that, as a sensualist, he supposes any more than Cabanis does that his fellow-men are capable of overcoming the conditioning they receive from the environment. To repeat once again an expression used by Cabanis, and with which Rousseau would probably have concurred, the inhabitants of Vendée are nothing more than 'the living image of their locale'[46] in the eyes of Leclerc.

Since men, to his mind, are so sensitive to music, it is not surprising that Leclerc wishes to use it as a decisive aid in the task of government. Music and poetry must be the monopoly of the Republican state, which will organise the themes to be developed, will select the genres and will, for each canton, decide the number and type of musical instruments, all of which are determined and imposed under threat of incurring fines.[47] It is thanks to such procedures that 'by impressing a *simultaneous* movement on *all men's hearts*, by giving them a *uniform* direction, we will succeed in putting some *unanimity* into men's passions'.[48] There is nothing new in all this, except perhaps that Leclerc would like the unanimity he seeks to be diachronic into the bargain. As an out-and-out enthusiast of *la Marseillaise* and the *Ça Ira*, those 'electrifying anthems', he predicts that their continued repetition over the years will place citizens once and for all in a Republican frame of mind: and hence it would appear to be necessary that in this way: 'in *all* periods, at *all* times, in *all* their games, in *all* their forms of relaxation, our children should be able to keep present in their minds the origins of their freedom'.[49] This stabbing repetition of the word *all* calls to mind a similar repetition in a famous phrase from Rabaut Saint-Étienne, dating from December 1792 which we have already quoted.⁵⁰

In a similar vein, in a report dated November 1797, that is to say once again just after fructidor and therefore at a time when the Republicans were deeply woried about the successful outcome of their enterprise, Jean-Baptiste Leclerc uses the following very strong words to evoke the task that falls to the legislator: '*None* of the moments in the life of a citizen, *none* of his actions, *none* of his sympathies, *none* of his interests, should be indifferent to him [the legislator]. In some way, he has to keep his *eye* on the *daily* acts of *each* individual in order to *guide* the citizens towards the *common* goal on which social *unity* rests'.⁵¹ To qualify such assertions as they would seem to deserve to be qualified would require that I once again risk using the word 'totalitarian'. To comment upon them as they deserve to be commented upon would lead me to risk repeating myself even more, and this consideration has at least the advantage of making it clear to what extent the theme of the human being as a purely passive entity, totally open to the forms of manipulation that the legislator deems to be necessary for achieving public happiness – a theme, issuing quietly and happily from the Enlightenment – can be traced throughout the Revolution, from beginning to end, provided that one is willing to take the trouble to look for it.

His eye on the daily acts of each individual ... The omnipresent eye of the law-maker: this could also remind us of the pedagogical theories prevalent throughout the Enlightenment, theories which focus on a set of problems that are so tightly intertwined with questions of a political nature. In *Émile*, we read that the pupil 'must not take a single step that you have not already foreseen; he must not open his mouth without you knowing what he is about to say'.⁵² 'The child in these somewhat totalitarian educational systems is always under supervision, especially when he doesn't realise it, therefore unbeknownst to him, during his games and his periods of recreation, and at mealtimes too'.⁵³ Jean-Baptiste Leclerc, as a faithful inheritor of the Enlightenment⁵⁴ took the trouble to emphasise '*Men are big children*', and law-making, according to Destutt de Tracy, is simply 'the education of grown men'.⁵⁵ We could also add, as far as the inquisitorial eye of the pedagogue is concerned that in October 1795, as the Thermidorean Convention went into its final phase, it envisaged that its law enforcement officers should 'carry in their hands a white stick of the same height as a man and mounted with an ivory sphere on which *an eye* would be engraved in black'.[56] Similarly, in 1796 a decree issued by the Directory determining 'the form of the engraving intended to serve as the frontispiece to the *Bulletin des Lois*' ruled that in one of its hands, Law would hold 'a stick mounted with an eye, as a symbol of watchfulness'.[57] The words of Leclerc on the onerous ocular task befalling the legislator and this article of the decree seem to offer each other mutual support and comfort. If the notion of the individual conscience tends to find itself invalidated by the anthropology of the age, a substitute is needed. The eye of the State appears to have replaced it and it is essential that all citizens should realise the fact. What we have here, in the event, is a symbolism with a very practical agenda.

Notes

1. L.-M. La Révellière-Lépeaux, *Réflexions sur le culte, sur les cérémonies civiles et sur les fêtes nationales* (read at the *Institut* 12th floréal Year V, 4 May 1797), Paris, Year V, 19. 'In matters concerning morality, purely metaphysical reasoning has little effect other than to make us feel exceedingly unenthusiastic about doing good'.
2. Ibid., 45; cf. 44: 'My ideas and my maxims will probably find little favour with both priests and with certain of the *philosophes*'.
3. Ibid., 19.
4. Ibid., 20.
5. Ibid., 21. 'Finally I must admit that when I see moral questions being taught from a metaphysical perspective and see fine and very serious treatises being produced which are founded solely on metaphysics, my soul grows cold as ice and my imagination dies within me; in such sad productions I am unable to see anything more than the seed of the most complete egoism, the most mind-numbing dullness, and often the most criminal as well as the most coldly calculating expression of naked ambition and vice working against the interests and the happiness of mankind'.
6. See above, 136 and thereafter.
7. Proclamation of 22nd frimaire Year VI, 12 December 1797: *Bull. Lois* no. 164, 13.
8. La Révellière-Lépeaux, *Réflexions sur le culte*, 10.
9. Ibid.,
10. To d'Argental, 20 April 1769: Voltaire, *Corr.*, vol. 9, 873.
11. This is a point on which the propagandists of the Revolution in general, and the spiritualists of the Directory in particular, envied Catholicism which, througout the ages, was supposed to have stood guarantor to the use of a terrible power, which 'infiltrates the minds of all men, spies out the secrets of every family' et cetera, (Message from the Directory, 13th ventôse Year VI, 3 March 1798 announcing the definitive collapse of pontifical Rome: *Bull. Lois*, no. 187. 3).

12. R.-M. Lesuire, *Le législateur du chrétien, ou l'Évangile des Déïcoles*, Paris, Year VI, 1.
13. Hence he remarks that 'people take a new-born child into an office to have it registered as they would take some bundle into the customs' (*Réflexions sur le culte*, 22–23); hence too, he describes the sordid atmosphere in which marriages are dispatched one after the other in Paris: the corridor blocked 'with hundreds of vulgar characters', the disorder and the filth of the rooms, the shoddy furnishings, et cetera (26–27).
14. Ibid., 29. The sentence continues: 'any other animal whatsoever that we seek to get rid of as quickly as we possibly can, and solely through official channels, so as not to infect the air', et cetera.
15. Ibid., 35.
16. Speech to the *Institut*, quoted below, note 30, 5.
17. Cabanis, *Rapports du physique et du moral de l'homme*, Paris, (1802), reprinted Paris/Geneva, 1980, 298.
18. In this respect, cf. several quotations and references in my study 'L'individualisme libéral en France autour de 1800', in *Revue d'Histoire des Facultés de Droit et de la Science juridique*, no. 4, (1987), [87–144], 95.
19. La Révellière-Lépeaux, *Réflexions sur le culte*, 18.
20. Ibid., 18–19.
21. Ibid., 15.
22. Ibid., 33.
23. 'Proclamation du Directoire exécutif aux Français' 23rd fructidor Year V, 9 September 1797: *Bull. Lois* no. 144, 7–13.
24. See above, 86.
25. D'Holbach, *Système de la Nature*, vol.1, 214.
26. Letter to La Condamine, 6 January 1759: *Corr. compl. de Rousseau*, vol. 6, 3.
27. Decree from the Directory, 14th germinal Year VI, 3 April 1798: *Bull. Lois* no. 194, 11.
28. Proclamation referred to above in note 23.
29. Ibid.
30. La Révellière-Lépeaux, *Essai sur les moyens de faire participer l'universalité des spectateurs à tout ce qui se pratique dans les Fêtes nationales*, read to the Moral and Political Sciences class at the *Institut* on 22nd vendémiaire Year VI (13 October 1797), Paris, Year VI.
31. Ibid., 21.
32. Ibid., 26.
33. Ibid., 11.
34. Ibid. This sensualist does not forget the sense of smell either: 21.
35. La Révellière-Lépeaux, *Du Panthéon et d'un Théâtre national*, Paris, frimaire Year VI (Nov.–Dec. 1797), 5.
36. H.Grange, Introduction to B.Constant, *Fragments d'un ouvrage abandonné sur la Possibilité d'une constitution républicaine dans un grand pays*, Paris, 1991, 56.
37. 'From their earliest years onwards the same principles, same views, same feelings united them in bonds of friendship that death alone will be able to break' (pluviôse Year VI, Jan.–Feb. 1798). Angers Municipal Library, Reserve, H 1567.
38. This is only relative: see beginning of chapter for a few details on Leclerc's career.
39. For more detail on this I refer readers to my study 'Jean-Baptiste Leclerc. Un Angevin des Lumières sous le Directoire', in *Travaux sur le XVIIIe siècle. 3. Hommage au professeur Jean Roussel*, Angers, 1995, 123–41.

40. *Opinion de J.-B. Leclerc, Député de Maine-et-Loire sur le jugement de Louis XVI*, Paris, 1792, 14.
41. J.-B. Leclerc, *Essai sur la propagation de la musique en France, sa conservation, et ses rapports avec le gouvernement* (Year IV), re-ed., Paris, Year VI, 13–15.
42. Ibid., 20–22.
43. Cabanis, *Rapports*, 405–06.
44. Ibid., 464.
45. J.-B. Leclerc, *Essai sur la propagation de la musique*, 66–67, footnote 16.
46. Cabanis, *Rapports*, 411.
47. See Martin, 'Jean-Baptiste Leclerc', 125–126.
48. Leclerc, *Essai sur la propagation de la musique*, 29.
49. Ibid., 50–51.
50. See above, 122.
51. *Corps législatif. Conseil des Cinq-Cents. Rapport fait par Leclerc sur les institutions relatives à l'état-civil des citoyens*, 16th brumaire Year VI (6 November 1797), Paris, Year VI, 8.
52. Rousseau, *Émile*, Book II, 150
53. M. Grandière, *L'Idéal pédagogique en France au XVIIIème siècle (1715–1789)*, University of Lille, 1991 III, 615.
54. Report mentioned in note 51 above, 7, (w.u.o.).
55. See above, 168.
56. Law of 3rd brumaire Year IV, 24 October 1795: *Bull. Lois* no. 202, 4.
57. 22nd floréal Year IV, 11 May 1796: *Bull. Lois* no. 47, 2.

Chapter 12

SUPERVISED SOVEREIGNTY

Those in charge of affairs in the post-Thermidor years were inhabited by an overweening ambition: that of assuming complete control of each and every individual, including their 'inner' space. The strength of this ambition was, in actual fact, directly proportionate to their own inability ever to realise it – an inability which in turn, somewhat paradoxically, constantly served to make the ambition grow ever stronger. Reality obviously threw a thousand and one obstacles in its path. To begin with, there was the 'pliant but almost invincible resistance of those governed', as Tocqueville put it;[1] an inert hostility then, to which Mme de Staël bore lucid testimony at the time.[2] In such a context it was a distressing problem and one which cruelly agitated the technicians working to inflict compulsory and happy unanimity on their fellow-men. A key element of the political scene was that so many of the men in charge quite reasonably thought that their most pressing need was to do everything they could to conserve power. It was they who had killed Louis XVI and Robespierre, and hanging on to power was therefore a matter of life or death for them. The Constitution made provision for elections to be held each spring to replace a third of the members of each assembly and one of the five Directors. And here, I would suggest, lies another major, underlying ambiguity, to be added to so many others that we have come across in the course of this study, namely, of a sovereignty that is located in an electorate whose members 'are nothing more than men', that is to say, in keeping with the spirit of the times, certainly something more than women (who were, even in such an age as this, simply excluded from all sectors of public life)³ but beings nonetheless to be considered, as Voltaire put it, 'pitiful things', always teetering on the verge of irrationality, over-vulnerable to 'impressions', and the passive and derisory prey to those who wished to modify the habits of humanity. There is little alternative but to accept that this was the lesson Enlightenment anthropology proposed to the Republicans. It was reinforced by the prolonged and difficult experience of the Revolutionary period and also by the men, whether *idéologues* or not, who continued to produce theories on man and on society, considering both as projects yet to be realised – in short it was reinforced by all those things that have solicited our attention in the preceding pages.

It would also seem to be the lesson that is taught by election results which, year after year, are never quite to the liking of the philanthropists, who have been condemned, by the accident of historical circumstance, to govern the country. The feverish defiance which they exhibit as their response to the crass immaturity of their fellow-citizens is particularly in keeping with the times. One has the strong feeling that the brief moment when the secret ballot is in operation is a moment of tremendous vulnerability for these men whose chief aspiration is to exercise absolute control over men's minds. It is a moment that seems to go on for ever and which allows the 'big children' the opportunity to demonstrate that they are capable of doing everything and anything whatsoever – an opportunity they assiduously seize upon year after year by voting in ways that run counter to the wishes of the government. Nor was it for want of precautions taken by the latter. There had been the return to census-based suffrage which divided the voters into two groups. The qualifying age for the first group had surreptitiously been put back to 22 and the qualifying age for the second group quite openly put back to 25, and this in a constitutional and mental setting which could, without exaggeration, be characterised as tending towards gerontocracy.⁴ There had also been the 'two-thirds decree' of October 1795, which in essence decided the result of the first elections before they had even taken place. This result, as one contemporary quite accurately said, was then ratified by 'a tiny minority'.⁵ There were also the fussy speeches, full of careful warnings and admonitions, which the Directory, La Révellière among them, saw fit, as executives of the Republic, to address to their fellow-citizens. It is no small order to prove to people in such circumstances that they are happy and that their happiness will continue to increase if they vote as instructed. Indeed, attempts to make the citizens believe such a thing were to no avail. And, as a last resort, necessity being a hard taskmaster, there were the constant 'corrections' that were forcibly applied to the results of the elections – the Directory's infamous series of *coups d'état*.

In all logic, these strong-arm tactics should not give rise to indignation or concern on the part of anyone. On the contrary, the recent commemoration of their bicentenary should have been a time for all lawyers desirous of keeping up to date with original and highly effective techniques to take note of them. Even when their obvious tactical usefulness has been set on one side, these strong-arm methods can in no way be considered as anomalous. Firstly they are quite in keeping with the whole logic of the *Contrat Social*, in which, at the sudden release of a spring, an omnipotent and omniscient legislator is suddenly propelled forth from some distant Olympian summit to philanthropically descend to earth and take the place of the masses (who are certainly sovereign but such insignificant small fry!) for the very laudable reason that 'a blind multitude ... often does not know what it really wants because it rarely knows what is good for it'; as a result, it is quite obviously necessary 'to oblige some people to really want what their reason tells them they want, and others to be taught to know what they want'.[6] At the time the mood was diffusely anti-Rousseauist, and this reminder therefore seems to add even greater weight to my argument. So the academic historiographer is perfectly within his rights to consider the repeated interventions to 'correct' the results of elections which took place under the Directory as anodine and quite unimportant. Secondly, this latter view would seem to be all the more true when one considers that there was a solid constitutional basis for these interventions. But maybe the facts are not sufficiently well known. We are referring here to article 376 of the Constitution of Year III: 'Citizens will constantly bear in mind that the length of rule, the preservation and the prosperity of the Republic principally depend on the wisdom of choices made in primary and electoral Assemblies'.

Now a man such as Barère, in times not very far removed from these, had already made the point: 'I must point out that the secrecy of the ballot box would give weak and corrupt men the opportunity of making a bad choice at the urns too often'.[7] It was therefore a thing to bear in mind that electoral majorities might forget 'the wisdom of choices'. It was therefore important that some provision should be made so that choices made unwisely could be declared unconstitutional, by means of a disposition in the law which, I am bound to agree, offered a clear justification for such votes being declared invalid, even if the ways in which they were so declared sometimes lacked a little formal rigour. The worst thing about all this is that it is all true. The law of 11 May 1798 invalidating the election of Barère and 105 other undesirable *députés* (the *coup d'état* of floréal), considered 'that it would be an outrage against the majesty of the French people to consider as its work elections which have clearly been prepared in order to destroy its sovereignty and to replace it either with demagogic tyranny or with the despotism of a single man', and the law expressly founds its argument on article 376 of the Constitution.[8] So if anyone has ever been so ill-advised as to use the words, 'permanent electoral cheating', when referring to the Directory, the choice of such an inappropriate expression must clearly have resulted from a momentary lapse in attention or betrayed the fact that the person who had the naïvety to use it simply possessed inadequate information. Those who follow the rules of the game are not really cheating, even if they have made the rules themselves so that they perfectly correspond to their own requirements. At least, it seems to me, this is a principle implicit in the French constitutional tradition which has tried so many experiments in its time. And if I may make so bold as to say so, this principle is perhaps even one of the reasons for the very existence of constitutional law in the first place, and especially its electoral branch. Under the Directory, therefore, it is not a question of waging attacks on the expression of the popular will, but, on the contrary, of treatment designed to set the popular will on the right road again when it has strayed in some way. It is merely a question of invalidating 'unwise choices', and of validating excellent ones, or, more precisely, of cancelling 'choices contrary to the will of the people'[9] (this very people which on occasion has to be taught 'to know what it wants') and, then, of 'respecting all those choices which bear the imprint of the national will',[10] that is to say, which do not threaten the interests of the political class in power. This eminently democratic way of reasoning commands our support all the more in that it is in complete conformity with what the century teaches us with regard to the lack of consistency in the will of men in general, and with regard to the concomitant omnipotence of the 'well-intentioned' will of the manipulators.

The fever and its symptoms had come to a head precisely as the spring of 1798 approached, for the elections following the *coup d'état* of fructidor which itself, rather pathetically, had been made necessary by an electoral victory by the monarchists. As early as 1 February, a law had instituted 'the annual celebration of a *fête* to mark the sovereignty of the people' on the grounds, expressed in the text of the law, that the national celebration 'is a powerful means of assembling *all* French people in the *same* sentiments; and that on the forthcoming occasion when citizens will exercise their right to sovereignty, it is important that love of the fatherland and the desire to maintain the Constitution of Year III should *burn in the hearts of all men* and predominate over *all* opinions'.[11] Once again, it is worth stopping to consider every single word. On 1 February, the festivities are fixed for 20 March, the eve of the primary Assemblies, and they are organised as only these people knew how, that is to say with great pomp and in laborious detail which is heavy with a symbolism designed to make an impression on recalcitrant minds.[12] Each commune had its altar, its branches and banners, and its parade of 'not unmarried' elders, and its tricolour sticks and ribbons. And since it is not certain that 'Citizens will *constantly* bear in mind' what is expected of them on election days (a fact which we know full well to be the case), and since, as the years go by, the opposite certainty would appear to be increasingly obviously true, it has to be *constantly* hammered home to them. In the event, it is worth mentioning that while one sign reproduces article 17 of the Declaration of Rights of Year III: 'In essence sovereignty resides in the universality of the citizens', another sign bears the text of article 376, saying 'Citizens will constantly bear in mind',[13] namely that 'the length of rule, the preservation and the prosperity of the Republic principally depend on the wisdom of choices', but also and especially, – what is left unsaid here is deafening – the length of rule, the preservation and the prosperity of those politicians who, according to Tocqueville 'considered the Republic as their personal security'.[14] To an elderly man who had been selected to recite a civic allocution on the importance of the 'choices' in question, the 'principal civic functionary' present would reply with a second allocution, including a word-for-word reading of the magic text of article 376,[15] that remedy of all woes and lifebelt of the democrats, which was treated with such utter contempt by the people themselves.

After which, but before the hymns and parades, there was to be a reading of quite a long and didactic proclamation from the Directory, the opening part of which admitted to the objective of unanimity and wasted no time in making quite explicit what was the real point at issue: 'It is the meaning of article

376 of your founding law that has to be *engraved upon your minds* by the memories of this day'.¹⁶ Indeed, what is needed on this day of festivities is that

> in these emotional meetings in which benevolence brings men's affections closer together and intermingles them with one another, French people, as they compare their present hopes with all that has gone before, should be able to exclaim *simultaneously, on the same day, at the same hour*, on the most far-flung points of their vast territory: It is true; the length of rule, the preservation and the prosperity of the Republic principally depend on the wisdom of choices made in primary and electoral Assemblies,

an exclamation which we can see was purely and simply a repetition of the article of the Constitution in question.¹⁷ The Directory goes on to admit quite candidly to the apprehension it feels at these 'primary Assemblies', 'in which the people holds its destiny in its own hands', a fact which hardly bodes well for democracy, and at the very least seems to suggest a future full either of 'incalculable dangers or tremendous advantages'.¹⁸ And speaking about itself, the Directory expresses the following wish: 'May the *impression* of this august occasion give weight to [our] advice and *engrave it on the hearts* of everyone'.¹⁹ Et cetera. In the recent past, whether the people voted unthinkingly for Royalists or for latter-day Jacobins, they were, 'without seeking to be so, without even suspecting it was the case' (unbeknownst to themselves), 'merely the instruments of Royalism'.²⁰ And the urgent advice continued to pour out, including the following piece which more or less says it all: 'Become perfect in the art of choosing the organs of your sovereign will'.²¹ Is this a case of following the advice of Rousseau and 'teaching' people 'to know what they want'? 'O sovereign people, you unflinchingly *desire* the Constitution of 1795, freedom, the Republic. These are the things your choices must guarantee for you'.²² There could be no better way of suggesting to what extent this sovereign but child-like nation, this nation of passive minors, as we learn from the teachings of Helvétius, and d'Holbach, and Voltaire (and Rousseau), desperately needs constraints and blinkers and reins: in this respect, we might suggest, the first years of the Revolution had regrettably corroborated Enlightenment anthropology.

On 27 February 1798, there was a new proclamation from the Directory, with an eye to the primary Assemblies of 21 March: 'Citizens, on 1st germinal next, you will be assembled *in full sovereignty*', immediately one feels that these words 'in full sovereignty' are the crux of the problem.[23] Pages and pages of advice and admonitions follow. 'Citizens, listen to the advice of your magistrates', they are once again telling you what you imperatively are *supposed to want*: 'The nation is a Republican nation. It chose freedom, it cannot be in contradiction with itself, in revolt against itself'.[24] We should note that against the 'senseless egoism' that leads to 'the mistaken ... calculation' of those who abstain from voting, is opposed the consideration of 'all their interests',[25] in other words the *correct calculation* of *sensible egoism*. This analysis is implicit throughout and provides yet a further example of the case I have been making.[26] As for any 'aristocrats' who might be thinking of standing in the elections, the five Directors dismissively invite them to think back on the events of the previous fructidor, which ensured that no such aberration could come to anything.[27] And so on. There are a dozen or so pages of this sort. On 8 March a law of mammoth proportions determined the arrangements for the holding of primary and communal Assemblies,[28] with a proliferation of details which once again included a reading of article 376 of the Constitution,[29] which, 'inscribed in large letters on a placard will, as soon as the reading has been completed, be placed in the most visible place in the room'.[30] All this simply demonstrates the Directory's utter terror at the approach of that dreadful day of reckoning, election day, in respect of which the Directory had even admitted to fellow-citizens, and with itself in mind: 'This is the only moment when the law refuses itself the right to speak in your name'.[31] And this is where the rub is. In the hull of a vessel that hankers after being totalitarian any election represents a hole below the water line. And in fact, the ballot held in 1798 required that all hands be called to the pumps for the emergency repairs of floréal, previously mentioned.

Notes

1. A. de Tocqueville, 'Fragments sur la Révolution: deux chapitres sur le Directoire', in Tocqueville, *De la Démocratie en Amérique*, Paris, 1986, 1,108.
2. Mme de Staël, *Des circonstances actuelles qui peuvent terminer la Révolution et des principes qui doivent fonder la République en France* (1798), Paris/Geneva, 1979, for example 322–23.
3. See the measures adopted at the beginning of prairial Year III (May 1795): *Bull. Lois* no. 145, 9, no. 147, 6, no. 157, 19.
4. See my study 'À tout âge? Sur la durée du pouvoir des pères dans le Code Napoléon' in *Revue d'Histoire des Facultés de Droit et de la Science juridique*, no. 13, (1992), [227–301], 251, 254 and passim.

5. Citizen Aimé from the Drôme who was, as a result, stripped of any 'legislative functions', 18th nivôse Year IV, 8 January 1796 : *Bull. Lois* no. 18, 3. The famous 'decree' had been ratified by about 200,000 votes to 100,000, from a potential electorate of about 5 million voters.
6. J.-J. Rousseau, *Contrat Social*, Book II, end of chapter 6, 380; see above, 67 and 68.
7. 12 June 1793, *Archives parlementaires*, 1/66/453/2.
8. Conseil des Anciens, *Bull. Lois* no. 200, 2–3.
9. Ibid., 2.
10. Ibid., 3.
11. Law of 13th pluviôse Year VI, 30 January 1798 (the text quoted is from the preceding day) : *Bull. Lois* no. 181 and 182, 1.
12. Decree from the Directory, 28th pluviôse Year VI: *Bull. Lois* no. 181, 2–5.
13. Ibid., 3–4.
14. Tocqueville, 'Fragments sur la Révolution,' 1,108.
15. *Bull. Lois* no. 181, 5.
16. Proclamation of the same day, *Bull. Lois* no. 181, 6.
17. Ibid., 7. The *fête* will be held on the eve of the elections.
18. Ibid., 8. A little further on, while dwelling on recent examples of its own political qualities, the Directory remarks: 'The final victory belongs to you alone: here the Directory cannot share your laurels; it can only tell you the true way to collect them, and that is by drawing your attention to the choices to be made in tomorrow's primary Assemblies'(11).
19. Ibid., 8.
20. Ibid., 10.
21. Ibid., 14.
22. Ibid.
23. 9th ventôse Year VI,*Bull. Lois* no. 186, 1.
24. Ibid., 3.
25. Ibid., 4.
26. See above, 136 and thereafter, and 178.
27. *Bull. Lois* no. 186, 7.
28. *Bull. Lois* no. 188, 1–40.
29. Ibid., 27.
30. Ibid., 28.
31. 28th pluviôse Year VI, 16 February 1798: *Bull. Lois* no. 181, 14.

Chapter 13

Madame de Staël and Constant

The identical problem occurs a year later, when once again at the *fête* for the sovereignty of the people, article 376 on the vital 'wisdom of choices'[1] is brought to people's attention. The Directory honours the citizens with a new proclamation which reiterates the happiness and the glory that are 'bound up with the wisdom of choices',[2] and seeks to penetrate the French people with 'tutelary and conservative principles which must guide choices', warns them against 'negligence in choices', expresses the fear that 'choice may go astray'[3] and recalls that past interventions in the processes of national representation will only be perpetrated in the name and in the place of the citizens themselves, and in such a way that they might better know what it was they wanted.[4] The Directory explains to these latter: We must also 'carry a torch to guide your steps', to ensure 'good choices',[5] and it sketches the profile of the ideal candidate for office as one who demonstrates something midway between 'apathetic coldness' and 'sulphurous enthusiasm', et cetera; 'the man of good character, in short, should be the object towards which your choice should direct itself'.[6] This is tantamount to saying that little else matters but choices, although people in fact have little choice. The French, 'on the eve of exercising one of the most important acts of sovereignty',[7] are still, as ever, being treated like children. Mme de Staël (1766–1817) reckoned at the time that 'it would be better ... to openly deprive [the nation] of its rights than to have it *play at elections* like children playing at being grown-ups'.[8] And lucid as she so often was, she went on to sum up the point of view that characterises the whole of the Directory when she remarked: 'Everything has to happen freely, *on condition that that is what people want*'.⁹

The politics of the Directory are *dirigiste*, or that is what they would like to be, at least surreptitiously, in the manner of Rousseau's pedagogic methods. 'Let him always believe himself to be the master', is what Rousseau advises the child's tutor, 'and let it always be you who is in command. There is no form of subjection so complete as that which preserves the illusion of freedom'.¹⁰ Perhaps we are beginning to realise more and more just to what extent this type of logic contains within it the true essence of the Enlightenment – a project which, as these interminable years drag on, comes to resemble more and more closely an attempt to square the circle. The problem is that the nation of adult-children, fed on a diet of fairytales and false hopes, refuses to consider itself as being in charge. How clumsy its leaders must have been to have managed to make such a recalcitrant lot out of this amorphous mass of men, 'whose will' the marquis de Condorcet disdainfully suggested, was there to be guided by 'whomsoever chooses to guide it'.¹¹ Given the length of time for which people had been claiming to remodel them, the French had good reason to consider themselves as having been well and truly remodelled. 'The word regeneration has led us to demolish everything', Benjamin Constant was to say later.¹² In these final years of the century, which are years of great disarray, the manipulation of the masses makes little progress. It no longer takes place without the people it targets knowing about it, and it even appears to admit as much quite openly as the preamble to the texts which still seek to ensure that it happens.¹³

We have already come across the *passive agent*, and *generous egoism*. The equally paradoxical moment has now arrived for us to be introduced to the notion of the *compulsory volunteer*. The expression does not appear in the *Contrat Social* but one is well aware that it could almost have done so, and one might be forgiven for considering that in substance it did appear there. In fact, the expression is once again from the pen of Mme de Staël.¹⁴ It very neatly sums up the impasse of an anthropological stance which for decades has appealed to scientific principles in order to support the claim that there is no such thing as the human will, that it simply does not exist, while *at the same time* appealing to that very concept as the foundation-stone of a contractual arrangement which establishes nothing less than society itself. Not surprisingly, this position is a little disconcerting. The decree issued by the Directory creating *fêtes* in honour of freedom bore the motto 'any man who carries a hatred of slavery in his heart, and who deserves to call himself a Frenchman, will be eager to associate himself with the pomp and ceremony of their celebration'.[15] With the added weight of a nice threat *a contrario*, this sentence seems to illustrate very well what Mme de Staël means by the collocation 'compulsory volunteer'. In a similar way, the decree creating a *fête* to commemorate the birth of the Republic appears to be seeking to make enthusiasm itself obligatory.[16] Mme de Staël writes: 'You would need to have no idea whatsoever as to the true nature of enthusiasm to imagine that it could be inspired by first producing a mere counterfeit of it'.[17] And she goes on to say, even if it 'were desirable that all men should be enthusiastic for freedom, devoted to their fatherland, the most oppressed country on earth would be the one in which such virtues were insisted upon'.[18]

And she goes on to remind us that 'virtue has to be voluntary and there is no spontaneous movement save that which comes from within'.[19] But what this statement seems to be supposing is that in every man there is an active principle, a supposition that is roundly contradicted by the anthropological doctrines of the age which argue quite to the contrary that habits can be manufactured to order, on command – exactly what Mme de Staël[20] refuses to accept:

> The habits of freedom can never have their origin in some form or other of command. We are doing our best to stand the natural order of things on its head; we ordain that everyone must attend such and such a *fête* and should give their support to this and that institution on the grounds that these things persuade the people who take part in them that Republican government is an excellent thing. But the very fact that we command, cajole and threaten in this way has the effect of destroying the very thing that we are trying to prove ... Any Republican government, which by an odd refinement sought to create a new form of obedience: *the compulsory volunteer*, would be infinitely more tyrannical than straightforward despotism and, overwhelmed by increasing difficulties on a daily basis, there would be no end to its tyranny as it sought to obtain by compulsion all the outward signs of consent.[21]

This shows great perspicacity. But it is worth noting nevertheless that under the Directory, Mme de Staël herself, in spite of the sharpness of her powers of observation, still does not manage to escape from the pull of reductionism. In this respect she is clearly a child of the Enlightenment, and in fact her dual position doubly reinforces the strength of our own argument, as, by the way, is the case for the majority of spiritualists I consider in these pages. As far as my own argument is concerned, all the spiritualists emphasise the importance of what they are denouncing: in the first place, by the very fact that they denounce it at all and, secondly, by succumbing to it themselves. The lines that I have quoted from her work could give the impression that Mme de Staël would be a staunch defender of human will, but in fact it is very often the case in her work that it is the *involuntary* which is endowed with favourable connotations and more or less becomes a synonym of all that is sincere and disinterested. Like Rousseau and Robespierre, she tends to set little store by reason and reasoning, which she herself used to such good effect, and prefers to favour the instinctive and the spontaneous. When she praises these '*instinctive virtues*, pity, delicacy, pride, which are, so to speak, mixed up in our blood and have become inner *physical movements* preceding any act of reflection',[22] it is obvious that she is imprudently venturing into the orbit of theories which she finds outrageous elsewhere. She exposes herself in a similar way too, when, for example, she waxes lyrical on the consequences that flow from the magic art of oratory: 'Eloquence is the life of thought: it makes ideas pass into the bloodstream, it transforms the conviction of reason and the analysis of duty into electrical energy and *bringing man back to his physical nature*, not in such a way as to debase him but to fire him with passion, it makes his heart beat, his tears flow; it inspires him with courage, virtue, self-sacrifice, as *involuntary* movements that no amount of reflection could prevent'.[23]

Expressions of this sort are very interesting. Mme de Staël, despite her sparkling intelligence, is still a woman of her times. 'We are no more the masters of our ideas than we are of the circulation of the blood in our veins', Voltaire has already been quoted as saying. Once again, it is a question of exploiting this passivity *in other people*, even if it means reinforcing it. We must 'force the animal economy', Rousseau advised us, which is not so very different from 'bringing man back to his physical nature', since both are examples of exerting control over man's psyche. According to this line of reasoning the manipulation is, of course, legitimate in that it is motivated by good intentions: it is not a question of 'debasing' man, but of 'firing him with passion' for the best of reasons. And this tends to prove that guiding man in a coldly calculated way to 'involuntary movements that no amount of reflection could prevent' was not to equivalent to debasing him in so far as the Mme de Staël of 1798 was concerned. This is an important point. It is the same sort of language as is used by a man like Robespierre when he tried to arouse in his fellow-citizens what he called a 'rapid instinct' which might dispense them from having to use their powers of reason. It is also the language used by La Révellière, in respect of whom Mme de Staël notices the inclination to perpetrate *compulsory volunteering* on his fellow men, for which she offers a lucid denunciation while simultaneously showing herself to be one of his unconscious disciples. In effect, Mme de Staël is very close indeed to the conceptions she so strongly vituperates. As far as the Directory is concerned, in a strange moment of weakness she thinks she discerns in its 'theoretical principles the most perfect Republic that has ever yet been proposed to men'.[24] And as to the eventual fate which awaits it, she feels that ballots can really only be free when all citizens have been broken to the yoke of Republicanism. Entry into this vicious circle reintroduces her to the logic of manipulation and she begins to ascend the foothills of utopia: 'When the whole nation has Republican views and ways of understanding, when public instruction has made wise and enlightened friends of freedom out of all men, if such a thing is possible, then not only will it be possible to elect everyone, but you could almost, so to speak, dispense with government';[25] which, we must admit, suggests a perfect social *mechanism* and brings us back to that masterpiece of political thinking proposed by Rousseau: the example of the man of state who can afford to 'idle away his time'.[26]

And at this point I feel obliged to mention a fact that is a concomitant of this way of thinking, namely that throughout the years of the Directory, Mme de Staël shows a strange propensity to judge some of the wilder claims made by the social mathematics that were in vogue at that time as containing a great deal of promise. This social mathematics, hitherto promoted in France by Condorcet (a man lost to his country at far too tender an age) also had its origins in enlightened scientism. The urgency accorded to the task of expressing the whole study of man and society in terms of mathematical formulae was not, during the Enlightenment, a crackpot idea pursued by merely a few discredited marginal figures. The idea that matters of morality and ethics might be proved to be intimately linked to a system capable of being expressed in a series of mathematical calculations, and that all that was required was to work at it in order to elucidate it more fully, are ideas in total conformity with the mental atmosphere of the age as the century draws to a close. 'Everything can be reduced to calculations; they extend to cover even purely moral things':[27] thus, in 1734, wrote Melon, an economist much admired by Voltaire. And 'Morality', said d'Holbach in 1770, 'is as much the science of the relationships that exist between the minds, the will and the actions of men, as geometry is the science of the relationships that exist between natural bodies'.[28] In April 1796 at the *Institut*, Destutt de Tracy was no less positive: 'The moral and social sciences are as open to precision as are the mathematical sciences; provided that the method of mathematics is applied to them too'.[29] A 'social science' worthy of the name, he felt, would allow us to 'predict the happiness and the misfortunes of different societies, and only to see them as the necessary and inevitable consequences of demonstrable laws'.[30] Germaine Necker, who, although not yet twenty years old, had already taken note of the fact that Condorcet had published a book on the applications of the mathematics of probability,[31] and she adopted this approach as her own. (The timing of this decision, and the profile so utterly devoid of scientism of the person who made it, once again serve to add weight to my argument.) The fact is noticeable in her *Influence des Passions*, written between 1793 and 1796.[32] It is even more noticeable in 1798 in *Circonstances actuelles*, from which I shall once more need to quote.

'Moral forces', she writes in the latter book, 'are calculated by laws that are as positive as physical forces'.[33] 'Descartes applied algebra to geometry, we must use mathematical calculations in politics – when they are perfectly adapted to it, political quarrels will cease. Men's passions are as capable of being calculated as is friction within machines',[34] 'and the statesman should study the movements of a temperament, as Newton observed a stone falling'.[35] These assertions are clear enough for there to be little need for further comment.[36] The author is convinced of the matter: 'All the moral and political sciences will be successively subjected to the geometric method. The mathematics of probability applies to human passions as it does to throws of the dice'.[37] And she goes on, in a pejorative way, to oppose to the happy certainties of arithmetic, everything that people can write 'on infinity, eternity, space, free will, all the vague ideas of the human mind'.[38] It is quite an interesting sight to see an author demonstrating such a lack of respect for *free will* when very soon she will be vigorously rebuking the Enlightenment for having made such short shrift of it. Even in 1800, she is still delighted at the prospect that the mathematical proofs of reasoning will 'put the very idea of opposition out of men's minds'.[39] No more opposition, 'political quarrels will cease', she tells us, 'the peace of mathematical proof',[40] will have descended upon us, we have seen too that there will be scarcely any purpose in having a government at all, or it will be one that functions so well it runs smoothly and automatically. This brings to mind another quotation from Rousseau: 'The movement of the machine should be as smooth as it is simple and always a noiseless affair if at all possible'.[41] Such a soberly perfect model can only have value in the absolute, when seen to be applicable for all times and in all places: 'A government founded on mathematical truths can be established in all places and at all times'.[42] With methods such as these, based on assurances that 'the ultimate degree of the perfectibility of the human mind is to be found in the application of mathematics to all branches of the moral system', man finds himself happily launched 'into the vast career of absolute truth'.[43] The utopianism of the century and of the Revolution had visibly contaminated the very person who, a little later on, would manage to transform herself into one of its most incisive analysts.

There is a lot to say, too, about Benjamin Constant (1767–1830) who was so close to Mme de Staël. They were not only close intellectually, but Constant also had an equally analytical mind and was equally talented as a critic of the paradoxes of the Directory. If the Directory was totalitarian it was precisely because of the enigmatic way it made freedom its ideal,[44] but above all because it insisted on doing so in an anthropological context that denied freedom – this was one paradox that Constant appears not to have clearly identified. The fact is apparent in his famous distinction between, on the one hand, the 'freedom of modern man' passionately seeking to limit the power available to any form of authority whatsoever, and consequently deserving the support of everyone, and on the other hand, the 'freedom of the ancients' which had become something to be outlawed[45] and which refers precisely to the fusion and integration of the citizen and the city. He reproached the revolutionaries for having used this latter model far too often and for having uncritically accepted a mythology associated with ancient Greece and Rome inherited from Rousseau, and even more perhaps from (Bonnot de) Mably,[46] one of the notorious absences from the preceding pages, and, incidentally, brother of (Bonnot de) Condillac, the chief sensualist of the whole eighteenth century. But in spite of his talent and the brilliance of his analyses, it would seem that Constant appears to have misunderstood to what extent the thing he hated about the Revolution, namely its impulse towards philanthropic totalitarianism, was a consequence of Enlightenment anthropology. Quite clearly this impulse was at the basis of the very real attacks on freedom, successful or merely attempted, that were perpetrated during the 1790s, far more than it was the basis for Constant's strenuous defence of individual autonomy which in a way encapsulates his political thinking and is indeed all the merit it possesses. Constant's intransigence on this point seems to me to express some sort of primordial instinct rather than to represent a doctrinal position. Certainly, despite what one may be accustomed to believe, the Enlightenment does not seem to provide any basis upon which to found such a doctrinal stance anyway. We are therefore left with something of a problem when it comes to examining exactly how the impetus towards political liberalism, which de Staël and Constant provide around 1800, should be viewed in relation to eighteenth-century thought, with which it is usual to consider it as being on an equal footing. To put it another way, if eighteenth-century thought should prove itself to be significantly different from what received wisdom generally teaches us it is, then there may be good grounds for reconsidering whether the received teaching on liberalism too is as accurate as it could be.[47]

When Constant offered his diagnosis of the tendency of revolutionary power to veer towards totalitarian hypertrophy, he expressed it in terms of the simple nostalgia for 'a succession of errors and prejudices' which he presumes to have permanently beset 'governments of classical times'. This led him to suppose that all that really interested the revolutionary government was 'reviving this tendency to prejudice to its own advantage'.[48] All of which belies a rather short-sighted perspective on the matter. His analysis fails to recognise, first of all, shifts in the political bases underpinning the monarchy which in its final years was torn between two quite different doctrines without even realising the fact. On the one hand, it had traditionally promoted the enjoyment of freedoms at a local level, but on the other hand, it was tending towards the creation of a coldly modern state in ways that were clearly not unsympathetic to Enlightenment thinking. Secondly, his analysis also fails to recognise the political logic behind both the Enlightenment itself and the Revolution, and above all the severely reductionist anthropology on which this logical position is predicated. In other words, Constant seems unaware of the fact that the majority of the great *Encyclopédistes*, Voltaire, and to an extent even Rousseau himself, persistently refused to accept the notion that human freedom was possible, and in so doing reduced the idea of a human 'will' to virtual insignificance, and cast serious doubt on the notion of human dignity and man's status as a responsible being. Hence they had, in advance, gone a long way towards relativising all the disadvantages associated with the inhuman methods and practices which proliferated under the Revolution, and which have occasionally continued to proliferate since then, inspired by similar doctrines. At the very least, Constant was not particularly concerned to examine such matters very closely and was therefore unable to recognise the logical inconsistencies they concealed. When he observes that the 'well-intentioned men' who were actively engaged in 'abuses' of governmental power under the Directory, 'had as their aim the belittling of the human species',[49] we may feel that he is 'getting warm', he can clearly sniff the reductionism that is in the air. But it is quite clear, in my view, that in this speech he misses the point somewhat. He is positing as an aim what is in fact a logical premise. At very least I would argue that if there was, under the Directory, such a concerted effort made at 'the belittling of the human species', it is because they were unconsciously working to reduce humanity to fit the shrunken conception of man that so many of the authors of the Enlightenment had passed down, including (and despite all his pleading to the contrary) Jean-Jacques Rousseau himself, notwithstanding the fact that he had criticised the *philosophes* for being in the business of 'shrinking the human heart and belittling men'.[50]

This nexus of misunderstandings may help to explain Constant's uneasiness and the way he rather too promptly expresses his allegiance to Rousseau while pillorying the dangerous risks involved in 'the subtle metaphysics' of the *Contrat Social*, which, he considered, 'is, nowadays, only fit to provide all forms of tyranny with weapons and ammunition as well as reasons for using them'.[51] And elsewhere he reiterates the same idea that 'this sublime genius who was inspired by the purest love of freedom nevertheless furnished arguments of deadly significance to more than one sort of tyranny', and so on.[52] It is clear that a more thoughtful and closer reading of Rousseau would have led Constant to be less forgiving in his judgements. But he too was a child of his age. He comes very close to singing from the very hymn-sheet that he himself criticises. In this respect he is far from being an exception, and in fact there are times when he actually does so. In Year IV, when he theorises: 'We must maintain the majority as though it were invariable. We have to remind the people what they wanted, *teach them to know what they want* by ensuring they find their happiness and repose under the law',[53] it is clear that he is adding grist to the mill of the philanthropic promoters of compulsory happiness, and that he is reiterating in his own right a precept that is typical of the subtleties of the *Contrat Social* and which justifies the sleight of hand which allows the general will to be by-passed by invoking the need to 'teach' such and such a person 'to know what he wants'.[54] The two verbs are tightly linked and justify a situation in which a small number of people think and act in the name of all. The usefulness of programming individuals to change their habits, which is one of the most frequently mentioned corollaries of Enlightenment anthropology, is an idea that was by no means alien to Constant and one which he occasionally draws upon himself.[55] All of which is tantamount to saying that his views are not very far removed from those held by the Directory, which he subjects to sincere and quite pointed criticism. Yet these are, almost genetically, his own views too and from time to time they surface rather violently. He shared, for example, the conviction that a carefully thought-out law of inheritance could play on hopes and expectations in such a way as to manufacture affectionate feelings within families. This, for him, went without saying and simply had to be exploited. In March 1800, he gave a proof of this attitude during the debate on the germinal law which marks a break in this respect with the egalitarian views on inheritance ushered in by the Revolution. Constant defended both the spirit and the letter of the new proposals.[56] In its inspiration this law prefigures the Napoleonic Code itself and the *Travaux préparatoires* for the Code illustrate the fact that this type of thinking was in fact a determining influence upon it. Indeed, the *Travaux* provided the material used in the introduction to this book and will be waiting for us in the final pages.

Notes

1. Beginning of 1799: *Bull. Lois* no. 258, 12.
2. 23rd pluviôse Year VII, 11 February 1799: ibid., 13.
3. Ibid., 15.

4. Ibid., 14 ('the tutelary authorities have had to act in your name, and do on your behalf what you should have done for yourselves in order to preserve your fundamental laws').
5. Ibid., 14.
6. Ibid., 14–15.
7. Ibid., 13.
8. Mme de Staël, *Des Circonstances actuelles qui peuvent terminer la Révolution*, Paris/Geneva, 1979, 176.
9. Ibid., 175.
10. J.-J. Rousseau, *Émile*, Book II, Paris, 1966, 150, see above, 75.
11. See above, 174–175.
12. B. Constant, *De l'Esprit de Conquête et de l'Usurpation dans leurs rapports avec la civilisation européenne* (1813–14), Paris, 1986, 251.
13. See above, 194.
14. De Staël, *Des Circonstances actuelles*, 175 and 323 (she always uses italics for this expression).
15. 17th messidor Year IV, 5 July 1796, *Bull. Lois* no. 56, 13.
16. 13th fructidor Year IV, 30 August 1796, *Bull. Lois* no. 72, 11.
17. Mme de Staël, *Considérations sur la Révolution française* (1818), Paris, 1983, 348.
18. De Staël, *Des Circonstances actuelles*, 284. She continues as follows; 'You must be generous, you must be sensitive, you must be sincere! What an unfortunate nation that would be, for whom the law had to insist upon these virtues!'
19. Ibid. Any number of passages in this book could be quoted.
20. Ibid., 277.
21. Ibid., 323, (w.u.o.).
22. Ibid., 225.
23. Ibid., 285.
24. Ibid., 323.
25. Ibid., 177.
26. See above, 139.
27. [J.Fr. Melon] (1675–1738), *Essai politique sur le commerce*, s.l., 1734, second-hand quotation.
28. D'Holbach, *Système de la Nature*, vol. 1, 236 (the words 'as much' in this quotation are our own addition).
29. Destutt de Tracy, *Mémoire sur la Faculté de penser*, op. cit., quoted from G.E.Gwynne, *Madame de Staël et la Révolution française. Politique, Philosophie, Littérature*, Paris, 1969, 88.
30. Destutt de Tracy, *Mémoire sur la Faculté de penser*, II, 6 (20 June 1796, 2nd messidor Year V), 127.
31. Letter of 22 June 1785: Mme de Staël, *Correspondance générale*, edited by Béatrice W. Jasinski, vol 1/1, Paris, 1962, 41.
32. Mme de Staël, *De l'Influence des Passions sur le bonheur des individus et des nations*, Œuvres Complètes, 17 vols, 1820–21, vol. 3, Introduction, 11 and 18; and 30.
33. De Staël, *Des Circonstances actuelles*, 305.
34. Ibid., 26–27.
35. Ibid., 267.
36. There are further references in my study 'Madame de Staël, Napoléon et les Idéologues' in *Himeji International Forum of Law and Politics*, no. 1, (1993), 46.

37. De Staël, *Des Circonstances actuelles*, 281, where she also writes that 'mathematics will make men lay down their arms'.
38. Ibid., 283.
39. Mme de Staël, *De la Littérature considérée dans ses rapports avec les institutions sociales*, ed. Van Tieghem, 2 vols, Paris/Geneva, 1959, vol. 2, 377. See also vol. 1, 13 and vol. 2, 371–77.
40. De Staël, *Des Circonstances actuelles*, 27
41. See above, 65.
42. De Staël, *Des Circonstances actuelles*, 63.
43. Ibid., 27.
44. 'They made a duty out of what should have been voluntary; they imposed by force what should have been spontaneous celebrations of freedom ... they called habitual actions malevolent. You might almost have said that malevolence was a sort of magical power, that ... constantly obliged the people to do the opposite of what they wanted to do' (B. Constant, *De l'Esprit de Conquête et de l'Usurpation dans leurs rapports avec la civilisation européenne* (1813–14), Paris, 1986, 174).
45. B. Constant, 'De la liberté des anciens comparée à celle des modernes. Speech made at the Royal Athenaeum in Paris', February 1819, published in B. Constant, *De l'Esprit de Conquête*, 265–91.
46. Ibid., 278–80.
47. See the remarks I make in my study mentioned above 182, note 18.
48. B. Constant, *Fragments d'un ouvrage abandonné sur la possibilité d'une constitution républicaine dans un grand pays*, ed. H. Grange, Paris, 1991, 416.
49. Constant, 'De la liberté des anciens', speech quoted above.
50. See above, 44.
51. Constant, *De l'Esprit de Conquête*, 169. He explains: 'to the tyranny of a single man, to that of many men, to that of all men, to legally constituted forms of oppression and to those exercised by the fury of the mob'.
52. Constant, 'De la liberté des anciens', 278. It is here especially that we find a proliferation of qualifying statements with regard to Rousseau.
53. B. Constant, *De la force du gouvernement actuel de la France et de la nécessité de s'y rallier* (Year IV, 1796), ed. Ph. Raynaud, Paris, 1988, 42.
54. Rousseau, *Contrat Social*, Book II, end of Chapter 6, 380.
55. For example, Constant, *De la force du gouvernement actuel*, 74: in questions of morality as in politics, 'form influences content. Corruption ... diminishes by taking on disguises ..., and what we first wished to appear to be through hypocrisy, we eventually become through habit'.
56. See my study quoted above, 191, note 4, 258–69, especially 265.

≈ Chapter 14 ≈

BONAPARTE: *IDÉOLOGUE* ?

It is generally agreed that the French Civil Code, as it was drafted between 1801 and 1804, bears the personal stamp of that exceptional lawmaker who, in 1807, was willing to give it his name: Napoléon. As a prelude to the last leg of the journey we have undertaken in these pages, it would seem to be fitting therefore, to examine in more detail Bonaparte's thinking on the theme we have been exploring and in the light of which I should now like to consider the celebrated Civil Code. Am I jumping the gun a little by beginning with the following statement? Bonaparte's anthropological instincts seem to me to be much closer to the position we have just been examining than they do to the image which French academics have created around him and which contributes to the myths that have become entrenched in the French national consciousness with regard to the Napoleonic code. In what is generally considered to be a 'classic' text on civil law, which appeared under the title *Spiritualité*, the author writes,

> In the Civil Code, man is treated essentially as a being endowed with a will: he is not a being of flesh and blood, with weaknesses and needs, labouring under oppressive economic forces; he is a being with a will which is always strong, clear, purposeful and free. The notion of responsibility presupposes the existence of will; the agreement of two individual wills, the contract, has the force of law (a.1134) as though to echo the words of Jean-Jacques Rousseau'.[1]

If we were to accept this assessment as accurate, it would imply that the Civil Code was some sort of spectacular anomaly, a flowering in the wilderness. It would also require us to believe that Rousseau placed great emphasis on the importance of individual wills: and it is certainly true that many people are led to believe as much, but especially people whose only acquaintance with him is through rather poor editions of his work.

The scientifically orientated view of man, which met with official approval at the time the Civil Code was being drafted, is all the more deserving of our fullest attention in that it also has a political dimension, and this sought to influence the legislation. It is not being unkind to say that this anthropological view was severely reductionist, since it openly professed to be so (and we know in what terms), and indeed saw this as a proof of its seriousness. More particularly, it was a view of man that was especially associated with the view proposed by the *idéologues*, under the leadership of Cabanis and Destutt de Tracy, and this would seem to indicate that it could never therefore be the view adopted by Napoléon since he had a reputation for having distrusted the *idéologues*, for having isolated them politically and for having at various times subjected them to verbal attack. In creating this impression, by the way, Napoléon ensured that they were seen by posterity as a courageous group of men who were proudly independent and who had the great merit of being fierce defenders of the cause of freedom. This is an opinion which many disagree with and we should examine the matter more closely.

First of all, it should be remembered that throughout these pages I have often stated that the reductionist anthropology of the Enlightenment is a phenomenon of huge proportions. It is a basic fact of life and it is shared by virtually all men, or at any rate by political thinkers of very different persuasions indeed, even including those who personally sought to oppose it: for example, Rousseau and Robespierre, who were singularly incapable of avoiding falling into the very trap they spent so much time warning others away from. So it would appear to be quite normal that Bonaparte should himself be infected by the very thing for which he attacked the *idéologues*, who were simply the men who were bold enough to turn it into a system and whom he was quite capable of disliking for totally separate reasons. But much more serious: when the *idéologues* were at their height under the Directory, Bonaparte actually belonged to the movement. He frequented the 'Auteuil circle', which met at the house of Mme Helvétius, and he became a member of the *Institut* which they controlled and which they considered as their private patch, a place where they could happily work away preparing for brumaire.

Now there are a number of reasons why this should all be considered quite natural. First of all, as a result of his training as an artillery officer and his education as a man of the Enlightenment, but above all for reasons to do with his temperament, Bonaparte is inclined towards *scientism*. He has a tendency to see the world through mechanicistic eyes. He followed the advice, proffered by Mme de Staël in her reductionist phase, when she suggested that, 'the statesman has to study the movements of *sensibilité*, in much the same way as Newton would watch a stone falling'.[2] He was interested in the mathematical side of things to what is possibly an abnormal extent. He confided that examining 'a book of logarithms' was 'always' a pleasurable 'form of relaxation'[3] for him. Other people read poetry. But it is true that in the Emperor's opinion 'a few months' are enough 'to understand the mechanism of poetry'.[4] In a word, things that are efficient, useful, positive and measurable define the only system of reference that he recognises. The human and the social side of things are thus exposed to a mental approach which is directly related to the approach adopted by the *idéologues*, whose materialistic tendencies he had completely shared when this group were at the height of their power. 'I do not believe in the immortality of the soul', he wrote in June 1796.[5] The hero's own words and the memories of those who were close to him constantly reveal that he would spontaneously adopt forms of expression that call to mind the sort of ideas that the *idéologues* themselves favoured.

Secondly, it goes without saying that a superb strategist such as he, who had just provided further proof of his abilities in the Italian campaign (March 1796–October 1797), possessed a certain quality of cool detachment in the way he looked at things and at men. Without wishing to denigrate the military skill of anyone, it is quite obvious that in the eyes of a leader involved in a battle, anything that tends to relegate soldiers to the status of machines that can be driven hither and thither as a unit (turning 'groups of men into a single mass' which, as Cabanis said, is available to anyone to use who knows how to do so), also provides him with a margin for manoeuvre that is at one and the same time moral, strategic and tactical, and is never likely to lessen his chances of victory. At Sainte-Hélène, the Emperor once again expressed his admiration for Frédéric II of Prussia for 'having known the secret of being able to turn men into real machines'.[6] As far as the war in Italy was concerned,

Bonaparte had boasted of having 'had to find within himself the means ... of inspiring several hundreds of thousands of men who were a long way from home with a single sense of purpose and common endeavour'.[7] Mechanicistic vision, single-minded manipulation of individual wills: we should be well aware that in the language of the age all this awakens echoes of a truly *doctrinal* nature. In the famous Italian campaign, which saw his fortunes waxing so strongly, he demonstrated a startling degree of insight into the techniques of propaganda, both in so far as the soldiers themselves were concerned and in respect of national opinion. In other words, he showed himself to be a past master in the collective massaging of mentalities, unbeknownst to the people concerned, a practice that has clear connections with that particular view of man that is discernible in the anthropological position of the *idéologues*, although it was by no means exclusive to them. He even went so far as to admit that Frenchmen 'will allow themselves to be led, provided however, that you carefully conceal from them the destination towards which you are making them march'.[8]

Thirdly, it is quite obvious that a theory that considers self-interest as the only motive underlying all human behaviour is hardly likely to meet with the disapproval of a man like Bonaparte. Such a view is absolutely and completely consistent with his own personal attitude to life as well as with his opinions about the people he employed or sought to influence. His whole career seems to identify him, and this in more than one respect, as the perfect prototype of the type of person whom Robespierre had attacked in floréal Year II – the man who sees 'the world as the skilful egoists' inheritance'.[9] The phrase could almost have been coined with Bonaparte in mind. He often talked of the omnipotence of self-interest as a power in human affairs and he is known to have been singularly annoyed whenever he came across examples of disinterested behaviour, which upset the fine balance of his mechanicistic system and lessened people's dependence upon him. Mme de Staël wrote that 'he was readier to forgive a piece of selfish scheming than a disinterested opinion'.[10] It would be quite mistaken to see such a remark as being made purely for the sake of argument: it reflects the fact that there was an undeniably 'technical' aspect to Napoléon's way of handling people and this was based on notions that are clearly associated with the anthropolgy in vogue at the time.

Fourthly, during the years 1797–98 Bonaparte's political ambitions were beginning to take shape and he was not slow to seize on this opportunity to add a 'cultural dimension' to his image and reputation, thus adding an aspect that had been missing from his earlier public image. This was a way of appearing more serious, of creating an impression and reassuring the public. It was clearly also a way of making the most of the political climate of the day by associating himself with the State scientism that was so much in vogue under the Directory and which was embodied (or perhaps reached its apotheosis) in the creation of the *Institut national*,[11] that mouthpiece of the *idéologues* to which Bonaparte had himself elected on 25th December 1797. Two weeks earlier, at the unprecedented triumphal celebrations organised by the Republican government in honour of the victor of the Italian campaign, Talleyrand had officially praised Bonaparte's 'love of the abstract sciences',[12] and had foreseen that perhaps it would one day be necessary 'to call him away from the pleasures of his *studious retreat*'. During this speech, the putatively soon-to-be-retired would-be student of twenty-eight years of age looked on with an appropriate expression of humility on his face: the official account[13] tells us that 'his simple and modest countenance was in marked contrast to his great reputation', as though to illustrate in advance the assessment made by Mme de Staël, when she wrote of the need (which she explained by reference to the 'mediocrity of the age') to 'steal men's admiration from them *unbeknownst to them*. It is important', she went on, 'not only to adopt a reassuringly modest demeanour, you must also feign indifference to the public's approval if you wish to secure it'.[14]

Having taken a place in the mechanical arts section of the physical sciences and mathematics class at the *Institut*,[15] Bonaparte later reckoned that he was tenth in order of merit out of a class of fifty students.[16] On successfully completing his course, alongside Monge and Berthollet, in January he made the following, particularly edifying remark: 'True conquests', he said, 'the only ones that leave us feeling no regrets, are the ones we achieve over ignorance. The most honourable as well as the most useful of occupations is to contribute to the extension of human ideas',[17] and the final part of this quotation is absolutely typical of the climate of the age. Bonaparte, aware of the advantages it brought with it, made a great show of his membership of the *Institut*. He later recalls that he made a tremendous impression there, discussing with the great minds of the day 'very deep and metaphysical matters. In those days he was called the *Geometrician* of war, the *Mechanic* of victory'[18] – 'loaded' expressions one might say. Mme de Staël accepted the whole thing at face value and thought of Bonaparte as 'the most intrepid warrior and *the deepest thinker* that history has ever produced'.[19] She also claimed: 'The French *Institut national* is the body of men which, given time, will win the highest consideration in France .... The nature of the French Revolution is such that it falls to the whole body of enlightened men to preserve its principles and to channel them in the right direction. By making the effort to be accepted as a member of the *Institut*, Bonaparte has demonstrated to public opinion where his true path lies'.[20] In 1799, the Director of the *École polytechnique* fondly recalled the frequency of the visits made by 'the hero of the Italian campaign' and how he so often used to drop in 'seeking to refresh himself by seeing how far the exact sciences had progressed, by calculating the amount of influence that the extraordinary impetus given to mathematical studies was likely to have upon the levels of intelligence in the general mass of the population'.[21]

The *idéologues'* scientism and their dream of applying mathematics to the moral and social spheres of activity were not things that he himself envisaged with trepidation. On the contrary, it was a natural step for him to take to have himself presented at Auteuil, at the house of Helvétius' widow, from early 1798 onwards (he left for Egypt in May). The most regular visitors to the circle counted among his colleagues at the *Institut*, and his brothers, Joseph and Lucien, were members of the group.[22] In a dedication to a book he had written in this same year, one of the group's friends alludes to the general's admiration for Helvétius.[23] In March, Bonaparte says to Roederer that, as far as ideas are concerned: 'We have those [ideas] that our organisation makes us have and not a single one more'.[24] This is quite straightforward materialistic determinism such as we have seen throughout the whole century but here expressed in quite a hard-line way. This same summer, he confides to his brother, Joseph, that he has taken the decision 'to become a really thoroughgoing egoist',[25] soon after having had dealings with the chief theoreticians of all-powerful and officially-endorsed egoism, the *idéologues*. *Really thoroughgoing egoist*: the expression suggests that previously he was an egoist in the same way that everyone is, but that from now on he will be an egoist in a systematic way. In itself, taking a decision of this sort would not have required him to be close to the *idéologues*, but could such an explicit decision be taken in such a self-conscious way had the climate of opinion been different? At the very least it would have been remiss of me not to point out the coincidence involved. And Benjamin Constant retrospectively judged this 'coincidence' to be a factor working in the despot's favour: 'When he heard the ideas that were being expressed in our salons at the time, why do serious thinkers say that the man had no other motive than his personal interest?'[26] We should point out here that Constant rebukes him for having said this rather more, in fact, than for having thought it.

But we should be clear about this: the real question in this whole affair, which is so full of interest from a historical point of view, combining as it does both events of great importance and doctrinal issues of great significance, the real question is not simply that the young Bonaparte was attracted to the Auteuil circle. In any event, we have already seen that this attraction can be explained in terms of expediency. The real question is the need to shed light on the very obvious infatuation which the leading *idéologues* felt for Bonaparte. It is true that for a number of years he had demonstrated his strong attachment to the Republic, that he could not be suspected of sympathy with Catholic obscurantism, that his scientism quite rightly had a true ring to it, and moreover, it was quite flattering that this warrior of legendary stature should condescend to treat the scientific rationalists, anthropologists and physicists as his equals. But for the leading figures among the *idéologues* to decide to rally in support of the brumaire *coup d'état* was a very big step to take, and one that was indeed taken. It was taken not only by Sieyès, whom we can consider in actual fact as a figure of essentially political importance, but also by someone like Cabanis whom we have already had occasion to identify as a character of major significance in that he acts as an epistemological linchpin between the modern and contemporary worlds.[27] Bonaparte and Cabanis, in fact, got on well together. The poison that came into their relationship under the Consulship of Bonaparte can be considered medicinal: it supposes the existence of (or helped to create) ties between them. And it is a fact that Cabanis was very much involved in the forefront of events of the 18th and 19th brumaire year VIII (9 and 10 November 1799),[28] in respect of which no one ever really took the trouble to try to find out what the opinion of the sovereign nation might have been: 'Everyone knows that this government [the Directory] was overthrown *unbeknownst to itself* and without its participation. Everyone knows that the government that replaced it did so also *unbeknownst to itself* and without its participation.'[29] But not, and this is the point, *unbeknownst to* and without the most active participation of Cabanis. One could almost say that in the event he contributed to providing 'close protection' for the saviour of France, he was also involved in a number of decisive interventions, and it was he personally who wrote the address designed to persuade the people to rally to the new régime.[30] Eight days before the *coup d'état* the newspaper *La Décade philosophique*, which a legitimately broad-brush approach allows us to consider as the official mouthpiece of the *idéologues*, innocently recorded: 'Within the *Institut*, Bonaparte is nothing more than a well-informed fellow traveller, a scientist in the midst of scientists, and he appears to no longer remember all his many other claims to glory.'[31]

The Constitution of Year VIII, which Cabanis helped to draft, possesses the great merit of doing away entirely with the major defect of its predecessor: it renders the electoral process incapable of having any political impact whatsoever. From this point onwards there is no need to worry about 'the wisdom of electoral choices', no need to lose any sleep at those times when 'the people holds its own destiny in its hands'.[32] This new constitution can in no way be remotely suspected of being democratic, and no one since has seen any reason to question this view. It is all the more striking therefore to record the fact that Cabanis, of all people, seemed quite happy to think it was and considered the Constitution founding the Consulate as the ideal of democracy: 'This is true democracy. Here we have democracy with all its advantages ... Everything is done on behalf of the people and in the name of the people, nothing is done by the people, nor in response to ill-considered popular demand'.[33] And this is hardly surprising. For the delight which Cabanis shows here is quite clearly in keeping with his position as the privileged inheritor of the century's philosophical tradition. The conception of man this tradition proposes is exactly the opposite of that which has been ascribed to it, and is a deeply pessimistic one. Here it is even more pessimistic since it has been hardened by the miscalculations of the Revolutionary period concerning man's ability to behave well on an individual and a collective level. Concomitantly, this view of man implies that he is destined to become an object to be manipulated by the very select club of those who possess knowledge, and who in Voltaire's words know how to enjoy 'the noble pleasure of feeling themselves to be *of a different nature* to that of common idiots',[34] the very idiots for whom the privileges of equality are consequently reserved. The functions of the great legislator have '*nothing in common* with the world of mere mortals', Rousseau believed.[35] The position adopted by Cabanis-the-Demiurge in respect of the 'collections of men taken *en masse*' he mentions in the boldly progressive text we have already discussed,[36] is exactly analogous to the position adopted by Cabanis-the-Democrat in year VIII, who would have everything done on behalf of men and nothing whatsoever done by them. And we may conclude from this that the *idéologues* felt that Bonaparte was going to become the enlightened 'legislator' whom the great minds of the century, including Rousseau, had been expecting to undertake the decisive remodelling of the substance of society.

The belief that this task of 'remaking' man required a fruitful collaboration between the legislator and the moralist, properly assisted by men of science, including doctors, was a familiar theme among the *Encyclopédistes,* the most important precursors of the *idéologues.* 'Let physicians, anatomists and doctors pool their experiences', writes d'Holbach, '... let the discoveries they make serve to teach moralists what are the true motivations behind men's actions; teach legislators what are the patterns they must adopt to stimulate men to work for the general well-being of society; instruct sovereigns as to the ways of making the nations which are subject to their rule really and truly happy'.[37] This is really a clear case of *scientism*, and of happiness being delivered to *subject nations* by rationalist planners, and has nothing whatever to do with questions of democratic freedom. And moreover, a huge psychiatric hospital is probably the last place one would wish to see democratic rule being established. We should not forget that d'Holbach also thought that 'although we are constantly told that man is a rational being, the human species includes only a very small number of individuals who really enjoy the powers of reason or who have the experience or the disposition that make their use possible';[38] nor should we forget that for Voltaire, the French 'will always be an ignorant and weak people, which needs to be led by the small number of enlightened men'.[39] 'The more I read Voltaire the more I like him', the first consul says shortly afterwards. 'He is a man [in his opinion] who is *always reasonable*',[40] whose great contempt for the masses, the 'populace',[41] Bonaparte himself adopted, and a man whom he felt he had to consider as being in the opposite camp to that occupied by Rousseau. Which seems to indicate that he was apparently unaware of the fact that Rousseau thought it inappropriate to waste knowledge on 'a populace unworthy of receiving to it' (a truly Voltairean theme),[42] or of the fact that the 'blind multitude' needed a great legislator to take on the task of putting the social contract in place;[43] and of the fact that 'a stupid and stultified populace ... secretly whipped up by clever schemers', was generally the reason for the existence of civil strife.[44]

Baron d'Holbach continues: 'Physical souls and physical needs require physical satisfactions ... Let us get to work on man's *physical* side ... and we shall soon see his *moral* side become better and much improved'.[45] The argument proposed by Cabanis in his *Rapports du Physique et du Moral de l'Homme* and the general tenor of this work quite patently belong to the same line of thinking as this piece of advice from d'Holbach. The latter goes on: 'The care taken by the legislator to work on the physical side of man will help create healthy, robust and well-formed citizens, who, because they are contented, will readily accept the useful impulses that it may be seen as desirable to bring to bear upon their souls'.[46] As we have often found in d'Holbach's writings, we have here a concentrated amalgam of the major themes of the present study, including eugenics, manipulation on a huge scale, a utopian conception of what constitutes happiness and finally also the theme which has led me to quote this piece in the first place, the inevitable cooperation of the political and scientific spheres. It is worth mentioning again that Helvétius himself thought that 'if we wish to know how to control the movements of the human doll, we first of all have to know which strings to pull to make it move'.[47] 'The science of man', he insisted, 'is part of the art of government ... Therefore, let the *philosophes* delve ever deeper into the abyss of the human heart: let them there seek out *all the principles which govern its movements* and let the Minister, benefiting from their discoveries, put them ... to good use'.[48] Doctor Cabanis, clinging to Bonaparte's coat tails, could have seen himself as a man on active service on behalf of his peers or his Enlightenment forebears. It would seem that he proposes for himself, and indeed that he is looking forward to, the task that d'Holbach had identified for medicine: providing whomsoever it may concern, for whatever reason they see fit, with the 'key to the human heart',[49] in order to ensure that 'politics' has all the 'advantages' that can 'possibly be gained from *Materialism*'.[50] In such conditions we can better understand how Cabanis was able to greet the Constitution founding the Consulate with a reference to 'true democracy', for the very express and unambiguous reason that under its aegis *nothing* would be done by the people.

To which we should also add that when Cabanis and his friends rather naïvely threw in their lot with General Bonaparte, they were simply in this respect too remaining true to the great Enlightenment tradition, which included a fascination on the part of the *philosophes* for despots of varying degrees of acceptability. Catherine II of Russia, Frédéric II of Prussia, heroes of Voltaire above all, but also of Helvétius and Diderot, had in fact been paragons of the virtues of 'true democracy' in the Cabanis version, but stripped of 'all its advantages'. The servile reverence they inspired in Voltaire is no great secret, but far less well known, in France at least, is the verbal delirium, sometimes of hallucinatory proportions, that they also triggered off. Voltaire speaks of Frédéric in terms redolent of passionate love,[51] he unreservedly offers him the gift of his person ('a great man for whom alone I live, feel and think'),[52] he places him far above all other mortals,[53] he likens him to God, and even Marcus Aurelius,[54] he debases himself by writing lines of astonishing vulgarity in his honour,[55] he judges him to be a better poet than David, who was nothing more than 'an abominable Jew, him and his psalms. I know a more powerful king than he and ... one who in my view writes better poetry'.[56] Before he imprudently risked the journey to Prussia, where in actual fact he came across 'a prodigious number of bayonets and very few books',[57] and from which he was to return having been morally horse-whipped,[58] his niece and mistress, Mme Denis, who was rather more clear-sighted than he, said that he was 'totally intoxicated with Berlin' and was making 'very admirable sketches of that country. The only quality they lacked was that of being true to life.' And above all, she was at pains to point out: but 'you know the weakness that M. de Voltaire has for kings and their courts'.[59] Two weeks earlier Voltaire had written of Frédéric, 'You should also know that he is the very best among men or I am the most stupid'.[60] Indeed, even after all the shameful treatment he had been subjected to in Germany, his vanity once more gained the upper hand and little by little the correspondence between them began again,[61] as did Voltaire's barely credible obsequiosness, examples of which are too numerous to cite here.

'I shall always have great respect for the powers that be', he announced,[62] and therefore naturally when *Système de la Nature* was published anonymously he attacked it for being 'too critical of the powers that be'.[63] The 'great respect' he felt for the 'autocrat of all the Russias' was indeed quite proportionate to the power she wielded, a power which Voltaire privately, quite lucidly, described as *'the most despotic power that exists anywhere on earth'*.[64] Soon after he informs us that the implacable Catherine has 'become my overriding passion',[65] he writes to her saying that she is 'an admirable, victorious, peace-bringing, law-making autocrat',[66] he proclaims her 'superiority over all other thinking beings'.[67] Quite literally, Voltaire envelopes 'this heroine who was born to change the face of the world'[68] in clouds of incense. Diderot and I, he says, 'are lay missionaries who preach fidelity to the cult of Saint Catherine'.[69] He even deifies her by dedicating 'a cult of worship' to her,[70] and he writes to her saying, 'Three of us, Diderot, d'Alembert and myself, have set up altars in your honour. You have turned me into a pagan. I prostrate myself in idolatry at the feet of your majesty, and much more than in deep respect, Mme, I am the priest of your temple. Voltaire'.[71] When the Russian army is victorious in battle, he claims that he breaks into a *Te Deam*, a *Te Catharinam*, and sometimes even a *Gloria*.[72] 'Your Imperial majesty brings me back to life by killing Turks', he admits to her, melting with gratitude;[73] for his own part he would like to contribute his own small piece by wiping out a few himself.[74] For indeed, Voltaire the well-known pacifist becomes an out-and-out bellicist for 'the sublime Cathy',[75] and Frédéric II, his militaristic friend from Berlin, chuckles at this recantation.[76] Voltaire and he once again renew their friendship and mockingly celebrate (in verse) the fate of these 'Turkish brigands cut to ribbons'.[77]

It is quite clear that as far as both Catherine and Frédéric are concerned, Voltaire's eloquence was capable of leading him far from the realm of common sense into the uncharted territory of hyperbole.[78] And yet the 'old Russian of Ferney', as Voltaire comes to call himself,[79] is not unaware of the fact that 'Cathy' was renowned for having first tried out her talents for despotic behaviour by having her captive husband done away with (1762); nor is he unaware that little Prince Ivan, whom she kept literally chained up, probably also owed his sad demise to her attentions (1764). 'Rather unfortunate rumours are abroad concerning the Russian Empress', he says to d'Alembert at the time,[80] conceding rather enigmatically: 'I think we should somewhat curb our enthusiasm for the North. It produces rather strange *philosophes*'[81] – both monarchs are targeted here. But Voltaire has already nailed his colours to the mast: 'the weakness that M. de Voltaire has for kings and their courts' is all the stronger. He declares himself to the tsarina as 'her champion in the face of the whole world' and these 'silly stories about her husband' are in his view, as he soon tells us, 'family matters that are nothing to do with me'.[82] He offers his friends in France jesuitical arguments seeking to demonstrate that the Empress was innocent of these two crimes.[83] And finally he produces the sledge-hammer argument suggesting that the merit she has had in spilling 'so much Turkish blood' surely weighs heavier in the balance than the blood of that 'drunkard', Pierre III.[84] In *De l'Homme*, Helvétius writes that for his own part, he considers these two episodes as 'minor misfortunes resulting from domestic difficulties'.[85]

The man whom the *idéologues* considered as their forebear, the great Helvétius, also cultivated a 'respect' for the 'powers that be', provided they could lay some claim to foreign origins. In 1764, when he was nominated to the Academy of Frédéric II (whose sister, the Queen of Sweden greatly admired *De l'Esprit*[86]) he honoured the king with a letter that could have been signed by Voltaire himself. He writes, for example: 'All the various gods have had their own priests whose function it was to honour their cult and to glorify them ... The priests of your temple are the *philosophes*'.[87] By the following year, the erstwhile tax-collector had assumed the role of adviser in fiscal affairs to the Prussian godhead. He managed to distance himself from his 'friend', Voltaire,[88] and came back from Prussia having been won over to the merits of militarism,[89] and would even have liked France to suffer a military defeat in order to ensure its own military regeneration. This very idea is formulated in the opening pages of his posthumous work, *De l'Homme* (1773),[90] which naturally (or perhaps rather unnaturally) quite obviously sings the praises of Catherine and Frédéric. Indeed it is worth remembering a fact that has enormous signifance in respect of this book, which through the scandal it caused and the success it enjoyed came to be considered as an emblem of the reductionist anthropology of the age, and that is, that its publication had in fact been expedited by the tsarina herself and that it was to her that it was dedicated.[91] Catherine, like Helvétius, had come to detest what Voltaire called the land of the Welches,[92] and this type of interference even caused a diplomatic incident.[93] Meanwhile Turgot, who was sympathetic to the *philosophes* and who had not yet been made a Minister, confided to Condorcet his irritation at the obscene lack of decency shown by Helvétius in managing to express an utter contempt for tyranny while simultaneously proving himself to be an admirer of the most thoroughgoing tyrants.[94]

And even Voltaire himself, and this is a little surprising, had the candour to express his astonishment, in an aside, that this book, which provides a summary of all the major ideas that the century had produced on the subject of man, should have paid homage through its dedication to Catherine, 'the most despotic power that exists anywhere on earth'. It was in this context that Voltaire used the expression,[95] and later, speaking of this very affair, he repeated to d'Alembert 'it is all very curious'.[96] But Voltaire's surprise is itself surprising on a number of levels. It highlights the relative lack of consistency, which we have previously identified in Voltaire's thinking and which is captured here as it unfolds before us. But in a historical sense, this lack of consistency (as the *idéologues'* attitude to Bonaparte bears witness) affected Enlightenment thinking as a whole. Superficially, the Enlightenment is reputed for its tendency to promote some vague form of political freedom, but this tendency derives from an explicit and irksome philosophical negation of the notion that man is in any way capable of freedom. And yet it seems to have been Frédéric II himself who had won Voltaire over to this negation of freedom, in two letters of 1737 and 1738.[97] Some ten years later Voltaire confessed as much.[98] He knew full well that it would have been dangerous in social terms to admit to such a belief, for the reasons we have already given,[99] and he also recognised the mutual attraction and appeal that a philosophical position of this sort and unfettered authoritarianism held for one another. Voltaire himself, in this respect, comes directly up against the absurdity of a system in which he had more or less allowed himself to be confined – roundly condemning despotism and speaking out in the name of freedom while simultaneously proclaiming that freedom is an illusion, yet those who defended the latter point of view with greatest vigour were also those who were prepared, of their own accord, to go crawling along the 'corridors of power' and wait service on the great and powerful, as Robespierre himself has reminded us.[100] As we have seen, Voltaire was greatly put out by *De l'Homme*, which drew unwelcome attention to his person.[101] It is quite clear that the whole affair surrounding its publication bothered him considerably, or rather that it served to highlight the weaknesses in his own intellectual position and drew attention to the theoretical and practical contradictions in his views when placed alongside the theoretical and concrete political ideas of his day. And this would seem to be the reason for the very disarming incongruity of Voltaire's surprise. If it was rather odd that the autocrat of all the Russias should take an interest in promoting *De l'Homme*,[102] Voltaire should obviously have been the last person to be in a position to take umbrage at the fact. But more than this, the connivence between despotic 'power' and Helvétius' reductionist anthropology is of necessity almost organic in nature and strictly within the order of things.

It is equally in the order of things and equally in tune with the mood of the age that there should be a connivence between the accredited successors to Helvétius and company and Bonaparte himself as he seizes power. The logical structure in evidence here could not be more clearly defined. At the risk of repetition. I should emphasise once again that the most important anthropological work to come from the pen of the writer whose widow provided the general headquarters of the *idéologues* and rented rooms to Cabanis, had been published twenty-five years earlier, under the protection of the most unashamed of all autocrats, who was in turn an object of worship for Helvétius, Voltaire and Diderot, to name but a few of the principal players in the orchestra. This is what Diderot has to say at the very moment when Catherine was promoting the publication of *De l'Homme*: 'Ah my friends! Just imagine that woman on the throne of France! What an empire! What a tremendous empire she would make out of France and in what a short space of time! ... Just come and spend a month in St Petersburg'.[103] In 1800 there was no need to make such a long journey. We have to hand, already practically 'on the throne of France' a man ready to create a 'tremendous empire ... and in what a short space of time!' It is therefore quite understandable that Diderot's admirers should opt for the same solution as he, even if the ambiguities we have already pointed out prepare the ground for later charges of inconsistency. Frédéric and Catherine both liked to think of themselves as enlightened codifiers, an area of activity in which Bonaparte was about to achieve total predominance. He too, both within the *Institut* and at Auteuil, was on very good terms with his friends the *philosophes* and, what is more, he could even be considered one himself. If Frédéric II was like Marcus Aurelius, Bonaparte could be compared at very least to Socrates: the similarity between Socrates and Bonaparte may not immediately have struck a chord in the public imagination but it did not escape Barras who, as one of the five Republican Directors, had made the comparison the theme of one of his official speeches.[104] Could anyone go one better? Yes. Mme de Staël, in her first period. This 'intrepid warrior'? 'The greatest thinker that history has yet produced', she was not afraid to suggest.[105] 'A *philosophe* who, chance would have it, felt himself obliged to win a few battles', said the *idéologue*, Garat.[106] And, in a simple letter from Potsdam, Voltaire had already had occasion to describe Frédéric II as 'a *philosophe* who has won five battles'.[107] The similarity in terminology here provides matter for reflection.

All this being the case, it is important to bear in mind two facts when considering the differences which begin to emerge between the first consul and the *idéologues*. The first fact is that the leading *idéologues* nevertheless remained important figures within the state and enjoyed to the full all the honours and advantages that the consular and imperial régimes had to offer. The second fact, and from our own point of view the more important one, is that despite appearances Bonaparte continued to share the same view of man as that adopted by the *idéologues*.

The fact that much of the intellectual baggage carried by the *idéologues* happened to find favour with Bonaparte[108] in no way implies that their systematic approach to all things did not profoundly irritate him. The military genius he first displayed in Italy relied quite heavily on flashes of intuition and on empirical judgements. This is the exact opposite of the normal way of working favoured by the official military schooling he had received and for which, for his own part, he had little time. 'The art of war is a simple art where all that matters is implementation', he confided, 'and *idéologie* has no place at all'.[109] Even before the days of brumaire he had recognised Sieyès as 'a man of systems' and detested him for it.[110] And once he had gained power, the myriad concrete demands that were made upon him could only serve to distance him yet further from what he pejoratively called, in August 1800, 'the metaphysics of principles'.[111] Laplace had hastily been appointed Minister of the Interior, on the basis that he had begun to publish a masterly work, his *Traité de Mécanique céleste* and was therefore the right man to restore the clockwork mechanism of French society to good working order, but he was immediately overwhelmed by minor details. The first consul remarked that he had proved himself to be a man obsessed with 'infinitely small details' and he was replaced as speedily as he had come.[112] One might well imagine that an episode such as this might have served to help Bonaparte to differentiate more clearly between his own innate tendency towards scientism and the infinite virtues that empiricsm offered him when it came to responding to practical needs. In May 1800, Mme de Staël remarked, 'This government uses every type of nuance, except that which could be considered purely philosophical'.[113] 'I am not seeking the best that is possible in an abstract or ideal sense, but to do positive good', the master proclaimed in 1802; 'old ways of getting things done are often better than new theories'.[114] And shortly afterwards, he scoffed at the political pretensions of 'a number of *idéologues* who have never been involved in practical matters and who do not understand the difficulties they entail'.[115]

What is more, 'new theories' aimed at regenerating society, in the style of those of Cabanis and Destutt de Tracy, may well have held out much promise, but the fact remains that at this particular moment of history it is difficult to see how they could be made to impinge upon the social fabric in any concrete way. Moreover, the bright future that they seem to suggest is on the horizon not only remains rather vaguely defined but seems also to imply the need to carry out a good deal of work upon 'successive generations'[116] before it can be achieved. Yet it is a well-known fact that Bonaparte's whole career was to be a hectic race against time: he had everything to do or to redo, to make or to remake within a very short time-span, as well as to try to establish roots of his own as he did so. Diderot, at least, had the intelligence to sense 'the immense distance that separates a systematically minded *philosophe*, making arrangements for the happiness of society from the comfort of his couch, from a great sovereign who spends the whole day from morn till night confronting all sorts of obstacles which threaten to prevent her realising the good she would achieve ... obstacles that the poor *philosophe* has never even thought about'.[117] Not all of the *idéologues* were necessarily capable of such lucidity, which possibly accounts for the sarcastic tone adopted by Fiévée, who was a secret adviser to the first consul, and who wrote to him in January 1803 in the following terms: 'The need to govern the whole of Europe has become such a *philosophically easy* thing to do that it would appear that this part of the world is only waiting on the agreement of scientists as to the *intellectual stamp* of government that is to be adopted. Doctors will probably have a great deal of say in this decision; for since they have been converted to materialism they show distinct aspirations to becoming the legislators of the whole universe'. There immediately follows a reference to Cabanis,[118] whose famous *Rapports* have just been published. Fiévée has touched on a very sore point indeed: what concrete proposals do these system-obsessed anthropologists have to offer? In 1807, Napoléon claims that grammar and the science of ideas are indistinguishable, and that together they provide 'the basis of sensations'.[119] The idea more or less succinctly expressed here, is pure *idéologue* orthodoxy. It is a theme close to the heart of Destutt de Tracy[120] and indeed is one he expounded upon himself, but one must wonder whether the Emperor was not in fact quite right to add that, exactly how the 'practical application' of these ideas could be achieved remained something of a 'great mystery'.[121]

We should add that Bonaparte was well placed to know the limitations of the sensualist methods which had been used under the Directory at the instigation of the *idéologues*, and of many others besides. He did not refute the anthropological premises on which such methods were based and had accepted that such methods should be used, and this for the simple reason that it was their failure which had created the conditions for his own success, politically speaking. And then, the vogue which these methods enjoyed under the Directory can be put down to the fact that they were seen as an alternative to the naked authoritarianism that the circumstances of the day seemed to demand but which, in these years following the Terror, was understandably rejected by all.[122] In the absence of any willingness to accept any form of authoritarianism there was no choice but to fall back on a search for ways to condition the mass of citizens without their realising it, by recourse to such techniques as the use of *fêtes nationales*. Now the repeated miscalculations that marked the period 1794–99 and the toll which these took on public opinion finally had the effect of throwing the gates wide open to an authoritarianism that was all the more precisely and markedly monocratic in that the hope that they might avoid falling into this particular trap had been 'ever more cruelly disappointed'[123] throughout the preceding years. In other words, authority was more able to speak its own name because it was more ardently desired as a symbolic solution. And the effect of this was that the less obvious methods of propaganda employed at the time of the Directory, although not thrown out overnight, nevertheless underwent something of a downgrading. This in turn meant that those whose technical specialism lay precisely in promoting such methods, that is to say, by and large, the *idéologues* themselves, were also invited to take something of a back seat. Or, to put it yet another way, the 'Hobbesian' tendency that had been ushered in in the aftermath of Thermidor[124] was now able to flower more freely. 'Hobbes, a philosopher with whom your Imperial Majesty is most certainly acquainted', Diderot wrote to Catherine,[125] whose 'power', according to that great admirer of hers whom we have already identified, was 'the most despotic that exists anywhere on earth', a phrase which calls to mind the biblical description of of the monster Leviathan: 'there is no power on earth that can be compared to it'.[126] Rousseau maintained that, in reality 'peace is more important than freedom',[127] a phrase which also has a Hobbesian ring to it. And, moreover, he confided to that Friend of Mankind, Mirabeau: 'I can see no tolerable middle ground between the most austere form of democracy and the most downright Hobbesianism'.[128] By making themselves absolutely intolerable, the post-Thermidor years would seem to lend weight to the contention that there could be no middle ground between Jacobin republicanism and the Caesar-like ambitions of a Napoléon.

The Concordat of 1801 was a source of great disappointment for the *idéologues*. There are those who have become so obsessed with this event that we might almost be led to think that a rejection of Catholicism and of its insistent and hateful emphasis on free will which ensured that individual consciences could remain vigilant, was one of the defining criteria of the whole Enlightenment (in the absence of any other supposedly defining criteria capable of standing up to serious scrutiny). But the *idéologues* and other rationalists of various types were fooling themselves if they sought to interpret the Concordat as a proof that the philosopher-General wished to mark out Catholicism for specially favourable treatment. In his view, this religion was merely one avatar, albeit one which historical circumstances made preferable to all others, of the socially necessary cult of civil observance which had been the dream of Rousseau, Voltaire and many others, as well as Robespierre and various other examples of deistically-minded men. 'Is Christianity not the simplest system of all ... the one best suited to our need to train good citizens?' This objection, which a pastor voiced in response to Rousseau's civic antichristianism,[129] was adopted *mutatis mutandis* by the first consul. He could see the absurdity of seeking to combat a religion that was followed by the vast majority of people living in France and which – as l'abbé Grégoire had not failed to point out – offered singular advantages to those whose job it was to govern. As far as the quality of the social fabric was concerned, it promised them such attractive things as 'conjugal chastity, filial piety, a respect for contracts entered into'.[130] As Portalis explained, the Revolution which saw the Concordat established may well have destroyed religion, but the 'good habits' which religion had instilled helped to limit the damage which the Revolution caused. 'France has suffered a great deal, but what would have become of her if these habits had not worked *unbeknownst to us*, as a counterweight to our passions?'[131] I should perhaps point out in passing that working on the masses, unbeknownst to them, is an aim that has in no way been abandoned in government circles.

Voltaire congratulated Catherine II on 'having managed to restrict priests to being simply useful and making them dependent'.[132] And this was entirely within the logic of the civil Constitution of the clergy, and later of the Concordat and the organic Articles which were appended to it on the sole authority of the Consulate. Far from being a 'strange conclusion', therefore, to the philosophy of the eighteenth-century,[133] the aims which the Concordat set out to achieve place it firmly in the tradition of the politicoreligious utilitarianism of the Enlightenment and of the Revolution – a tradition which Robespierre, too, illustrated in his own special way,[134] and which included within itself elements of subjectivism and relativism, both of which are equally discernible in the speeches of Bonaparte and his followers. Vigorously defending the Concordat to the *Corps législatif*, Bonaparte's brother, Lucien, calmly pointed out that cults '*even if they are based on mistakes*, these mistakes become sacred because they are necessary to men's happiness; and that the sort of absence of belief that coldly calculates and cynically analyses, *even if it were based on truth*, would nevertheless be the worst enemy of individuals, families, nations and governments'.[135] A comment such as this could hardly be clearer. The speech goes on to underline the fact that religious faith promotes a useful sense of responsibility, that it makes oppressors feel, 'secret remorse and a vague and terrible fear which go beyond the punishments meted out by human justice' and that it 'comforts the victim by giving him hope which is holy and infinite in nature and totally unconnected with his surroundings'.[136] The Emperor also strongly condemned the unyielding atheism of the astronomer, Lalande, as containing a 'principle capable of destroying all social organisation, since it robs man of all the *consolations* and all the hope he might have':[137] this, naturally, brings Rousseau and Robespierre to mind. He also says, 'Take away their faith from the people and you will be left with only highway robbers', a remark which brings to mind Voltaire. But in the final analysis, it is always the same logic at work with the added bonus, in this case, of a little (or perhaps quite a lot of) cynicism: *'Religion is the vaccine of the imagination'*, adds the Emperor,[138] and if the idea is expressed in strong terms it is important to realise that the content of the expression is fairly commonplace. What all of this points to, of course, is the political importance of religion for Napoléon: 'In religion I see all the mystery of society',[139] he says. Moreover, he classifies both the Bible and the Koran as political books.[140]

For it matters little what the actual religion is, if it is appropriate to the people governed. 'From Mohammedanism to the religion of the desert elders, his mind is ready to understand and his character to act in accordance with what the circumstances dictate', says Mme de Staël.[141] How true this is. It is an oft-voiced opinion that if Bonaparte had settled in the Middle East his pragmatism would have led him to become a Muslim. When his soldiers disembarked in Egypt he warned them: 'Show respect to their Muftis and their imams, as you have shown respect to rabbis and to bishops'.[142] And later he boasted: 'I put an end to the war in Vendée by becoming a Catholic, I established myself in Egypt by becoming a Muslim, and I won over the Italians by becoming an ultramontane. If I had to govern a nation of Jews I would rebuild the temple of Solomon'.[143] The very sequence he enumerates here shows the extent to which Bonaparte was basically indifferent to matters theological.

But, in the event, the men of progress proved themselves to be far more rigid than their erstwhile colleague of Auteuil and the *Institut*. It is of course easy to understand that the Concordat morsel, hastily cooked up by the pragmatic Bonaparte, should have been a little too much for them to swallow. The promulgation of the Concordat is the signal for the introduction of an official rhetoric which would henceforth be very hostile to materialism and to atheism. Many *idéologues*, and Cabanis not least among them, felt good cause to be unhappy at this turn of events. It was Lucien Bonaparte himself, in the same speech of 1802, who attacked Cabanis, the 'cold materialist' and his 'murderously false metaphysics', who 'proudly claims to be analysing everything from a moral point of view' and 'only manages to break everything down into pieces' including the notion of 'generous passions'. He also pillories those 'hardened hearts' for whom the idea of something holy is 'incomprehensible'.¹⁴⁴ This attack, coming as it does from a former member of the Auteuil circle and someone so close to the hero who was governing France, is severe indeed for the aforementioned Cabanis, whose *Rapports du Physique et du Moral de l'Homme*, had set out, with particularly bad timing, to make its lonely way in the world that very same year. It was perhaps equally cruel for him to hear Portalis, this time, saying that thanks to religion even non-believers find themselves being swept up by 'a sort of general spirit which carries them along *in spite of themselves* and which, up to a certain point, controls their actions and their thoughts *without them realising it*'.¹⁴⁵

What we have to understand about this episode is that the political about-turn involved is by no means indicative of a personal recantation on the part of the first consul but rather quite simply an illustration of his astonishing ability to adapt to circumstances. In a situation where less supple minds than his own refuse to see anything other than inconsistency and a desire to rehabilitate a disgraced clergy along with their superstitious practices, this former colleague of theirs is looking for ways to ensure a much better harnessing of every individual's involvement in civic duties – an aim which they themselves were crying out to see realised just as much as he.¹⁴⁶ In his own heart the consul, and later Emperor, has in no way abandoned rationalism and the reductionist anthropology of the *idéologues*. If anything, we might argue that the opposite is true. If everything can be explained in material and mechanical terms, if man is neither free nor responsible for his actions, 'usefulness is the sole criterion in all things', and one is authorised to do anything whatsoever that promotes usefulness, or indeed anything else, for that matter. So here we have Bonaparte facing up to concrete problems like a master empiricist and with a degree of flexibility that the mental mind-set of the *idéologues* would never have allowed them to envisage. Voltaire and Diderot, among any number of others, would have welcomed the Concordat because it made priests 'useful and ... dependent'.

And Voltaire would have coveted the *Légion d'Honneur* too. For the creation of this distinction in 1802 offers a similar case in point: even though it offends certain egalitarian sensibilities, it is none the less strictly in line with the Enlightenment principle of political usefulness that Helvétius and d'Holbach so often mentioned. Helvétius argued that an honours system was essential. 'With an order of merit, a ribbon or some other external sign of distinction, you can make men do whatever you want them to do'.¹⁴⁷ D'Holbach too spoke of the civic advantages of 'marks of distinction, titles, pensions (which are often quite modest), ribbons'.¹⁴⁸ And we know very well the extent to which men of the Enlightenment appreciated titles, honours and wealth, with the exception of Rousseau, who kept his distance from such things. In this respect too, Bonaparte's line of reasoning cannot be accused of departing from orthodoxy.

No. In his heart of hearts Bonaparte has not changed at all. The best part about it is that when Bonaparte slights the *idéologues* in this way, not only is he happily carrying on like one of the enlightened despots of the past rather than being the man to put an end to tyrannical behaviour – Voltaire too believed he had allowed himself to be 'used like a fool'¹⁴⁹ by the tsarina after having been so atrociously treated by the King of Prussia, although he expressed the point more discreetly – he is also (and this is what the *idéologues* fail to understand) merely putting into effect the principle of egoistical utilitarianism that their theories have instilled in him, or at the very least have served to legitimise. Constant rightly observed that Bonaparte had very quickly spotted the inanity of the 'subtle interpretations by which they tried to avoid the consequences of the principles they had proclaimed'.¹⁵⁰ In just as candid a way as the author of *Candide* had done,¹⁵¹ the *idéologues* could wonder 'What a curious thing is this' when they saw what a strange bird they had hatched. Napoléon had enough worldly-wise intelligence to leave to people more slow-witted than himself the problem of explaining away the ambiguities and the intellectual absurdity of events, which was fair enough since they, rather then he, were ultimately responsible for them. But the way he made light of the fine distinctions the system sought to establish, does not mean that in broad terms he did not remain within its spirit. Such an attitude is condoned, if not by the *idéologues* themselves, at least, and whatever they might think, by their own system, in the sense that in the long run it could be made to justify anything whatsoever. Throughout his whole career, the words and deeds of the great man show him deferring in a very straightforward way not only to what people had to say about him but also to the enlightened reductionism of the century's *philosophes* and their successors, the *idéologues*.

There is considerable evidence for this. Mme de Staël has clearly demonstrated the importance of calculated egoism in various aspects of the whole Napoleonic enterprise and I shall not dwell on this point here,¹⁵² except to mention an example which is typical of the spirit of the age. The Emperor, in an attempt to show that he is capable of benevolence, says, 'Do you really believe that I don't enjoy giving pleasure to people too? *It does me good* to see a happy face';[153] this is indeed altruism with an egoistic and subjectivist stamp: the wording is typical and could easily have come from Rousseau or d'Holbach.[154] Many other elements associated with the Enlightenment's reductionist view of man, can be discerned in Napoléon. For example, the absence of any real ontological or axiological boundary between man and the animals. Speaking of individuals of the human kind, he was wont to say 'Every animal has its own instincts and each must follow them'.[155] After playing the part of the ethnologist in the East, he allowed himself to extrapolate on his experience thus: 'Uncivilised man is a dog'.[156] Later the Emperor voices his admiration for a cavalry general who has, 'the art ...of communicating the spark of electricity to men as well as to horses';[157] we have already seen several times that these two species are interchangeable.[158] Much could be said too about the choice of the bee as the imperial symbol, in that it makes a clear reference to a social model which, if applied to humans, connotes absence of freedom and the perfect mechanicistic utopia, and so on. 'My arms are a bee which ... collects honey to carry back to its hive, and the motto they bear is *Usefulness*'. These words, which could have been spoken by Napoléon, were written by Catherine II,[159] who crops up yet again. Diderot referred to these social insects in the advice he himself offered to the tsarina.[160] As far as Enlightenment doctrine is concerned, this is a very rich theme and one I have barely touched upon here.

Likewise, traces of the propensity of Enlightenment thinking for racist or imprudent attitudes to eugenics[161] can also be picked up in various comments made by Bonaparte. Indeed, if the opposite were true it would probably be much more surprising. He shows a marked contempt for Jews, for example, and referred to them as the 'most contemptible of men'.[162] At times, this idea was expressed with a vigour that would have delighted Voltaire himself. Thus, the Emperor explains that it is wrong to consider that Jews have been 'rendered vile' by the ill treatment they have received since in Poland, where they enjoy high social status, 'they are none the less vile, ill-kempt and given to all forms of behaviour of the greatest improbity'. Jews? 'a mass of bad blood'. We should force them to exogamy, he advises, and 'Jewish blood will cease to have a special character'.[163] 'Correcting' them by 'changing' them: is this not simply one special case of the desire to remodel mankind that we have already encountered in Rousseau and Cabanis? Bonaparte also showed a contempt for blacks, a fact which is borne out by the restoration of slavery in 1802. On the very subject of Enlightenment thinking in respect of these two groups, Léon Poliakov wrote the following: 'Putting on one side Voltaire's frenzied outbursts, comments of this type are to be found in the majority of authors'.[164] He also showed a contempt for Arabs, either directly, in Egypt, where 'its people ... is made up of several different species',[165] or vicariously in Spain, where its 'people ... are vile and cowardly, rather like what I found with the Arabs'.[166] Kant put the cruelty of Spaniards down to the influence of Arab blood.[167] Here again, I am barely scratching the surface of a topic on which there is a great deal to say.[168]

In exactly the same way, mechanicist forms of expression are a commonplace for Bonaparte, who uses them himself and hears them being used all around him.[169] They are applied to both the cosmos and to individuals, to both society and to institutions, since in theory everything is linked.[170] When Bonaparte uses such terms, they at times take on a very particular resonance. 'I shall create', he says, 'institutions which will strengthen my system, the machine I have organised'.[171] And he refers elsewhere to, 'this immense machine',[172] a phrase which is echoed by Mollien when he talks about 'that very complex machine at the centre of which Napoléon had positioned himself to act like a pivot, strong enough through his own power to resist all movements in opposing directions'.[173] Often too, the Emperor talks of, 'my system', 'because I govern by a system',[174] which for him, as we know, implies rigour but not rigidity and includes an ability to adapt to circumstances as well as a not-disinterested respect for 'the nature of things'.[175] The Emperor speaks of the 'governmental machine' and 'the human machine', of the 'mechanism' of language and that of poetry.[176] Chaptal observes, 'Men were, in his eyes, no more than machines that he believed himself to have been destined to set in motion'.[177] In fact, he would have wished to have as a secretary 'a writing machine',[178] and he speaks of considering judges as 'physical machines through whose offices laws are executed just as the hands of a clock indicate the time'.[179] After our journey through the Enlightenment and the Revolution, there is nothing in all this to make us feel we are breaking new ground here.

And it is worth noting that the Emperor is consistent enough not to exclude himself from the great mechanism. 'I am the timepiece which exists and which does not know itself but which functions without knowing who made it', he says again in later life.[180] Once more the very Voltairean flavour of such an expression is striking (albeit on a theme which was far from restricted to Voltaire's pen alone, as we have already seen). Voltaire had also written, 'We are born and we grow up, we live and we die without ever knowing ourselves'.[181] Specks of dust or pieces of straw blown in the wind, balls bouncing along into infinity: these are frequent images which Voltaire uses to describe human destiny and to minimise man's sense of responsibility – which explains how timely it was, for the good of society, that he 'should believe himself to be free', and accountable to a God.

The Emperor too demonstrates that his mechanicism is sufficiently consistent to allow him to deduce that human beings cannot be held responsible for their actions. But this is a difficult exercise to maintain and one which it is impossible to assume to the full. On a matter of administrative detail the master remarks, 'it is not a question of seeking to understand the metaphysics of blame here but of finding the person responsible'.[182] The point at issue here is precisely the risky dialectical ground we find ourselves on in so many chapters of d'Holbach.[183] And, moreover, both men make value judgements on the behaviour of others. With these reservations in mind, we can nevertheless recognise that this is a very 'meritorious' tendency in a man immersed to such an extent in concrete political activity. In Bonaparte's opinion, the Revolution was a blind whirlpool of cause and effect which excluded any possibility of holding responsible those people who had became caught up in it.[184] One advantage of looking at past events in this way is that it is easier to persuade people to let bygones be bygones, and we know full well that this was an aim dear to Bonaparte's heart. But it was still his aim, even at St Helena, where he spoke of the Revolution in terms of a volcanic combination – an expression which brings to mind certain 'hyper-deterministic' pages in d'Holbach which deal with 'the terrible convulsions which shake the very roots of political societies from time to time'.[185]

And Bonaparte's tendency to view things in this way applied equally to those who had rebelled against him. In the final analysis, all he reproaches Malet's accomplices with is the fact that they were 'blind, even to their own real interests'[186] – and here the theme of ill-advised egoism reappears yet again. Quite rightly, Caulaincourt sees a connection between his 'lack of esteem for human kind' and 'the indifference which he often showed for the obvious wrongs committed by a number of people'; and he goes on to say that in Bonaparte's view, as far as some people are concerned, acting in honour and good faith are quite simply 'feelings which, according to him, are totally absent from their make-up'.[187] Indeed, on his return from Elba, Napoléon reassured those who had rallied to the cause of the monarchy by declaring that 'there are events of such a nature that they go way beyond the ability of the human make-up to cope with'.[188] And we would be justified in thinking that he really believed this because from his final island retreat, St Helena, his opinion of people reflects very similar views. Las Cases writes, 'It is certainly the case that he speaks objectively ... without any resentment about the circumstances of his life and the people he has known'.[189] At St Helena, too, the deposed Emperor explained, 'There are virtues and vices that fit the circumstances. The latest difficulties we have experienced are above anything human strength could be expected to bear'.[190]

It is also worth remarking that Napoléon did not consider himself as in any way distinct from those who voiced the general tendency to reject the notion that man can be held responsible for his actions. Apparently, around the very date at which Bonaparte was coming into the world, d'Holbach had said: 'Maybe at this very moment imperceptible molecules are collecting together and combining in such a way that the finished assemblage will make up a sovereign who will be the scourge or the saviour of a vast empire'.[191] The determinism of this remark would not have displeased Bonaparte, who was wont to describe himself as a 'timepiece', or as 'a stone thrown through space'. It is even from within this very perspective that he is able to argue that what people refer to as his ambition is not ambition at all: 'it is so natural to me', he explained in 1804 'it is so bound up with my very existence that it is like the blood flowing in my veins, like the air that I breathe; it doesn't make me go any quicker, nor behave any differently than the other natural drives that are within me'.[192] Mme de Staël allusively ranged Napoléon among those who are capable of exaltation *'unbeknownst to themselves'*.[193] She said that the seductive powers of Talleyrand had 'captured Bonaparte, unbeknownst to himself'.[194] Bonaparte himself would not necessarily have disagreed with this view, for reasons we have already outlined. As Condillac had explained, the governor 'is the machine operator who must reset the springs and rewind the whole machine as often as circumstances demand'.[195] But for good or ill, as far as Condillac was concerned, the machine operator is himself logically a part of the general mechanism he is regulating: 'Every government has maxims: or rather every government has a way of doing things which presupposes the existence of maxims which often do not in fact exist at all, or which it doesn't realise exist. It acts for reasons *unbeknownst to itself*, through habit; and without offering explanations for acting the way it does, it continues to act as it has always done'.[196] It seems quite clear to us that, despite a 'style' of government that was so alien to the idea of determinism, Napoléon would have acknowledged the logic behind such opinions.

We would not go so far as to suggest that this way of thinking was in any way an absolute or a constant for the Emperor. The thing would have been impossible in any case, and it would be easier to prove the opposite to be true. But nor can it be seriously doubted that this way of thinking provided the framework for his whole mental outlook. And this outlook remains quite happily the one inherited from the Enlightenment and therefore the outlook adopted by the *idéologues*. If one examines the matter more closely, it seems evident to me that many aspects of the Napoleonic enterprise and of Bonaparte's way of thinking, which one might be tempted to explain away as being somehow related to the fact that he was an exceptional man living in an exceptional period of history, in fact are more exactly and more simply seen as merely an amplification or an exacerbation (and not at all a rejection) of tensions and potentialities issuing from the Enlightenment and the Revolution. His unbridled utilitarianism is one proof of this, and another is the deep disdain in which he held 'metaphysics' – a view we have already encountered in Voltaire and Rousseau. So many other examples provide yet further proofs. His contempt for his fellow-men, which is so often alluded to by himself and others, is merely a concretised version of the anthropological reductionism which is omnipresent in the present study. 'That is how men are', he concluded. 'I am reproached for not holding them in very high esteem. Am I wrong?'[197] It is impossible not to imagine the whole of the Enlightenment answering him in chorus, with a resounding 'No'. It would be foolhardy indeed to try to rule out any connection whatsoever between this sort of contempt, founded as it is in doctrine, and Napoléon's prowess in war, based as it was on losses of human life that are a matter of common knowledge. This 'contempt' cannot but imply, almost of necessity, a value judgement which the scientistic or scientific approach should exclude completely, if followed rigorously. But it should be said, too, that even the most coldly technical of the eighteenth-century anthropologists of the ilk of d'Holbach fall into the very same trap, as do even more so some of those writings which are more obviously tainted with subjectivism. Voltaire springs to mind here. His contempt for mankind was at least as strong as that demonstrated by Napoléon, although the latter was probably colder and more neutral in his contempt than Voltaire ever was. Voltaire's contempt for humanity even extended to include himself and, face to face with his own mirror, he uses language that makes us stop and think, and to which the notorious Mme Denis gives a form of endorsement when she says: 'Where feelings are concerned you are the worst of men'.[198]

But certainly not where the mind is concerned. The firmly-held belief that by far the greater part of humankind is not equipped for the task of thinking, the feeling that in this respect he belongs to a very restricted élite, these ideas – which we have encountered several times within these pages, in Voltaire and many others – reach their apotheosis, one might say, with Napoléon. In his person, the élitism of the Enlightenment in a sense enters its final phase by elevating Bonaparte alone over and above all others, as somehow distinct from the very species which produced him. 'My Italian peoples know me well enough', he pronounced in 1806, 'to never forget that I know more about it in my little finger than they know about it in all their heads put together'.[199] And where the affairs of this nether world of ours are concerned he also felt himself able to treat directly with the very highest authority of all: 'When I undertook to regenerate France, I asked Providence to accord me a determined number of years', which to this day remains a secret between the two of them.[200] He would even like to be seen as someone who can see into people's innermost hearts. 'I could ask each and every one of you to provide me with a full explanation for the most secret feelings which are harboured in your hearts, for I know everything, even what you have never told anyone at all': this, in 1798, is what he would like to have the inhabitants of Cairo believe.[201] He is certainly taking them for the idiots he believed them to be. Here once again we come across the very 'Directory-style' ideal that is the obsessional ambition to make the inner man utterly crystal clear and transparent (without which, by the way, it would have been necessary to greatly extend the police service). But in addition, this type of pronouncement shows an obvious tendency on the part of Bonaparte to claim to possess an ability which 'has nothing in common with the world of mortal men', an ability which the *Contrat Social* has already informed us is one which also characterises the exceptional legislator.[202] It is true that the man in question had, as Mollien explained, 'only studied power in military camps, where in order to turn men into *docile instruments*, in order to take them over and make them of a like mind, the leader needs to have himself proclaimed in some way the *universal providence* of all those who are under his command'.[203]

In accordance with the course of events described in the *Contrat Social*, the will of this exceptional man substitutes itself for the individual wills of the 'blind multitude' in order to reveal to them what they didn't even know they wanted. Mme de Staël, whose judgement was sharpened rather than blunted by the persecution to which she was subjected, more than once remarked upon this Napoleonic will of iron, forcibly supplanting all other wills and expanding its influence so forcefully that only the continental blockade was finally able to check its expansionist impetus. Mollien had recognised this insatiable Napoleonic ambition 'to fuse all wills into a single will', and the views he proposes are entirely consistent with certain pages from Rousseau: 'He wanted to make himself the regulator of every opinion on all matters ... the arbiter of all public affairs, the hope of all private enterprises, in a word to centralise everything in his own person', and 'he felt himself capable of single-handedly retaining in place the knot that held together all the different strings of that vast network which included all the local needs of communities, all the private hopes of individuals; and wherever he happened to be, his hand felt the vibration passing up each of these strings'.[204] The hypertrophy of the Leviathan-state in the interests of maximum efficiency, the undervaluing of the totality of those governed and who are absolutely vulnerable and unprotected, the omnipotence of the one person who alone knows, who alone exercises his will and who alone possesses power and authority: these features of the times merely describe the continuation of a trajectory which can be traced through the Revolutionary period and the decades which preceded it.

There is so much more that could be said on this score. The way he ploughed up the politico-institutional landscape like a man possessed, both in France itself and even more so round about (one thinks of the republics he established, the mushrooming of satellite kingdoms, the replacement of this monarch by that one, the bartering of one crown for another), can all of this not be seen quite legitimately as a corollary of the political artificialism which goes to the very heart of the doctrines on which the social contract was founded? The artificialist view of the family, which is a concomitant and which is equally discernible in Bonaparte, is typical of the climate created by these same doctrines and revolutionary ideas. It was especially visible in relation to his own family, which was held in such high esteem that it was frequently allowed to take precedence over the interests of the state. Even the way he tended to refer to his soldiers as 'my children' can possibly be seen as belonging to the same logic. The revolutionary tradition constantly refers to children as belonging, in the first instance, to the fatherland and to the Republic.[205] And since, henceforth, he is a single-handed embodiment of the state, it is logical and doctrinally *modern* that he should take verbal possession of his soldiers in this way, and refer to conscripts to the army as his 'annual income' – we know only too well what kind of investment he had in mind for them. The Napoleonic experience frequently involves exaggeration and over-emphasis. Even at the moments when I would like to be able to speak in terms of a break with the past, very often it is merely a continuation of it in some paroxysmal form. At bottom, the Revolution saw itself as, and wished itself to be, a *regeneration*. Bonaparte frequently repeated that very word and even admitted on St Helena that he would have liked to 'march peacefully towards *universal regeneration*'.[206]

In truth, all this is not enough to pluck Napoléon free from the intellectual current in which the *idéologues* themselves moved. And what is more, despite what one may be tempted to suppose, neither do we see the *idéologues* themselves move too far away from the current of imperial thinking. People happily talk of the exclusion of the *idéologues* from the *Tribunat* in 1802. But in the event the meaning of the word '*idéologue*' is rather vague and its use allows people to rather conveniently forget that the principal founders of the *idéologie* movement and its two great intellectual leaders, namely Cabanis and Destutt de Tracy, held seats in the 'conservative Senate'. This was a most prestigious political forum whose richly endowed functions were only offered to a very select group, among whom were also numbered Garat and Volney, and also Berthollet, Laplace, Monge and Lagrange, who, without belonging to the *idéologues'* group in the strictest sense of the word, nevertheless had much in common with them through their belief in scientism. Bonaparte held sway over these men through the lever of the honours system and by what they also stood to gain from his rule. Consistent with their own doctrines, and as pious successors to the *philosophes* whom Rousseau had called 'the privileged children of our age', they had the human weakness to be tempted by such things. Without ever sinking to the depths of the pathological servility demonstrated by some of their forebears with regard to the enlightened despots of their own age,[207] these men were nevertheless prepared on occasion to eat their hats and to swallow hard when circumstances demanded it. To begin with, they had to grin and bear the Concordat. They were not necessarily proud of this and they made a show of hiding behind their dignity, but whatever they could or could not do, what really mattered above all for them was their *dignity*. In 1803, Bonaparte confided that 'these men of absolute principles ... sell these same principles rather cheaply once it is a matter of putting a price on them'.[208] And the ever-incisive Fiévée observed of his master – and this in January 1804 – 'That one may say of the first consul that, if he is fattening up the old *philosophes* and the old revolutionaries, it is in order to get them out of the way, in much the same way that athletes in ancient Greece were obliged to retire from the ring when they had grown too stout'.[209]

As Marc Regaldo has pointed out, 'it was only in order to allow themselves to be decorated and endowed with pensions and coats of arms', that certain *idéologues* 'remained quarrelsome'.[210] 'The *idéologues* suffered Napoléon's charm and his authority ill-temperedly'.[211] But this was the discreetest of quarrelsomeness and ill-temper. In 1804 they decided to grin and bear the creation of the Empire which would bring ennoblement to some of their number. But we cannot disagree that the first consul's address to the Senate, justifying his imminent mutation into imperial guise, in all respects corresponds to the definition of 'good democracy' offered by Cabanis: 'Sovereignty resides in the French people *in this sense that* everything, everything without exception, must be done in its interests, for its happiness and for its glory'.[212] The same year, Destutt de Tracy continues to demonstrate that 'judging, speaking and wanting derive from a common source', which, when studied in detail, reveals 'the principles of education and lawmaking'.

But this is preaching, mechanically, in the wilderness.²¹³ Garat was not one to haggle over the price to be paid for marks of allegiance, and in 1805 in a speech to the Academy, he provides a very indirect justification for his views on the subject with a reference to those *philosophes* of the *ancien régime*, who 'living at the court without being courtiers saw that no barriers existed to separate them from the ear of the man who was in a position to broadcast a truth and make it useful to a whole nation'.²¹⁴ And in this same year, in a letter to Mme de Staël, Cabanis rather weakly denies the accusation of materialism levelled against him, explaining that such an accusation 'is perhaps not without its inconveniences these days'.²¹⁵ We might conclude from this that he too, like Voltaire, has come to 'set greater store by the happiness life has to offer than by a single truth'.²¹⁶

It is indeed true that Napoléon continues to castigate the *idéologues* but, on the one hand, the occasions when he does so usually make it difficult to believe that the word really refers in any strict sense to the *idéologie* movement. *Idéologie* is a pejorative term used to designate what Bonaparte also understands by the term 'metaphysics': the narrow belief in systems, the excesses of a theoretical approach which neglects to take account of practical necessities,²¹⁷ and more generally, it has to be said, any line of reasoning that was likely to end up criticising his own policies. (In my view, it was a relatively rare thing that the *idéologie* movement, as it has been specifically defined, became the target of a direct attack on his part.)²¹⁸ On the other hand, the chief *idéologues* continue to prosper, providing they tone down their theories. For, clearly, the wind had changed direction. Royer-Collard, who energetically refuted sensualism in an 1806 article in the *Journal des Débats*, was soon afterwards offered the chair of philosophy at the Sorbonne. Nevertheless, Cabanis, who died in 1808, was given the honour of being inhumed in the Panthéon and it was Destutt de Tracy who succeeded him at the *Académie française*. It is true that he immediately started complaining about the poor state of intellectual debate at that time, about the opprobrium in which were held certain 'useful speculations' and 'so many felicitous attempts to perfect the art of reasoning and improve the lot of humanity'.²¹⁹ And then, as if to safeguard the memory of the man who had 'loved him with the greatest tenderness', he assures us that Cabanis had in no way laid down his arms, and, in a phrase that sounds rather like a reheating of yesterday's menu, he claimed that he was still tirelessly 'working on the plan of a major work on possible ways to improve the human species'.[220] To which the Comte de Ségur, himself a solid disciple of the Enlightenment and a confirmed traveller on the 'path to glory' in vogue at that time, made the following cruel reply: that 'anybody who has an idea in his head is, whether he likes it or not, involved in *idéologie*'.[221] Cold comfort here for the *idéologues*. And, as far as Cabanis was concerned, he went on to remind us that 'when on the 18th brumaire his every wish had been that the hero whose name had since come to adorn the *Institut* should be called to govern us, it had been a portent of the glory that was to follow'.[222] This is rather like turning the knife in the wound and a way of reminding the *idéologues* that their own logic had trapped them in a golden cage of their own making, in which they were not a little embarrassed to be seen enjoying the comforts that their support for the master afforded them.

The heart of the matter, which is also the heart of the present study, is that whatever the dialectical contorsions one might wish to undertake, the decision to opt for materialism is, philosophically speaking, a handicap of Himalayan proportions for anyone who wants to talk about freedom. When Cabanis' *Rapports* had come out, Dégerando remarked to Mme de Staël that 'men who only believe in determinism and matter cannot be true friends of freedom'.[223] And from this time onwards, or thereabouts, Mme de Staël begins to think along lines which, deepening as they go, will eventually lead her to express with increasing insistency and lucidity the *idéologiste* and reductionist basis of the whole Napoleonic enterprise. The culmination of this line of thinking, which we do not have the space to go into here, was probably *De l'Allemagne* in 1810.[224] Afterwards, she again speaks of this 'tyranny which had used a development of the very ideas of the Enlightenment the better to enslave all sorts of freedoms'.[225] For my own part, I would have simply spoken of a 'development of the ideas of the Enlightenment' and I hope readers will understand why. As far as enslavement and the suppression of freedoms is concerned, it should be remembered that in 1802 assemblies made up of ex-revolutionaries raised no opposition whatsoever to the re-establishment of slavery for blacks. It is probably impossible for us to try to imagine what kind of self-justificatory sophistry this matter was an occasion for. It is also impossible to let this event pass without seeing it as highly significant to our attempts to understand this particular view of man, and of his freedom, if we can assume that such a view can include any meaningful notion of freedom. It is worth remembering that the former member of the Constituent Assembly, Regnaud from Saint-Jean d'Angély, who spoke at the time in his capacity as a *conseiller d'état*, defended the proposal 'in the name of holy humanity'.[226] Such a request, in defence of a law of this sort, can be considered, I believe, as a confirmation of some of the risks associated with Enlightenment anthropology. The political class that was in charge of this piece of legislation at the time was simultaneously working on the major question of the French Civil Code – a project which it now seems difficult to believe, or to make others believe, was unequivocally inspired by a desire to exalt the notion of human individuality.

Notes

1. J. Carbonnier, *Droit civil*, vol.1, Paris, 1974, 66. In recent re-editions the author has replaced the rather ill-advised word 'spirituality' by the word 'will' and undertaken a re-jigging of the paragraph so as to retain the essential thrust of it. But the whole thing still seems to me to be in relative disharmony with the sources of the time.
2. See above, 204.
3. According to Lord Holland, quoted in *Correspondance de Napoléon. Six cents lettres de travail (1806–1810)*, ed. M.Vox, Paris, 1943, 443.
4. Napoléon, 'Observations sur un projet d'établissement d'une École spéciale de Littérature et d'Histoire au Collège de France', 19 April 1807: ibid., 198.
5. Letter to Joséphine, 26th prairial Year IV, 14 June 1796: *Napoléon, Bonaparte. L'Œuvre et l'Histoire*, 12 vols, Paris, 1969–71, (abbreviated to *N.B.O.H.*), vol. 1, 366–367.
6. Las Cases, *Mémorial de Sainte-Hélène* (1823), pres. Joël Schmidt, Paris, 1968, 14 November 1816, 572/2.
7. *Mémoires* de Mollien (1845), in *N.B.O.H.*, vol. 9, 267.
8. *Mémoires* de Miot de Melito, ibid., 555.
9. Speech of 18th floréal Year II, 7 May 1794 (See above, 127 ff) *Archives parlementaires*, 1/90/137/1.
10. Mme de Staël, *Considérations sur la Révolution française* (1818), Paris, 1983, 366.
11. See above, 152.
12. 20th frimaire Year VI, 10 December 1797 (Bonaparte had been in Paris since the fifth): *Bull. Lois* no. 165, 4.
13. Ibid., 5.
14. Mme de Staël, *De la Littérature considérée dans ses rapports avec les Institutions sociales* (1800), 2 vols, Paris/Geneva, 1959, vol. 1, 63.
15. G. Lacour-Gayet, 'Bonaparte, membre de l'Institut' in *Compte rendu des séances et travaux de l'Académie des Sciences morales et politiques*, 1922/2. 89–150.
16. Las Cases, *Mémorial*, 12 May 1816, 253/2.
17. A. Guillois, *Le Salon de Mme Helvétius. Cabanis et les Idéologues*, Paris, 1894, 121.

18. Reference to note 16, (w.u.o.).
19. Mme de Staël, *Des circonstances actuelles qui peuvent terminer la Révolution*, (1798), Paris, 1979, 122.
20. Ibid., 289. And again, shortly afterwards, in *De la Littérature*, vol.2, 330, she considers it beneficial 'to the progress in human understanding that a man should combine together a career as a soldier, as a legislator and as a philosopher, as was the case in classical times'.
21. Ambr. Fourcy, *Histoire de l'École Polytechnique* (1828), repr. Paris, 1987, 164.
22. Guillois, *Le Salon de Mme Helvétius*, 120–22.
23. Lefebvre de la Roche, begging Bonaparte to accept 'the feeble homage of the disciple and friend of a *philosophe* whose writings you admire' (*Corr.gén. d'Helvétius*, Toronto/Oxford, vol.3, 1991, 296/2).
24. Guillois, *Le Salon de Mme Helvétius*, 121.
25. See above, 157–158.
26. B. Constant, *De l'Esprit de Conquête et de l'Usurpation dans leurs rapports avec la civilisation européenne* (end of 1813 – beginning of 1814), Paris, 1986, 260. On Constant's failure to fully understand the anthropology of the Enlightenment, see above, 207.
27. See above, 171–172 et circa.
28. 'It was, by the way, in the 'Salon d'Auteuil' that the *coup d'état* of 18th brumaire 1799 was worked out with Cabanis' (H. Tribout-Morembert, 'Helvétius Anne-Catherine', in *Dictionnaire de Biographie française*, vol. 17, 1989, 877/1).
29. *Manifeste des Royalistes des Provinces de l'Ouest de la France, en Réponse à la Proclamation des soi-disant Consuls de la prétendue République française*, s.l., Press of the Royal and Catholic Army, 1800, 10.
30. Guillois, *Le Salon de Mme Helvétius*, 129–32; L. Picavet, *Les Idéologues. Essai sur l'histoire des idées et des théories scientifiques, philosophiques, religieuses, etc. en France depuis 1789*, Paris, 1891, repr. Hildesheim-New York, 1972, 220–22. On the great importance of the role played by Cabanis in the *coup d'état*, see also the entry on A. Cabanis in J. Tulard, ed., *Dictionnaire Napoléon*, Paris, 1987, 317/1.
31. *La Décade philosophique*, 10th brumaire Year VIII. 1 November 1799, 242.
32. See above, 195.
33. P. Cabanis, *Quelques considérations sur l'organisation sociale en général et particulièrement sur la nouvelle constitution*, Paris, Year VIII (end of Dec. 1799); quoted by Picavet, *Les Idéologues*, 223, footnote 1.
34. Voltaire, *Corr.*, vol. 7, 711 (1764).
35. J.-J. Rousseau, *Contrat Social*, Book II, cha 7, in *Œuvres complètes*, vol. 3, 382.
36. See above, 165–167.
37. D'Holbach, *Système de la Nature* (1770), Paris, 1990, vol. 1, 129.
38. Ibid., 161, (w.u.o.).
39. To Chamfort, in 1764; Voltaire, *Corr.*, vol. 7, 624.
40. *Journal* de Roederer, quoted in *Corr. Nap.*, 487.
41. For example at the *Conseil d'état*, June and July 1804: *N.B.O.H.*, vol.7, 293 and 294.
42. J.-J. Rousseau,*Discours sur les Sciences et les Arts* (1749–50), in *Œuvres complètes*, vol. 3, 29. Cf. for example, Voltaire, *Corr.* vol.8, 819, in 1767, to Frédéric II, on 'the riffraff not worthy of being enlightened'.
43. J.-J. Rousseau, *Contrat Social*, Book II, chap. 6, ibid., 380.
44. Rousseau, *Lettres écrites de la Montagne* (1764), Ninth Letter, ibid., 889.
45. D'Holbach, *Système de la Nature*, vol. 1, 129–30, (w.u.o.).
46. Ibid., 130.

47. Helvétius, *De l'Homme* (1773), vol.1, 45.
48. Ibid., 46.
49. D'Holbach,*Système de la Nature*, 153.
50. Ibid., 154, (w.u.o.) 'Indeed, there can be no doubt that man's temperament may be corrected, altered, modified by causes which are just as physical as those of which he is constituted'. We should remember that Rousseau, too, spoke of the modification of man's make-up by means of legislation, and of 'forcing the animal economy', et cetera. (See above, for example 55–56 and 68).
51. For example, Voltaire, *Corr.* vol.3, 211, and 500 (where he fears 'being like a cuckold who tries to convince himself that his wife is faithful') See above, 34 and 35.
52. Ibid., 356; and 472, et cetera.
53. Ibid., 433 ('the rarest man that ever existed') et cetera.
54. Ibid., 124, 323. Numerous allusions to Marcus Aurelius.
55. Like this verse on 9 April 1751, *Corr.*, vol.3, 387:

    On this very day of Good Friday
    When we're all asked to swallow the story
    That a God chose to suffer for us
    I dare to address the king of true glory.

56. To Frédéric, 1 February 1766: *Corr.*, vol. 8, 364.
57. *Corr.*, vol. 3, 777, 5 September 1752, to d'Alembert. 'The king has made Sparta very attractive but he has transported Athens only as far as his private study'.
58. See above, 33–35.
59. Letter to Cideville, 3 September 1750: D2411 in *The complete Works of Voltaire*, 95 vols, ed. Theodore Bestermann (and collaborators), *Correspondence and related documents*, vol. 11, Geneva, 1970, 345.
60. To d'Argental, 21 August 1750: Voltaire, *Corr.*, vol. 3, 218.
61. See the study by C. Mervaud, *Voltaire et Frédéric II: une dramaturgie des Lumières, 1736–1778*, Studies on Voltaire, 234, Oxford, 1985.
62. Voltaire, *Corr.*, vol. 7, 602, 4 March 1764, to Damilaville.
63. *Corr.*, vol. 8, 789. The anonymous work was by d'Holbach.
64. *Corr.*, vol. 11, 390, to d'Alembert, 1773.
65. To Catherine II, 28 August 1770: *Corr.*, vol. 10, 398.
66. Ibid., 6 October 1774: *Corr.*, vol. 11, 804.
67. Ibid., 2 March: ibid., 624 ('for I count other beings as of no significance').
68. Ibid., 1 November 1773: ibid. 497.
69. Ibid., 496.
70. Voltaire, *Corr.*, vol. 10, 430 ('The adoring worshipper of your Imperial Majesty'); vol. 11, 625.
71. To Catherine II, 22 December 1766: *Corr.*, vol. 8, 789.
72. For example, *Corr.*, vol. 10, 22 ('*Te Catherinam laudamus, te dominam confitemur*') and 430.
73. 30 October 1769: *Corr.*, vol. 10, 22
74. To Catherine II, 11 August 1770: ibid., 375 ('I would at least have liked to have contributed to killing a few Turks for you'). It is true that, at the time, the French monarchy supported the Turks.
75. To d'Alembert, 26 June 1773: *Corr.*, vol. 11, 390.
76. On this theme, see my sketch 'Liberté, Égalité, Fraternité. Inventaire sommaire de l'idéal révolutionnaire français', in *Himeji International Forum of Law and Politics*, no. 1, (1993), [3–25], 21.

77. The verse is by Frédéric, and destined for Voltaire, who redirects this fine joke towards the tsarina, 5 September 1770: Voltaire, *Corr.*, vol. 10, 407.
78. And it is also quite something when he begins talking about the 'white feet' of the heroine that he himself is kissing.
79. To Catherine II, 9 August 1774: Voltaire, *Corr.*, vol. 11, 748.
80. 19 September 1764: *Corr.*, vol. 7, 844.
81. 7 September : ibid., 829.
82. To Mme du Deffand, 18 May 1767: *Corr.*, vol. 8, 1,142.
83. To d'Argental, 23 January 1768: *Corr.*, vol. 9, 280.
84. To Mme du Deffand, 2 September 1770: *Corr.*, vol. 10, 403.
85. Helvétius, *De l'Homme* (1773), Paris, 1989, vol. 1, 432.
86. *Corr. gén. d'Helvétius*, Toronto/Oxford, vol. 3, 1991, 5.
87. To Frédéric II, 1 February: ibid., 89–90.
88. Ibid., 193.
89. Ibid., 289/1.
90. Helvétius, *De l'Homme*, vol. 1, 11 where he says that 'this degraded nation is today the scorn of all Europe. No salutary crisis can give it back its freedom. It will perish through consumption. The only remedy to its ills is military conquest'.
91. Prince Golitsyne, Catherine's ambassador to the Hague, was given the task of arranging this. On this very interesting, and rather complex affair, see *Corr. gén. d'Helvétius*, vol. 3, 381, passim, and 399 (from the Prince: 'As far as the the printing of this book is concerned, there would be no danger in it for the author's heirs or for his friends provided thay have nothing to do with it – indeed they impatiently await its publication'), and 444 (facsimile of the actual dedication).
92. Ibid., 349/1. From the French *chargé d'affaires* in Russia: 'She hates us with the most thorough hatred ... It is really quite strange that despite the strength of her animosity all her natural leanings make her tend to prize anything that comes from France ... You must ... not be at all surprised if you see her use all the public and private means in her power to do us as much harm as she finds it possible to do'.
93. Ibid., 454–55.
94. Letter of December 1773: 'What can one make of a bombastic fellow like Helvétius who ... broadcasts everywhere the most bitterly sarcastic remarks one can imagine about governments in general ...; and who, while deploring the misfortune that his own country has suffered, so he reckons, in sinking to the lowest depths of baseness and oppression, a view which in no way reflects the truth, then goes off and makes heroes out of the King of Prussia and the Czarina? In my view, all that is nothing more than vanity, wrong-headedness and over-excited nonsense: I fail to see any love of humankind in it, nor any philosophy' (ibid., 465–466: and *Corr. complète de Rousseau*, vol. 39, 207).
95. Voltaire, *Corr.*, vol. 11, 390, to d'Alembert, 26 June 1773. But a week earlier to Prince Golitsyne, a rather different tune: 387.
96. Ibid., 426, 2 August. There is another pejorative (and discreet) allusion to the 'absolute power' of Catherine on 8 July 1774: ibid., 725.
97. Letters to Frédéric, 25 December 1737 and 19 February 1738: *Correspondence*, vol. 4 (vol. 88). D. 1413, 435–41, and vol. 5 (vol. 89), D 1459, 44–50. See especially, 437, where there is a particularly mechanicist passage with a reference to God as a 'clockmaker'.
98. To Frédéric II, 26 January 1749: Voltaire, Corr., vol. 3, 20; some passages from this letter have already been quoted, above, 29.

99. See above, e.g. 134.
100. See above, 128.
101. See above, 31 and 33.
102. Like Frédéric (and Voltaire, and many others) she disagrees with the view expressed by Helvétius that at birth all human beings are totally equal intellectually.
103. D. Diderot, *Mémoires pour Catherine II* (1773–74), Paris, 1966, 43.
104. 20th frimaire year VI, 10 December 1797: *Bull Lois* no. 165, 6. 'Your heart is the temple of republican honour', he also said to him (10).
105. De Staël, *Des Circonstances actuelles*, 122, already quoted.
106. Reported by Roman d'Amat, article 'Garat, Dominique-Joseph', in *Dictionnaire de Biographie française*, vol.15, 1982, 371/1, who sees no reason to think there is 'anything strange' about this comment.
107. Voltaire, *Corr.*, vol. 3, 404, 8 May 1751.
108. See above, 211–213.
109. Quoted in *N.B.O.H.*, vol. 6, 529.
110. Remark made on 24 October 1799, to Bourrienne, who transcribes it in his *Mémoires*, extracts to be found in *N.B.O.H.*, vol. 9, 242.
111. *Conseil d'état*, 22nd thermidor year VIII, 10 August 1800: *N.B.O.H.*, vol. 7, 282.
112. I consider the significance of this episode in my article on the Revolutionary calendar: 'Une tentative de désacralisation du temps: le calendrier révolutionnaire' in Thireau, J.-L., ed., *Le droit entre laïcisation et noéscralisation*, Paris, 1987, (215–27).
113. To Dupont de Nemours: Mme de Staël, *Correspondance générale*, ed. Béatrice W. Jasinski, IV/1, Paris, 1976,271.
114. *Mémoires* de Mollien, extracts in *N.B.O.H.*, vol. 9, 242.
115. In 1803: *Mémoires* de Mollien, ibid., 266.
116. Cabanis, *Rapports du Physique et du Moral de l'Homme*, 298; See above, 166.
117. Diderot, *Mémoires pour Catherine II* , 109–10.
118. J. Fiévée, *Correspondance et relations avec Bonaparte,1802–1813*, Paris, 1836, vol.1, 113.
119. Napoléon, 'Observations' on education (quoted above, note 4): *Corr. Nap.*, 199.
120. Question already touched upon above, 163–164.
121. Napoléon, 'Observations' on education: *Corr. Nap.*, 199.
122. See above, 145–147.
123. Duveyrier, to the *Tribunat*, 8th ventôse year VIII, 27 February 1800: *Archives Parlementaires*, 2/1/271/2.
124. See above, 145–146.
125. Diderot, *Mémoires pour Catherine II* , 110.
126. Quoted by J.-J. Chevallier, *Les grandes Œuvres politiques de Machiavel à nos jours*, Paris, 1964, 53.
127. Letter to Moultou, 7 March 1768: *Corr. complète de Rousseau*, vol. 35, 180–81.
128. Letter of 26 July 1767: ibid., vol. 33, 238–41.
129. From Pastor Meister to Bodmer, 13 March 1768: ibid., vol. 35, 197.
130. Grégoire, *Discours pour l'ouverture du concile national de France, prononcé le 29 juin 1801...*, Paris, undated, reprinted in *Œuvres de l'Abbé Grégoire*, vol. 11, Paris-Nendeln, 1977, 33–34.
131. To the *Corps législatif*, 15th germinal year X, 5 April 1802: *Archives Parlementaires*, 2/3/415/2.
132. Letter to the Empress, 24 July 1765: Voltaire, *Corr.*, vol. 8, 141.

133. Chassin, *La Vendée patriote* (1894), reprinted Mayenne, 1973, vol. 3, 167.
134. See above, especially 134.
135. 18th germinal year X, 8 April 1802, *Archives parlementaires*, 2/3/451/1, (w.u.o.). Lucien is speaking in his role as *rapporteur* to the *Tribunat*.
136. Ibid., 450/2.
137. Quoted in *Corr. Nap.*, 509.
138. To the *Conseil d'état*, 26 March 1805: ibid., 519.
139. Reported by Molé, ibid.
140. *Mémoires* de Bourrienne, extracts in *N.B.O.H.*, vol. 8, 318.
141. De Staël, *Considérations sur la Révolution française*, 374.
142. Proclamation of the 4th messidor year VI, 22 June 1798 : *N.B.O.H.*, vol. 1, 410.
143. To the *Conseil d'état*, on 28th thermidor year VIII, 16 August 1800: Boulay de la Meurthe, ed., *Documents sur la négociation du Concordat*, vol. 1, Paris, 1891, 77.
144. Reference to note 136.
145. Speech quoted in note 130; *Archives Parlementaires*, 2/3/412/2.
146. See my own study: 'L'individualisme libéral en France autour de 1800', 109–113.
147. Letter to Prince Chouvalov, 10 June 1761: *Corr. gén. d'Helvétius*, vol. 3, 17.
148. D'Holbach, *Ethocratie ou le Gouvernement fondé sur la Morale*, (Amsterdam, 1776), Paris, 1967, 289.
149. To Frédéric II, 15 February 1775: Voltaire, *Corr.*, vol. 12, 48. We should add that the recipient somewhat severely diagnosed Helvétius as being intellectually totally worthless: to d'Alembert, 7 January 1774, *Corr. gén. d'Helvétius*, vol. 3, 471.
150. Same reference as above, note 26.
151. See above, 226–227.
152. See my own study already mentioned, 'Mme de Staël, Napoléon et les Idéologues: pour un réajustement des perspectives', in *Himeji International Forum of Law and Politics*, no. 1, (1993), 39–62.
153. December 1812, *Mémoires* de Caulaincourt, in *N.B.O.H.*, vol. 11, 239.
154. See above, 58–61.
155. Reported by Joseph Bonaparte, 19 February 1809: *Corr. Nap.*, 560.
156. From 21th nivôse year XI, 12 January 1803: *Journal* de Roederer, quoted in *Corr. Nap.* 488.
157. This was said of Letort: *Œuvres* of Napoléon at St Helena, in *N.B.O.H.*, vol. 6, 398.
158. See above, 23 (Voltaire), 163 (Destutt de Tracy), and 167 (Cabanis).
159. Letter to Voltaire, 2 September 1765: Voltaire, *Corr.* vol. 8, 1,279, (w.u.o.).
160. Diderot, *Mémoires pour Catherine II*, 197–98.
161. See above, 170–71.
162. To King Jérôme, 6 March 1808: *Corr. Nap.*, 365.
163. To Champagny, 29 November 1806: ibid., 461.
164. L. Poliakov, *Mémoires*, Paris, 1981, 197.
165. From Bonaparte to the Directory (Cairo, 16th vendémiaire year VII, 7 October 1798): *N.B.O.H.*, vol. 1, 428.
166. In 1808: *N.B.O.H.*, vol. 6, 90 (and 71). In 1812, the Emperor speaks of 'the barbarous state of this half-savage people' (ibid., vol. 11, 206).
167. L. Poliakov, *Le Mythe Aryen*, 170.
168. See once again the very suggestive article, to which we have already referred, by J. de Viguerie, 'Les Lumières et les Peuples' in *Revue Historique*, (1993), 161–89.

169. As is testified by the rhetoric of those of his collaborators for whom there exists some recorded account.
170. In this respect, see the very significant appointment of Laplace as Minister of the Interior to which we have already referred.
171. In December 1812, *Mémoires* de Caulaincourt, in *N.B.O.H.*, vol. 11, 194.
172. Beginning of 1807: *Corr. Nap.*, 509.
173. *Mémoires* of Mollien, in *N.B.O.H.*, vol. 9, 190.
174. April 1807: ibid., 354; cf. 307, 347, 356, 554.
175. Ibid., 41, 74, 186.
176. *N.B.O.H.*, vol. 7, 296; *Corr. Na*, 78,196, and 198. In his vocabulary, the word 'machine' is also used to refer to a bank or a section of an administration.
177. *Mémoires* of Chaptal, in *N.B.O.H.*, vol. 9, 63.
178. *Corr. Nap.*, 452.
179. To the *Conseil d'état*, 7 May 1806: ibid., 455.
180. *Mémorial*, 311/1 and 420/2 (8–9 June and 17 August 1816).
181. Around 1767–68 (?): Voltaire, *Corr.*, vol. 9, 238.
182. September 1807: *Corr. Nap.*, 44.
183. D'Holbach, *Système de la Nature*, vol. 1, 249.
184. April 1808: *Corr. Nap.*, 215.
185. *Mémorial*, 460/2, 3 September 1816; d'Holbach, *Système de la Nature*, vol. 1, 84–85.
186. December 1812, *Mémoires* de Caulaincourt, in *N.B.O.H.*, vol. 11, 284.
187. Ibid., 252.
188. Address to the French people, 1 March 1815: ibid., vol. 3, 145.
189. *Mémorial*, 99/2, 16 November 1815.
190. Ibid., 100/1.
191. D'Holbach, *Système de la Nature*, vol. 1, 274. Napoléon was born in 1769. These lines *appeared* in 1770.
192. *Journal* de Roederer, in *N.B.O.H.*, vol. 8, 192.
193. De Staël, *De l'Allemagne* (1810), Paris, 1968, vol. 2, 302.
194. De Staël, *Dix Années d'Exil* (1811), Paris, 1966, 11.
195. Condillac, *Traité des Systèmes* (1749) (1798 edition), C.O.P.L.F., Paris, 1991, 249.
196. Ibid., 254.
197. *Mémoires* de Caulaincourt, in *N.B.O.H.*, vol. 11, 278.
198. Reported by Voltaire to d'Argental, 10 March 1754: Voltaire, *Corr.* vol. 4, 85.
199. To Prince Eugène, 14 April: *N.B.O.H.*, vol. 2, 329. And he also sets himself up as 'a man who has proved that he was more far-sighted than others'.
200. To the Senate, 20 December 1812; ibid., vol. 3, 32.
201. 1st nivôse year VII, 21 December : ibid., vol. 1, 439.
202. See above, 68. He also warns the inhabitants of Cairo that he is 'guided by orders from above', and that 'all human efforts are to no avail' against him (loc. cit.).
203. *Mémoires* of Mollien, in *N.B.O.H.*, vol. 9, 190.
204. Ibid., 190–91.
205. On this theme, see above, 109 ff.
206. *Mémorial*, 211/1, 13 April 1816.
207. Garat (who made a very lengthy speech indeed in December 1799 justifying the events of brumaire) is probably the exception which proves the rule. Hence, in 1806, he proclaimed that the Emperor 'like the eternal geometrician will concern himself only with eternal laws' et cetera. (1 January, *Archives Parlementaires*, 2/9/7/1).

208. *Mémoires* of Mollien, in *N.B.O.H.*, vol. 9, 266.
209. Fiévée, *Correspondance et relations avec Bonaparte*, vol. 1, 193.
210. M. Regaldo, 'Un milieu intellectuel: la Décade philosophique (1794–1807)', thesis University of Paris IV, 1976, 5 vols., vol. 2, 651.
211. Guillois, *Le Salon de Mme Helvétius*, 188.
212. Message to the Senate (of which Cabanis is a member), 5th floréal year XII, 25 April 1804: *N.B.O.H.*,vol. 2, 70. See above, 218.
213. Preface to the 1804 edition of his *Élémens d'Idéologie*, xv. On this point, see above, 231.
214. From 26 December 1805:*Recueil des Discours, rapports et pièces diverses lus dans les séances publiques et particulières de l'Académie française, 1803–1819*, 1st part, Paris, 1847, 17.
215. In R. de Luppé, *Les idées littéraires de Mme de Staël et l'héritage des Lumières (1795–1800)*, Paris, 71 and 165.
216. See above, 23.
217. Numerous possible references. To Cambacérès, 24 April 1805: 'States never prosper through *idéologie*' (*N.B.O.H.*, vol. 2, 374).
218. It is the case in the *Conseil d'état* on 25 November 1809 when he attacks 'this false philosophy which slips into sophistry by seeking to submit *everything to analysis*, and thus substitutes new errors for old errors'; but it is worth mentioning that he doesn't use the word *idéologie* here (ibid., vol. 7, 257). It is also the case in December 1812 on his return from Russia – the link is an obvious one– when he ranges 'Tracy' among the 'empty headed' (*Mémoires* de Caulaincourt, ibid., vol. 11, 261.), and, showing what a poor loser he is into the bargain, quite wrongly and hastily blames the misfortunes of France 'on *idéologie*, on that obscure metaphysics which, while seeking with great subtlety to identify first causes, simultaneously seeks to base national legislation on them' et cetera. (Address to the *Conseil d'état*, 20 December, ibid., vol. 3, 33).
219. Speech made on 21 December 1808: *Recueil des Discours ... lus dans les séances ... de l'Académie française...*, op. cit., 301 and 312.
220. Ibid., 314.
221. Ibid., 322.
222. Ibid., 332.
223. Quoted by J.-F.Braunstein, 'Degerando, le social et la fin de l'idéologie'. in *Corpus, Revue de Philosophie*, no. 14–15, (1990), 200–01.
224. I refer readers to my own study, already mentioned in note 152.
225. De Staël, *Considérations sur la Révolution française*, 428.
226. To the *Corps législatif*, 30th floréal year X, 20 May 1802: *Archives Parlementaires*, 2/3/754/2.

~ *Chapter 15* ~

The Napoleonic Code

It goes without saying that when the 'Civil Code of the French people' came to fruition it was the result of a longstanding and yet recent process which went far beyond the set of problems which the *Travaux préparatoires* had set out to resolve and which preoccupied us at the start of this study. As we approach the end, we return to that same problem.[1] The lines which follow, therefore, are not intended to offer an overview of the whole Napoleonic Code but only, if at all possible, to focus on the particular impetus that it received as a result of the influence of anthropological views that held sway at the precise moment in time when it was being drafted. One would be very much inclined to believe that such influence works, to a significant extent, in a diametrically opposite direction to that in which it is commonly assumed to work, especially by university academics.[2] It also goes without saying that the views I shall describe cannot be considered as having been fully accepted, like some sort of monolithic credo, by all the various individuals: members of the drafting commission, *conseillers d'état*, orators at the *Tribunat* and magistrates at the Court of Appeal, who at various times expressed their opinions in writing on this or that article of the Code that was being drafted.[3] I would simply argue that such views tended to be predominantly the sort of views they held in a very general and diffuse way, as, moreover, one might expect of a political class whose mental universe had been fashioned by all that has been described thus far in these pages and who, in addition, had as their charismatic leader a man offering a clear and constant example, to those in his immediate entourage, of applied anthropological reductionism.

It is probably true that at this precise moment in history, on account of the Concordat, the official line had taken on an anti-materialist tone. Sufficiently so, in any case, for some people to be concerned. But we know that an interplay of self-reflecting mirrors is at work here. In October 1802, Fiévée, Bonaparte's secret adviser, while quietly scoffing at a typically 'ideological' subject that had been chosen for the entry examination to the *Institut* – which invited candidates to muse on ways of decomposing thought – added, with great lucidity and with Bonaparte in mind, that to pour 'public derision' on such a subject would outrage *'every single man in the first consul's immediate circle'*.[4] This is simply a very eloquent way of confirming that in the very highest echelons of the state, the nebula of doctrines we have been considering reigned supreme, even at the very moment when historical circumstances dictated that they no longer represented the official line of thinking.

The case of Portalis, who unconsciously illustrates the phenomenon, is exemplary in this respect. One of the principal figures behind the implementation of the Concordat and the drafting of the Civil Code, he was a Catholic by conviction and was an opponent of materialism.[5] Now in April 1802, on the promulgation of the Concordat, it is he who *publicly* expressed his delight that thanks to the 'organic articles', 'even people's consciences had been subjugated'.[6] In speaking such words, he seems to be joining forces with that very long line of men who for some forty years or so have congratulated themselves on 'subjugating' and 'captivating' man's inner being, seizing control of it, using scientific methods to take command of it, in order to subject it to political manipulation for the benefit of all. And then, when this same Portalis argues that the Civil Code should refuse to recognise marriages contracted on the death-bed, on the grounds that it is not possible to marry 'what is beginning to turn into a corpse',[7] it is very clear indeed that this *unquestionable spiritualist* is allowing himself to reason like an orthodox materialist because he is subject to the influence of the age in which he lives. In the event, he calls to mind what Helvétius said about the loved one who is gradually losing the use of all his senses: 'We shall continue to show respect for their body: but in fact we can no longer love them'.[8] And we cannot avoid agreeing that in the 'organised mucus', which is all that the foetus represents to Cabanis,[9] and the being which 'is beginning to turn into a corpse', which is the way Portalis sees human beings on the verge of death, we have the alpha and omega of a coherent version of human destiny which has very little that is spiritualist about it at all. To sum up, in the case being presented here, someone like Portalis following in the footsteps of a Rousseau, and a Robespierre, or a La Révellière-Lépeaux, is really one of those sorts of spiritualists who, through their own mental vulnerability, provide ammunition for the opposite camp. Indeed, as one of the four drafting commissioners of the Napoleonic Code, Portalis quite rightly had the reputation for being the most 'theoretically-minded' of the lot.

This is tantamount to saying, therefore, that under the aegis of Bonaparte and Portalis, and in the mental atmosphere described throughout this study, the archetypal subject on whose behalf the Code is being enacted would not appear to amount to very much. Among the leading figures of the Enlightenment there is hardly a single one who has not worked to prepare the ground in this respect, and mentioning them here again would be simply repetitive. Man's lack of any aptitude for reasoning and his incurable immaturity are major themes which structure their thinking, while they themselves, in all modesty, present themselves as exceptions which prove the rule.[10] Men in general are 'big children', or something similar in so far as their powers of reasoning are concerned. And d'Holbach claimed that most men don't even possess these powers. The series of disasters, one following upon another, that marked the revolutionary period would indeed seem to confirm this diagnosis. As far as the lawmaker of the the Consulate is concerned, blacks remain 'in the obscure regions of childhood' and this counts in their favour, 'in the name of holy humanity' as a reason for allowing them to become slaves.[11] Women, too, 'although endowed with sense and reason' are mentally immature, and neither subsequent education nor the 'maturity that comes with age'[12] can in any way affect this, since 'time' is also seen as bringing 'for a woman ... only ravages'.[13] Voltaire had already said to d'Alembert 'Many women, as you know, are big children', and he had gone on to prescribe 'the whip and sweets' for them as a result.[14]

But in fact, in Voltaire's view, French people suffer the disgrace of not being 'worthy of freedom', since they are 'nice little children' who 'need to be guided', 'a nation of naughty children' who must, as a result, be 'given the whip and sweets'.[15] Now an extension along these lines is discernible, albeit discreetly, in the *Travaux Préparatoires* of the Civil Code.

The tendency to infantilisation is only explicit, and we might say has only crystallised out, as far as women are concerned. Consequently it is necessary 'to defend them *unbeknownst to themselves* and even against their own wishes'.[16] But all *male adults* are targeted rather more covertly, as I was able to illustrate at the beginning of this study. One could even say that this is one of the obsessions of those who drafted the Code. Thus, their decision to maintain the age of majority at twenty-one years (which many see as a proof that they were remaining true to the revolutionary spirit) is, in my view, far too often overemphasised both in terms of its significance and its effect. This venerable tree hides a little-suspected forest of afterthoughts and of measures more or less directly designed to mitigate this enfranchisement by age which Portalis called a 'purely civil invention'.[17] It is at this point in our consideration of the Civil Code of 1804 that, contrary to all generally received wisdom on the matter, we might begin to suspect that it contains a low-key but 'universal presumption of minority' in those for whom it is designed, the concomitant of which is a propensity to promote gerontocracy. There is, however, neither time nor space here to reiterate this thesis, which has been fully developed elsewhere.[18]

The notion of the human being posited here is not only archetypally impoverished, it is also far from sure that it possesses free will. As a result, man would find it difficult to stake any serious claim to being considered as being honoured with individual responsibility. Too many ideas that have been in vogue for so many years conspire to deny that option[19] and Bonaparte himself, above all others, is imbued with such notions. It is probably true to say that things were not as clearcut as this all of the time for those to whom the task fell of drafting the Civil Code, since even if they had been consummate technicians of the anthropology of the day, pure force of circumstance would have obliged them from time to time to think counter to their express principles. But the reductionist mood surrounded and enveloped them[20] and it clearly tended to make them objectivise a sense of responsibility, empirically conceived of as a pure necessity of social life.

It is true that the famous article 1382 mentions the word 'fault': 'Any *deed* whatsoever performed by a man and which causes prejudice to others, makes it incumbent upon the person by whose *fault* this has come about, to repair the damage'. But in the particular historical moment that we are dealing with, one might be excused for concluding that the 'fault', rather like an asymptote, has a tendency to be equated with the 'deed' itself. It may well be that there are lingering traces of the notion of individual responsibility influencing discussions and being voiced in speeches: it would be humanly impossible for the opposite to be the case. But at the moment when it comes to a final vote on this question, the proposer, as he approaches the end of his speech, quite incidentally and unexpectedly refers to: 'that constant and invariable rule according to which the person who suffers prejudice *by the deed or the fault* of another must in all cases have the possibility of seeking redress'. It was in February 1804 that these words were spoken[21] and specialists have been musing over them ever since. In March, speaking on another matter entirely, Fiévée points out to Bonaparte that 'in this thoroughly materialist century of ours, no one concerns themselves with the intentions behind actions but only with the consequences they have'.[22] Soon afterwards, Mme de Staël makes the following comment, as though she were describing a symptom of all the ills of the age: 'Actions are no longer considered in relation to where they originated but in relation to the effects they have'.[23] No, subjective responsibility is not really a notion that carries much weight in these days when people worship above all at the altar of 'usefulness'. And all the less so in that the idea of subjective responsibility begins to look like an existential debt contracted by all those who had wreaked the havoc of the revolutionary period and survived. In spite of first appearances, the title of article 1382 cannot therefore necessarily be taken to presuppose that man's inner being is a rich treasure house of qualities: a notion which is generally understood as implying that among these qualities is that of individual responsibility.

The reactivation of religious activity brought about by the Concordat brought with it some compensation on a political level in that it maintained among the commonalty of the people an acute *feeling* of subjective responsibility with regard to an omniscient transcendent being. The idea is hardly a new one.[24] It is not devoid of significance that Portalis should have found himself simultaneously in two different front lines: working for the Concordat and working on the Civil Code. To see in this accumulation of functions nothing more than 'a somewhat schizophrenic undertaking' would seem to constitute a rather uninspired attempt at analysis.[25] For the Concordat and the Civil Code cannot really be dissociated the one from the other: they both play an important role in the reconstruction of society from the defective links in the chain that we already know have been provided.

Thus the usefulness of religion will also be to largely neutralise the right to divorce that the law has unenthusiastically maintained, while recognising the social consequences that flow from it. And religion also promises a great deal as far as 'respect for contractual obligations' is concerned: something that is of particular importance for the quality of the social fabric. Anyone who imagines, in this respect, that the authors of the Civil Code were moved by a deep respect for the '*autonomy* of the individual will' of human beings – that is, a source of energy with the capacity to provide a juridical basis for entering into contractual obligations – anyone who believes this is seriously underestimating, among many other things, the sensualist propensity of the age and its view of man's inner being as a realm of pure passivity. Lack of space prevents me from going into this point in any greater detail.[26] But what is apparent is that, once again in direct contrast to academic opinion on the matter, the whole politico-anthropological context of the few decades which preceded the drafting of the Code corroborates the view that the inability of human beings to assume responsibility for the obligations they have contracted makes it essential that, in the interests of society, the dagger of the law be pressed closely to the back of anyone who enters into a contract in order to ensure they respect it. This is diametrically opposed to any notion of the 'autonomy of the individual will'. And besides, what sort of will could possibly be at issue here? 'Human will is of itself so weak, so slight, so inconstant', and this diagnosis is offered by Cambacérès no less.[27] As Voltaire himself said, speaking precisely about a contractual agreement, 'it is much better to rely on the punishment meted out by the law than on the will of men'.[28] Similarly, and this time it is Napoléon speaking: 'In a state of society man does *almost nothing* by the sole action of his will'.[29] He also says elsewhere: 'In the system of the world, nothing is left to chance: in the system of societies, nothing should be left to depend on the *whims* of individuals'.[30] This is the context, then. Once again, doubt must be cast upon a good number of commonly held beliefs.

For, quite to the contrary, it is right and proper that these passive beings should be taken in hand so that their behaviour can be socialised. In order to achieve this there is a lever that can be used on them, and that is the universal lever of self-interest. Within families it can be brought to bear in such a way that it induces feelings of affection which can themselves become fixed and durable, thus favouring social stability. It is in this sense that Mandeville, in his *Fable des Abeilles* (what an evocative title!), maintained that 'private vices are for the public good'.[31] Rather than put obstacles in the way of men's weaknesses and passions, we should exploit them so that they produce useful outcomes. The idea is present in Rousseau too,[32] as well as in d'Holbach, who considers this to be 'the *great art* of the moralist'.[33] 'In England, the way the State is organised, everything, including men's vices, is to the country's advantage', Helvétius commented approvingly.[34] And in 1798, Mme de Staël explained that 'in order to correct a man's character, the resources for helping him are to be found in the very passion which leads him astray'.[35] The idea that 'the great art of the legislator' is to make use of men's weaknesses rather than to combat them, underpins the whole project of elaborating the Civil Code and surfaces within it on a number of occasions: 'Leave man with the defects that are his by nature; the *great art* of the legislator is to turn them to the advantage of society'.[36] Later, Napoléon echoes much the same idea: 'The legislator's *secret* must be knowing how to gain best advantage from the worst aspects of those he would seek to govern'.[37]

Hence the law governing rights of succession is conceived of, in the first instance, as a reservoir of ways and means of ensuring externally harmonious relationships between a potential legatee and his presumptive heirs. It is the pressure generated by the testament that aims to create such relationships, and the force of habit will automatically reinforce them and make them 'sincerely felt', *unbeknownst* even to those who have an *interest* in them, and in this particular context the word is doubly appropriate. Legislation under the Consulate involved feverish attempts to reinstate paternal authority, which the Revolution had actively sought to undermine: a process which had come to be seen as synonymous with social anarchy. Even before the Civil Code was enacted, demands were made for the reintroduction of some way of using inheritance law as a means of bestowing favours and inflicting punishment ('the whip and sweets'). Such was the aim of the law of germinal year VIII (March 1800).[38] So children, even after reaching full maturity, were subjected to a very real form of blackmail throughout the whole of a father's lifetime, and one which could be guaranteed to be effective because of the power of calculated self-interest in all circumstances. Yet again then, as always, it is a matter of manipulating individuals, modifying them and 'making them better', by applying a specially programmed version of the simple force of habit. Just as, for Rousseau, mammary pain and the lactation process that it induces provides a totally physical and mechanical explanation for maternal love;[39] and just as, if Cabanis is to be believed, artificially irritating a capon's abdomen can make it experience the relief felt by a brooding hen and actually make it feel 'a sort of artificial motherly love' for its chicks;[40] in the same way, the itching set in train by the last will and testament as programmed by the law, in so far as it encouraged children and nephews to pay visits to ageing parents, would in the long run work on their psyche in such a way as to lead them quite mechanically to feel a sort of affection towards them. Indeed, 'it has been said that elderly people might be looked after, and sometimes seduced: but they will always at least have the consolation of company',[41] and the social fabric will be all the better for that.

Hence, the harmony that exists within each and every household is the result of a subtle balance of self-interested calculations, of second-guessing the thoughts that individuals may actually be having or are presumed to be having, and of implicit blackmail. This situation is not without similarities to the order which reigns within the seraglio in the *Lettres persanes*, where the head of every individual harbours a storm of calculated hypothesising on a variety of levels, but where sweetness 'is constrained to be in evidence at all times'.[42] Nor is it dissimilar to the model of the ideal household proposed in *La Nouvelle Héloïse*, which is peopled by schemers who are 'united, so to speak, in spite of themselves';[43] nor to the demographic harmony imagined by Condorcet on the basis of self-interested calculations made by both sexual partners which give neither of them any reason to feel very proud.[44] It is also similar to the sort of 'happy' atmosphere that Napoléon would have liked to see existing at Longwood on Saint Helena, as he explained to his retinue: 'You should try to form a single family here', and if 'mutual liking' is not quite enough, 'you must be guided at least by reason and calculation; you must learn to reckon up your difficulties and sacrifices against your moments of pleasure, ... just as we add and subtract in any type of calculation'.[45] All of which demonstrates that the originality of Bentham, with regard to the age in which he lived, has probably been overestimated. For reasons that have never really been made clear this has perhaps allowed the age of the Enlightenment to be let off rather lightly when attempts have been made to evaluate its true nature.

Mme de Staël would have liked the legislator to apply 'the principles of reckoning to every branch of the moral system'.[46] This is precisely what was done when matters relating to rights of succession and family relationships were articulated around the mainspring of self-interest. In this way, the law was seen as manufacturing lasting affections, which was a precious thing to do indeed, given the proven lack of sociability in the human make-up. D'Holbach had warned that it is 'through liberal treatment' that we 'enslave hearts'.[47] 'They loved me dearly too; but always a little less than if I had been dead', wrote Paul-Louis Courier of those who stood to be his heirs and who were kept on tenterhooks by the dangers of the military life he led. This was in 1807.[48] But in order for the pressure to work there has to be something with which to be liberal in the first place. Which explains the vital importance of property in the minds of the authors of the Civil Code. Property emerges as one of the most important justifications for the Code's existence at all, albeit one which is not always acknowledged as such. Yet we read in the *Travaux Préparatoires* that, because of the feelings it inspires in would-be heirs, property is 'the source of *all moral affections*'.[49] Which is saying a great deal, and if we remain within the perspective of that text, it is also saying perhaps just a little too much.

Property: 'the source of all moral affections': how can this be saying a little too much? In the sense that, within the family, affections exist prior to any thoughts about inheritance, which therefore cannot be the source of the affections but will simply be – and this is already a great deal – the indispensable means of maintaining them. It is true that human beings are, incidentally, prone to their 'little preferences'. These are ephemeral inclinations which give life a little 'touching' charm, but which on the one hand tend to upset the general mechanism of self-interest, and on the other hand, have too little substance about them to actually offer any serious leverage for the purposes of the legislator. Spontaneous affections occurring within the family have no greater importance than 'little preferences' and the laws of inheritance aim to perpetuate these artificially and to turn them into something 'synthetic', that is, something that clearly lacks the freshness of the original but also does away with its inconveniently transient, evanescent nature too. Throughout this same period, Destutt de Tracy was teaching that 'what seems to us to be the most natural part of our make-up is totally artificial ..., even if it is so *unbeknownst to ourselves*'.[50]

Behind a couple's coming together therefore, we might well suppose there exist 'tender feelings', or 'touching sentiments', and what Bonaparte has the great delicacy to refer to as an 'animal friendship'. But with the exception of 'poor marriages', where the partners have no choice but to run the risks of following the dictates of pure affection, the need for stability presupposes that well-organised pecuniary arrangements take precedence over all else. Thus, ensuring the revocability of gifts made during the marriage is an excellent way of guarding against fits of impulsive 'affection'. And thus, too, during the debate over the relative merits of a system of goods held in common or a dowry system, the question was asked as to which of these will best guarantee 'the greater number of affectionate wives' and which will inflict 'the greater number of cold companions' on their husbands. An important consideration indeed. In the dowry system, one orator alleges, because of the fact that immovable goods are inalienable, the wife will have the blissful certainty of knowing that 'if techniques of seduction are used as a way of awakening her tenderest feelings', they can never be a prelude to extorting her signature. 'Confidence in such matters is the balm of the heart and the charm of life.'[51] We should point out that such an approach to matrimony is in no way at variance with the sometimes disconcerting anthropology inherited from the Enlightenment and the Revolution. Within marriage, 'law follows in the wake of instinct', is the way Portalis sums up the matter,[52] and here again, his 'spiritualism' is very discreet indeed.

In 1801 one orator explained: 'What determines the nature of an institution is the nature of the relationships it is intended to *maintain*'.[53] What we have here is the application of this principle. More generally, within the family, the law maintains affections and renders them submissive through its use of the lever of self-interest trained upon the prospect of a future inheritance. This is precisely what Bigot-Préameneu means when he says that the Articles of the Code relating to gifts and testaments 'call to mind all the things that are likely to be of the greatest interest to man, everything that is likely to *captivate his affections*',[54] in other words to fix them in a useful way, to make them congeal once and for all, in the expectation or the fear of the benefits or the reprisals that are contained in the will. Captivate, take hold of, subjugate – we continually come across the vocabulary of manipulation. Destutt de Tracy said that the wish to 'take possession of the will of one's fellow-man' was 'the source of all morality',[55] which brings us back once again to the idea of property as the 'source' or, more exactly, as the way of maintaining 'all moral affections'. In all logic therefore, it is its function as 'the guardian of property' that makes the Napoleonic Code 'the depository of those laws *which preserve all the human affections*', as one orator put it.[56] In this respect, it is worth pointing out that notions of 'maintenance' and 'preservation' became quite obsessive preoccupations during the years of the Directory.

Speaking about the Civil Code, the same orator makes the following further point: 'Even when it is dealing with people it is *always* in consideration of some property or other that belongs to them or which could belong to them'. And he adds, 'Even the most superficial reading of the Civil Code will convince anyone that this is true'.[57] The highly significant word *always* is not used here inadvertently. The idea that the Code is more concerned with possessions than with people is ensconced within the *Travaux Préparatoires*, although among university academics it is quite usual for the opposite to be suggested. I would suggest that this relative disregard for people provides an illustration of, and indeed is one of the outcomes of, the anthropological reductionism that has been our central concern throughout this study and which, in this instance, is at the very least tinged with materialism in so far as it bathes in a materialist atmosphere. For Portalis, the section that 'is like the universal soul of the whole legislation' (*universal ... of the whole*) is well and truly article 544 which defines property as 'the right to use and enjoy in the most absolute way'. And Portalis drives the point home: '*The whole body of the Civil Code* aims at providing a definition concerning everything that has anything to do with the exercising of the right to property'. This is no small task if you think about it, and if you think about all those themes relating to individual rights which, in the process, are denied any significance as a source of specific values or as an end in themselves. We also learn that 'The most precious maxim of the Civil Code, the first and the most important of its dispositions, is therefore that which proclaims the right to property; *all others are merely* extensions or consequences of it'. And Tribune Grenier, when he came to make his final report to the *Corps législatif*, and sought to convey what he thought to be its very *essence*, described property in the following, quite remarkable way, as a 'moral quality inherent in *things*'. He, in turn, goes on to clarify: '*All the various sections* of the Civil Code *are merely* the development of rules relating to the exercising of the right to property'. 'The respect for property is evident in *every page* of the Code' we also hear. And as a further example: 'There is more certainty in possessions than in people'. It would be rather a pity to go on neglecting this whole corpus of quotations which surely cannot be dismissed as being totally unimportant.

Napoléon makes a similar point when speaking of himself: 'The man who is made for business and to wield authority does not see people; he sees only things and the importance and the consequences they have'.[58] Such a comment provides a clear confirmation of the organic relationship existing between, on the one hand, the impetus that was the driving force behind the Civil Code and, on the other, the general mentality of a period which had been formed by the sort of influences we have been discussing. 'Family ties exist to provide inheritances', one *enfant du siècle* will soon appear to complain.[59] He probably did not know that Tronchet, the chairman of the Commission called upon to draft the Civil Code, had purposely dared to describe 'kinship' as the 'right to property', in that it always implies 'reciprocal successibility'.[60]

This attraction felt for possessions and property should not, however, be seen as implying that the authors of the Civil Code held the *natural* right to the ownership of property in particularly high esteem. While such a view is not entirely absent from their deliberations, it is not openly and clearly expressed, and the opposite idea, that of a right to property seen purely and simply as a social creation, is mixed up with it (and possibly predominates?). The question of the disposal of the *biens nationaux* is obviously an important element in this thinking, even if its true significance is really much wider. This is what Tribune Sédillez has to say when voicing his support for the section of the Code devoted to Donations and Testaments (and we well know the sort of logic underpinning this particular part of the Code); he allows himself to leave on one side what he calls 'the material of the law in order to consider the wider context'[61] and he says: 'Animals merely enjoy the use of things, man alone *believes himself* to be their owner'. Well, well, now. 'This idea is perhaps merely *an illusion*, but there are a small number of similar sorts of illusions just like this one, which serve to make the world go round and which activate all the levers in political societies',[62] and we can bet on it that among them he would include the notion of subjective responsibility. The illusion of property, he added, 'precisely because it is of our own making, is dearer to us than if it were a reality'. Can an illusion that is dearer to us because it is an illusion really be considered an illusion? At very least it is an illusion for those who are not aware of its existence, for the mass of the people for whom the Civil Code is being written – a Code inspired, unbeknownst to itself, by an interplay of legislative afterthoughts that I have been at pains to illustrate in these pages, alas all too sketchily.

The premeditated promotion of an illusion to what we might call the ontological status of reality (which has, at least hypothetically, the handicap of being less attractive than the illusion) and therefore having axiological significance, is one of the philosophical miracles of the Code of 1804. This is an example of the type of consequence that flows from the view of the human being as purely passive and open to various types of manipulation, which has been passed down from the Enlightenment. The same theme has already been seen several times in the context of religion, including the whole Concordat episode. Now it is clear that a single and identical political objective underpins and explains both the Concordat and the Civil Code, and the dual role played by Portalis is there to symbolise this fact.

As we have seen, the universal mainspring of self-interest, if it is sufficiently well primed, should manufacture within the family a subtle web of synthetic affections. The appropriateness of such affections would seem to be founded on ideas such as the following expressed by Maleville, that 'often the semblance of virtue has effects equivalent to virtue itself'.[63] And so order reigns both within families and within the state. The elderly mother whose inalienable dowry is an object of affection will enjoy the very timely illusion, 'this last sweet illusion', of being tenderly loved by her family.[64] And does the father believe he lives on through his offspring? 'Sweet and consoling idea! If it were merely an illusion common to soft-hearted fathers, we should have to be wary indeed of denying it them'.[65] And what about adoption then, that strange *ersatz* version of paternity? 'Probably another illusion too, but an innocent one'.[66] Should a father not have the reward of contemplating the 'image of the family', in other words, 'the sweetest of all illusions'.[67] In this respect, logic demands that we acknowledge that the best possible results will be achieved, both for families and for the state, when 'rich men ... go to choose a child in the hospital'.[68] Lequinio wrote: 'The man who knows what pleasure is, worries little about what causes it so long as the effect is to secure his happiness'.[69] As for Jean-Jacques, if Rousseau is to be believed, 'for him, happy fictions take the place of real happiness'.[70]

All this in order to demonstrate that when the authors of the Civil Code think along these lines, they are merely reflecting the views of their age. To those members of his clan who persist in telling him that Joséphine 'is false and that the tender feelings expressed by his children are a studied counterfeit', Napoléon replied: 'So what! I am happy with that; they treat me like an old uncle; it nevertheless brings joy to my whole life'.[71] And his brother Joseph writes to him from Spain in 1809 saying that 'the illusion' of 'his friendship' is necessary for his 'happiness'.[72] Although Mme de Staël objected: 'Seeking to create any form of illusion whatsoever is tantamount to *forcing love* to obey orders',[73] she nevertheless also considered 'the illusions of the heart'[74] as a positive thing, and claimed that 'there are no illusions except in happiness'[75] – an expression that deserves deeper analysis. Paul and Virginie too, through the arbitrary toponymy that they bestowed here and there on their exotic island 'were maintaining' ... 'the sweet illusions of their country'.[76]

The taste for reassuring and consoling illusions, which can be used as a branch of government, is a characteristic of the Enlightenment which seems to illustrate a certain affinity between philosophical idealism and the propensity to materialism.[77] Writing to his wife about the love he supposes her to feel for him, Helvétius notes: 'Perhaps I am mistaken but the mistake is agreeable to me ... we believe all the things that we long for'.[78] And in the specific case of the man who imagines he is going to live on through his own offspring, d'Holbach sees 'useful illusions' on which the laws of inheritance should capitalise. 'Happy make-belief! sweet illusion that *comes true* for those with fertile imaginations', and which leads men to follow the path of virtue because they live in fear of what others may think.[79] Voltaire himself nibbles at the fruit of illusion – the world is a place which offers 'so little consolation' that he adopts Mme du Châtelet's precept, according to which: 'In order to experience happiness one has ... to be ready to believe in illusions'.[80] 'Delude me just a little, I beg of you, deign to help me to fool myself honestly', Voltaire implores Frédéric II.[81] He fears and deplores 'the unhappiness of being made to see the truth'[82] and in particular, with regard to man's final ends, he speaks of 'the cruelty there is in letting us know about them'.[83] It is far preferable and a far more comfortable thing that so much happens here on earth unbeknownst to us. Moreover, the very acute metaphysical anguish expressed in his letters, an anguish which grew ever more acute with the passing years, seems to derive from Voltaire's inability to rid himself of his vague belief in the existence of certain supernatural realities – a belief which he tried so hard to put out of his mind.

So Rousseau is most certainly far from alone in feeling the attractions that the charms of 'consoling' illusion hold, even if he is the out-and-out champion in this domain. This is a title Rousseau richly deserves, reckoning as he did that the only things that are 'beautiful are those which do not exist'. Speaking of his religion, he is not afraid to admit 'An illusion perhaps, but if I had a more consoling one I should adopt that instead'.[84] He has Julie, the 'nouvelle Héloïse', say: 'Oh sweet illusions! Oh fantasies! last resort for the unfortunate soul! ah! if it is possible, take the place of reality!'[85] Abbé Trublet observes that: 'The true hypocrite pretends in order to seem to be; Rousseau pretends in order to be'.[86] The latter praises 'this sweet illusion that is friendship',[87] he rails against 'the cruel confidences' which come along 'to dispel sweet illusions'.[88] He holds that men should only use imagination, 'that consoling faculty', 'in order to soften the sense they have of their misfortunes', and in order to seek refuge 'above the foggy vapours of our atmosphere'.[89] He recognises himself in this practice, advantaged as he is by his 'weak understanding' which, by laying him open to the influence of 'sensitive objects, makes his meditations less dry, more sweet, *more illusory*',[90] and so on. The same theme is expressed in the writings of Rousseau's correspondents and admirers.[91] Hence his friend, Moultou, writing about Mably's book, *De la législation, ou principes des loix* (1776), says: I have found in it 'the dreams of my whole life, and dreams from which I have not yet woken up'. This work 'confirms me in my illusions. It has unearthed the true principles of happiness for men'.[92] Once again these are strong words. True happiness to be found in illusion: as we have just seen, the same idea is equally deeply entrenched in the writings of those *philosophes* who could be considered Rousseau's opponents.

And so, in seeking to propagate 'useful illusions', the authors of the Napoleonic Code are merely men of their times. They think that in order to achieve the happiness of society they have to manipulate the inner beings of those whom they govern *unbeknownst to them*. Tribune Sédillez, in the speech of May 1803 from which we have already quoted, sums up the deeper aims of the Civil Code that is in the process of being elaborated, and identifies the 'effects' that it is expected to produce in their most 'imperceptible ramifications' (working therefore *unbeknownst* to the people concerned): 'to *take hold of man* even in *the most secret refuge of his thought*', touch 'the most sensitive fibres of his affections in order to alter his habits and make him adopt new ones; for *the great secret* of the legislator is to act in such a way that the citizen who obeys the law thinks he is merely obeying the dictates of his own will'.[93] All of which confirms the fact that the Civil Code, in so far as the 'big children' it seeks to coordinate into a society are concerned, has very ambiguous intentions.[94] Among other things, it calls to mind *Émile* and the supreme secret contained therein regarding pedagogical manipulation:

> Let him [the pupil] always believe himself to be the master and let it always be you who is really in command. There is no form of subjection so complete as that which preserves *the illusion of freedom*; the will itself thus becomes subjected. Is the poor child, who is ignorant of everything, who can do nothing and who knows nothing, not completely at your mercy? In your relation to him, are you not in control of everything that surrounds him? Are you not in a position to influence him as you see fit? When he is at work or at play, in his moments of pleasure or pain, is he not entirely in your hands, *unbeknownst to himself*? No doubt he should only do what he wants to do; but he should only want to do what you want him to do.[95]

In the report already quoted, Sédillez said he was departing from 'the material of the law in order to consider the wider context'. It is quite normal that in 'the wider context' he should see what we have constantly seen since we began this study, namely the boldly manipulative and discreetly totalitarian intention to 'take hold of man even in the most secret refuge of his thought': an intention which *Le Moniteur*, although 'universal',[96] never actually bothered to convey to its readers. It is indeed remarkable – and so far as the Civil Code is concerned the event is apparently unprecedented – that this overly explicit speech, which received its *imprimatur*, was published only in a much reduced version, the most revealing two-thirds having been cut out. As a result, these sections do not appear in Fenet's *Recueil* (1827), which is the only collection commonly in use among members of the legal profession.[97] When one believes oneself to be responsible for fashioning citizens *unbeknownst to them*, there are some things it is better not to let them know.

Notes

1. On the origins of the Napoleonic Code, and more precisely on the attempts at codification made during the Revolutionary period, I strongly recommend the work by J.-L. Halperin, *L'impossible Code civil*, Paris, 1992.
2. For a typical example of an academic point of view on this matter, see above, 209–10.
3. The members of the commission were as follows: Tronchet (in the chair), Portalis, Bigot-Préameneu and Maleville. There exist the minutes of a hundred or so sessions of the *Conseil d'état* dealing with this matter, as well as the text of more than a hundred and fifty speeches and reports. Numerous collections of these have been published. The best-known is the collection by P.-A. Fenet, *Recueil des Travaux préparatoires du Code civil*, 15 vols, Paris, 1827.
4. J. Fiévée, *Correspondance et relations avec Bonaparte 1802–1813*, Paris, 1836, vol. 1, 18.
5. J.E.M. Portalis, *De l'usage et de l'abus de l'esprit philosophique durant le XVIIe siècle* (posthumous, 1820, 1827) 3rd edn, 2 vols, Paris, 1834, Chapters IX to XIII.
6. To the *Corps législatif*, 15th germinal year X, 5 April 1802, *Archives parlementaires* 2/3/424/2.
7. *Conseil d'état*, 24th brumaire year X, 15 November 1801, in Fenet, *Recueil des Travaux préparatoires du Code civil*, vol. 10, 59.
8. Helvétius, *De l'Esprit* (1758), Paris, 1988, 315, footnote.
9. P. Cabanis, *Rapports du Physique et du Moral de l'Homme*, Paris, (1802), reprinted Paris/Geneva, 1980, 234.
10. Excepting, however, Rousseau, who 'until the very end of his life will never cease to be an old child' (*Rousseau juge de Jean-Jacques, Deuxième Dialogue*, in *Œuvres complètes*, vol. 1, 800); in which respect he remains true to the common lot as he himself sees it : see above, 77.
11. *Tribunat*, 29th floréal year X, 19 May 1802: *Archives parlementaires* 2/3/730/2. See above, 252.
12. *Corps législatif*, 28th ventôse year XII, 19 March 1804: *Archives parlementaires* 2/6/165/2. See above, 161–162.
13. *Tribunat*, 19th pluviôse year XII, 9 February 1804: *Archives parlementaires* 2/5/435/2.
14. Voltaire, *Corr.*, vol. 10, 327, 9 July 1770.
15. April 1771, ibid., 702 and 704.
16. See above, 10.
17. *Conseil d'état*, 30th frimaire year XII, 22 December 1803: *Archives parlementaires* 2/7/742/1.
18. I refer readers to my study: 'À tout âge? Sur la durée du pouvoir des pères dans le Code Napoléon' in *Revue d'Histoire des Facultés de Droit et de la Science juridique*, n° 13, (1992).
19. See, for example, above, concerning an expression used by Sieyès, 100–103.
20. Thus we read in the *Travaux préparatoires* that prodigality 'could be merely the effect of an unfortunate organisation' (*Archives parlementaires* 2/4/534/2), and that 'the gambler, for example, is an individual whose organs are diseased' (Fenet, *Recueil*, vol.10, 688). Et cetera.
21. *Corps législatif*, 19th pluviôse year XII, 9 February: *Archives parlementaires* 2/5/429/1.
22. Fiévée, *Correspondance*, in *N.B.O.H.*, vol. 10, 537.

23. Mme de Staël, *Correspondance générale*, ed. B.W. Jasinski, vol. 6, Paris, 1993, 475, letter of 8 July 1808.
24. See above, 134.
25. The expression is from C. Langlois, article on 'Portalis', in J. Tulard, ed., *Dictionnaire Napoléon*, Paris, 1987, 1,365/2
26. A number of these arguments will be collated in a study already in preparation on this particular problem.
27. Shortly after thermidor: Fenet, *Recueil*, vol. 1, 105, 23rd fructidor year II, 9 September 1794.
28. Voltaire, *Corr.*, vol. 7, 928.
29. Bonaparte, to the *Conseil d'état*, 4th nivôse year X, 25 December 1801: Fenet, *Recueil*, vol. 10, 350.
30. *Mémoires* de Mollien, in *N.B.O.H.*, vol. 9, 224.
31. See above, 78, note 196.
32. See above, 77–78.
33. D'Holbach, *Système de la Nature*, vol. 1, 241–42, 169, 175.
34. Letter to Servan, 1765: *Corr. gén. d'Helvétius*, vol. 3, 150.
35. Mme de Staël, *Des circonstances actuelles qui peuvent terminer la Révolution*, Paris, 1979, 273.
36. Tribune Favard, 13th floréal year XI, 3 May 1803: *Archives parlementaires* 2/5/86/1.
37. *Mémorial*, 368/2, 18 July 1816.
38. On all of this, see my article quoted in Chapter One, note 4, and even more so, Chapter Twelve, note 4, as well as various other of my studies to which they refer here and there.
39. See above, 57–58.
40. Cabanis, *Rapports*, 127–28, footnote.
41. Tribune Jaubert, 9th floréal year XI, 29 April 1803: *Archives parlementaires* 2/5/41/2.
42. Montesquieu, *Lettres persanes* (1720), Paris, 1949, 136, Letter XCV.
43. See above, 74.
44. See above, 90–91.
45. *Mémorial*, 212/2, 17 April 1816.
46. De Staël, *Des circonstances actuelles*, 27.
47. D'Holbach, *Ethocratie ou le Gouvernement fondé sur la morale* (1776), Paris, 1967, 273.
48. P.-L. Courier, *Œuvres complètes*, Paris, (1951), 1964, *Correspondance*, 750; 'when I want them to do some service or other on my behalf, I let them know that I am close to death; I am making my will, and straight away they jump into action'.
49. Tribune Grenier, to the *Corps législatif*, 6th pluviôse year XII, 27 January 1804: *Archives parlementaires* 2/5/247/2.
50. See above, 174.
51. References quoted in my study (somewhat outdated in respect of the analysis it proposes) : 'L'insensibilité des rédacteurs du Code civil à l'altruisme', in *Revue historique de Droit français et étranger*, vol. 60, 1,982/4. [589–618], 590–91.
52. *Corps législatif*, 7th ventôse year XI, 7 March 1803: *Archives parlementaires* 2/4/85/2.
53. Garat-Maillia, to the *Tribunat*, on the 'establishment of a special criminal tribunal': *Archives parlementaires* 2/2/293/1.
54. *Corps législatif*, 2nd floréal year XI, 22 April 1803: *Archives parlementaires* 2/4/719/2.

55. In October 1796: see above, 174.
56. Sédillez, 10th floréal year XI, 30 April 1803: *Archives parlementaires* 2/5/61/1.
57. All the references to quotations in this paragraph figure in our own study 'À tout âge? Sur la durée du pouvoir des pères dans le Code Napoléon' in *Revue d'Histoire des Facultés de Droit et de la Science juridique*, n° 13, (1992), 295–97.
58. *Mémorial*, Paris, 1961, vol.2, 611. Once again therefore, when Mme de Staël says that Napoléon 'looks upon a human creature as though he/she were an object or a fact' (*Considérations sur la Révolution*, 338), far from giving way to polemical excesses, it seems to us that she is describing very exactly what is actually the case.
59. A. de Musset, *Les Confessions d'un enfant du siècle* (1836), Lausanne, 1968, 1st Part, Chapter 2, 36.
60. *Conseil d'état*, 4th nivôse year X, 25 December 1801: Fenet, *Recueil*, vol. 10, 351.
61. 10th floréal year XI, 30 April 1803: *Archives parlementaires* 2/5/60/1.
62. Ibid., 61/1.
63. *Conseil d'état*, 30th nivôse year XI, 20 January 1803: *Archives parlementaires* 2/7/427/1.
64. See above, 9–10.
65. Tribune Chazal, 16th floréal year VIII, 6 May 1800: *Archives parlementaires* 2/1/563/2.
66. Sédillez (see note 61): *Archives parlementaires* 2/5/61/2.
67. Tribune Perreau, 30th ventôse year XI, 21 March 1803: *Archives parlementaires* 2/4/414/2.
68. Abrial, Minister of Justice, to the *Conseil d'état*, 4th nivôse year X, 25 December 1801: Fenet, *Recueil*, vol. 10, 340.
69. Lequinio, *Les Préjugés détruits*, Paris, 1792, 148.
70. *Rousseau juge de Jean-Jacques, Deuxième Dialogue*, vol. 1, 814.
71. *Journal* de Roederer, in *N.B.O.H.*, vol. 8, 199.
72. 19 February: *Corr. Nap.*, 561.
73. De Staël, *Des circonstances actuelles*, 64.
74. De Staël, *Corinne* (1807), Paris, 1985, 28.
75. Letter to Hochet, 30 April 1805: De Staël, *Correspondance*, vol. V/2, Paris, 1985, 546; see also 427.
76. Bernardin de Saint-Pierre, *Paul et Virginie* (1788), Lausanne, 1961, 116.
77. Marcel de Corte, *L'Intelligence en péril de mort*, Dismas, 1987, Chapter 1, 'Les intellectuels et l'utopie', 72: 'Because it has rejected the identity principle: being is what it is and *not* what it appears to us to be, intelligence is split by the contradiction between two positions which are equally untenable and between which it constantly oscillates'.
78. 28 May 1765: *Corr. gén. d'Helvétius*, vol. 3, 190.
79. D'Holbach, *Système de la Nature* (1770), vol. 1, 315 and 316.
80. Mme du Châtelet, *Discours sur le bonheur* (around 1747), ed. R. Mauzi, 1961, 4. From Voltaire to Mme du Deffand, 2 July 1754: Voltaire, *Corr.*, vol. 4, 201.
81. Around 20 August 1752: Voltaire, *Corr.*, vol. 3, 767.
82. To Mme du Deffand, 11 October 1763, ibid., vol. 7, 404.
83. Ibid., 692–93.
84. To Mme d'Épinay: quoted by J. Maritain, *Trois Réformateurs, Luther, Descartes, Rousseau*, Paris, 1925, 215.
85. Rousseau, *La Nouvelle Héloïse* (1761), Paris, 1988, 268. See also 588, 728: 'For a long time I deluded myself. This delusion was good for me'.
86. *Corr. complète de Rousseau*, vol. 3, Appendix 142, 351.

87. Rousseau, *Premier Dialogue*, 727
88. Ibid., 729.
89. Rousseau, *Deuxième Dialogue*, 815.
90. Ibid., 816.
91. Hence, from Alexandre Deleyre, in 1757: if his admiration for Rousseau and Diderot 'were merely an illusion, would that it could be forever thus' (*Corr. complète de Rousseau*, vol. 4, 206). In respect of the future Mme Roland, twenty years later: even were he an atheist Rousseau would have shown himself in the colours of a deist , and would not have used 'his talents to undermine a *useful belief*, even if it were a mistaken one' (ibid., vol. 40, 167; and 161).
92. Letter to Meister, 16 January 1777: ibid., vol. 41, 121.
93. *Archives parlementaires* 2/5/63/1.
94. See my article, already referred to: 'la durée du pouvoir des pères dans le Code Napoléon', for example, 294.
95. Rousseau, *Émile* (1762), Paris, 1966, Book 1, 150.
96. [The full title of the publication was *Le Moniteur universel*. Translator's note]
97. The sections cut out only appear in the *Archives parlementaires* , 2nd series, vol. 5, in 1865 (see 60/1, footnote, and 63/1; and compare with Fenet, vol. 12, 623–27). At the end of the speech, the orator in question is nevertheless nominated as one of the three Tribunes invited to support the project before the *Corps législatif*.

Conclusion

In a masterly book investigating 'the politics of the asylum' during the first half of the nineteenth-century, *La Pratique de l'Esprit humain*, Marcel Gauchet and Gladys Swain[1] are struck by the way psychiatrists of that period persisted in trying to reconstruct the personality of mad persons 'unbeknownst to them', through the use of a premeditated and precalculated series of sense-impressions. Thus Esquirol writes that it is a question, above all, of 'producing new sensations'.[2] He explains that in the universe of the mental asylum, 'the most stubborn, the most defiant manic-depressive finds that he is *forced, unbeknownst to himself,* to live outside of himself, carried along by ... *sense-impressions* ... which *perpetually* bombard his senses'.[3] Likewise, Pinel says of the asylum that 'the distributions of the establishment are calculated in such a way as to produce *a continual impression* on the imagination of the patients', conditioning even those who don't realise the fact or pretend to be unaffected by it'.[4] Gauchet and Swain sum up by saying that it is a question of 'formulating an indirect but methodical and complete strategy for reconstructing the psychic individuality of the patient through the sense-impressions they have received and the general influence of a predetermined environment'.[5] In their presentation of this treatment, the two authors in question patently have considerable difficulty in controlling their emotions as they underline what an aberration was being perpetrated in this approach to madness, based as it was on incredibly totalitarian, demiurgic and utopian ambitions: this 'naive and coldly calculating desire to rebuild the individual from scratch, to begin him anew, to reform him totally'.⁶ In speaking this way, they are, perhaps unbeknownst to themselves, railing against what I have continued to identify, over and over again, in an almost obsessively repetitive way, as a fundamental impulse triggered by the French Revolution in respect of *all citizens*.

For it is clear that those who are, in this case, medically diagnosed madmen, are hardly subjected to different *treatment* than other people, or, should we say: than the rest of humanity, with the exception of the small number of *planners* – those who know, and theorise and pass laws and decide the inner nature of (and what the future holds for) those whom we hardly dare to call their fellow-men. Conditioning the inner being of all men, unbeknownst to them, by bombarding them with sense-impressions in an appropriate environment: this is the leitmotif that I have followed throughout the Enlightenment, throughout the Revolution and throughout the legislative work of the Consulate. If, by definition, the madman is bereft of reason, it is difficult to say what distinguishes him from virtually the whole of the 'individuals in the human species', as seen by the *Encyclopédiste*, d'Holbach, who said, 'there are only a very small number ... who really enjoy the power of reason or [even] the disposition and the experience that make it possible'.⁷ And Voltaire reckons: 'The multitude of brutish animals called men compared with the small number of those who think, is *at least* in the ratio of a hundred to one in many nations', a little later he says, 'a thousand to one'.⁸ And from this point of view, religion has the particularly useful social function of 'enslaving fools', he says.⁹ As for Diderot, he admits that it is useful to maintain priests to act 'as *warders for madmen*, and I would let their churches remain too, as the asylums or 'petites maisons'¹⁰ for certain kinds of imbecile who might possibly become enraged if they were completely neglected'.¹¹ The troubles that antireligious policies stoked up in Revolutionary France would have confirmed Diderot in this view of things which, as we have seen, was more or less the view of the consular government when it undertook to arrange the Concordat.

Gauchet and Swain object quite strongly to seeing mentally ill patients being considered by the doctors of that period as 'big children' and suggest that this naturally leads to 'medicine's constant use of educational metaphors' and a radicalistaion of the desire to completely restructure the personality of patients.¹² But we might well object that, in fact, it is not a metaphor at all, and *infantilisation* is by no means restricted to those mental patients who have been clearly diagnosed as being infantile. The idea that the generality of mankind is made up of 'big children' is a commonplace in the rhetoric of the legislators for at least a fifteen-year period around 1800. Indeed, the 'universal presumption of minority' that I identified in the minds of the authors of the Civil Code may be seen as a discrete but systematic application of the same idea. It is true that women alone are expressly assimilated to minors and certified persons, but we know that tacitly or obliquely the normally-endowed male adult does not enjoy the confidence of the legislator to any appreciably greater extent.[13] Whether he is an 'old child' or a 'big child', the same idea recurs explicitly in Voltaire, Diderot and the others, as well as in Rousseau – Rousseau, whose fundamentally manipulative educational principles cannot really be dissociated (as I have had occasion to remark) from those political principles which he helped to disseminate as the Revolution approached, without, for all that, being the sole propagator of them. The techniques he described for the conditioning of the pupil in his care are, word for word, those which the Revolutionary propagandists used on the citizen, and word for word those that the psychiatrists of the day considered appropriate for treating 'the most stubborn manic-depressives'. All this is well documented and it leaves one wondering, and not a little sceptical, when one is expected to feel awe and gratitude for the way the founding of the Republic by the Revolutionaries supposedly ushered in 'the sacred period when man came of age, *the era of human majority*'.[14] From a historiographical point of view, it is sometimes not without its disadvantages to subject a master of antiphrasis such as Michelet to a very literal reading.

'Know men in order to act upon them'. Stendhal appreciated this expression which, if I may recapitulate, so admirably sums up the whole problematic which this study has constantly sought to elucidate and illustrate. The expression puts the whole problematic in a nutshell, providing we read it from a perspective tending towards materialism and scientism. We must presume, firstly, that the knowledge of man in question is assumed to be total and to contain no lingering residue of mystery, and, secondly, that the action it sets in train is subjected to no technical or moral limits. 'Know men in order to act upon them': we find this expression quoted by André Malraux in the preface to Choderlos de Laclos' *Les Liaisons dangereuses*,[15] which is not generally considered to be a text that is in any way marginal with respect to the mental universe of the

Enlightenment. And Stendhal had noted it in the work of Destutt de Tracy, whom he greatly admired, as he also admired Helvétius.[16] Destutt was, of course, one of the two masters of the *Idéologie* movement whose key importance I have been at pains to reiterate, just as I have sought to demonstrate the movement's capital role as a pivotal link in that continuous process which I have attempted to describe as it has unfolded before our eyes. An interlocking of ideas such as this is hardly likely to undermine the coherence of the case which has been developed in these pages. All the less so in that Cabanis, Destutt de Tracy's *alter ego* in this combat to secure the happiness of the human beings whom they were so intent on regenerating in such radical ways, doctor Cabanis himself, on several occasions, studied the question of madness. In essence, he even predicted that it would disappear as soon as a good state of society had finally normalised human animals: and we have already seen what kind of dreams he concocted in this respect.[17] Gauchet and Swain, who have difficulty in stopping themselves from quoting from Cabanis, do not attempt to hide their stupefaction at his extravagant social claim to 'fashion personalities' and 'hold sway over men's souls *unbeknownst to them*', nor at his ambition, which they considered to be totally utopian, 'of being able to prevent men from being mad'.[18]

The two authors go on to underline 'the character, so clearly foreshadowing totalitarianism, that a number of aspects of the world of mental asylums unquestionably took on'.[19] Nor are they afraid to posit a connection between the totalitarian tendencies of the psychiatrists of the day and the establishment at that time of technically *alienating* conditions of industrial labour, alongside the burgeoning of the nascent 'omnipresent and omniscient' contemporary state. They clarify this point:

> From the factory to the totalitarian states of the present day ... the *way power is organised* remains fundamentally the same and involves a basic division into two groups: on the one hand, there are those who are simply agents and who are destined never to emerge from the opacity of their blissful ignorance, and on the other hand, there are those who lead them and who are defined by the sovereign knowledge they are supposed to possess – a knowledge which envelopes others, pierces them through *unbeknownst to themselves* and claims in a very literal sense to *constitute* them as they are.[20]

The very least we can say is that such words and expressions are in no way new to us. They sum up the programme of the whole

Enlightenment and so many aspects of the Revolution. Deciding what sort of programme of a more contemporary nature they may also be deemed to be summing up must, provisionally at least, be left to the responsibility of the reader to decide.

Notes

1. M. Gauchet and G. Swain, *La Pratique de l'Esprit humain. L'institution asilaire et la révolution démocratique*, Coll. 'Bibliothèque des Sciences humaines', Paris, 1980.
2. Quoted ibid., 138, footnote 21.
3. Ibid., 144. [Gauchet and Swain refer to *lypémanie*, which is a type of depressive madness. I have chosen the more general term manic-depressive. Translator's note]
4. Ibid., 145, footnote.
5. Ibid., 138.
6. Ibid., 138, footnote 22.
7. D'Holbach, *Système de la Nature*, (1770), vol. 1, 161.
8. Voltaire, *Dictionnaire philosophique* (1764), article 'Homme', *Œuvres complètes*, Paris, vol. 19, 1879, 383; and Voltaire, *Corr.*, vol. 8, 426.
9. To Mme du Deffand, 6 November 1765: Voltaire, *Corr.*, vol. 8, 239.
10. Les Petites-Maisons was a well-known Parisian asylum for the mad in the eighteenth century.
11. Diderot, *Plan d'Université*, quoted by J.-A. Naigeon, *Mémoires historiques et philosophiques sur la vie et les ouvrages de Denis Diderot* (1821), repr. Geneva, 1970, 360–61.
12. Reference to note 6.
13. See above, 256.
14. J. Michelet, *Histoire de la Révolution* (1847–1853), Paris, 1979, vol. 2, 622.
15. Choderlos de Laclos, *Les Liaisons dangereuses* (1782), Lausanne, 1968, 9.
16. Stendhal, *Vie de Henry Brulard* (1835–36), Grenoble, 1988, for example 203, 261, 316 and 317.
17. See above, 165 ff.
18. Gauchet and Swain, *La Pratique de l'esprit humain*, 140, and, as far as Cabanis is concerned, 140–41, footnote.
19. Ibid., 144. They insist that it is really and truly a question of 'authentic prefiguration'.
20. Ibid., 106–07. Only the first expression is underlined by the authors. 'To be thought/to think in place of other people: this is the ultimate and absolute form of the power relationship in modern societies, and what makes it essentially and very specifically totalitarian in nature'.

Select Bibliography

Anon. 1773. *L'Élève de la Raison et de la Religion*. Paris.
Aquinas, Thomas. *Summa Theologica*.
Archives Parlementaires de 1787 à 1860. 1ère série, 1787–1794, Paris, 1879–1995; 2e série en cours, Paris, depuis 1862.
Armogathe, J.-R. 1990. 'L'École normale de l'an III et le cours de Garat', in *Corpus, Revue de Philosophie*, no. 14–15, 143–54.
Aulard, F.-A. (ed.) 1892. *La Société des Jacobins. Recueil de Documents pour l'Histoire du Club des Jacobins de Paris*, vol. 4. Paris.
Baczko, B. 1982. *Une Éducation pour la Démocratie. Textes et projets de l'époque révolutionnaire*. Paris.
Ballanche, P.-S. 1991. *Essai sur les institutions sociales dans leur rapport avec les idées nouvelles* (1818). Paris.
Béjin, A. 1988/3. 'Condorcet, précurseur du néo-malthusianisme et de l'eugénisme républicain', in *Histoire, Économies, Sociétés* 347–354.
Belaval, Y. 1973. dir. *Histoire de la Philosophie*, 3 vol., t. 2. Paris.
Bonaparte, N. 1969–1971 *L'Oeuvre et l'Histoire*, ed. J. Massin, 12 vols. Paris.
Bonnet, C. 1755. *Essai de Psychologie, ou Considérations sur les opérations de l'âme, sur l'habitude et sur l'éducation*. London.
Bonnet, C. 1760. *Essai analytique des facultés de l'âme*. Copenhagen.
Bonnet, C. 1770. *Contemplation de la Nature*. Neuchâtel.
Bouley de la Meurthe, A. 1891. *Documents sur la négociation du Concordat*, t. 1. Paris.
Braunstein, J.-F. 1990. 'Degerando, le social et la fin de l'idéologie', in *Corpus, Revue de Philosophie*, no. 14-15, 200–01.
Bulletin des Lois de la République française. 1793-1804. Paris.
Cabanis, P.-J.-G. 1799. *Quelques considérations sur l'organisation sociale en général et particulièrement sur la nouvelle constitution*. Paris, an VIII (fin décembre 1799).

Cabanis, P.-J.-G. 1980. *Rapports du Physique et du moral de l'Homme* (1802). Reprint de l'éd. de 1844, Paris-Geneva.

Carbasse, J.-M. 1994. 'Les Responsables de la Terreur en Vendée: les hommes et le système', in *La Vendée dans l'Histoire*, published papers from colloquium held at La Roche-sur-Yon, April 1993. Paris, 341–57.

Carbonnier, J. 1974. *Droit civil*, vol. 1. Paris.

Carbonnier, J. 1995. 'Langue de la nation et "idiomes grossiers": le pluralisme linguistique sous le niveau jacobin', in Van Goethem, H., Waelkers, L. and Breugelmans, K., dir. *Libertés, Pluralisme et Droit*. Bruxelles, 157–72.

Chassin, C.-L. 1973. *La Vendée patriote, 1793–1795*, vol. 4 (1895). Mayenne.

Chevallier, J.-J. 1964. *Les Grandes Oeuvres politiques de Machiavel à nos jours*. Paris.

Condillac, É. 1991. *Traité des Systèmes* (1749; 1798 edition). Paris.

Condorcet, J.-A.-N. 1994. 'Rapport sur les Prisons', in Condorcet, *Arithmétique politique. Textes rares ou inédits* (1767–89). Paris.

Constant, B. 1986. *De l'Esprit de Conquête et de l'Usurpation dans leurs rapports avec la civilisation européenne* (1813–14). Paris.

Constant, B. 1988. *De la Force du gouvernement actuel de la France et de la nécessité de s'y rallier* (1796), ed. Ph. Raynaud. Paris.

Constant, B. 1991. *Fragments d'un ouvrage abandonné sur la possibilité d'une constitution républicaine dans un grand pays*, ed. H. Grange. Paris.

Courier, P.-L. 1964. *Oeuvres complètes*. Paris.

Crétineau-Joly, J. 1979. *Histoire de la Vendée militaire* (1840–42), 4 vols. Paris.

Décade philosophique, littéraire et politique, 1794–1807.

De Corte, M. 1987. *L'Intelligence en péril de mort*. Dismas.

De Frénilly, A.-F. 1908. *Souvenirs*. Paris.

De la Caze, A. 1764. *Lettre sur le meilleur moyen d'assurer le succès de l'éducation*. Paris.

De la Fare, M. 1768. *Le Gouverneur, ou Essai sur l'Éducation*. London.

De la Madeleine, P. 1783. *Vues patriotiques sur l'Éducation du Peuple tant des villes que des campagnes*. Lyon.

De Laclos, C. 1968. *Les Liaisons dangereuses* (1782). Lausanne.

De Luppé, R. 1969. *Les Idées littéraires de Mme de Staël et l'héritage des Lumières (1795–1800)*. Paris.

De Montenoy, P. 1760. *Les Philosophes*. Paris.

De Musset, A. 1968. *Les Confessions d'un enfant du siècle* (1836). Lausanne.

De Saint-Pierre, B. 1815. *Harmonies de la Nature*. Paris.

De Saint-Pierre, B. 1961. *Paul et Virginie* (1788). Lausanne.

Deschepper, J.-P. 1973. 'Le Spinozisme', in Y. Belaval (ed.), *Histoire de la Philosophie*, vol. 2. Paris.

Desné, R. 1987. 'Voltaire et Helvétius', in *Le Siècle de Voltaire. Hommage à René Pomeau*, 2 vols. Oxford.

De Staël, Mme 1820–1821. *De l'Influence des Passions sur le bonheur des individus et des nations*, in *Oeuvres Complètes*, 17 vols, vol. 3. Paris.

De Staël, Mme 1959. *De la Littérature considérée dans ses rapports avec les institutions sociales*, ed. P. Van Tieghem, 2 vols. Paris-Geneva.

De Staël, Mme 1962–1993. *Correspondance générale*, ed. Béatrice W. Jasinski, 9 vols. parus. Paris.

De Staël, Mme 1968. *De l'Allemagne* (1810), 2 vols. Paris.

De Staël, Mme 1979. *Des Circonstances actuelles qui peuvent terminer la Révolution* (1798). Paris-Geneva.

De Staël, Mme 1983. *Considérations sur la Révolution française* (1818). Paris.

De Staël, Mme 1985. *Corinne* (1807). Paris.

Destutt de Tracy, A.-L.-C. 1970. *Élémens d'Idéologie. Première Partie, Idéologie proprement dite*. Paris.

Destutt de Tracy, A.-L.-C. 1992. *Mémoire sur la Faculté de penser*. Paris, C.O.P.L.F..

De Tocqueville, A. 1986. 'Fragments sur la Révolution: deux chapitres sur le Directoire', in *De la Démocratie en Amérique*. Paris.

De Viguerie, J. 1981. 'Le Mouvement des idées pédagogiques aux XVIIe et XVIIIe siècles', in *Histoire mondiale de l'Éducation*. Paris, 273–99.

De Viguerie, J. 1990. 'Quelques réflexions critiques à propos de l'ouvrage de Paul Hazard *La Crise de la conscience européenne*', in *Études d'Histoire européenne. Mélanges offerts à René et Suzanne Pillorget*. Angers.

De Viguerie, J. 1993. 'Les "Lumières" et les peuples. Conclusions d'un séminaire', in *Revue Historique*, no. 287/1, 161–89.

De Viguerie, J. 1995. *Histoire et dictionnaire du Temps des Lumières. 1715–1789*. Paris.

D'Holbach, P.-H. 1773. *Système social, ou principes naturels de la morale et de la politique, avec un examen de l'influence du gouvernement sur les moeurs par l'Auteur du Système de la Nature*. London.

D'Holbach, P.-H. 1776. *La Morale universelle, ou les Devoirs de l'Homme fondés sur sa nature*, 3 vols. Amsterdam.

D'Holbach, P.-H. 1967. *Ethocratie ou le Gouvernement fondé sur la Morale* (Amsterdam, 1776). Paris.

D'Holbach, P.-H. 1971. *Le Bon Sens, ou idées naturelles opposées aux idées surnaturelles* (1772). Paris.

D'Holbach, P.-H. 1990. *Système de la Nature, ou des loix du monde physique et du monde moral*, 2 vols. Paris.

Dhombres, J. (ed.) 1992. *L'École normale de l'an III, Leçons de mathématiques. Édition annotée des cours de Laplace, Lagrange, Monge*. Paris.

Diderot, D. 1955–1970. *Correspondance*, ed. G. Roth et J. Varloot, 16 vols. Paris.

Diderot, D. 1965a. *Le Neveu de Rameau* (1761). Paris.

Diderot, D. 1965b. *Entretien entre d'Alembert et Diderot* (c. 1770). Paris.

Diderot, D. 1966. *Mémoires pour Catherine II* (1773–74), ed. P. Vernière. Paris.

Diderot, D., d'Alembert, J.-B., eds. 1751–1772. *Encyclopédie, ou Dictionnaire raisonné des Sciences, des Arts et des Métiers, par une Société de Gens de Lettres*. Paris.
Du Châtelet, É. 1961. *Discours sur le bonheur*, ed. R. Mauzi. Paris.
Faiguet de Villeneuve, J. 1763. *L'Economie politique. Projet pour enrichir et pour perfectionner l'espèce humaine*. London.
Du Deffand, M. 1805. *Correspondance complète*, ed. M. de Lescure, 2 vols. Paris.
Fenet, P.-A. 1827. *Recueil des Travaux préparatoires du Code civil*, 15 vols. Paris.
Fiévée, J. 1836. *Correspondance et relations avec Bonaparte, 1802–1813*, 3 vols. Paris.
Fourcy, A. 1987. *Histoire de l'École Polytechnique* (1828). Paris.
Garaud, M. and Szramkiewicz, R. 1978. *La Révolution française et la famille*. Paris.
Gauchet, M. and Swain, G. 1980. *La Pratique de l'Esprit humain. L'institution asilaire et la révolution démocratique*. Paris.
Gilson, É. 1932. 'La méthode de M. De Wolmar', in *Les Idées et les Lettres*. Paris.
Gilson, É. 1979. *Le Thomisme* (6th edn). Paris.
Grandière, M. 1991. *L'Idéal pédagogique en France au XVIIIe siècle (1715–1789)*, Doctorat d' État, University of Lille III.
Grégoire, H. 1789. *Essai sur la Régénération physique, morale et politique des Juifs* (1788). Metz.
Grégoire, H. 1977. *Oeuvres de l'Abbé Grégoire*. Paris-Nendeln.
Grimm, M. and Diderot, D. 1830. *Correspondance littéraire, philosophique et critique*, t. 8. Paris.
Guillaume, J. 1891–1907. *Procès-verbaux du Comité d'Instruction publique*, 6 vols. Paris.
Guillois, A. 1894. *Le Salon de Mme Helvétius. Cabanis et les Idéologues*. Paris.
Gusdorf, G. 1984. *L'Homme Romantique*, Paris.
Gwynne, G.-E. 1969. *Madame de Staël et la Révolution française. Politique, Philosophie, Littérature*. Paris.
Halperin, J.-L. 1992. *L'impossible Code civil*. Paris.
Helvétius, C.-A. 1981, 1984 and 1991. *Correspondance générale d'Helvétius*, 3 vols (4th vol. in preparation). Toronto-Oxford.
Helvétius, C.-A. 1988. *De l'Esprit* (Paris, 1758). Paris.
Helvétius, C.-A. 1989. *De l'Homme, de ses facultés intellectuelles et de son éducation* (London, 1773). Paris.
La Révellière-Lépeaux, L.-M. 1797a. *Réflexions sur le culte, sur les cérémonies civiles et sur les fêtes nationales*. Paris, an V.
La Révellière-Lépeaux, L.-M. 1797b. *Essai sur les moyens de faire participer l'universalité des spectateurs à tout ce qui se pratique dans les Fêtes nationales*. Paris, an VI.
La Révellière-Lépeaux, L.-M. 1797c. *Du Panthéon et d'un Théâtre national*. Paris, an VI.

Las Cases, E. 1968. *Mémorial de Sainte-Hélène* (1823), prés. Joël Schmidt. Paris.
Lesuire, R.-M. 1797–1798. *Le Législateur du chrétien, ou l'Évangile des Déïcoles*. Paris, An VI.
Le Camus, A. 1753. *Médecine de l'Esprit, où l'on cherche 1º Le Méchanisme du corps qui influe sur les fonctions de l'âme, 2º Les causes physiques qui rendent ce méchanisme ou défectueux ou plus parfait, 3º etc.*, 2 vols. Paris.
Leclerc, J.-B. 1797–1798. *Essai sur la propagation de la musique en France, sa conservation, et ses rapports avec le gouvernement*. Paris, an VI.
Le Mercier de la Rivière, P. 1775. *De l'Instruction publique; ou Considérations morales et politiques sur la nécessité, la nature et la source de cette instruction. Ouvrage demandé pour le roi de Suède*. Stockholm.
Lequinio, M.-J. 1792. *Les Préjugés détruits*. Paris.
Mandeville, B. 1985. *La Fable des Abeilles, ou les vices privés font le bien public* (1714), trans. and ed. L. and P. Carrive. Paris.
Maritain, J. 1925. *Trois Réformateurs. Luther, Descartes, Rousseau*. Paris.
Maritain, J. 1927. *Art et Scolastique*. Paris.
Martin, X. 1982/4. 'L'Insensibilité des rédacteurs du Code civil à l'altruisme', in *Revue historique de Droit français et étranger*, vol. 60, 589–618.
Martin, X. 1987. 'L'Individualisme libéral en France autour de 1800', in *Revue d'Histoire des Facultés de Droit et de la Science juridique*, no. 4, 87–144.
Martin, X. 1988. 'Sur l'Homme de la Déclaration des Droits', in *Droits, Revue française de Théorie juridique* no. 8, 83–89.
Martin, X. 1992. 'À Tout Age? Sur la durée du pouvoir des pères dans le Code Napoléon', in *Revue d'Histoire des Facultés de Droit et de la Science juridique*, no. 13, 227–301.
Martin, X. 1993a. 'The Mythology of the Napoleonic Code', *Himeji International Forum of Law and Politics* (University Dokkyo, Himeji, Japan) no. 1, 27–38.
Martin, X. 1993b. 'Madame de Staël, Napoléon et les Idéologues ...', in *Himeji International Forum of Law and Politics*, no. 1, 39–62.
Martin, X. 1993c. 'Liberté, Égalité, Fraternité. Inventaire sommaire de l'idéal révolutionnaire français', in *Himeji International Forum of Law and Politics*, no. 1, 3–25.
Martin, X. 1995a. 'Jean-Baptiste Leclerc. Un Angevin des Lumières sous le Directoire', in *Travaux sur le XVIIIe siècle. 3. Hommage au professeur Jean Roussel*. Angers.
Martin, X. 1995b. *Sur les Droits de l'Homme et la Vendée*. Bouère.
Martin, X. 1997. 'Une tentative de désacralisation du temps: le calendrier révolutionnaire', in Tireau, J.-R., dir. *Le Droit entre laïcisation et néo-sacralisation*. Paris, 215–27.

Melon, J.-F. 1734. *Essai politique sur le commerce*. s.l.
Mervaud, C. 1985. *Voltaire et Frédéric II: une dramaturgie des Lumières, 1736–1778, Studies on Voltaire* 234, Oxford.
Michel. 1769. *Essai sur les moyens d'améliorer les études actuelles des collèges*, Nancy-Paris.
Michelet, J. 1979. *Histoire de la Révolution*. Paris.
Mirabeau, H.-G. 1982. *Deuxième discours sur l'Éducation publique*. Paris.
Mirabeau, H.-G. 1776. *Essai sur le Despotisme*, 2nd edn. London.
Montesquieu, C.-L. 1949. *Lettres persanes* (1721). Paris.
More, T. 1978. *L'Utopie* (1516), ed. A. Prévost. Paris.
Morelly, E.-G. 1970. *Code de la Nature* (1755). Paris.
Müller-Hill, B. 1989. 'La génétique après Auschwitz', in *Les Temps Modernes*, no. 511, 52–85.
Naigeon, J.-A. 1970. *Mémoires historiques et philogophiques sur la vie et les ouvrages de Denis Diderot*. Geneva.
Ozouf, M. 1989. *L'Homme régénéré*. Paris.
Papazu, M. 1993. 'L'Utopie face à ses habitants', in *Bulletin de la Société française d'Histoire des Idées de d'Histoire religieuse*, no. 9, 33–72.
Picardet, H.-C. 1756. *Essai sur l'Éducation des petits enfans*, Dijon.
Picavet, L. 1972. *Les Idéologues. Essai sur l'histoire des Idées et des Théories scientifiques philosophiques, religieuses, etc. en France depuis 1789* (Paris, 1891). Reprint Hildesheim–New-York.
Poliakov, L. 1981. *L'Auberge des Musiciens. Mémoires*. Paris.
Poliakov, L. 1971. *Le Mythe aryen*. Paris.
Portalis, J.-E.-M. 1834. *De l'usage et de l'abus de l'esprit philosophique durant le XVIIIe siècle*, 3rd edn., 2 vols. Paris.
Prévost, F. 1990. *Manon Lescaut* (1731). Paris.
Recueil des Discours, Rapports et Pièces diverses lus dans les séances publiques et particulières de l'Académie française, 1803–1819. 1847. Paris.
Regaldo, M. 1976. *Un milieu intellectuel: la Décade philosophique (1794–1807)*, thesis, University of Paris IV. Paris.
Rostand, J. 1978. *Pensées d'un Biologiste* (1954). Paris.
Rousseau, J.-J. 1959a. *Dialogues* (1772–75), in *Oeuvres complètes*. Paris.
Rousseau, J.-J. 1959b. *Rousseau juge de Jean-Jacques. Dialogues*, in *Oeuvres complètes*, vol. 1. Paris.
Rousseau, J.-J. 1960. *Les Rêveries du Promeneur solitaire* (1778). Paris.
Rousseau, J.-J. 1964a. *Discours sur les fondemens et l'origine de l'inégalité parmi les hommes* (1755), in *Œuvres complètes*, vol. 3. Paris.
Rousseau, J.-J. 1964b. *Discours sur l'Économie politique* (1755), in *Oeuvres complètes*, vol. 3. Paris.
Rousseau, J.-J. 1964c. *Contrat Social*, (1762), in *Oeuvres complètes*, vol. 3. Paris.
Rousseau, J.-J. 1964d. *Lettres écrites de la montagne* (1764), in *Oeuvres complètes*, vol. 3. Paris.

Rousseau, J.-J. 1964e. *Considérations sur le Gouvernement de la Pologne* (1770), in *Oeuvres complètes*, vol. 3. Paris.
Rousseau, J.-J. 1965–91. *Correspondance complète de Jean Jacques Rousseau*, ed. R.A. Leigh, 50 vols. Geneva-Oxford.
Rousseau, J.-J. 1966. *Émile ou de l'Éducation* (1762). Paris.
Rousseau, J.-J. 1980. *Les Confessions* (1766–71). Paris.
Rousseau, J.-J. 1988. *Julie ou la Nouvelle Héloïse*, (1761). Paris.
Sieyès, E. 1982. *Qu'est-ce que le Tiers État?* (1789). Paris.
Serna, P. 1993. 'Aux origines culturelles d'un engagement politique: les notes de lecture d'Antonelle', in *Annales historiques de la Révolution française*, no. 292, 169–202.
Spinoza, B. 1967a. *L'Éthique*, in *Oeuvres complètes*. Paris.
Spinoza, B. 1967b. *Traité de l'Autorité politique*. Paris.
Starobinski, J. 1979. *1789. Les Emblèmes de la Raison*. Paris.
Stendhal. 1988.*Vie de Henry Brulard*. Grenoble.
Testu, F.-X. 1987. 'Un texte méconnu: l'article premier du décret du 1er floréal an II', Conférence donnée à la Première Chambre civile de la Cour d'Appel. Paris, 13 janvier, 1987.
Tulard, J. dir. 1987. *Dictionnaire Napoléon*. Paris.
Tulard, J. Fayard, J.-F. and Fierro, A. 1987. *Histoire et Dictionnaire de la Révolution française*. Paris.
Vauréal, Comte de,. 1783. *Plan ou Essai d'Éducation général et national, ou la meilleure éducation à donner aux hommes de toutes les nations*. Bouillon.
Vellay, C. (ed.). 1908. *Correspondance de Marat*. Paris.
Volney, C.-F. 1980. *La Loi naturelle, ou Principes physiques de la Morale* (1793). Paris.
Voltaire. 1977–1993. *Correspondance*, 13 vols (notes trans. Fr. Deloffre). Paris.
Vox, M. (ed.). 1943. *Correspondance de Napoléon. Six cents lettres de travail (1806–10)*. Paris.
Zac, S. 1973. 'Spinoza', in Y. Belaval (ed.) *Histoire de la Philosophie*, vol. 2. Paris.

Index

A
Abrial, A.-J. 269
Aimé, see Aymé
Alembert, J.-B. d' 11, 18, 20, 21, 22, 25, 29, 30, 31, 32, 33, 65, 100, 102, 154, 169, 220, 222, 245, 246, 248, 253, 279, 280
Andlau, F.-A.-H. d' 168
Antonelle, P.-A. d' 88, 89, 95, 98, 100, 283
Aquinas, Thomas 4, 79, 133, 139, 277
Argental, C.-A. d' 29, 32, 33, 140, 170, 185, 245, 246, 249
Armogathe, J.-R. 167, 277
Arnaud, abbé F. 11, 139
Arouet, see Voltaire
Aulard, F.-A. 137, 277
Aymé, J.-J. 196

B
Babeuf, F., 'Gracchus' 89
Baczko, B. 99, 100, 118, 119, 277
Ballanche, P.-S. 153, 168, 277
Barère, B. 107, 108, 118, 191, 192
Barras, P. de 223
Baudelaire, C. 86
Beauharnais, E. de 249
Beauzée, N. 31
Béjin, A. 99, 277
Belaval, Y. 13, 99, 277, 278, 283
Belloy, P.-L. Buyrette, Dormont de 66
Bentham, J. 78, 258
Bernardin de Saint-Pierre, J.-H. 66, 67, 269
Berthollet, C.-L. 213, 240
Bestermann, Th. 29, 68, 245
Bigot-Préameneu, F.-J.-J. 260, 267
Bodmer, J.-J. 247
Bonaparte, Joseph 154, 214, 248, 264
Bonaparte, L. 214, 228, 229, 248
Bonaparte, N., see Napoléon

Bonnet, C. 68, 75, 80, 139, 169, 277
Bordes, C. 32
Boulay de la Meurthe, A, 248
Bourrienne, L. de 247, 248
Boy de la Tour, see Delessert
Braunstein, J.-F. 250, 277
Bréard, J.-J. 131
Buyrette, see Belloy

C

Cabanis, A. 244
Cabanis, P.-J.-G. 87, 99, 149–172, 173, 174, 179, 183, 186, 187, 210, 211, 215, 216, 217, 218, 219, 223, 225, 226, 229, 230, 233, 239, 240, 241, 242, 243, 244, 247, 248, 250, 252, 258, 267, 268, 274, 275, 277, 278, 280
Cambacérès, J.-J.-R. 250, 256
Carbasse, J.-M. 65, 140, 278
Carbonnier, J. 243, 278
Carrier, J.-B. 164
Carrion-Nisas, F. 4
Catherine II 11, 69, 120, 219, 220, 221, 222, 223, 227, 228, 232, 245, 246, 247, 248, 279
Cato 139
Caulaincourt, A. de 235, 248, 249, 250
Caze, L. de la 75, 79, 278
Cérutti, J.-A.-J. 69
Chamfort, S. R. N. 244
Champagny, J.-B. de 248
Chaptal, J. 233, 249
Charette, F. de 131
Charles X 168

Chassin, C.-L. 119, 120, 138, 139, 140, 248, 278
Châtelet, E., Mme du 22, 157, 264, 269, 280
Chazal, J.-P. 269
Chénier, M.-J. 105
Chevallier, J.-J. 247, 278
Choderlos de Laclos, P. 273, 275
Choiseul, E. F., duc de 16
Choiseul, L.-H., Mme de 16, 21
Chouvalov, I. I. 248
Cideville, P. R. de 31, 140, 245
Collot d'Herbois, J.-M. 102
Condillac, E. de 18, 30, 45, 53, 62, 67, 69, 84, 151, 203, 236, 249, 278
Condorcet, J. A. N. de 31, 41, 66, 78, 86, 99, 137, 152, 154, 167, 168, 171, 198, 201, 202, 221, 258, 277, 278
Constant, B. 108, 118, 137, 186, 197–208, 215, 231, 244, 278
Courier, P.-L. 259, 268, 278
Cramer, G. 31
Craveri, B. 34
Crétineau-Joly, J. 139, 278
Cubières-Palmézeaux, M. de, see Morton

D

Damilaville 65, 139, 140, 245
Damilaville, E. N. 29
Danton, G. J. 106, 107, 118
Daunou, P. C. F. 146, 150, 159
De Corte, M. 269, 278

Deffand, M., Mme du 18, 20, 25, 28, 29, 30, 31, 33, 34, 68, 93, 101, 246, 269, 275, 280
Degerando, J.-M. 250
Delessert, M.-C. 81
Deleyre, A. 66, 68, 270
Delisle de Sales, J.-B. 30
Deloffre, F. 29, 33, 283
Denis, M., Mme 32, 33, 139, 219, 237
Descartes, R. 19, 139, 202, 269, 281
Deschepper, J.-P. 99, 278
Desné, R. 25, 32, 33, 278
Destutt de Tracy, A. 119, 149–172, 184, 202, 207, 210, 225, 226, 239, 240, 241, 248, 259, 260, 274, 279
Dhombres, J. 167, 168, 279
Diderot, D. 6, 7, 8, 11, 18, 19, 34, 40, 53, 66, 69, 91, 93, 97, 100, 101, 102, 116, 120, 129, 134, 136, 138, 140, 154, 158, 169, 219, 220, 223, 225, 227, 230, 232, 247, 248, 270, 272, 273, 275, 279, 280, 282
Dompierre d'Hornoy, see d'Hornoy
Dormont, see Belloy
Du Peyrou, P.-A. 66
Duchesne, N. 79
Dulaure, J.-A. 110
Dupont de Nemours, P. S. 247
Dutens, V.-L. 10
Duveyrier, H.-N.-M. 247

E
Epicure 40, 84, 124

Epinay, F., Mme d' 11
Esquirol, J. E. D. 271
Eugène, prince, see Beauharnais

F
Fabre d'Églantine, P. Fabre, 116, 117, 120, 121
Faiguet de Villeneuve, J. 164, 170, 280
Favard, G. 4, 268
Fayau, J. P. M. 119
Fenet, P.-A. 266, 267, 268, 269, 270, 280
Fiévée, J. 170, 225, 226, 240, 247, 250, 252, 255, 267, 280
Florian, P.-A. de 34
Fouché, J. 111, 119, 123
Fourcy, A. 168, 244, 280
Francastel, M.-P.-A. 140
Frédéric II 23, 30, 31, 32, 33, 84, 169, 211, 219, 220, 221, 222, 223, 224, 244, 245, 246, 248, 264, 282
Frédéric-Guillaume, de Prusse 21, 31
Frénilly, baron de 34, 278
Fréron, E. 139
Freytag, F. von 33

G
Garat, D.-J. 150, 159, 167, 224, 239, 241, 247, 249, 277
Garat-Maillia, J.-J. 268
Garaud, M. G 118, 280
Gauchet, M. 271, 272, 274, 275, 280
Gilson, E. 4, 46, 67, 280

Goebbels, pseudonyme de Voltaire 24
Golitsin, A.-M. prince 33
Grandière, M. 76, 79, 80, 117, 187, 280
Grange, H. 181, 186, 208, 278
Grégoire, H., l'abbé de 106, 108, 110, 118, 119, 134, 139, 227, 247, 280
Grenier, J. 261, 268
Grimm, F. M. 31, 34, 280
Guillaume, J. 100, 118, 170, 280
Guillois, A. 243, 244, 250, 280
Gusdorf, G. 29, 78, 79, 81, 151, 167, 280
Guyenet, I. 71
Gwynne, G. E. 207, 280

H
Halperin, J.-L. 267, 280
Hazard, P. 118, 279
Helvétius, A. C., Mme 151, 154, 210, 214, 243, 244, 250, 280
Helvétius, C.-A. 5–14, 21, 22, 23, 24, 25, 28, 29, 30, 31, 32, 33, 34, 37, 40, 46, 50, 54, 65, 66, 67, 68, 69, 73, 77, 78, 79, 80, 87, 89, 93, 97, 99, 100, 101, 105, 106, 118, 122, 124, 126, 134, 137, 138, 139, 140, 151, 152, 153, 154, 155, 156, 157, 158, 159, 168, 169, 170, 194, 214, 218, 219, 221, 223, 230, 244, 245, 246, 247, 248, 252, 257, 264, 267, 268, 269, 274, 278, 280
Hentz, N. 131, 140

Hobbes, T. 142, 227
Hochet, C. 269
Holbach, P.-H. d' 5–14, 18, 19, 20, 21, 25, 29, 31, 34, 50, 52, 56, 58, 61, 64, 67, 68, 69, 70, 73, 76, 77, 78, 79, 80, 81, 83, 84, 92, 93, 94, 95, 98, 99, 100, 101, 119, 136, 139, 140, 151, 154, 155, 156, 163, 168, 169, 180, 186, 194, 202, 207, 217, 218, 230, 231, 232, 234, 235, 237, 244, 245, 248, 249, 253, 257, 259, 264, 268, 269, 272, 275, 279
Holland, H.-R., Lord 243
Hornoy, A.-M.-F., de P. d' 30
Hornoy, L.-S., Mme d' 17
Houdetot, E.-S.-F., Mme 66, 68
Hume, D. 65

I
Ivernois, F.-H. d' 65, 69, 71

J
Jacob, J. 109
Jaubert, F. 268
Joséphine, l'impératrice 243, 264
Jullien, M.-A., de la Drôme 128

K
Kant, I. 233
Kirchberger, N. A. 71

L
La Chalotais, L. R. de 164

Index

La Condamine, C. M. de 186
La Fare, M. de 76
La Mettrie, J. de 18, 19, 30, 151
La Révellière-Lépeaux, L.-M. 173–188, 253, 280
La Rochefoucauld, F. de 68
La Tour du Pin, A.-G., Mme de 29
Lacour-Gayet, G. 243
Lagrange, J. L. 167, 240, 279
Lahary, J.-T. 4
Laignelot, J.-F. 140
Lakanal, J. 100, 150, 163, 170
Lalande, J. J. de 228
Landois, P. 11, 101
Langlois, C. 268
Lanthenas, F. X. 110
Laplace, P. S. 167, 168, 224, 240, 249, 279
Las Cases, E. de 235, 243, 281
Le Camus, A. 75, 79, 80, 281
Le Mercier de La Rivière, P.-P. 57, 69, 75
Le Monnier, abbé G.-A. 66, 102
Le Peletier de Saint-Fargeau, M. 106
Leclerc, J.-B. 107, 173–189, 281
Lefebvre de La Roche, M.
Lefebvre de La Roche, M. 244
Lequinio, J. M. 96, 97, 98, 101, 102, 103, 106, 118, 119, 129, 139, 263, 269, 281
Lesuire, R.-M. 186, 281
Letort, L.-M. 248

Levasseur, T. 41
Locke, J. 16, 151
Louis XIV 54, 105
Louis XV 16, 168
Louis XVI 168, 187, 189
Louis XVIII 168
Luppé, R. de 250, 278
Lycurgus 56

M
Mably, G. de 203, 265
Maine de Biran, F.-P. 173
Malesherbes, C. G. de Lamoignon de 25
Malet, C.-F. de 234
Maleville, J. de 263, 267
Malraux, A. 273
Mandeville, B. de 63, 71, 257, 281
Marat, J.-P. 38, 59, 66, 283
Marcus Aurelius 219, 223, 245
Maritain, J. 75, 79, 80, 139, 269, 281
Marmontel, J.-F. 168
Massin, J. x, 168, 277
Maupertuis, P. L. de 149
Meister, J. H. 247, 270
Melon, J.-F. 202, 207, 282
Merlin, A.-C., de Thionville 135
Mervaud, C. 32, 245, 282
Michel 75, 77, 80, 282
Michelet, J. 78, 273, 275, 282
Miot de Melito, A.-F. 243
Mirabaud, J.-B. de 11
Mirabeau, H. G. de 42, 66, 67, 69, 83–103, 109, 124, 137, 154, 161, 170, 227, 282
Mirabeau, V. de 119
Mohammed 229

Molé, M.-L. 248
Mollien, N.-F. 233, 238, 243, 247, 249, 250, 268
Monge, G. 167, 213, 240, 279
Montesquieu, C. de 17, 30, 120, 133, 139, 163, 170, 268, 282
Montmollin, F.-G. de 65
More, T. 113, 119, 282
Morellet, abbé A. 29, 33
Morelly, E.-G. 16, 29, 90, 100, 167, 282
Morton, chevalier de, pseudonyme de M. de Cubieres-Palmézeaux 31
Moultou, P.-C. 65, 71, 137, 247, 265
Müller-Hill, B. 170, 282
Musset, A. de 269, 278

N
Naigeon, J. A. 275, 282
Napoléon x, 34, 64, 150, 154, 159, 168, 170, 174, 178, 195, 207, 209–270, 277, 280, 281, 283
Necker, G., *see* Staël
Newton, I. 202, 211

O
Ozouf, M. 109, 110, 111, 113, 114, 117, 119, 120, 143, 147, 282

P
Palissot de Montenoy, C., Palissot 126, 138, 147, 278
Papazu, M. 119, 282

Perreau, J.-A. 269
Petit, M.-E. 107
Phlipon de la Madeleine, L. 77, 80
Picardet, H.-C. 80, 282
Picavet, L. 244, 282
Pierre III 221
Pillorget, R. 118, 279
Pillorget, S. 118, 279
Pinel, P. 271
Plato 106, 118
Poliakov, L. 165, 167, 170, 233, 248, 282
Pomeau, R. 32, 278
Portalis, J. 228, 230, 252, 253, 254, 255, 260, 261, 263, 267, 268, 282
Portiez, L. 105
Prévost, A.-F., l'abbé de 119, 140, 282

R
Rabaut Saint-Etienne, J.-P. 109, 110
Raynaud, P. 208, 278
Regaldo, M. 240, 250, 282
Regnaud de Saint-Jean-d'Angély, M.-L.-E. 243
Richelieu, L. F. A., duc de 30, 32, 33, 138
Ripault de la Cathelinère, C. 136
Robespierre, M. 86, 106, 107, 108, 117, 118, 119, 120, 121–140, 147, 152, 153, 174, 175, 176, 178, 179, 189, 200, 201, 210, 212, 222, 227, 228, 229, 253
Roederer, P.-L. 214, 244, 248, 249, 269
Roland, M. J., Mme de 25, 270

Index

Roman d'Amat, J.-C. 247
Rostand, J. 19, 31, 64, 93, 101, 170, 282
Roth, G. 11, 101, 279
Roume de Saint Laurent, P.-R. 66
Rousseau, J.-J. 10, 16, 28, 29, 30, 34, 35–72, 73, 74, 75, 77, 78, 79, 81, 84, 85, 88, 90, 91, 93, 95, 97, 98, 101, 102, 105, 106, 108, 111, 113, 114, 115, 116, 118, 119, 120, 121, 123, 126, 127, 128, 130, 131, 132, 133, 134, 135, 137, 138, 139, 152, 153, 155, 157, 158, 162, 163, 165, 166, 167, 168, 169, 171, 173, 175, 176, 179, 180, 183, 186, 187, 191, 194, 196, 198, 200, 201, 203, 205, 207, 208, 209, 210, 217, 227, 229, 231, 232, 233, 236, 238, 240, 244, 245, 246, 253, 257, 258, 263, 265, 267, 269, 270, 273, 281, 282, 283
Royer-Collard, P. P. 241

S

Sabatier de Castres, A. 137
Saint-Just, L. 106, 117, 135, 138
Saurin, B.-J. 33
Saxe-Gotha, L. D., duchesse de 31
Sédillez, M.-L.-E. 262, 265, 266, 269
Séguier, A.-L. 12
Ségur, L.-P. de 242
Serna, P. 100, 101, 283
Servan, J.-M.-A. 268

Sieyès E. J. 83–103, 111, 150, 159, 164, 170, 215, 224, 267, 283
Socrates 8, 34, 138, 223
Solomon 229
Spinoza, B. 8, 12, 13, 21, 83, 84, 92, 101, 283
Staël, G., Mme de 27, 34, 35, 64, 92, 101, 152, 168, 189, 195, 197–208, 211, 212, 213, 224, 225, 229, 231, 235, 238, 241, 242, 243, 244, 247, 248, 249, 250, 255, 257, 259, 264, 268, 269, 278, 279, 280, 281
Starobinski, J. 69, 83, 86, 99, 120, 137, 283
Stendhal, H. Beyle, 273, 274, 275, 283
Swain, G. 271, 272, 274, 275, 280
Szramkiewicz, R. 118, 280

T

Talleyrand, C.-M. de 213, 235
Testu, F. X. 137, 283
Thellusson, M.-J. 81
Thomas, see Aquinas
Tocqueville, A. de 189, 193, 195, 196, 279
Tribout-Morembert, H. 244
Tronchet, F.-D. 262, 267
Tronchin, T. 64, 169
Trublet, N.-C.-J., l'abbe 265
Tscharner, V. B. 67
Tulard, J. 120, 244, 268, 283
Turgot, A. R. J. 25, 137, 154, 168, 221
Turreau, L.-M. 125

V

Vauréal, Comte de 76, 80, 107, 283
Viguerie, J. de 79, 117, 118, 171, 248, 279
Volland, L.-H., Sophie 11, 102
Volney, C.-F. 130, 139, 150, 159, 239, 283
Voltaire, F. M., Arouet, 10, 11, 15–34, 36, 38, 40, 45, 51, 52, 54, 55, 64, 65, 68, 80, 84, 90, 93, 94, 95, 98, 99, 101, 102, 123, 128, 133, 134, 136, 138, 139, 140, 142, 147, 152, 155, 157, 162, 168, 169, 170, 177, 178, 185, 190, 194, 200, 202, 205, 216, 217, 218, 219, 220, 221, 222, 223, 224, 227, 228, 229, 230, 231, 232, 233, 234, 236, 237, 241, 244, 245, 246, 247, 248, 249, 253, 256, 264, 265, 267, 268, 269, 272, 273, 275, 278, 282, 283

W

Walpole, H. 28, 30, 34

Z

Zac, S. 13, 283
Zeno 139